Human
Smoke

Also by Nicholson Baker

Human
Smoke

The Beginnings of World War II,
the End of Civilization

Nicholson Baker

SIMON &
SCHUSTER

London · New York · Sydney · Toronto

A CBS COMPANY

First published in Great Britain in 2008 by Simon & Schuster UK Ltd
A CBS COMPANY

Copyright © 2008 by Nicholson Baker

1 3 5 7 9 10 8 6 4 2

Simon & Schuster UK Ltd
Africa House
64–78 Kingsway
London WC2B 6AH

www.simonsays.co.uk

Simon & Schuster Australia
Sydney

A CIP catalogue for this book is available
from the British Library.

ISBN: 978-1-84737-274-1 (Hardback)
ISBN: 978-1-84737-303-8 (Trade paperback)

Designed by C. Linda Dingler
Printed and bound in Great Britain by
Mackays of Chatham Ltd

Human
Smoke

ALFRED NOBEL, the manufacturer of explosives, was talking to his friend the Baroness Bertha von Suttner, author of *Lay Down Your Arms*. Von Suttner, a founder of the European antiwar movement, had just attended the fourth World's Peace Conference in Bern. It was August 1892.

"Perhaps my factories will put an end to war even sooner than your congresses," Alfred Nobel said. "On the day when two army corps may mutually annihilate each other in a second, probably all civilized nations will recoil with horror and disband their troops."

STEFAN ZWEIG, a young writer from Vienna, sat in the audience at a movie theater in Tours, France, watching a newsreel. It was spring 1914.

An image of Wilhelm II, the Emperor of Germany, came on screen for a moment. At once the theater was in an uproar. "Everybody yelled and whistled, men, women, and children, as if they had been personally insulted," Zweig wrote. "The good-natured people of Tours, who knew no more about the world and politics than what they had read in their newspapers, had gone mad for an instant."

Zweig was frightened. "It had only been a second, but one that showed me how easily people anywhere could be aroused in a time of a crisis, despite all attempts at understanding."

WINSTON CHURCHILL, England's first lord of the admiralty, instituted a naval blockade of Germany. "The British blockade," Churchill later wrote, "treated the whole of Germany as if it were a beleaguered fortress, and avowedly sought to starve the whole population—men, women, and children, old and young, wounded and sound—into submission." It was 1914.

STEFAN ZWEIG was at the eastern front, gathering Russian war proclamations for the Austrian archives. It was the spring of 1915.

Zweig boarded a freight car on a hospital train. "One crude stretcher stood next to the other," he wrote, "and all were occupied by moaning, sweating, deathly pale men, who were gasping for breath in the thick atmosphere of excrement and iodoform." There were several dead among the living. The doctor, in despair, asked Zweig to get water. He had no morphine and no clean bandages, and they were still twenty hours from Budapest.

When Zweig got back to Vienna, he began a pacifist play, *Jeremiah*. "I had recognized," Zweig wrote, "the foe I was to fight— false heroism that prefers to send others to suffering and death, the cheap optimism of the conscienceless prophets, both political and military who, boldly promising victory, prolong the war, and behind them the hired chorus, the 'word makers of war' as Werfel has pilloried them in his beautiful poem."

JEANNETTE RANKIN OF MONTANA, the first woman to be elected to the House of Representatives, voted against declaring war on Germany. It was April 6, 1917.

"I leaned over the gallery rail and watched her," said her friend Harriet Laidlaw, of the Woman Suffrage Party. "She was undergoing the most terrible strain." Almost all of her fellow suffrage leaders, including Laidlaw, wanted her to vote yes.

There was a silence when her name was called. "I want to stand by my country," Rankin said. "But I cannot vote for war. I vote no." Fifty other members of the House voted no with her; 374 voted yes. "I felt," she said later, "that the first time the first woman had a chance to say no to war she should say it."

One of her home-state papers, the Helena *Independent,* called her "a dupe of the Kaiser, a member of the Hun army in the United States, and a crying schoolgirl."

A YOUNG PRO-WAR PREACHER, Harry Emerson Fosdick, wrote a short book, published by the Young Men's Christian Association.

War was not gallantry and parades anymore, Reverend Fosdick said. "War is now dropping bombs from aeroplanes and killing women and children in their beds; it is shooting by telephonic orders, at an unseen place miles away and slaughtering invisible men." War, he said, is "men with jaws gone, eyes gone, limbs gone, minds gone."

Fosdick ended his book with a call for enlistment: "Your country needs *you,*" he said. It was November 1917.

MEYER LONDON, a socialist in the House of Representatives, voted no to President Wilson's second declaration of war, against Austria-Hungary. It was December 7, 1917.

"In matters of war I am a teetotaler," said London, in a fifteen-minute speech. "I refuse to take the first intoxicating drink."

Representative Walter Chandler walked over to where London sat and stood in front of him as he delivered his rebuttal.

"It has been said that if you will analyze the blood of a Jew under the microscope, you will find the Talmud and the Old Bible floating around in some particles," Congressman Chandler said. "If you analyze the blood of a representative German or Teuton you will find machine guns and particles of shells and bombs floating around in the blood."

There was only one thing to do with the Teutons, according to Chandler: "Fight them until you destroy the whole bunch."

ELEANOR ROOSEVELT and her husband, Franklin D., the assistant secretary of the navy, were invited to a party in honor of Bernard Baruch, the financier. "I've got to go to the Harris party which I'd rather be hung than seen at," Eleanor wrote her mother-in-law. "Mostly Jews." It was January 14, 1918.

A CAPTURED GERMAN OFFICER was talking to a reporter for *The New York Times.* It was November 3, 1918, and the German government had asked for an armistice.

The German officer claimed that his army was not defeated and should have continued the war. "The Emperor is surrounded by people who feel and talk defeat," the officer said. He mentioned men like Philipp Scheidemann, the leader of the socialists.

New tanks were coming, the captured officer observed, and war was expected between the United States and Japan. "Japan and the United States would surely clash some day," he said, "and we would then furnish both sides with enormous quantities of material and munitions." The ceding of Poland and Alsace-Lorraine, the officer believed, meant social upheaval, the ruin of German industry, and the impoverishment of the working class. "Our enemies will have what they have desired—the complete annihilation of Germany. That would be a peace due to Scheidemann."

WINSTON CHURCHILL, now England's secretary of state for war and air, rose in Parliament to talk about the success of the naval blockade. It was March 3, 1919, four months after the signing of the armistice that ended the Great War.

"We are enforcing the blockade with rigour," Churchill said. "It is repugnant to the British nation to use this weapon of starvation, which falls mainly on the women and children, upon the old and the weak and the poor, after all the fighting has stopped, one moment longer than is necessary to secure the just terms for which we have fought." Hunger and malnutrition, the secretary of war and air observed, had brought German national life to a state of near collapse. "Now is therefore the time to settle," he said.

WINSTON CHURCHILL published a newspaper article. It was February 8, 1920. Churchill had a different enemy now. Now his enemy wasn't Germany, it was the "sinister confederacy" of international Jewry.

"This movement among the Jews is not new," Churchill said. It was a "world-wide conspiracy for the overthrow of civilisation and for the reconstitution of society on the basis of arrested development, of envious malevolence, and impossible equality." He listed Marx, Trotsky, Béla Kun, Rosa Luxemburg, and Emma Goldman as some of the malefactors. The conspiracy had been, he said, the "mainspring of every subversive movement during the Nineteenth Century." It had played a recognizable part in the French Revolution. All loyal Jews, he advised, must "vindicate the honour of the Jewish name" by rejecting international bolshevism.

AYLMER HALDANE, the commander of British forces in Iraq, telegraphed Winston Churchill for more troops and airplanes. It was August 26, 1920.

"Jihad was being preached with frenzied fervour by the numerous emissaries from the holy cities of Najaf and Karbala," Haldane wrote. Churchill, secretary of state for war and air, sent him an encouraging note: "The Cabinet have decided that the rebellion must be quelled effectually, and I shall endeavour to meet all your requirements."

Several days later, Churchill wrote Hugh "Boom" Trenchard, the head of the Royal Air Force, a memo. Churchill and Trenchard were developing the notion of policing the British empire from above, thereby saving the cost of ground troops—a policy that became known as "air control."

"I think you should certainly proceed with the experimental work on gas bombs, especially mustard gas, which would inflict punishment on recalcitrant natives without inflicting grave injury on them," Churchill wrote Trenchard. Churchill was an expert on the effects of mustard gas—he knew that it could blind and kill, especially children and infants. Gas spreads a "lively terror," he pointed out in an earlier memo; he didn't understand the prevailing squeamishness about its use: "I am strongly in favor of using poisoned gas against uncivilised tribes." Most of those gassed wouldn't have "serious permanent effects," he said.

HALDANE'S MEN BOMBED and strafed rebellious tribes, fired on them with gas-filled shells, burned villages, and repaired the railway. The official death toll on the British side was forty-seven English officers and troops and 250 Indian Gurkhas. "It is impossible to give the Arab casualties with any approach to exactitude," Haldane wrote, "but they have been estimated at 8450 killed and wounded." Haldane offered his thoughts on how to deal punitively with a village. "Separate parties should be detailed for firing the houses, digging up and burning the grain and bhoosa, looting, &c.," he advised. "Burning a village properly takes a long time, an hour or more according to size from the time the burning parties enter."

Churchill wrote Haldane a congratulatory telegram: "During these difficult months your patience and steadfastness have been of great value, and I congratulate you upon the distinct improvement in the situation which has been effected by you." It was October 18, 1920.

A WING COMMANDER in the Royal Air Force, J. A. Chamier, published his views on how best to deal with tribal rebellions.

The commanding officer must choose the most inaccessible village of the most prominent tribe, said Chamier, and attack it with all available aircraft. "The attack with bombs and machine guns must be relentless and unremitting and carried on continuously by day and night, on houses, inhabitants, crops and cattle," Chamier wrote. "This sounds brutal, I know, but it must be made brutal to start with. The threat alone in the future will prove efficacious if the lesson is once properly learnt." It was 1921.

FRANKLIN ROOSEVELT, now a lawyer in New York City, noticed that Jews made up one-third of the freshman class at Harvard. He talked the problem over with Henry Morgenthau, Sr., and he went to the Harvard Board of Overseers, of which he was a member. "It was decided," Roosevelt later explained, "that over a period of years the number of Jews should be reduced one or two per cent a year until it was down to 15%." It was about 1922.

MOHANDAS K. GANDHI was arrested for sedition. He had written an article that began: "How can there be any compromise whilst the British Lion continues to shake his gory claws in our faces?" It was March 10, 1922.

That Sunday, John Haynes Holmes, a pacifist preacher, gave a sermon in the Lyric Theater in New York. "Gandhi is disciplining three hundred million Indians to struggle for liberty," Holmes said, "to throw off the British yoke by nonviolence, and he is doing this with a degree of success which is shaking the empire to its foundations. He would save India in time, and therewith perhaps save the world."

Gandhi gave a statement at his trial. "I am endeavoring to show to my countrymen that violent non-cooperation only multiplies evil and that as evil can only be sustained by violence, withdrawal of support of evil requires complete abstention from violence," he said. He would, he told the court, cheerfully submit to the highest penalty for his crime.

He was sentenced to a term of six years in jail.

LORD HUGH CECIL, a member of Parliament for Oxford, rose to say that the Royal Air Force was unnecessarily large and should be smaller. It was March 21, 1922.

Winston Churchill, the secretary of state for war, secretary of state for air, and secretary of state for the colonies, rose in reply to say that the Royal Air Force should stay large. Churchill recalled the end of the Great War, when British airplanes had been on the verge of bold accomplishments. "Had the War lasted a few more months, or possibly even a few more weeks," he said, "there would have been operations conducted from these coasts upon Berlin and in the heart of Germany, and those operations would have increased in magnitude and consequence had the campaign been prolonged all through the year 1919." But those operations were not to be. Peace intervened, "owing to our having run short of Germans and enemies before the experiments were completed."

Churchill went on to make a prediction. "In an aerial war," he said, "the greatest form of defence will undoubtedly be offense."

STEFAN ZWEIG was on vacation in Westerland, on the island of Sylt in the North Sea. He read in the paper that his friend Walter Rathenau, the foreign minister of Germany, a Jew, had been assassinated. It was June 24, 1922.

The German mark plunged in value. "Now the real witch's sabbath of inflation started," wrote Zweig. To repair a broken window now cost more than the whole house would have cost before the inflation; a single book now cost more than a printing company with one hundred presses had. "The unemployed stood around and shook their fists at the profiteers and foreigners in their luxurious cars who bought whole rows of streets like a box of matches," he said. "Towering above them all was the superprofiteer, Stinnes."

With the collapse of values, Zweig said, Berlin became a Babylon: "Every high school boy wanted to earn some money, and in the dimly lit bars one might see government officials and men of the world of finance tenderly courting drunken sailors without any shame."

Authoritarian countermovements grew amid chaos, said Zweig. Men "aligned themselves in readiness for any slogan that promised order."

BOOM TRENCHARD, head of the Royal Air Force, was chatting with his staff. They were wondering whether it was better to have lots of fighter planes, in order to fight off the enemy, or lots of bombers to bomb the enemy on his home ground. Trenchard said that it was really like playing football. You can't just defend your own goal, you have to go over onto the other side of the field. The nation that could stand being bombed longest, he said, would win in the end. And, in his opinion, "The French in a bombing duel would probably squeal before we did." It was July 9, 1923.

THE *DAILY MAIL,* a conservative London paper, published a forged letter. It was October 25, 1924.

The letter was purportedly signed by Grigori Zinoviev, a Russian communist leader, and addressed to the Communist Party in England. It appeared four days before the general election of 1924—an important race for Winston Churchill, who had lost two previous campaigns.

The letter, marked "very secret," talked of a "successful rising in any of the working districts of England." Its prose had faintly Churchillian cadences in places—there were phrases such as "strain every nerve" and "pronounced its weighty word"—but with an admixture of bolshevistic pastiche. "It would be desirable to have cells (nuclei?) in all the units of troops, particularly among those quartered in large centres of the country, and among factories working on munitions and at military store depots," the letter said. The headline in the *Daily Mail* was "Civil War Plot by Socialists' Masters."

Churchill's devoted supporter Esmond Harmsworth was the son of Lord Rothermere, publisher of the *Daily Mail.* Churchill's close ally in Secret Intelligence, Desmond Morton, first forwarded the letter from an obscure Latvian source to the British Foreign Office, attesting to its authenticity.

Moscow called the letter a "clumsy forgery" and a "crude fabrication" and demanded an apology. Members of Parliament said it was a "fake" and a "malicious hoax." "How did Conservative headquarters become possessed of that letter?" the Labor prime minister, Ramsay MacDonald, asked. "It is a most suspicious circumstance that a newspaper and headquarters of the Conservative Association seem to have had copies of it at the same time as the Foreign Office, and if that is true, how can I, a simple-minded, honest person who puts two and two together, avoid a suspicion—I will not say conclusion—that the whole thing is a political plot?"

CHURCHILL AND OTHER CONSERVATIVES used the Zinoviev letter to unseat Prime Minister MacDonald. Churchill compared MacDonald to Alexander Kerensky, the weak Russian socialist leader who allowed the Bolsheviks to triumph.

"You all know the story of Kerensky," Churchill said in a campaign speech, "how he stood there, like Mr. MacDonald, pretending that he meant to do the best he could for his country, and all the time apologizing behind the scenes to the wild, dark, deadly forces which had him in their grip."

Churchill won his election. Still he couldn't stop talking about the Zinoviev letter. Conspirators and revolutionaries "of every race under the sun" had assembled in Russia to plan world revolution, he asserted in the *Weekly Dispatch.* "Everywhere they have endeavoured to bring into being the 'germ cells' from which the cancer of Communism should grow," he wrote. "There was, therefore, nothing new and nothing particularly violent in the letter of Zinoviev, alias Apfelbaum, to the British Communists." It was November 2, 1924.

Ramsey MacDonald watched his Labor cabinet pack up. He felt, he said, like a man sewn in a sack and tossed into the sea. Churchill returned to power: He became chancellor of the exchequer in the new Conservative government.

He reinstated the gold standard, triggering a massive depression.

JOSEPH GOEBBELS was working on his diary-novel *Michael.* "I lie awake for a long time and think of the quiet pale man of Nazareth," he wrote. Then Adolf Hitler came into his life.

Hitler had just gotten out of Landesberg prison, where he'd dictated *Mein Kampf* to his friend Rudolf Hess. Goebbels finished reading *Mein Kampf.* "Who is this man?" he asked himself. "The real Christ, or only St. John?" Hitler offered Goebbels the job of editor of the National Socialist newspaper, the *Völkischer Beobachter.* They spoke at meetings together. "He jumps to his feet, there he is," Goebbels wrote in his diary in November 1925. "Shakes my hand. Like an old friend. And those big blue eyes. Like stars. He is glad to see me. I am in heaven."

A few weeks later, Goebbels saw him again. "Hitler is there. Great joy. He greets me like an old friend. And looks after me. How I love him! What a fellow! Then he speaks. How small I am! He gives me his photograph. With a greeting to the Rhineland. Heil Hitler! I want Hitler to be my friend. His photograph is on my desk."

A few months later still, the two of them had another meeting. Goebbels gave a two-and-a-half-hour speech. "I give it all I have. They rave, they shout. In the end Hitler embraces me. Tears are in his eyes. I feel something like true happiness."

They had dinner together that evening—Hitler allowed Goebbels to pay. "And even in that, what greatness!"

Goebbels had found his man of Nazareth. "Adolf Hitler—I love you."

REVEREND HARRY FOSDICK gave a sermon in Geneva, at the Cathedral of Saint Pierre. It was September 13, 1925, the opening of the League of Nations Assembly. Reverend Fosdick had renounced his previous fervent militarism; he was a well-known antiwar preacher now.

Fosdick had seen men come freshly gassed from the trenches, he said. He had heard the cries of those who wanted to die and could not.

"I hate war," he said, "for what it forces us to do to our enemies, rejoicing over our coffee cups at the breakfast table about every damnable and devilish evil we have been able to inflict upon them. I hate war for its results, the lies it lives on and propagates, the undying hatreds that it rouses, the dictatorships that it puts in the place of democracy, and the starvation that stalks after it." Fosdick's speech was quoted in newspapers. Twenty-five thousand copies of it were printed and distributed. Most people agreed with it. Most of the world was pacifist.

THE ROYAL AIR FORCE dropped more than 150 tons of bombs on India. It was 1925.

WINSTON CHURCHILL visited Rome. "I could not help being charmed by Signor Mussolini's gentle and simple bearing, and by his calm, detached poise in spite of so many burdens and dangers," Churchill said in a press statement. Italian fascism, he said, had demonstrated that there was a way to combat subversive forces; it had provided the "necessary antidote to the Russian virus."

"If I had been an Italian I am sure I should have been entirely with you from the beginning to the end of your victorious struggle against the bestial appetites and passions of Leninism," Churchill told the Romans. It was January 20, 1927.

THE ROYAL AIR FORCE announced the staging of a mock bombing exercise at its annual air pageant in Hendon, north of London. It was June 11, 1927.

The New York Times described the Hendon event in advance: "The 'town,' which will be built largely of airplane wings, will be bombed to bits. Airplanes will drop food and ammunition to the European 'refugees,' who will be fleeing after having escaped from the citadel in which they have been 'beleaguered' by the town's native inhabitants." The town was located in the imaginary land of Irquestine.

Two hundred airplanes were going to fly to the music of a song called "Chick, Chick, Chick, Chick, Chicken." When the singer sang "Lay a little egg for me," the planes were to release their bombs.

A SQUADRON of British planes bombed the sacred pyramid of the Nuer at Dengkur, in the African Sudan. They blew up herds of cattle—"mangled flesh and splintered bones crescendoed high," reported *Time* magazine—and strafed Nuer tribesmen. One of the tribesmen shot back, wounding a pilot in the thigh. "Not more than 200 Nuers were killed," according to an official estimate. It was February 1928.

WINSTON CHURCHILL published an extraordinary work of history called *The Aftermath,* the last volume in his history of the Great War. It was March 1929.

The Great War exhibited novel features, Churchill said. For example: "Whole nations were methodically subjected, or sought to be subjected, to the process of reduction by famine." But what had happened was nothing compared to what would have happened if the Germans had kept fighting into 1919, he said. Poison gases of "incredible malignity" would have ended all resistance. "Thousands of aeroplanes would have shattered their cities."

Instead, suddenly, the fighting ended: "In a hundred laboratories, in a thousand arsenals, factories, and bureaux, men pulled themselves up with a jerk, and turned from the task in which they had been absorbed."

But those whose noncombatant labors had been interrupted would get another chance, sooner or later, to carry forward their plans from 1919, Churchill predicted. "Death stands at attention," he wrote, "obedient, expectant, ready to serve, ready to shear away the peoples en masse; ready, if called on, to pulverise, without hope of repair, what is left of civilisation. He awaits only the word of command."

BARON PONSONBY, author of *Falsehood in Wartime,* remembered something that Winston Churchill had said to him years before. "I like things to happen," he had said, "and if they don't happen I like to make them happen." It was March 11, 1929.

WINSTON CHURCHILL, on a speaking tour in the United States, gave a talk at the Bond Club in New York City. It was October 9, 1929.

Churchill's speaker's fee of $12,500 was paid by Sir Harry McGowan, chairman of African Explosives and deputy chairman of Imperial Chemical Industries, a British conglomerate that made fertilizer, rayon, gunpowder, TNT, bombs, ammunition, and poison gas. Imperial Chemical was the descendant of Alfred Nobel's explosives company, where McGowan had started working at the age of fifteen; it had agreements with munitioneers DuPont and, in Germany, I. G. Farben.

McGowan and Churchill had developed a financial intimacy: McGowan was investing some of Churchill's wealth for him in the American stock market. Sir Harry had, Churchill confided to his wife, Clementine, "profound sources of information."

During his multicity tour, Churchill praised big navies, large weapons programs, and Anglo-American cooperation. "We don't want all the good people in the world to disarm while the bad ones remain heavily equipped for war," he told the Iron and Steel Institute later that month. "You are the friends we would like to see most strongly armed."

MOHANDAS GANDHI walked to the ocean with his followers. He had decided to resist the British imperial salt monopoly. "Watch, I am about to give a signal to the nation," he said, lifting a few grains of sea salt. It was April 6, 1930.

Lord Irwin, the tall, bony viceroy of India, had already arrested many of Gandhi's disciples. He hoped he wouldn't have to arrest Gandhi, though, which would cause unrest:

> I was always told that his blood pressure is dangerous and his heart none too good, and I was also told a few days ago that his horoscope predicts that he will die this year, and that is the explanation of this desperate throw. It would be a very happy solution.

But Mohandas Gandhi didn't die. He and sixty thousand followers were imprisoned. In Peshawar, near India's Northwest Frontier, British troops fired on a crowd of Muslim salt protesters, killing some of them. Air raids "cleaned up" the Peshawar region afterward, according to *The New York Times*.

MUSSOLINI GAVE A SPEECH to a crowd of blackshirted Fascisti in Florence. "Words are beautiful things," he said, "but rifles, machine guns, ships, and airplanes are more beautiful still." It was May 17, 1930.

MAJOR FRANK PEASE, the president of the Hollywood Technical Directors Association, a Red-baiting group, saw *All Quiet on the Western Front,* from Universal Pictures. The movie, about the pointlessness and horror of the Great War, was based on a novel by Erich Maria Remarque.

Major Pease disliked the movie; he wrote telegrams to President Hoover and others asking them to ban it. "Its continued uncensored exhibition especially before juveniles will go far to raise a race of yellow streaks, slackers and disloyalists," he said. "Moscow itself could not have produced a more subversive film."

When the movie wasn't banned, Pease sent out a newsletter. "The mesopotamian mongrels guilty of such a criminal film as ALL QUIET were bound to over-reach themselves some time, and this looks like the time," he wrote. "THE TIME TO CALL A HALT IS NOW."

It was May 24, 1930.

THE ASSOCIATED PRESS sent in a story from Peshawar. It was August 17, 1930. "Chastened by a daily rain of bombs from British planes, raiding Afridi tribesmen were reported today in full retreat to the hills of the northwest frontier," the story said. "Punishment inflicted on the villages by raiding airplanes was said by officals to have had a salutary effect. The disaffected sections are expected to sue for peace in a short time."

The Times of London, in an editorial, blamed the deaths of Afridi tribesmen on Gandhi's propagandists.

IN BERLIN, Albert Einstein was talking to reporters. It was September 18, 1930. The Hitlerites had triumphed in an election. "There is no reason for despair," Einstein said, "for the Hitler vote is only a symptom, not necessarily of anti-Jewish hatred but of momentary resentment caused by economic misery and unemployment within the ranks of misguided German youth." Einstein observed that during the Dreyfus affair most of the population of France had become anti-Semitic. And then that had changed. "I hope that as soon as the situation improves the German people will also find their road to clarity," he said.

JOSEPH GOEBBELS, Reichstag member and party leader of Berlin, led two hundred Brownshirts into a movie theater. It was December 8, 1930. Goebbels had gotten them tickets to *All Quiet on the Western Front,* which was just out in Germany. Goebbels described Erich Maria Remarque as a "slicked-over fashion-monkey." He said that the film was a "work of filth." His recruits had weapons—briefcases full of white mice, stink bombs, and sneeze powder. They would defend the honor of the two million who had died in the Great War against naysayers and defeatists such as Remarque.

As the film played, and as Goebbels observed from the balcony, the Brownshirts leaped up and began shouting, "Jews out! Jews out!" They freed the mice and flung the stink bombs and the sneeze powder. There was confusion; the film was stopped. The police arrived and emptied the theater.

The next night, the storm troopers were there again, and there were more of them. Police on horses tried to keep control. Goebbels denounced the film as "Jewish," and then the protestors marched toward a fancy shopping district in Berlin, the Kurfürstendamm, where there were Jewish-owned businesses. "Many a proprietor of a stylish café trembled for its plate-glass front as he saw the young anti-pacifists approaching," reported *The New York Times,* "but apparently no windows were broken." Twenty-seven people were arrested.

The next night, there was another disturbance; and the night after that; and the night after that. The theater stood empty. The German government, intimidated, suppressed the film. "The film of shame has been banned," wrote Goebbels in his diary. "With that action the National Socialist movement has won its fight aginst the dirty machinations of the Jews." It was, he wrote, "a victory that could not have been any grander."

Erich Maria Remarque had been watching the first demonstration. "Nobody was older than twenty," he wrote later. "None of them could have been in the war—and none of them knew that ten years later they would be in another war and that most of them would be dead before they reached thirty."

GANDHI HAD REPLACED LENIN as Churchill's arch-nemesis. "The truth is," Churchill wrote, "Gandhi-ism and all it stands for will, sooner or later, have to be grappled with and finally crushed. It is no use trying to satisfy a tiger by feeding him with cat's-meat." It was December 11, 1930.

A month later, Gandhi was released from jail. He wrote a letter to the viceroy, Lord Irwin. "Dear Friend," he said. "I have received suggestions from friends whose advice I value that I should seek an interview with you."

Irwin invited him to the palace. The two men met and talked. They met again and talked—and again. Winston Churchill was disgusted. The British government must, he said in a speech, dissociate itself from this "weak, wrong-headed" rapprochement: "It is alarming and also nauseating to see Mr Gandhi, a seditious Middle Temple lawyer, now posing as a fakir of a type well known in the East, striding half naked up the steps of the viceregal palace, while he is still organising and conducting a defiant campaign of civil disobedience, to parley on equal terms with the representative of the King-Emperor. Such a spectacle can only increase the unrest in India." It was February 23, 1931.

ALBERT EINSTEIN gave a speech at the Ritz-Carlton in New York. There were two ways of resisting war, Einstein said. In countries where there was a draft, the pacifist could refuse military duty. In countries where no draft currently existed, such as the United States and England, the pacifist could publicly declare that he will not, under any circumstances, take up arms.

"If only 2 percent of the men liable for war service were to refuse," Einstein said, "there would not be enough jails in the world to take care of them." He and Mrs. Einstein got an ovation. It was December 14, 1930.

Two EDITORS from a conservative newspaper presented themselves at a house on an elegant street in Munich. It was May 4, 1931. The house was called the Brown House, and it was the headquarters of the National Socialist German Workers Party—the Nazi Party. A steel magnate, Fritz Thyssen, had helped the party leader, Adolf Hitler, buy it. There was a swastika flag flapping on the roof. Guards checked the two editors' papers, and then Rudolf Hess, Hitler's longtime private secretary, greeted them. Hess had an odd look, one of the visitors thought: in his face there were traces of fanaticism and "mental turmoil." Hess was the man to whom, some years earlier, Hitler had dictated the long monologues that became *Mein Kampf.*

Hitler was busy for the moment, so Hess took the two of them on a tour. They went down to the basement and saw the fireproof cabinets that held files on half a million party members. They went back upstairs and saw swastikas in the ceiling stucco and swastikas in the window glass. They saw a room called the Hall of the Senators, which held sixty-one chairs covered in red leather. Its ceiling was of marble, and it bore an image of the party emblem done in mosaic; on its floor were "vast priceless carpets into which were woven innumerable swastikas." Hess took them up to the courtroom of the National Socialist Party, which had a table in it bearing a gold swastika and a figure of Christ.

After an hour, Hess showed the guests into Hitler's office and made the introductions. Hitler was friendly. He shook hands with them and said, genially, "I know the part which you and your paper play among the German intelligentsia and bourgeoisie." There were two pictures visible: a small one of Mussolini on the desk and a big one of Frederick the Great, in oil, on the wall. Hitler began talking—sometimes banging his fist on the table, sometimes shouting—about the communists, the Vatican, the Jews, Freemasonry, the press, Karl

Marx, Trotsky, and the city of Berlin, which he called an "international muckheap." One of the editors, Richard Breiting, had worked as a shorthand recorder in the Reichstag, the German Parliament, so he was able to keep up with this stream of excited speech.

"We can achieve something only by fanaticism," said Hitler. "We do not intend to nail every rich Jew to the telegraph poles on the Munich-Berlin road," he said. "That is nonsense." But there will be cases of hardship. "If you use a plane, there will be shavings."

Breiting asked who would supply the administrative brains to run the government, assuming the National Socialist party came to power. Hitler eyed him intently. "I am the master mind and my secret General Staff will produce the brains we need," he said. He flushed and grew angry. "Any resistance will be broken ruthlessly. I will tolerate no opposition." They finished the interview.

Afterward, Breiting wrote a summary. "Hitler exerts over his staff semi-hypnotic influence," he noted. "I was told he sometimes rages around the Brown House like a madman." He was, Breiting thought, a neurasthenic, a man of enormous egotism, with a tendency toward megalomania. Sometimes, it was said, he burst into tears. He left a strong impression, in any case; his chin, under the centerpiece of the mustache, showed great energy. "As he speaks he frequently grimaces as if he would like to crush his opponent with his teeth."

RICHARD BREITING returned to the Brown House for a second interview. It was June 1931. Hitler began to talk quickly. He talked about the need for monumental architecture and beautiful cities and new highway systems, and about the decadence of art. Also about the Jews in Parisian finance, and about election returns, about the Viennese Jews who had interfered with his ambitions to be an architect, about the imprisonment of Dr. Goebbels for slandering the Jews, about the usefulness of brutality in politics, and about the ugliness of the Reichstag building. The Reichstag, Hitler said, looked like a synagogue. The sooner the Reichstag was burned down, he said, "the sooner will the German people be freed from foreign influence."

The greatest threats to Germany, Hitler said, were the Soviet Union and the United States. The German nation must complete its reconstruction soon, "before the Soviet Union becomes a world power, before the three million square miles possessed by the United States turns into an arsenal for world Jewry." That was the danger. "These two colossi are still asleep," he said. "When they wake up, that is the end of it for Germany."

Breiting ventured to say, rather daringly, "But, Herr Hitler, one should not see Jewish conspiracies behind every tree." People have to work things out, he said; nothing will be accomplished "merely by whipping up anti-Semitism."

Hitler became indignant. The Jews wanted to divide people. Henry Cabot Lodge was a tool of the Jews. Woe to Germany if the Jewish "string-pullers" were to get their way. There were "forces" in New York behind Governor Franklin D. Roosevelt.

"The Jews should tremble before us," he said, "not we before them."

A GERMAN FIRE ENGINEER, Hans Rumpf, wrote about the future of firebombing. One hundred airplanes, he said, each carrying a few thousand firebombs, might fly to the capital of an enemy country—for instance, Paris or London. They might release the bombs, starting one hundred thousand fires simultaneously. "The hot air rising from the innumerable centers of conflagration," Rumpf wrote, "would cause the so-called fire wind, which would carry the flames to points not yet affected. And in the end, all the fires would flow together into one roaring conflagration, against which no fire-fighting organization or machinery could stand up. The city, the whole city, would burn to the ground, from one single well planned and well executed attack."

Rumpf ended his hypothetical air raid with: *"Der rote Hahn hat fliegen gelernt."* Which means: "The red rooster has learned to fly." It was 1931.

THE JEWISH TELEGRAPHIC AGENCY issued a news dispatch, which was published in *The New York Times*. In the Grenadier-strasse in Berlin, where there was a synagogue, a group of Nazis had gathered. They had shouted "Down with Judea!" and attacked some pedestrians. "A Jewish crowd soon collected, however, and offered resistance to the attackers, causing their retreat."

The news dispatch also quoted from a plan to "rid Germany of the Jews, without arousing foreign opinion." When the Nazis came into power, according to this plan—published in a legal journal—they would make lists of Jewish citizens. Once the Jews were listed, their citizenship could be withdrawn. "When the government is sufficiently strong it will introduce the fullest measures against the Jews with the customary 'Nazi' severity." It was December 2, 1931.

MOHANDAS GANDHI arrived in England. It was September 12, 1931. He chose to stay at Kingsley House, a home for the poor in London's East End. He made a live broadcast to the United States on CBS radio. "I personally would wait, if need be for ages, rather than seek to attain the freedom of my country through bloody means," he said. "The world is sick unto death of blood-spilling. The world is seeking a way out and I flatter myself with the belief that perhaps it will be the privilege of the ancient land of India to show the way out to the hungering world."

Gandhi talked to the king and queen, the Archbishop of Canterbury, the Master of Balliol, George Bernard Shaw, Lord Lothian, textile workers in Lancashire, and leading Quakers.

He wanted to talk to Winston Churchill, but Churchill declined to meet him.

LILIAN MOWRER and her husband, Edgar Mowrer, the journalist, went to a Nazi ceremony at the Sports Palace. It was about 1931. The Sports Palace was, Lilian wrote, "a handsome modern building with walls painted in brilliant futuristic colours." Making their way to the stage were Joseph Goebbels, "peaked, thin, limping slightly," and Rudolf Hess, "a regular Clark Gable of a man," and Hitler himself, in a trench coat and leather belt, "his lank lock of hair already straying over his low forehead, a happy nervous smile on his long shapeless lips."

Goebbels took the microphone. "Why do we trust our Führer?" he asked. "We hold to our Führer because—he holds to us." A roar rose from twenty thousand throats.

Hitler began speaking, in his odd, croaking voice. He listed off the misdeeds and corruptions of the Weimar regime. He wept over the woes of the people—"two fists in the air and tears pouring down each side of his flabby nose," Lilian Mowrer wrote. Then he excoriated the Jews and the socialists, and he promised lower taxes, higher wages, more jobs, better housing, and cheaper fertilizer. Mowrer was not swept away. "Hitler was talking nonsense, making the grossest mis-statements, garbling history in a voice that was raucous and suggested the parade ground, and with gestures uncouth and unconvincing," she thought. Yet when she looked around at the audience, she saw not just assent but ecstasy: a young girl with lips parted, eyes fixed on her leader; an old man nodding; the sixty-year-old woman next to her, saying "Richtig! Richtig!" after every promise Hitler made.

THE CHINA CORRESPONDENT for *The New York Times,* Hallett Abend, was having caviar and cocktails on a ship in the Shanghai harbor. Abend was talking to Shiozawa Koichi, a rear admiral in the Japanese navy. It was January 28, 1932.

"At eleven o'clock tonight I am sending my Marines into Chapei," Admiral Shiozawa said, "to protect our nationals and to preserve order."

Chapei was a part of Shanghai where more than half a million people lived. Five Japanese Buddhist monks had been beaten there, one fatally; in revenge, a Japanese patriotic association had burned down a towel factory. Admiral Shiozawa had already warned the Chinese of drastic measures if the anti-Japanese activity didn't stop. Other countries were keeping a close watch, too. President Hoover and Henry Stimson, his secretary of war, had announced that they were ready to protect American interests; two American destroyers were nearby, and a troop of U.S. Marines had paraded, bayonets held high, in Shanghai's international zone.

Shortly after midnight, Hallett Abend's taxi turned a corner on a side street of Chapei; its headlights lit up a group of Japanese marines and British policemen crawling forward with a machine gun in tow. An officer stood. "Lights out, you fools!" he called to Abend's taxi. There was a gunshot. "The officer flung both arms wildly into the air, gurgled strangely, and crumpled into a quiet heap," Abend wrote in his memoir.

More Japanese forces, on motorcycles, drove around shooting. Chinese snipers from the revolutionary Nineteenth Route Army were on the roofs. American and European onlookers gathered on the North Szechuen Road to watch the skirmish—drinking, laughing, smoking, and eating sandwiches. Abend and his coworker, Douglas Robertson, stayed up all night writing dispatches to the *Times,* fortified by the occasional absinthe frappe.

Early the next morning, the two of them were back on the scene, standing on the North Szechuen Road. They heard planes drone overhead.

> "The little yellow bastards are going to bomb Chapei," Robertson said in a breathless tone.
> "Never!" I ejaculated. "Bomb 600,000 civilians in an unfortified city? Not even the Japs."
> "Wait and see; bet you a bang-up dinner," said Robbie, that clever and canny young Scot.

"Airplanes Spread Terror," said headlines. "One Square Mile Burned." And also: "Wounded Children Lie All Night in Streets."

Four days later, Abend was back on Admiral Shiozawa's flagship, having another cocktail. "I see your American newspapers have nicknamed me the Baby-Killer," said the admiral. He seemed embarrassed. "They should give me some credit. I used only 30-pound bombs, and if I had chosen to do so I might have used the 500-pound variety."

GEORGE WESTERVELT, an ex-navy man, now a salesman for the Curtiss-Wright airplane company, watched the bombing of Shanghai from his hotel room window. Then he wrote a letter to China's wealthy minister of finance, T. V. Soong. It was March 10, 1932.

Westervelt described the kinds of things that China could do with its own fleet of bombing planes. "Such planes could easily carry sufficient inflammable bombs of small weight to burn down the major portion of most Japanese cities," Westervelt wrote. He recommended that China hire a seasoned American air force officer to set up a training program for Chinese pilots.

T. V. Soong liked the idea of a pilot-training program, and so did the new American air attaché, Colonel Drysdale, who wrote a memo to the State Department. "The presence of such a mission in China," Drysdale wrote, "will be invaluable in increasing the use here of American planes and equipment."

EDGAR MOWRER, in Berlin, learned something troubling about the pope. Mowrer's German assistant, Otto Brock, rushed into the office and said that he'd been to a meeting of the German Center party, or Zentrum. Somebody at the meeting had read aloud a letter from Cardinal Pacelli in Rome.

"The Cardinal wrote that the Pope was worried about the rise of communism in Germany and advised our Party to help make Hitler chancellor. The *Zentrum*'s leaders agreed." Brock was in tears.

Mowrer asked if he could write about the cardinal's message.

"No," said Brock, "it was a secret meeting. But you will see." As Brock predicted, from then on, the Center party supported Hitler. It was the summer of 1932.

BENITO MUSSOLINI was writing an article on fascism for volume fourteen of the *Enciclopedia Italiana*. Pacifism was cowardice, Mussolini said: "Only war brings to the highest tension the energies of man and imprints the sign of nobility on those who have the virtue to confront it." It was 1932.

COLONEL JACK JOUETT, a veteran pilot, began teaching eighty-eight Chinese cadets at a new military flying school south of Shanghai. The cadets showed up at class holding copies of Charles Lindbergh's *We*. They were eager to learn how to fly the school's new fleet of Curtiss-Wright airplanes. It was September 1932.

EDGAR AND LILIAN MOWRER were guests of a German banker. It was late in 1932.

"After dinner," Edgar later wrote, "while the men, all Jews but me, sat over coffee, several boasted of giving money to the Nazi party at the request of Aryans like Schacht and Thyssen."

Mowrer was silent. The banker, whom Mowrer identified as "Arnholt"—possibly Hans or Heinrich Arnhold—asked him what he was thinking.

"Merely wondering," said Mowrer, "how the People of Israel have managed to survive so many thousands of years when they obviously have a strong suicidal urge."

The banker scoffed at Hitler's rhetoric. "Just talk," he said.

LION FEUCHTWANGER, the popular German novelist, gave a talk at the Hotel Commodore in New York. It was February 8, 1933. There were 450,000 Jews in Germany, Feuchtwanger said, in a country of sixty-five million people. And yet every day, eighteen million copies of anti-Semitic papers were published: "Forty copies for an average Jew per day," he said.

In March, while Feuchtwanger was in Switzerland, Brownshirts raided his house in Berlin. They took his wife's car and the manuscript of a half-finished novel. They tore up a portrait of Eleanor Roosevelt. "I believe it was their intention to shoot me, but this failed owing to my absence," Feuchtwanger said. "The unfortunate thing is that these people have taken the former wild speeches of Hitler too literally."

THE REICHSTAG caught fire. It was February 27, 1933.

A young Dutch-born bricklayer, Marinus van der Lubbe, a professed communist, was found shirtless on the scene and arrested. Hitler went in the middle of the night to the offices of the *Völkischer Beobachter,* where an assistant told him to come back during business hours. "Are you mad?" said Hitler. "Don't you realize that an event of incalculable importance is actually now taking place?" He and Goebbels worked the rest of the night getting the next issue ready.

Civil rights in Germany were suspended. "Goering let loose his hordes, and at one blow all justice in Germany was smashed," wrote Stephan Zweig.

THE NEW YORK TIMES REPORTED, on page one, that the Central Union of German Citizens of the Jewish Faith, a group with sixty thousand members, had issued a statement saying that the reports of atrocities by Nazis against Jews were "pure invention." It was March 25, 1933.

Anti-Semitism existed, and it was, the society said, a matter of grave concern, but it was a domestic affair. "Let us take an energetic stand against everybody attempting criminally to influence the shaping of Germany's future through foreign newspapers."

JAMES G. MCDONALD, chairman of the Foreign Policy Association of the United States, had dinner in Berlin with Ernst Hanfstaengel, Hitler's friend. It was April 1, 1933. McDonald told Hanfstaengel that he'd just had a meeting with Hitler, in which he'd said that Hitler's anti-Semitic policies were injuring Germany. Hitler had said, "The world will yet thank us for teaching it how to deal with the Jews."

Hanfstaengel sipped his wine. He was an ardent booster of Aryanism, but he was a dark-haired man, not particularly Nordic-looking—except that, as he had been heard to say, his underarm hair was quite blond. "Do you know," he said to McDonald, "that we have arranged to wipe out the entire Jewish population in the Reich? Each Jew has a Storm Trooper assigned to him. Everything is ready and can be done in a single night."

McDonald walked back through the Tiergarten to his hotel. Lovers were sitting on park benches. "I felt as if I'd had a nightmare," he wrote.

LILIAN MOWRER heard Chancellor Hitler say, in a speech, "Our enemies will be brutally and ruthlessly exterminated." Mowrer thought she must have misheard. The leader of a great nation wouldn't say something like that. She looked up the official text. Yes: *Brutal und rücksichtslos ausgerottet.* And then the nighttime disappearances and beatings began, the murders, she wrote, "of hundreds and hundreds done in cold blood by sexual sadists and lads not out of their teens, upon orders by their 'party superiors.'" Then the yellow signs went up on Jewish-owned stores. At the

Kaufhaus des Westens, a department store, Mowrer, showing her American passport, pushed past the linked arms of the storm troopers. The place was almost empty. The only customers were foreigners protesting the boycott. "The salesfolk stood around, silent and miserable. I wanted to buy up everything in sight," she said. "All morning I shopped in Jewish places." It was April 1933.

How could this be happening? she wondered. The country was calm. The streets were clean. The traffic flowed smoothly.

"Germans are among the most likable people in Europe and surely average no greater number of bullies and sadists than any other nation," she wrote. "The difference was that Hitler's régime was built on sadists and bullies, from the top down."

SAMUEL FULLER, an executive in the rayon-fiber business, wrote a memo to his old friend Franklin Roosevelt, now president of the United States. It was May 8, 1933.

Roosevelt had asked Fuller, when he visited Berlin, to find out the answers to some questions about Hitler. One of the questions was: "Is he going to keep the Jews out for good? Or is he just punishing them temporarily to make them be good?"

"Regarding the Jews," wrote Fuller to Roosevelt, "Dr. Schacht stated that the Jewish situation had been much exaggerated in the American press." Nobody had been killed, Schacht—the head of the German bank—told Fuller: No Jews had suffered personal violence. Schacht described the situation this way:

> A large number of Jews entered Germany after the War.
> These had joined, to a great extent, the Communists' party.
> The Government for the past 10 years had been filled, in the

bureaucratic places to a very large extent by Jews. The majority of places were held by Jews. Germany is not a Jewish nation. The appointed judges of the Courts were largely Jewish. The ministry of education was filled with Jews. The Chief of Police of Berlin was a Jew. 2600 out of the 3200 Berlin lawyers were Jews. In the University of Berlin 3 per cent to 4 per cent of the student body were Jews, and 40 per cent of the professors were Jews. Germany felt that this was wrong; and they put them out and filled their places, or places where necessary, with Gentiles.

Fuller had another conversation with Schacht later on. "If I were a Jew I would be concerned," Schacht told him then. "I am not a Jew and I am concerned."

Roosevelt passed the "extremely interesting" letter on to Cordell Hull, his secretary of state. "Please let me have it back when you and the Chief of the Division of Western Europe have read it," he wrote.

GOEBBELS STOOD at a swastika-bedecked rostrum on the Unter den Linden, a wide, tree-lined street in Berlin running past the University and the State Opera House. He said: "The age of extreme Jewish intellectualism has now ended." He threw a book into a fire.

"It was like burning something alive," Lilian Mowrer said. "Then students followed with whole armfuls of books, while schoolboys screamed into the microphone their condemnation of this and that author, and as each name was mentioned the crowd booed and hissed." Lion Feuchtwanger's books, which had already been banned from stores, went into the flames, as did books by Albert Einstein, Thomas Mann, Brecht, Lenin, Marx, Engels, Zinoviev, Heine, Emil Ludwig, Helen Keller, Upton Sinclair, and Jack London. Bertha von Suttner's pacifist novel *Lay Down Your Arms* was condemned as "un-German" and burned. *All Quiet on the Western Front* got the most booing. Stefan Zweig's books were nailed to a pillory as well as burned. Pacifism masked a "seeping poison," one speaker said. It was May 10, 1933.

Goebbels said: "Brightened by these flames our vow shall be: the Reich and the Nation and our Führer: Adolf Hitler. Heil! Heil!"

HARRY EMERSON FOSDICK, now the minister of Riverside Church in New York, organized a petition of protest. It was May 1933. "We acknowledge the grievous provocations which have led to the German revolution," Fosdick's petitioners said, "especially the condemnation of unborn generations of German children to economic servitude by the terms of the peace." Nevertheless, the time had come to speak. "Herr Hitler for years has preached relentless hatred against Jews," they said. "One of the fundamental doctrines of the Nazis, explicity acknowledged by them, is that the Jews are poisonous bacilli in the blood of Germany to be stamped out like a plague." That belief they were now putting into practice:

> Systematically they are prosecuting a "cold pogrom" of inconceivable cruelty against our Jewish brethren, driving them from positions of trust and leadership, depriving them of civil and economic rights, deliberately condemning them, if they survive at all, to survive as an outlawed and excommunicated people, and threatening Jews with massacre if they so much as protest.

One thousand two hundred American clergymen signed the protest; their names filled most of a page of *The New York Times*.

At a dinner of the Federal Council of Churches a few months later, Reverend Fosdick said: "Nothing so barbarous as the deliberate persecution of a whole race by the official powers of a nation has been heard of in Western civilization in a thousand years."

There was a German professor of theology at the dinner, a certain Julius Richter, an oil-on-the-waters man. The wave of German anti-Semitism would pass, he said. "Chancellor Hitler is a very clever, a very sound man," Richter said. "He doesn't drink; he doesn't smoke; he leads an exactly moral life. We can rely on Hitler not to let such things go on for a long time."

EDGAR MOWRER—who had just won the Pulitzer Prize for an anti-Nazi book, *Germany Puts the Clock Back*—received a politely worded threat. The German government didn't like his opinions and wanted him to resign from his post as president of the Foreign Press Association. Mowrer went to see Goebbels, who sat in a large room decorated with orchids in Chinese vases. "We will not have you swindle the public," Goebbels said.

A well-known newspaperman, Dr. Goldmann—unwell, not young, with a humpback—was arrested. Mowrer felt that Goldmann wouldn't live long in a prison camp. He offered to resign from the presidency if Goldmann was released. The Nazis agreed.

Four detectives began tracking the Mowrers' movements. One night, the couple noticed a group of storm troopers with a searchlight outside their house—clearly, it was time to leave Berlin. Edgar and Lilian still went out for walks, though, admiring the trees on the Tiergarten, the five elms where the rabbits played, the island where the cygnets hatched every year. They tried not to talk about German politics. "Think of their love of flowers," said Edgar Mowrer. "If ever there is a judgment on these people I hope someone will get up and say, 'But remember their window-boxes.'"

Edgar was informed that the German government could no longer guarantee his safety. He left for France. Lilian packed and joined him there. "Nowhere have I had such lovely friends as in Germany," she wrote afterward. "Looking back on it all is like seeing someone you love go mad—and do horrible things."

JAMES G. McDONALD, of the Foreign Policy Association, gave a speech at the Chatauqua festival. A reporter was there for *The New York Times* and covered it. It was July 10, 1933. McDonald didn't say what Hitler and Hanfstaengel had told him about their plan for the Jews. But he did say that the attempts on the part of Nazi apologists to deny that Jews were being cruelly treated were an "insult to the intelligence." "The Nazis believe the myth of the supremacy of the Aryan race, and are determined to crush Jewish economic life," he said. Hitler had exploited prejudices and postwar humiliations: "The war, the Versailles treaty and the treatment of Germany since the war have made Germans turn to new leaders," he said. "Hitlerism is in a very real sense a gift of the Allies and the United States."

HITLER MADE JULIUS STREICHER the party leader of Franconia. Streicher, a paranoiac with a shaved head, was the publisher of two newspapers, one of which was the luridly anti-Semitic tabloid *Der Stürmer,* or "The Stormer."

Streicher ordered the arrest of several hundred Jews, mostly shopkeepers, in Nuremberg, the capital of Franconia. "They were made to march in procession through the streets, flanked on either side by storm troopers and treated with derision and brutality," reported *The Times* of London. Some were imprisoned awaiting ransom; some were "set to plucking the grass out of a field with their teeth." *The Times* said: "As the need for a pretext to 'confiscate' funds is believed to have played a powerful part on the last occasion, a repetition of these occurrences is feared by many people in the near future." It was July 1933.

Streicher's newspaper ran an article called "The Dead Jew." It was about a man who committed suicide after being persecuted. "We would raise no objection at all if all his racial equals were to make their adieu in the same manner," the article said.

MAJOR JAMES DOOLITTLE, the American flying ace, was in China demonstrating airplanes for Curtiss-Wright. It was summer 1933. Doolittle did stunts for the mayor of Shanghai and a crowd of seventy-five thousand in his Curtiss Hawk, and afterward the Nanking government ordered thirty-six Hawks, the company's biggest order that year. "We sold 24 Hawks to the Turkish Government last fall," said T. P. Wright, Curtiss-Wright's president, "and several are in service in South America."

Major Doolittle had also been talking about Hawk airplanes with Ernst Udet, the blue-eyed German flying ace—the two of them flew at American air shows together. Udet fancied the new Curtiss Hawk II; he'd seen it at the air races in Cleveland. It was a good stunt plane and a good dive-bomber. But it was expensive.

IN NUREMBERG, storm troopers took a nineteen-year-old girl to a cabaret. They cut off her hair, shaved her head, and tied a placard around her neck. "I have offered myself to a Jew," said the placard. It was August 13, 1933.

A group of tourists who witnessed the scene wrote a letter to the authorities in which they said that while they had no desire to interfere in the municipal affairs of the city, incidents of that kind could not but be disgusting to all foreign visitors. Some weeks later, the girl was pronounced mentally ill and taken to an asylum.

JOSEPH STALIN, the leader of Russia, ordered operatives to remove all the stores of food from farming towns in the Ukraine. Millions of people had no bread—they ate field mice, insects, husks, and dead children. It was 1933.

A Russian-born American couple visited a Ukrainian village. "We are all dying of starvation," a villager told them. "They want us to die. It is an organized famine. There never has been a better harvest, but if we were caught cutting a few ears of corn we would be shot or put in prison and starved to death." It was August 1933.

DAVID LLOYD GEORGE, who had been prime minister of England during the Great War, gave a speech. The English government should not bully Germany, Lloyd George said. "I know there have been horrible atrocities in Germany and we all deplore and condemn them," he said. "But a country passing through a revolution is always liable to ghastly episodes owing to the administration of justice being seized here and there by an infuriated rebel." If the Allied powers managed to achieve the overthrow of Nazism, what would take its place? "Extreme communism," said Lloyd George. "Surely that cannot be our objective."

It was September 22, 1933.

ERNST UDET, the German pilot, was in Buffalo, New York, shopping for dive-bombers. He told the sales manager at Curtiss-Wright that he wasn't sure he could afford to buy a Hawk II. "But Mr. Udet," said the sales manager, "the money has already been lodged with our bank."

Hermann Goering, German aviation minister and president of the Reichstag, had bought two Curtiss-Wright Hawk IIs for Udet. Udet rejoined the Luftwaffe—the German air force—and with his help Junkers Aviation began designing a German plane called the Ju 87, the Stuka. It was even better at dive-bombing than the Curtiss Hawk II.

FREDERICK BIRCHALL, Berlin correspondent for *The New York Times,* published an article about Germany's preparations for war. It was October 8, 1933.

Birchall quoted from a recent book by Ewald Banse, a teacher at the Technical High School in Brunswick, Germany. The book was called *Wehrwissenschaft*—"Military Science." War was no longer a matter of marches and medals, Banse observed: "It is gas and plague. It is tank and aircraft horror. It is baseness and falsehood. It is hunger and poverty." And because war is so horrible, Banse said, it must be incorporated into the school curriculum and taught as a new and comprehensive science: "The methods and aims of the new science are to create an unshakable belief in the high ethical value of war and to produce in the individual the psychological readiness for sacrifice in the cause of nation and state."

Birchall's eye rested on one passage in particular of Banse's book. In it, Banse charged that in the Great War the French had attempted to use bacteriological warfare against German crops and livestock. The plan had failed, Banse said, but the technique deserved investigation. For a weak nation that has been disarmed and rendered defenseless, such as postwar Germany, biological warfare—tainting drinking water with typhus germs and spreading plague using infected rats—"is undoubtedly the given weapon." The League of Nations had forbidden such techniques, but when it came to national survival, "every method is permissible to stave off the superior enemy and vanquish him."

AT AN AIR PAGEANT on Long Island, Ernst Udet did amazing stunts in his red and silver Flamingo, and a fleet of U.S. Army airplanes bombed and strafed a papier-mâché village. The demolished village was named "Depressionville." It was October 8, 1933.

THE GERMAN GOVERNMENT ordered all copies of Ewald Banse's book confiscated. It was October 20, 1933.

"Single sentences and passages from it have been quoted abroad to throw suspicion on Germany's peaceable disposition," said an official pronouncement. "Professor Banse's ideas do not correspond with those of the Government and should be regarded merely as his private opinion."

The government also banned two songs: "We Shall Fight and Conquer France" and "German People, to Arms!"

AN EXECUTIONER in white gloves and a top hat strapped Marius van der Lubbe, convicted arsonist of the Reichstag, to a guillotine. His head fell into a basket of sawdust. It was January 10, 1934.

ELEANOR ROOSEVELT addressed the ninth annual Congress on the Cause and Cure of War. There were five hundred delegates at the congress, representing eleven organizations with a combined membership of eleven million people. "Any one who thinks, must think of the next war as suicide," Eleanor Roosevelt said. "How deadly stupid we are that we can study history and live through what we live through, and complacently allow the same causes to put us through the same thing again!" It was January 17, 1934.

A week later, Clark H. Woodward, a rear admiral in the U.S. Navy, gave a fierce speech before the assembled delegates at the ninth annual meeting of the Women's Patriotic Conference on National Defense, a promilitary, anti-immigrant umbrella group. Admiral Woodward had won many medals and fought in many wars—he had helped crush insurrections in Nicaragua and Haiti.

Subversive propaganda in favor of disarmament was being "viciously pushed by radical aliens, foreign-born and un-American Americans," Admiral Woodward said to the patriotic women. "Proselytizing parlor pinks and treacherous paid lobbyists have renewed their sinister, intensive and destructive efforts to convince our statesmen by insidious appeal and academic reasoning of the futility of further preparedness."

A BRITISH SPY, Frederick Winterbotham, visited Hitler in his new quarters in the Reich Chancellery in Berlin. It was February 1934.

Winterbotham, a tall, sandy-haired Englishman, mounted the grand stairway with his host Alfred Rosenberg, a racial theorist. Men in black uniforms stood at attention, touching their holstered guns with white gloves. The visitors entered a large office hung with tapestries and blue brocade curtains. Hitler was sitting behind his desk, wearing a brown shirt and a black tie.

"Maybe Hitler wasn't used to people smiling broadly at him, but it seemed to work for he stood up, out shot a hand, not in the now familiar salute but to be shaken in the ordinary civilised way," Winterbotham wrote. He was struck by Hitler's eyes. "Many people have commented on their apparent hypnotic quality but to me they looked as if they stood out a bit too far from their sockets. Nevertheless, they were friendly."

Hitler told Winterbotham that the Luftwaffe would be up to five hundred aircraft by the early part of 1935. "There should be only three major powers in the world," Hitler said, "the British Empire, the Americas, and the German Empire of the future." The British empire would oversee Africa and India, while Germany would control Russia. The fate of China would be determined in time. Versailles was dead. "All we ask," Hitler said, "is that Britain should be content to look after her empire and not interfere with Germany's plans of expansion."

Winterbotham then said that he gathered Hitler disliked the communists. Hitler's neck went red. "His eyes started to bulge even further; he stood up and, as if he was an entirely different personality, he started to yell in his high-pitched staccato voice, which now echoed round the walls of the great room; he addressed not three people but an imaginary three thousand," wrote Winterbotham. Then Hitler finished, smiled, and sat down. "That is what I think of the Communists," he said.

SOME QUTAIBI TRIBESMEN attacked a caravan in southern Yemen, a country that was part of the British empire. It was March 1934. Group Captain Charles Portal, of the Royal Air Force, believed that the tribesmen ought to be disciplined. He had his fliers drop leaflets, asking the tribesmen to pay a fine and hand over the wrongdoers. "Until you have complied with the terms your villages and fields may be bombed or fired on at any time by day or night, and you are particularly warned not to touch any bombs that do not go off, as if you do so you will probably get killed," said the leaflets.

The Qutaibi did not comply. Portal ordered his pilots to drop "a few small bombs in the principal villages" and also to bomb heavily the houses of the sheikh and his uncle. They used delayed-action bombs in order to keep the villagers away from their houses—a technique known as "inverted blockade." After two months of bombing, the Qutaibis accepted the terms. Three tribesmen were killed, Portal wrote, when they tried to take apart a delayed-action bomb; none of his own men was injured. "The most remarkable thing, and the most satisfactory," he said, "is the way the tribe came back into the fold with practically no ill-will."

H. C. ENGELBRECHT, author of *Merchants of Death,* a bestseller about arms dealers, spoke at a conference of the American Academy of Political and Social Science. "Armament is an industry that knows no politics, friends, right or wrong—but only customers," Engelbrecht said. "If you can pay, you can buy."

The French arms company Schneider had recently sold four hundred tanks to Hitler's Germany, Engelbrecht observed; the company disguised the sale by shipping the tanks via the Netherlands.

The Germans had also ordered sixty airplanes from Vickers, the British maker of bombers.

"In every war," said Engelbrecht, "the armament maker who sells internationally is arming a potential enemy of his own country—and that, practically, if not legally, is treason."

It was April 14, 1934.

CLARENCE PICKETT, the executive secretary of the American Friends Service Committee, met Rabbi Leo Baeck in Berlin. The American Friends Service Committee was a Quaker relief organization founded by a Haverford College professor named Rufus Jones; it had fed millions of people in Germany, Austria, Poland, and Russia during the famines in the late teens and early twenties. Pickett, an undemonstrative man with a crooked smile, was in Europe "to explore whether we could do anything to help prevent the barbaric treatment of Jews and to assist the immigration of those who were so fortunate as to be able to go to the United States or elsewhere." It was May 1934.

Rabbi Baeck said he didn't want to visit Pickett at the Friends Center in Berlin because he didn't want the center to be marked as a Jewish hideout; they met instead in a black-curtained room in the American Women's Club.

Since before the time of Christ, Baeck said, Jews had been a part of what was now Germany. The synagogue at Worms had recently celebrated its nine hundredth anniversary of continuous existence. The Jews loved Germany, and they wanted to stay there.

Baeck told Pickett that there had been an upsurge of religious feeling as a result of the racism and persecution. The rabbi's congregation used to number fifty or sixty people; now he held four separate services every Saturday. The crowds came, even though when they left the synagogue they were sometimes pelted with stones. It was a good time to be a rabbi, he said.

Baeck told Pickett that his constant theme was: "Let no drop of bitterness enter your hearts, to defile them."

REINHARD HEYDRICH, head of the intelligence branch of the German secret police, read a position paper prepared for him concerning Jewish policy. It was May 24, 1934.

"The aim of Jewish policy must be the emigration of all Jews," the paper said. Jewish "assimilationists"—those who wanted to live their lives as Germans within Germany—should be discouraged; while Zionists—those who wanted to emigrate to Palestine—should be encouraged, according to the memo. "It is the aim of the State Police to support Zionism and its emigration policy as fully as possible":

> Every authority concerned should, in particular, concentrate their efforts in recognizing the Zionist organizations and in supporting their training and emigration endeavors; at the same time the activities of German-Jewish groups should be restricted in order to force them to abandon the idea of remaining in Germany.

In this way, Germany would eventually become a country "without a future for the Jews."

Heydrich, a blond man with a high forehead and long, spidery fingers, began helping Zionist organizations set up agricultural-training centers, so that Jews would know how to farm when they reached Palestine.

PRESIDENT ROOSEVELT was using money from the National Recovery Act—part of the New Deal—to build thirty-two warships. He visited Pearl Harbor, a naval outpost near Honolulu: Hawaiian singers sang traditional songs for him, and three hundred Japanese girls danced by lantern light in a historical pageant at the Iolani Palace. In a speech, the president praised the richness of Hawaii's past, the cleanliness of Hawaii's houses, and the efficiency and spirit of Hawaii's American military forces, of which he was commander in chief. "These forces must ever be considered an instrument of continuing peace," he said. He thanked everyone and expressed a wish to return someday. "I say to you 'Aloha' from the bottom of my heart." It was July 28, 1934.

In the *Japan Advertiser,* General Kunishiga Tanaka, a former military attaché to Washington, wrote a response to Roosevelt's visit. "President Roosevelt has traveled to Hawaii, and there inspected the Pearl Harbor base, which is regarded as the centre of American offensive operations in the Pacific," said General Tanaka, "telling the world in loud tones its equipment is perfect." This event was accompanied, the general noted, by news of the Navy League's lobbying in favor of vast American fleets and by the creation of U.S. air bases in Alaska and the Aleutian Islands. "Such insolent behavior makes us most suspicious. It makes us think a major disturbance is purposely being encouraged in the calm Pacific. This is greatly regretted."

GEORGE SELDES, a muckraking journalist, published an article in *Harper's Magazine.* "It is an axiom that nations do not arm for war but for *a* war," Seldes wrote. He had just interviewed an official at the Navy League, a pro-preparedness pressure group.

"Do you accept the naval axiom that you prepare to fight a specific navy?" Seldes had asked the Navy League man.

"Yes," the man said.

"Do you contemplate a fight with the British navy?" Seldes asked.

"Absolutely, no," said the man.

"Do you contemplate war with Japan?"

"Yes."

It was October 1934.

STUDENTS IN THE NEW U.S. Air Corps Tactical School, at Maxwell Field, Alabama, were learning how to wage modern war with airplanes. It was the 1934–35 school year.

"Sound strategy requires that the main blow be struck where the enemy is weakest," the students learned. "Large urban populations and high standards of living broaden the possible range of dislocation and add length to the lever that an air force can apply against morale."

Water supplies were particularly vulnerable: "Reservoirs can be gassed, aqueducts cut, and dams or pumping facilities destroyed. The effects upon the civil population will be immediate and far reaching: sanitation will fail and the possibility of epidemic disease will become acute."

THE BOEING CORPORATION, in Seattle, sold three two-engine airplanes to Germany. These planes "might be regarded by a military expert as admirable potential bombers," said *The New York Times*; German engineers were studying them attentively. Pratt and Whitney maintained a Berlin office—BMW had bought the rights to build one of Pratt and Whitney's engines. The Sperry Corporation, maker of bombsights and gyroscopic stabilizers, had a patent-sharing agreement with a German company, Askania.

In Berlin, an American commercial attaché wrote that American manufacturers were selling Germany crankshafts, cylinder heads, control systems for anti-aircraft guns, and components sufficient to make about a hundred planes a month. There were, the attaché reported, orders outstanding to equip two thousand planes.

It was May 1934.

PRESIDENT ROOSEVELT placed Wake Island, a reef in the Pacific Ocean, under the administration of the U.S. Navy. He granted Pan Am Airways a permit to build runways on Wake Island, Midway Island, and Guam. It was March 14, 1935.

The Japanese military authorities were not pleased; the airports could become military bases, they said. "The islands are natural 'aircraft carriers,' affording enemy squadrons ideal places from which to operate," wrote a retired commander in chief in the Japanese navy. "Should they be occupied by an enemy they would at once endanger our defense."

CLARENCE PICKETT, the Quaker, and Harry Emerson Fosdick, the antiwar preacher, had tea in the Oval Office with President Roosevelt. It was April 1935. The navy was proposing to hold war games and maneuvers near the Aleutian Islands and Midway Island. The islands were far away from the United States and close to Japan. "This was," so it seemed to Pickett, "a deliberate effort to flex our muscles where Japan could see us, to warn her of what she might expect if she did not respect our power."

Roosevelt was a talker; he told stories, he reminisced. "We began to wonder whether we would get our concern expressed," Pickett wrote. Eventually, Reverend Fosdick broke in and warned of the danger of large naval maneuvers so near Japan. Roosevelt said that one of his Harvard classmates had been Japanese, and this Japanese classmate had talked about conquest. "We did not succeed in persuading him to move the navy's playground," Pickett said.

ONE HUNDRED and sixty American ships and 450 American airplanes began war games in the Pacific—the largest war games in American history. It was April 1935. The Fellowship of Reconciliation, a peace group, sent an open letter to the people of Japan, with a copy to President Roosevelt: "We desire to convey to you," the letter said, "the knowledge that many thousands of our citizens, especially those who constitute the membership of our churches and our synagogues, have protested against the holding of these maneuvers."

Japan and the United States had maintained friendly relations for eighty-one years, the letter said. "Multitudes of our people, whether connected with the institutions of religion or not, oppose these maneuvres and join us in spirit as we convey to you our assurances of continued and undiminished friendship." Rufus Jones, John Haynes Holmes, and fifteen others signed the letter.

Admiral Kanji Kato, former Japanese chief of staff, said that the American naval manifestation was like "drawing a sword before a neighbor's house."

"That's too damn bad," said Admiral Standley, the chief of naval operations of the United States.

SOMEONE THREW A STONE through the studio window of an immigrant painter named Michael Califano. The next day, three men came to the door. It was May 16, 1935, in New York City. The men asked to see some postcards of Califano's anti-Nazi painting, *The Ignominy of the Twentieth Century*. The postcards were being sold to benefit Jewish refugees. The painting, which had been exhibited at the Independents' Show in Grand Central Palace, showed Hitler expelling Einstein from Germany; near Hitler was an iron fist holding a bloody knife.

Califano turned to get the postcards, and the men grabbed him, beat him, and tied him to a steam pipe. One put the muzzle of a gun in his mouth and told him to be quiet. They began slashing his paintings. They slashed Einstein, Rudolph Valentino, and Adolph Ochs, publisher of *The New York Times*. They spared the image of Hitler. Califano fainted. A neighbor found him unconscious but alive, hanging from the pipe. He was taken to a hospital. He'd been planning on exhibiting his paintings at the World Jewish Congress.

TEN THOUSAND PEOPLE marched up Fifth Avenue from Washington Square Park. They carried signs that said: NO NATION CAN AFFORD BOTH WAR AND CIVILIZATION and PROMOTE JAPANESE FRIENDSHIP. The Women's International League for Peace and Freedom formed a "marching war cemetery," and there was a sort of float: a turf graveyard of white crosses with two mourners, a mother and child, and a sign that said, WHAT PRICE GLORY?

Among those leading the march were two famous religious leaders—John Haynes Holmes of the Community Church (the admirer of Gandhi) and Rabbi Stephen Wise of the Free Synagogue—along with leaders of other denominations, a group of Quakers, and some socialists carrying red banners. A dog wore a sign that said, I'M NOT GOING TO BE A WAR DOG.

The crowd turned onto Twenty-sixth Street, then went down Madison Avenue to Union Square, where three hundred policemen stood in lines keeping order. Socialist Charles Solomon told the crowd that capitalism breeds imperialism, "which is the parent of those international frictions that cause war." John Haynes Holmes promised that the jails would overflow if war came, and he led the crowd in a pledge:

> If war comes I will not fight.
> If war comes I will not enlist.
> If war comes I will not be conscripted.
> If war comes I will do nothing to support it.
> If war comes I will do everything to oppose it.
> So help me God.

It was May 18, 1935.

BENITO MUSSOLINI wanted an empire like the British had. He gave a demonstration of Italy's military resources, in advance of a planned annexation of Ethiopia. It was May 18, 1935. Bombs, poison gases, smoke screens, and flamethrowers were all on display in Rome before an admiring crowd. "Signor Mussolini himself took a hand and displayed considerable skill in throwing hand grenades, showing he had not forgotten the lessons he learned in the war," wrote *The New York Times*.

LEO ROSTEN, a young writer and teacher, published an article for *Harper's Magazine*. Never had the peace movement been so visible and so articulate, Rosten observed, and yet militarism was on the upsurge. Why? Because murderousness was "deeply encysted" in the human personality. "Man's primitivism vibrates to the call of militarism because it recognizes, through no 'conscious' mechanism, opportunities for murder, sadism, and violence," Rosten wrote. Think, he said, of those veterans of the Great War who cheerfully recalled "the time I ripped that Hun open."

> The vast majority of men enjoy seeing two prize fighters batter each other into a gratifying pulp, or take a perverse pleasure in "lynching a nigger," or are thrilled at the opportunity to bash in the head of a "radical," a conscientious objector or, more recently, a Jew.

To stop war, we needed to do several things, Rosten believed. We needed to reduce poverty, and we needed to produce more peace petitions and more muckraking articles about corrupt munitions makers. We also needed to offer convincing war substitutes—football, boxing, the Olympics, the World Court, the National Recovery Administration—arenas of conflict in which people could participate in group glories without millions dying.

The title of Rosten's article was "Men Like War." It was July 1935.

JOHN HAYNES HOLMES's antiwar play, *If This Be Treason,* had its world premiere in Westport, Connecticut. It was July 29, 1935.

In the play's first act, Japanese ships make a surprise attack on the American fleet at Manila. The newly inaugurated president of the United States, pledged to pacifism, decides not to counterattack. Amid cries for blood and vengeance, and at risk of impeachment, President Gordon flies unarmed to Japan in a private plane. The Japanese people, touched by this bold gesture, revolt nonviolently against their militaristic leader, install a populist named Koyé, and everything turns out fine.

Holmes wrote the drama with the help of a minor playwright named Reginald Lawrence. He based his plot, he said, on Gandhi's visit to England in 1931.

"They have managed to achieve moments of such dramatic intensity," wrote the *New York Times* reviewer, "that the audience tonight was frequently fired to applause." Luigi Pirandello was in the audience, and so was George M. Cohan.

Later, *Asahi Shimbun,* a major Tokyo paper, carried an article about the play. There was a long review in *The Nation* and praise in *The Times* of London. The play ran for six weeks at the Music Box Theater in New York and was then forgotten.

"It has been to me an innocent source of pride that my play anticipated, point by point, the Japanese attack on Pearl Harbor," Holmes later wrote.

A NAZI PARTY propagandist in Bavaria filed a report. The anti-Semitic campaign in his district was making no headway, he said. "Every child learns about the Jewish menace; anti-Semitic propaganda is delivered in lectures everywhere," he wrote. Anti-Jewish posters and issues of *Der Stürmer* were prominently on view. "And despite all this, the campaigns have not the slightest success," he said. "The peasants do not wish to sever their ties with Jews."

It was October 1935.

THE GOVERNOR OF NEW YORK, Herbert Lehman, asked President Roosevelt to increase the Jewish immigration quota. It was November 1, 1935.

"The type of immigration from Germany is of the highest," Lehman wrote Roosevelt. "I have met many of those who have come over here in recent months and they have impressed me as very much the type of men like my father, Carl Schurz, and other Germans who came over here in the days of 1848 and who later were among our best citizens." Lehman mentioned the current immigration quota from Germany, which was twenty-five thousand. In recent years, however, only 2,500 of the spaces in that quota had been filled, Lehman said, and he passed on a request from banker Felix Warburg and others: "They ask that the immigration quota of German Jews to this country be increased from 2,500 to 5,000. This, of course, is almost a negligible number."

Roosevelt's stiff reply—drafted by the State Department— said that there was no immigration quota for "persons in the class described." The State Department had, however, issued 5,117 immigration visas to natives of Germany in 1935: Felix Warburg's request was thus already granted. Anyone who sought to escape from the conditions of the country of their regular residence would receive, Roosevelt said, "the most considerate attention and the most generous and favorable treatment possible under the laws of this country."

THE U.S. GOVERNMENT released its monthly statistical summary of licensed arms sales to foreign governments. Under the provisions of the Neutrality Act, all arms sales had to have the approval of the Munitions Control Board of the State Department.

China was again, in February 1936, the largest purchaser of arms, followed by Chile, followed by Germany. China had bought airplanes, tanks, and ammunition. Germany bought "non-military" aircraft, revolvers, and ammunition.

IN A LONDON COURTROOM, Sir Harry McGowan, the chairman of Imperial Chemical Industries—Winston Churchill's friend and investment adviser—sat before a royal commission that was investigating the armaments trade. It was February 6, 1936.

McGowan was asked about the sales of arms to opposing nations—to China and Japan, for instance. "I have no objection to selling arms to both sides," McGowan answered. "I am not a purist in these things." Imperial Chemical Industries wasn't, McGowan said, producing any war gasses at the moment—but they could begin at any time, at the government's request.

The company broke ground on a new mustard-gas factory in Lancashire later that year.

ALDOUS HUXLEY, a novelist and prominent member of the British Peace Pledge Union, wrote an article for *Time and Tide* about "collective security"—the idea that groups of countries should band

together to threaten belligerent dictatorships with violent consequences.

Was it of any use, Huxley wondered, to have a large bomber
force at hand to deter a dictator from doing objectionable things?
No, it wasn't, because a dictator may well weigh risk very differ-
ently from the way we expect him to. "If he is crazy, he doesn't
perceive the risk. If he is coldly Machiavellian, he sees that in desperate circumstances he personally may risk less by going to war
than by submitting to the threats of foreign governments."

It may be very difficult, Huxley admitted, to keep some nations
from attacking others. "What is quite certain is that threatening them
with war if they do so or making war upon them, even with a collective bombing force, will not achieve what is desired," he wrote. "An
evil act always produces further evil acts."

It was March 7, 1936.

ON MUSSOLINI'S ORDERS, Italian airplanes dropped gas bombs
on Ethiopia. "Beginning at 7:30 A.M., a squadron of seven bombers
dropped steel containers, some containing phosgene and others
mustard gas," reported *The New York Times*. "Several fell among
peasant huts." It was March 16, 1936.

A month later, Walter Holmes, a reporter for *The Times* of London, wrote about a new means of Italian attack on Ethiopian troops
and civilians: aerial spraying. "From a fine rain of corrosive liquid
descending from the planes there seems to be little protection, unless possibly something in the nature of a diving suit were devised,"
he wrote. Consequently, a large number subjected to this form of
attack received ghastly injuries on the head, face and upper parts of
the body."

WINSTON CHURCHILL published an article in the *Evening Standard* called "How to Stop War." It was June 12, 1936.

Fine speeches were useless, Churchill said, and platitudes were a crime. There was only one way to stop war, and that was through military might. "Safety will only come," he wrote, "through a combination of pacific nations armed with overwhelming power, and capable of the same infinity of sacrifice, and indeed of the ruthlessness, which hitherto have been the attributes of the warrior mind."

THE EMPEROR OF ETHIOPIA, Haile Selassie, walked to the podium of the League of Nations in Geneva, Switzerland. It was June 30, 1936.

Selassie began arranging his papers to speak. Suddenly, from the press gallery, came noise and confusion. "Led by a red-faced man with a bull voice the Fascisti hurled execrations and abuse," *The New York Times* reported. "Several mechanical whistles were turned loose." Police removed the disturbers, and the emperor spoke.

He described the gas bombing of his people. First the Italians used tear gas, then barrels of mustard gas. Neither of these methods was very effective. Then came the battle for Makale, in northern Ethiopia. "Special sprayers were installed on board aircraft so they could vaporize over vast areas of territory a fine, death dealing rain," the emperor said.

> Groups of nine, fifteen or eighteen aircraft followed one another so that the fog issuing from them formed a continuous sheet. It was thus that, as from the end of January, 1936, soldiers, women, children, cattle, rivers, lakes and pastures were drenched continually with this deadly rain.

The aircraft passed over again and again, in order to be sure to poison the water. "The deadly rain that fell from the aircraft made all those whom it touched fly shrieking with pain," said Selassie. "All those who drank poisoned water or ate infected food also succumbed in dreadful suffering. In tens of thousands the victims of Italian mustard gas fell."

NEWSPAPERS IN TOKYO all carried the same lead story: the U.S. government was loaning one hundred million yuan to China so that China could buy American armaments. It was July 21, 1936.

According to one document, Arthur Campbell, a representative of the Treasury Department, had recently brought a draft trade agreement with him to China. In it, the United States agreed to buy twenty-six million dollars' worth of silver from China, and China agreed to buy airplanes, ships, oil, tractors, and railroad equipment from the United States. Campbell was going to be staying on in China as an adviser.

If the reports of the arms deal were true, said an official from the Japanese Foreign Office, the Japanese government could not remain indifferent.

HENRY "CHIPS" CHANNON, a conservative member of the British Parliament, went to Hermann Goering's party at the Ministerium in Berlin. It was August 13, 1936, during the Olympic Games. Goering, "wreathed in smiles and orders and decorations," seated

Channon and his wife at a table with the future queen of Greece. There were more than seven hundred guests. After dinner, some dancers performed a ballet in the moonlight—"the loveliest coup-d'oeil imaginable," thought Channon—and then, at the end of the garden, a procession suddenly appeared, of white horses, donkeys, and peasants. The guests followed them into a private amusement park. "There has never been anything like this since the days of Louis Quatorze," someone said. "Goebbels," Channon noted in his diary, "was in despair with jealousy."

Of Goering himself, Channon said, "People say that he can be very hard and ruthless, as are all Nazis when occasion demands, but outwardly he seems all vanity and childish love of display."

A SUBCOMMITTEE of English planners thought about a future air war with Germany. "If our attacks could demoralise the German people, by methods similar to those we foresee the Germans themselves using against us, their Government might be forced to desist from this type of attack," the war planners wrote. The difficulty, however, was that London was easier to find and hit than landlocked Berlin. "Moreover, a military dictatorship is likely to be less susceptible to popular outcry than a democratic Government." Therefore, bombing the German people in the expectation that they would make an outcry and overthrow their government probably wasn't going to work. It was October 26, 1936.

ALBERT WEDEMEYER, a handsome captain in the U.S. Army, went to Berlin to study advanced strategy and tactics at the German War College. He and his wife had traveled from Fort Leavenworth, Kansas, where Wedemeyer, a West Point graduate, had studied military science at the Command and General Staff School. Classes began in October 1936.

Wedemeyer rented an apartment from a man named Rossbach, who had been a close friend of Ernst Röhm, the pederastic chief of the storm troopers, whom Hitler had had executed in 1934. Rossbach gave a party and invited Wedemeyer. Goering, Hess, Bormann, Ley, and other top Nazis were there, as was Goebbels—"a dynamo with a brain," Wedemeyer called him.

At the German War College, Wedemeyer studied the campaigns of Frederick the Great, Napoleon, Caesar, Alexander, and Philip of Macedon. That curriculum wasn't too different from what he'd just been through at Fort Leavenworth, where they'd studied Frederick the Great, Napoleon, Caesar, Alexander, and Philip of Macedon. But the Germans were better teachers, and their military science was more purposeful. "One of the map problems given while I was a student in Berlin involved a hypothetical attack against Czechoslovakia," Wedemeyer wrote. "Later, it developed that the problem was not so hypothetical."

When he got to school in the morning, there were women cleaning the halls on their hands and knees. They threw up their right arms and said, "Heil Hitler." Wedemeyer saluted back and said, "Heil Roosevelt." The cleaning women thought this was funny, and they eventually began greeting Wedemeyer with "Heil Roosevelt."

"To which I replied 'Heil Hitler.'"

CAPTAIN PHILIP S. MUMFORD, a former British officer in Iraq, joined the Peace Pledge Union. He gave a speech about why. "What is the difference between throwing 500 babies into a fire and throwing fire from aeroplanes on 500 babies?" he asked. "There is none."

It was January 5, 1937.

IN POLAND, right-wing nationalists rioted, beating up Jews. The budget committee of the Polish Parliament in Warsaw had a meeting. The Jews of eastern Europe had a dark economic future, a Colonel Meidzinski warned, because there weren't enough jobs for them all. "The Polish government, in trying to find an outlet for its surplus population, has in mind the Jews first of all. We would appreciate the Jews if we had 50,000 of them," he said. "Our negative attitude is caused by the fact that there are 3,000,000. A change in this abnormal situation is the only way to a solution of the thorny Jewish problem."

Colonel Józef Beck, the Polish foreign minister, said that immigration to Palestine wasn't enough. "Without giving up Palestine as an outlet for our Jewish surplus," the colonel said, "we must treat our problem on a wider basis."

Another member of Parliament, Deputy Minzberg, criticized the notion of treating Jews as if they were surplus goods available for export.

It was January 13, 1937.

A DELEGATION FROM WARSAW went to Madagascar, an island off the coast of Africa that once had been a center of the slave trade. The Polish government was talking to the French government about whether Polish Jews could be sent to Madagascar, which was at the time a French colony. The delegation—including a colonization expert from Tel Aviv and the director of the Jewish Emigrant Aid Society—reported, according to *The New York Times,* that "the central plateau was quite suitable for settling white men of the peasant type." It was 1937.

Others pointed out later, however, that there wasn't much territory left on the plateau, and that the lowland was "unfit for white habitation."

A DENTIST FROM NEW YORK, Dr. Howard Blake, talked with Rafael Trujillo, president of the Dominican Republic. Blake was representing the American Jewish Congress. He and Trujillo were trying to determine whether one million eastern European Jews could move to Trujillo's country. It was January 1937.

Blake toured the proposed area of resettlement with the president's engineering aide and the secretary of agriculture. The island was, Blake said, a "veritable paradise."

President Trujillo wrote a letter to Rabbi Stephen Wise, president of the American Jewish Congress. "The Dominican people and government, over which I have the honor to preside, received the proposal with the greatest sympathy," Trujillo said, "and expect to be able to offer a hospitable reception to that immigration of Jewish agriculturalists whom you propose to bring to my country to dedicate themselves to the land and development of industrial enterprises."

Trujillo wanted Jewish immigrants because they were white: Later that year, Trujillo's troops massacred twelve thousand Haitian peasants because they were black.

TWENTY THOUSAND cheering people were in Madison Square Garden. It was March 15, 1937, at an anti-Nazi rally and boycott-Germany night. A big banner onstage showed a workingman using pliers to crush a swastika. Rabbi Stephen Wise spoke on the menace of Hitlerism, Mayor Fiorello LaGuardia said a few sentences, and so did the head of the CIO labor union. Joseph Tenenbaum, chairman of a coalition that was advocating the boycott of German goods, said that the four years since Hitler and his cabal had come to power had been a "nightmare of dread terror and savagery." And the nightmare was coming to the United States:

> Every German boat anchoring on our shores discharges a fresh cargo of Nazi rats which spread the bubonic plague of anti-Semitism and racial hatred, and nibble away at the fundamentals of our great commonwealth.

"No one is safe from the Nazi holocaust," Tenenbaum said.

STANLEY BALDWIN, prime minister of England, said to a deputation of peace workers, "I know some of you think I should speak more roughly to Hitler than I do, but have you reflected that the reply to a stiff letter might be a bomb on your breakfast tables?" There was, Baldwin said, no Christian public opinion in Europe to which England could appeal. "The peace of the world lies in the hands of these dictators. For all I know they may be insane, and unlimited power drives men mad." It was March 21, 1937.

THE NATIONAL COUNCIL of Jewish Women had a meeting in Utica, New York. Baruch Braunstein, a rabbi from Allentown, Pennsylvania, who directed the Jewish division of the Emergency Peace Campaign, asked the delegates to think about what the Great War had done. The Great War "turned three-fifths of Europe back to the middle ages," Braunstein said. "We went to war to save democracy and our experience has been that democracy has died a thousand deaths." The next war, he said, would be even more destructive, and it would be "co-educational."

The Council of Jewish Women resolved to oppose conscription and to urge arms limitation, neutrality, and the elimination of military drill in schools. It was April 13, 1937.

THE CHURCH BELLS in Guernica began ringing. It was market day, Monday, at 4:30 P.M., on April 28, 1937. German pilots were in the air. They wore the badge of the Kondor Legion: a condor plunging earthward with a bomb held in its claws.

They were over the town for three hours. The curate of the Church of Santa Maria de Guernica wrote: "Before God and my country I bear witness that the airplanes threw incendiary bombs." *The Times* of London wrote: "The whole town of 7,000 inhabitants, plus 3,000 refugees, was slowly and systematically pounded to pieces." A reporter for the *Daily Mail* wrote: "A sight that haunted me for weeks was the charred bodies of several women and children huddled together in what had been the cellar of a house. It had been a refugio."

Later Hermann Goering said that Guernica had been a testing ground for the Luftwaffe. "It was a pity," he said, "but we could not do otherwise, as we had nowhere else to try out our machines."

RICHARD BREITING, the editor who had interviewed Hitler at the Brown House, was asked, in 1937, to travel from Leipzig to Berlin, to appear at Goebbels's propaganda ministry. He had already been questioned several times, and he'd been accused of being a "Jewish lackey." Two agents took him out to a restaurant for a talk. By the time he got back home, he was feverish. He began having convulsions. He suspected poison, he told his family. When he died, the attending physician refused to perform an autopsy. Breiting's body was cremated.

WINSTON CHURCHILL was readying his book *Great Contemporaries* for the press. It was August 1937. In it was his article on Hitler, written a few years earlier. "Those who have met Herr Hitler face to face in public business or on social terms," he said, "have found a highly competent, cool, well-informed functionary with an agreeable manner, a disarming smile, and few have been unaffected by a subtle personal magnetism." Despite the arming of Germany and the hounding of the Jews, "we may yet live to see Hitler a gentler figure in a happier age," Churchill wrote. He was doubtful, though.

Churchill also included a short piece on Leon Trotsky, king in exile of international bolshevism. Trotsky was a usurper and tyrant, Churchill said. He was a cancer bacillus, he was a "skin of malice," washed up on the shores of Mexico. Trotsky possessed, said Churchill,

> the organizing command of a Carnot, the cold detached intelligence of a Machiavelli, the mob oratory of a Cleon, the ferocity of Jack the Ripper, the toughness of Titus Oates.

And in the end what was Trotsky? Who was he? "He was a Jew," wrote Churchill with finality. "He was still a Jew. Nothing could get over that." He called his article "Leon Trotsky, *Alias* Bronstein."

THE JAPANESE government announced that it was disturbed by a report that 182 American airmen, each accompanied by two mechanics, were going to be flying warplanes in China. The enlistment of Americans was at odds with America's recently expressed hopes for peace in northern China, said the Japanese statement, and was in violation of the American Neutrality Act. It was August 5, 1937.

HALLETT ABEND, the *New York Times* correspondent, was sitting in a car outside Wing On's, Shanghai's largest department store. It was August 23, 1937.

Abend's assistant, Anthony Billingham, was inside buying field glasses. Abend, smoking a cigarette, noticed that some Chinese pedestrians were looking at the sky. A moment afterward, a large bomb hit the department store. "The worst part of a bombing experience," Abend wrote in his China memoir, "is that period of utter paralysis which follows the concussions."

> For as much as four minutes, if the bomb is a big one, nothing moves except swirling smoke and thick dust, and there is no sound except the continued tinkle of falling broken glass and the rumble of crumbling masonry. After about four minutes the wounded begin to moan and shriek and try to drag themselves away.

Abend, limping, hurried through the dim department store in search of his assistant. At the field-glasses counter on the second floor, he found two Chinese corpses. Back at the car, he discovered Billingham crumpled in the backseat, with a flayed left arm and arterial blood spouting from his armpit. "I threw the car into low gear," Abend wrote, "and started carefully up the street, avoiding the helpless wounded but of necessity sometimes driving crunchingly over the scattered dead."

The bomb that hit Wing On's department store—a single 750-pound fragmentation bomb, made in Italy—was, as it turned out, not dropped by a Japanese plane. A Chinese air-force pilot, alarmed at the sight of three Japanese pursuit fighters, released his load so that he could climb to safety at twenty thousand feet.

Billingham recovered.

JAPAN INSTITUTED a naval blockade against Chinese ships. "Peaceful commerce carried on by third powers will be fully respected," the Japanese government said. It was August 28, 1937.

A freighter, the *Wichita,* owned by the U.S. government was on its way to China carrying bombing planes and barbed wire, according to the Associated Press. There were those who wondered whether the Japanese would regard this shipment as "peaceful commerce," the reporter wrote.

CHINESE AIRPLANES tried to destroy a group of Japanese ships with hundred-pound bombs. It was August 30, 1937.

A large American vessel, the *President Hoover,* filled with Americans leaving China, was anchored at the mouth of the Yangtze River. One of the Chinese pilots thought the *Hoover* was a Japanese troopship and dove to bomb it. Other Chinese planes followed. One crewmember was killed by flying shrapnel, and several passengers and crew were injured. A niece of Generalissimo and Madame Chiang Kai-shek was on board the boat.

Madame Chiang Kai-shek, secretary-general of aviation, was horrified. She summoned her husband's pilot, an American named Royal Leonard. "I want you to take charge of all Chinese bombardment," Madame Chiang said.

Royal Leonard said he would be happy to take charge of Chinese bombardment. In Hankow, Leonard and another American, Julius Barr, founded a new, better bombing school with a hundred students. A thousand laborers helped to improve the airfield. "Working day and night, each carrying material in baskets suspended from the ends of their yo-yo poles, they built a paved runway one thousand yards long in a few days," Leonard recalled.

CHURCHILL FOUND that he still nursed admiring feelings for Mussolini. "It would be a dangerous folly for the British people to underrate the enduring position in world-history which Mussolini will hold," he wrote in the *News of the World,* "or the amazing qualities of courage, comprehension, self-control and perseverance which he exemplifies."

It was October 10, 1937.

Boom Trenchard invited Churchill to a party for a delegation of German air-force officers. It was October 11, 1937.

"I have asked them privately to dinner at Brooks's Club on 20th October at 8:15 p.m. to meet only unofficials," Trenchard said. Camrose, Kindersley, Weir, Amery, and others would be there, he said—could he, Churchill, come? "*I hope you will,* because I think it might amuse you and interest them enormously."

Churchill went to the private party for the German air force.

Joseph C. Hyman, of the Joint Distribution Committee, a Jewish relief organization, gave a speech in Pittsburgh. "It is vitally necessary to send funds immediately to get our people out of Germany as soon as possible," Hyman said. But Germany wasn't their only problem.

> In Poland, though nominally protected by the constitution and the public law, only too often the Jewish population of over 3,000,000 souls are the victims of pogrom, riot, assault, boycott; only too openly the objects of a strong and effectively directed propaganda, which has one leit-motif— out with the Jews!

And in Romania, anti-Semitism "takes on a brutality of action and frequently a venomousness of expression which makes effective comparison with Nazi Germany," Hyman said.

It was October 17, 1937.

ALDOUS HUXLEY was in Hollywood writing *Ends and Means,* an inquiry into the philosophy of nonviolence. It was 1937.

The international police force that people were clamoring for was a mistake and a misnomer, Huxley believed. "The police act with the maximum of precision; they go out and arrest the guilty person," he wrote. "Nations and groups of nations act through their armed forces, which can only act with the maximum of imprecision, killing, maiming, starving and ruining millions of human beings, the overwhelming majority of whom have committed no crime of any sort." An international police force was in actuality a force for international massacre. "If you approve of indiscriminate massacres, then you must say so," he wrote. "You have no right to deceive the unwary by calling your massacre-force by the same name as the force which controls traffic and arrests burglars."

Nonviolence was, Huxley thought, the only intergovernmental response to violence that had any practical chance of working. It worked with nations as it did with individuals:

> We have all seen how anger feeds upon answering anger, but is disarmed by gentleness and patience. We have all known what it is to have our meannesses shamed by somebody else's magnanimity into an equal magnanimity; what it is to have our dislikes melted away by an act of considerateness; what it is to have our coldnesses and harshnesses transformed into solicitude by the example of another's unselfishness.

Violence made men worse, Huxley said; nonviolence made them better.

COLONEL CLAIRE CHENNAULT, a retired army flier now working for the Chinese, was in his apartment with Royal Leonard, the bombing instructor. It was sometime in 1937.

"The room was crowded with American pilots," Leonard remembered. "The topic under discussion was the immediate bombing of Tokyo."

> We had the men in that room, all of them experts in piloting and navigation. China had plenty of money with which we could purchase the fast, light Martin bombers.

But the plan was squelched by the Chinese, Leonard said, who didn't want to risk involving Americans in a Tokyo raid.

"Oh well," said Chennault. "It will be batter up sometime! We'll mow 'em down!"

The Chinese pilots called Chennault "Leatherface."

IN LONDON, LORD HALIFAX, the leader of the House of Lords, told his friend Chips Channon about a trip that he'd taken to talk things over with the Nazis. Lord Halifax used to be Lord Irwin, the viceroy of India. Now he was Lord Halifax.

Channon was eager to hear everything. Lord Halifax told Channon that he had liked all the Nazi leaders—even Goebbels. "He thinks the regime absolutely fantastic, perhaps even too fantastic to be taken seriously," Channon wrote in his diary.

Halifax told Channon about Hitler's black breeches, his patent-leather evening shoes, and his khaki shirt. "I was riveted by all he said," wrote Channon, "and reluctant to let him go." It was December 5, 1937.

JAPANESE AIRPLANES dropped leaflets over the city of Nanking, China. It was December 7, 1937.

"We have surrounded the city of Nanking," the leaflets said. "If your troops continue to fight, war in Nanking is inevitable. The culture that has endured for a millennium will be reduced to ashes, and the government that has lasted for a decade will vanish into thin air."

The Japanese waited. There was no reply from within the city. The Japanese bombed, shelled, and went in. Rape and massacre followed.

Royal Leonard, the American in charge of Chinese bomber command, wrote: "I remember people running along the streets in Nanking, the tops of their heads blown off, their mouths open and shrieking, gushing blood in little fountains, dying as they ran."

ALBERT SPEER, Hitler's architect, showed his father the room of the models. The room of the models was a large space set up in the former Berlin Academy of Arts, connected by a passageway to the Reich Chancellery, where Hitler lived. Hitler took guests there after dinner sometimes, to show them his private city, the city of Berlin as it would be, perhaps only after his death. The spotlights would come on, shining at an angle like sunlight on the elaborately rendered streets, the façades, the roofs, the allées of trees—all of them fabricated under Speer's close supervision. At the end of the grand boulevard in miniature—crowded with miniature movie houses, a new miniature opera house, hotels, and theaters—was to be the great domed assembly hall, inspired by one of Hitler's sketches. It was to be the biggest domed structure in the history of humanity, sixteen times more voluminous than St. Peter's, held aloft on ninety-eight-foot-high columns of red stone, surmounting a space that would hold one hundred and fifty thousand standing Reich worshippers.

Hitler, lost in happy megalomaniacal contemplation, would lean close to the grand boulevard, his eyes inches from the modelwork, discussing fine points. "In no other situations did I see him so lively, so spontaneous, so relaxed," Speer recalled.

Speer and his father entered the model room. The lights came on. Speer's father looked, then turned to Speer. "You've all gone completely crazy," he said.

That same night, at a play, Hitler invited Speer and his father to his private box. When introduced to Hitler, Speer's father turned pale. He could say nothing. "He was overcome by a violent quivering such as I had never seen him exhibit before," wrote Speer. Speer and his father never spoke of the incident afterward.

LOUIS LUDLOW, a member of the House of Representatives, introduced a bill to amend the U.S. Constitution. It was January 1938.

Under the amendment, any declaration of war by the United States would require a referendum—a national vote—except in the case of direct invasion or attack. The form of the question would be: "Shall the United States declare war on _____?"

President Roosevelt said that the amendment would cripple a president's ability to conduct foreign relations: "I fully realize," Roosevelt said, "that the sponsors of this proposal sincerely believe that it would be helpful in keeping the United States out of war. I am convinced that it would have the opposite effect."

A REPORTER for *The New York Times* interviewed Alexander Cuza, an elderly minister in the Romanian government. Jews were the spawn of the devil, Cuza said; every Jew must leave Romania; there would be terrible pogroms if they didn't go. "It is for the world to find a residence for the world's Jews," Cuza said. "Madagascar seems a suitable spot." It was January 21, 1938.

A little over a week later, the same reporter interviewed several Jewish students who had been attacked at a medical school. One woman said: "While working in the dissecting room, students surrounded me and took me to the basement. After a period of waiting six powerful students said: 'We will teach you to study at the university.' They then rushed at me with clenched fists, striking my face and body." She woke in a pool of blood. "My face was unrecognizable," she said.

MILTON MAYER, a writer who worked for the president of the University of Chicago, heard a story.

A Jew is riding a streetcar, reading the *Völkischer Beobachter,* the main Nazi paper. A non-Jew sits down next to him and says, "Why are you reading the *Beobachter?*" The Jew says: "Look, I work in a factory all day, my wife nags me, my kids are sick, and there's no money for food. What should I do on my way home, read the Jewish newspaper? 'Pogrom in Romania.' 'Jews Murdered in Poland.' 'New Laws against Jews.' No, sir, a half hour a day, on the streetcar, I read the *Beobachter.* 'Jews the World Capitalists.' 'Jews Control Russia.' 'Jews Rule in England.' That's *me* they're talking about. A half hour a day I'm somebody. Leave me alone, friend."

HERMANN GOERING, the second in command in the Nazi party, appeared at a reception for the Diplomatic Corps. He wore green boots and held a six-foot spear.

Goering was a morphine addict. He was rich and corpulent. He changed his clothes several times a day. In the morning, he would wear, perhaps, something with short, puffy white sleeves; at dinner, a "violet kimono with fur-trimmed bedroom slippers." Once he reclined on an ottoman with his pant legs pulled up, showing cardinal-red silk stockings. At hunting parties, he was accompanied by beaters and dog leaders carrying boar spears, "whose flashing tips were protected by tasselled leather sheaths."

JEANNETTE RANKIN made a statement on CBS Radio. "I want to urge mothers and fathers everywhere to work against war while there is time," she said. "I voted no in 1917, and I still vote no today, because I believe war is a futile method of trying to settle disputes."

At the Broadway Tabernacle Church, Allan Knight Chalmers addressed a large "peace consecration" service. Several hundred New York religious leaders had signed a new pledge. "Suddenly it does not seem so far off, the war that nobody wants and everbody dreads," the pledge said. "In the spirit of true patriotism and with deep personal conviction, I therefore renounce war and never will I support another." John Haynes Holmes, Rabbi Sidney Goldstein, and Reverend Fosdick were signers.

It was March 1, 1938.

GENERAL ARCHIBALD WAVELL, commander of British forces in Palestine, called for air support. An area known as the Bloody Triangle was under siege by the English. "Nine Royal Air Force planes bombed and machine gunned a band of Arabs, killing between fifty and sixty of their number in the encounter," the Associated Press reported. "Mopping up operations" followed. It was March 6, 1938.

IN VIENNA, a radio announcer said, in a voice of rapture, *"Der Führer ist hier!"* Hitler Youth and Hitler Girls filled the streets, roaring in unison. It was March 12, 1938.

Kurt von Schuschnigg, the chancellor of Austria, had resigned, announced a radio newsman from the Mutual Broadcasting Network. "He was told he was free to go where he liked, but that his eleven year old son, Kurt, must remain as a hostage, as a pledge of his father's discretion," said the newsman. Schuschnigg said that he wouldn't abandon his boy.

The SS put him in solitary confinement. Every Friday, he was allowed to talk to his wife for eight minutes.

MURIEL LESTER, a Christian relief worker and follower of Gandhi, was in Shanghai. It was 1938. Lester thought: Life has never been so painful. "Torture, starvation, and sex horrors surrounded us," she wrote. "Thousands slept on the city roads and pavements without even a piece of sacking to protect them from stone and concrete." Municipal employees picked up frozen corpses every morning; babies were born on the pavement. "Running over the battlefields in packs, like wolves, were native dogs which fattened and battened on human dietary."

Lester went on to visit Japan, where people were being arrested for dangerous thoughts. Yet there were some Japanese people who sent fraternal messages to China, Lester said. "Dear brothers and sisters in China," wrote Christian pacifist Toyohiko Kagawa. "Though a million times I should ask pardon, it would not be enough to cover the sins of Japan which cause me intolerable shame. I ask you to forgive my nation."

AT THE FRIENDS MEETING HOUSE on East Fifteenth Street in New York, some Quakers got together to oppose one of Roosevelt's new war-readiness bills. It was April 2, 1938.

A strong navy wasn't a deterrent, said Mary McDowell, a high school teacher. "Warships themselves," she said, "are the carriers of the disease, increasing the hate, fear, suspicion, and threat of destruction and domination, which are the atmosphere of war." The group sent letters off to Roosevelt and to Cordell Hull, the secretary of state.

THE SUNDAY MAGAZINE SECTION of *The New York Times* published a long article on President Roosevelt's fascination with the navy. "The navy is being run from the White House these days," wrote Hanson Baldwin, the *Times*'s military-affairs correspondent. Roosevelt, said Baldwin, was "the power behind the gradual extension of our naval strength across the Pacific." He took a personal interest in questions of ship design, armament, and officer promotion; he was more enthusiastically and knowledgeably "big navy" than the admirals themselves.

In the president's office, according to Baldwin, were an ashtray with a ship on it, a cigarette lighter in the shape of a ship's wheel, a barometer, a ship's clock, paintings of sea scenes and battles, and a model of the four-smokestack flush-deck destroyer—a craft produced under Roosevelt's supervision during the Great War. In nearly every room of the White House were paintings and lithographs of boats and naval engagements, and there were many ship models on display, too—so many that the White House chief usher was, said Baldwin, "almost at his wit's end to know how to dispose of all this fleet."

Accompanying the article was a charcoal portrait of Roosevelt looking thoughtfully at a three-masted schooner, with four massive battleship guns looming behind him. "The sea and things of the sea, the navy and its ships and men and guns are probably the outstanding passions of the President's life," the caption said.

It was April 3, 1938.

BERNARD BARUCH wrote a memo to the president. It was April 1938.

Millions of strong, courageous European refugees could settle, proposed Baruch, in a place to be called the United States of Africa—a large nondenominational republic assembled from pieces of Kenya, Tanganyika, and Northern Rhodesia, all under the "sovereign control of England." Baruch opposed changing American immigration policies—the United States was in a depression, after all.

"Messrs. Baruch and Morgenthau are preoccupied with saving their own hide and their own 'positions' in America, and care next to nothing about the lot of Hitler's victims," wrote law professor and future Supreme Court Justice Felix Frankfurter in a letter to a friend. "These men are behaving precisely as did the rich and powerful Jews who helped bring on Hitlerism as a way of avoiding Bolshevism."

ARTHUR "BOMBER" HARRIS, of the Royal Air Force, got off the *Queen Mary* in New York. It was April 25, 1938.

Harris had commanded bombing expeditions in India, Iraq, Palestine, Kenya, and Uganda. Now he was in the United States to buy airplanes. He went to Washington, D.C., and then he visited the Lockheed factory in Burbank, California. There, he and his team looked over the Model 14 Super Electra airliner, which they thought would suit British needs well, with some adjustments—a big bomb bay and some machine guns. "To my astonishment," Harris wrote, "only twenty-four hours later a car arrived to fetch me out to the Lockheed works, and there I saw a mock-up of all our requirements in plywood, fitted complete in every detail, with two alternative noses hinged onto a real aircraft all ready for our inspection."

The British Air Ministry ordered two hundred planes. It was, according to *The New York Times,* "the largest foreign order ever placed with an American aircraft company."

SOMEONE ASKED MOHANDAS GANDHI about English pacifists. It was May 1938.

The problem with the English pacifists, Gandhi said, was that they made moral calculations: "When they speak of pacifism they do so with the mental reservation that when pacifism fails, arms might be used." A true pacifist never calculated. "Someone has to arise in England with the living faith to say that England, whatever happens, shall not use arms," said Gandhi. "They are a nation fully armed, and if they having the power deliberately refuse to use arms, theirs will be the first example of Christianity in active practice on a mass scale. That will be a real miracle."

GEOFFREY TUTTLE, a commander at the Royal Air Force base at Rawalpindi, bombed a troublesome tribe on India's Northwest Frontier. "We were all trained as professional assassins and we wanted to see if we could kill people," Tuttle said later. They were required to bomb groups of ten or more people, after giving warning. "In my case I can remember actually finding nine people and saying 'That's within ten per cent and that's good enough,' so I blew them up." It was mid-1938.

THE JAPANESE GOVERNMENT placed an airplane order. They wanted twenty-nine Lockheed Model 14 transport-bombers. A sales booklet from Lockheed said that the Model 14 was a "very formidable weapon for offensive or defensive tactical purposes." It was May 1938.

The Tachikawa Aircraft Company and the Kawasaki Aircraft Company liked the design of the Lockheed airplanes so much that they began building them under license. Tachikawa and Kawasaki built more than two hundred Lockheed Model 14s.

RESIDENTS OF FARMINGDALE, Long Island, got a leaflet announcing a simulated air raid. "Please cooperate with your War Department, city, State and county officials, and the New York State park officials to make this, the first American Black-Out, 100 per cent successful," said the leaflet. Some children dug a bomb shelter in their yard and were photographed peering up at the sky. A loudspeaker truck drove around the town, exhorting residents to turn off their lights when they heard three siren wails from the Fire Department. It was May 16, 1938.

The sirens wailed, and the Long Island Light Company turned out the streetlights, at 10:30 P.M. Police told drivers to shut off their headlights. A platoon of eight hundred-million-candlepower searchlights pierced the darkness, as the "enemy" force's Douglas bombers, camouflaged with black paint for night raiding, dropped a hundred parachute flares on the nearby Seversky aircraft factory, while a squadron of pursuit planes tried unsuccessfully to intercept them. Thousands watched the war games at the Seversky airport and from pulled-over cars; air-force men and some members of the press sat on a small platform near the factory. "Is it realistic enough, Sascha?" a general asked Alexander Seversky, one-legged pilot and prophet of city bombing. Seversky said yes, it reminded him of 1915.

Henry "Hap" Arnold, chief of the Army Air Corps, gave a talk on NBC Radio afterward. "These national defense exercises demonstrated in a manner quite realistic just what we might expect if invaders came within striking distance of our shores," Arnold explained. "Fortunately we have been spared the sickening whine of dropping bombs, with the death-dealing crash of their explosions."

TWO MARTIN B-10 BOMBERS, flown by American-trained pilots, flew from Hankow, China, to Nagasaki, Japan. They flew around Nagasaki for half an hour, dropping leaflets that denounced Japanese militarism. The flying visit, one leaflet asserted, was a gesture of goodwill. The bombers also passed over Kyushu and the naval base at Sasebo.

Premier H. H. Kung, brother-in-law to Madame and Generalissimo Chiang Kai-shek, was waiting with a group of reporters at Hankow air base for the Nagasaki mission to return. Kung, a graduate of Oberlin College, said to the oil-spattered airmen: "You did not drop bombs, as the Japanese air force is doing in China, but dropped leaflets, because China champions humanitarianism."

It was May 20, 1938.

THE UNITED PACIFIST COMMITTEE sponsored a protest march. Eighty people carried posters written in green paint. WAR MEANS FASCISM, said one poster. THOU SHALT NOT KILL, said another. Another said: 2 PLUS 2 MAKE 4, GUN PLUS GUN MAKE WAR—DISARM. The marchers walked down Fifth Avenue. A spectator patted one of them on the back. "Good for you," he said, "but don't worry—we're not going to have any more war." It was May 21, 1938.

A BRITISH DEFENSE MINISTER announced that the government was planning on raising a large army through conscription. A large British army was "one of the surest bulwarks of peace," wrote Winston Churchill in one of his fortnightly newspaper columns. In the next war, Churchill pointed out, British cities and towns would be bombed frequently. "Our manhood will experience an irresistible incentive to fight from the fact that they will see around them women and children killed by this cowardly method," he pointed out. "No man worthy of the name but will demand to take part in the struggle."

It was June 9, 1938.

THE LOCKHEED CORPORATION had a new name for the Super Electra airplanes that it sold to the British government. It called them Hudson bombers. The Hudson River flowed past the estates of the two American leaders most keenly interested in the sale: Franklin Roosevelt and Henry Morgenthau, Jr. It was June 1938.

"The aircraft manufacturing industry outshone all other industries of the country in the first quarter of 1938," *The New York Times* reported. Profits were up 82 percent.

"These foreign orders mean prosperity in this country and we can't elect a Democratic Party unless we get prosperity," Roosevelt said later. "Let's be perfectly frank."

OSWALD GARRISON VILLARD, an editor of *The Nation,* wrote that great armaments were the road to fascism. "They bring with them increased worship of the State, increased nationalism, increased State service, and therefore play into the hands of those like Hitler and Mussolini who declare that the citizen is made for the State and not the State for the citizen," he said. It was July 2, 1938.

EMMA CADBURY, who ran a Quaker relief house in Vienna, wrote a letter to Clarence Pickett, who ran the American Friends Service Committee. Cadbury was passing on a request for phone books from the American consul in Vienna. "People come and pore over them looking for possible relatives, and their Brooklyn book is already worn out," Cadbury wrote—the only practical way to get into the United States was to find some relative there who could vouch for you.

"Old books are perfectly good for this purpose," Cadbury wrote, "and from any city." It was summer 1938.

THE EVIAN CONFERENCE, convened at a French resort on Lake Geneva to find a home for Jewish refugees, was a failure. Myron Taylor, a retired executive from U.S. Steel, asserted to the thirty national delegates that existing American immigration quotas were liberal. Lord Winterton, a member of the British cabinet, said that England wasn't a "country of immigration" and that British colonies and territories weren't, either. "Powers Slam Doors Against German Jews," was the headline in the New York *Herald Tribune,* and the subheadline was: "Gloom Engulfs Parley as Even Thinly Populated South American States Refuse to Offer Asylum." A German newspaper said: "Jews For Sale—Who Wants Them? No One." It was July 1938.

"Despite warm words of wisdom doled out at Evian-les-Bains," said *Time* magazine shortly afterward, "the hard fact remains that no nation is willing to receive penniless Jews." No nation, except for the Dominican Republic: Generalissimo Trujillo offered to receive one hundred thousand refugees; a tiny settlement called Sosua was the result.

ALBERT WEDEMEYER, the U.S. Army captain, was at a goodbye dinner at his professor's house in Berlin. Wedemeyer had successfully completed his studies at the German War College, and he and his wife and children were sailing back to the United States. It was the summer of 1938.

Wedemeyer's professor, Colonel Lohmann, a Luftwaffe officer, seemed nervous and upset after dinner, and so did his wife, Maria. Over liqueur in the library, Lohmann revealed the reason for his unhappiness. "Maria is a Jewess," Colonel Lohmann said. "I hope this will not affect our friendship."

Wedemeyer replied that he had no religious or racial prejudices. "I made it clear," Wedemeyer wrote, "that I had several good friends who were Jewish and that I accepted as loyal citizens of my country those who professed Judaism or any other religion."

Colonel Lohmann then made a request. Would Wedemeyer be willing to look after the Lohmanns' two children if something happened? Wedemeyer said he would do everything he could for the children.

Lohmann seemed greatly relieved and shook Wedemeyer's hand warmly as they said goodbye.

GEORGE BELL, the bishop of Chichester, gave his first speech in the House of Lords. It was July 27, 1938. "I cannot understand—and I know many Germans—how our kinsmen of the German race can lower themselves to such a level of dishonour and cowardice as to attack a defenceless people in the way that the National Socialists have attacked the non-Aryans," he said. Bishop Bell asked for more liberal immigration policies in England and in the colonies. Refugees should be thought of as assets, not as liabilities, he insisted.

It was, Bell wrote a few weeks later, "hard to understand the seeming apathy with which the fate of the Jews and the non-Aryan Christians is being regarded by the people of the British Empire." The refugees really couldn't be called refugees, he said, "for they have as yet no countries of refuge."

RABBI LEO BAECK put out a distress call. It was July 28, 1938.

"In a situation that has scarcely been equaled in the oft severe history of our people we have endeavored not without success to banish the spectre of chaos," Baeck wrote in a Jewish newspaper in Berlin. "But there can be no doubt that this continual and extraordinary strain on all our energies has its limit," he said. "The domain of our existence becomes daily narrower."

He said: "Our strength threatens to give out."

And he said: "We may therefore call for help."

THE GERMAN CONSUL of Cleveland went to Henry Ford's birthday party in Detroit. Ford was turning seventy-five, and the German consul had a gift for him from Adolf Hitler. It was a big gold-and-white medal with four gold eagles and four little swastikas on it, and with it came a wide red silk neck sash that stood out dramatically against Henry Ford's white suit. It was July 30, 1938.

ADOLF HITLER began talking about the conquest of Czechoslovakia. He had in mind a grand entrance into Prague—crowds, newsreel cameras, swastika banners. It was August 1938. Hitler's chief of staff, General Ludwig Beck, was opposed. His army had no enthusiasm for war, and the German people hadn't any either. Only the young, handpicked indoctrinees in Hitler's private militia, the SS, were eager for it.

Beck wrote a memo recommending that his generals refuse to obey Hitler's orders to invade Czechoslovakia, if the orders came. "Abnormal times require deeds that are also out of the ordinary," Beck wrote: A united opposition would save them all from "blood guilt." Hitler got word of Beck's opposition and demanded his resignation. Beck quietly complied, leaving his deputy, Franz Halder, in charge of the general staff. "Now all depends on you," Beck said.

General Halder, a man whose wick of conscience flickered fitfully, had been watching Hitler for a while. He believed Hitler to be both mentally ill and evil. He met with some well-placed co-conspirators who wanted to mount a coup right away. Halder, full of doubts and mindful of public sentiment, wanted to wait for the perfect moment. He asked for a detailed coup plan; he wanted incontestable proof that Hitler intended to lead the country into another world war before he gave the go-ahead. And there was a further disagreement. Halder and Beck wanted Hitler arrested and put on trial; another faction wanted him examined by a psychiatrist and declared insane; the radicals wanted him assassinated outright.

Then, suddenly, British prime minister Neville Chamberlain flew to Munich, averting war by signing over Czechoslovakia without violence. An overwrought General Halder, believing that the best chance for overthrowing Hitler was lost, put his head down on his desk and wept.

BERNARD BARUCH disembarked from the *Queen Mary.* It was September 12, 1938. Baruch had been shooting grouse on the Scottish moors and talking to Winston Churchill and Pierre Laval about airplanes. He wouldn't reveal to reporters whether Roosevelt had asked him to reorganize American industry for war, as he had done last time around for President Wilson. He wanted to eliminate the war-profit motive in industry, he said: "Everyone knows today that no country wins anything in a war."

The next month, Baruch stayed over at the White House. Bombers were the answer, he told the president: The United States should be turning out fifty thousand long-range bombers. He didn't mention long-range bombers to reporters, though. To reporters he said, "I believe America is unprepared." France and England had been tragically unprepared, he said, and that was the reason for what happened at Munich. He didn't want the United States to be in the same "humiliating position."

A few days later, Roosevelt said at a news conference that mass production in airplane manufacturing hadn't received adequate consideration and that it was time for a fresh look at military spending. "Roosevelt Moves to Rush Expansion of Army and Navy" was the headline in *The New York Times* on October 15, 1938. This prompted a predictable headline from the Goebbels people in Germany: "The Jew Baruch Smells Business Profits." There were other German headlines, too: "Is Washington Dancing to Baruch's Tune?" And, "Inflammatory Lies as Basis for Tremendous Rearmament in United States of America"—with the subhead "Jew Baruch's Mental Cobwebs."

MURIEL LESTER was in Germany, talking to a woman who had been forced by the racial laws to divorce her Jewish husband. The woman had just had lunch with him, illegally. "Discovery would have led to a concentration camp," Lester wrote. "In an insignificant café down a back street they had spent an hour together and parted."

Lester went to Vienna, where she saw the *Eternal Jew* exhibit, which was crowded. "It demonstrated by greatly enlarged photographs, posters, and pictures, all the bad things Jews had ever done, all the highly paid jobs they held, all the honours they had won in music, literature, art, drama, philosophy, and every branch of science. The massing together of so many proofs of genius seemed to reflect discredit on us Gentiles rather than on them, but it had the desired effect on the young Nazis, who conducted ever fiercer pogroms." It was the fall of 1938.

EXPULSIONS BEGAN in Czechoslovakia. Small groups of Jews subsisted in encampments on the outskirts of towns where their families had lived for generations. Czech and German authorities prohibited gifts of food or water. It was the middle of October 1938.

HEINRICH HIMMLER's Blackshirt newspaper, *Das Schwarze Korps,* carried a front-page article: "The Jews living in Germany and Italy are hostages given into our hands by fate so that we may defend ourselves in the most effective manner against attacks by world Jewry." It was the end of October 1938.

IN HANOVER, GERMANY, a policeman knocked on the door and told Sendel Grynszpan, an impoverished Polish tailor, that he and his family had to report to the police station with their passports. It was October 27, 1938.

Grynszpan and six hundred other Polish citizens were kept overnight in a concert hall; then they were trucked in groups of twenty to the train station. People on the street shouted, "Send the Jews to Palestine." They arrived at a border station near Poland. "There were trains from all over Germany: Leipzig, Berlin, Cologne, Düsseldorf, Bielefeld, Essen, Bremen," Grynszpan wrote to his daughter. "We were about 12,000 in all." The SS men ordered the crowd to walk to the border. "Those who couldn't walk were beaten until the road was wet with their blood."

The New York Times called the expulsion of the Poles from Germany "perhaps the greatest mass deportation of recent times."

CLARENCE PICKETT and his wife were on the *Ile de France,* returning from Europe. It was October 28, 1938.

Pickett had just been to Germany, Czechoslovakia, and Austria; he had a sense of impending doom. "What can be done?" he asked, in a memo. "We may feel penitent for our part in the vicious Versailles Treaty and war settlement. But the Jews are the ones on whom now the burden for that war settlement falls hardest. We can do no less than give every aid possible to help those who come to us to make a new and fruitful start. This is and will be our chief relief work for some time."

CHARLES LINDBERGH and his wife, Anne, went looking for a house to rent in Berlin. It was October 28, 1938. Lindbergh was an American pilot and Nordic supremacist; in Germany, Goering had given him an eagle-and-swastika medal in a red box—"by order of der Führer"—and Lindbergh was learning a great deal about Junkers bombers and Messerschmitt fighters and the organization of the German air force.

In Wannsee, a pleasant suburb, the Lindberghs saw a house they liked—"well-, though heavily, furnished," he wrote in his journal, "and large enough for our needs. The most attractive feature was the garden—a large one, well planted with trees and shrubs, and running downhill to a river with swans." It was October 28, 1938.

A man at the German Air Ministry made some calls about the house. The owner was Jewish, and he wanted foreign currency: "Colonel Wendland advised us not to go any further," Lindbergh wrote. Albert Speer, however, offered powerful assistance: If the Lindberghs were interested in building a new house, he could get them land almost anywhere in Berlin.

The Lindberghs weren't sure; they took the night train back to Paris.

HITLER CALLED WINSTON CHURCHILL a warmonger, in a speech to one hundred thousand cheering Nazis. "Mr. Churchill said he opined that the German Government had to be swept away with the help of forces within Germany that would place themselves at his disposal," Hitler said. There were no such forces, said Hitler. "There is only one power and that is the National Socialist movement, its leadership and its followers in arms." It was November 6, 1938.

Churchill issued a mild statement to the press in reply, expressing surprise at being singled out. He and his fellow advocates of a strong defense intended no aggression against Germany, he said; they wanted England, France, and Germany to dwell in peace side by side. And he added some words of praise: "I have always said that if Britain were defeated in a war I hoped we should find a Hitler to lead us back to our rightful position among nations." The world would now rejoice, Churchill said, to see a mellowed Hitler of peace and tolerance. "Let this great man search his own heart and conscience before he accuses any one of being a warmonger."

SENDEL GRYNSZPAN'S SON, Herschel Grynszpan, who lived in Paris, got a postcard from his sister. Grynszpan's sister briefly described his family's forced deportation. He bought a gun from a store in Paris called The Sharp Blade and took the Metro to the German embassy. He shot two bullets into a man—Ernst vom Rath—who happened to work there. It was November 7, 1938.

Hitler sent his personal physician, Brandt, to help vom Rath, who was bleeding internally from a ruptured spleen and stomach.

CLARENCE PICKETT had lunch at President Roosevelt's country house in Hyde Park, New York. Pickett told the president something of what he'd seen in Europe. "We were sure things would grow worse for the Jews and other noncomformists in Germany, and we could see nothing to stop the drift toward war," Pickett wrote. He said that he wished that Roosevelt could have a talk with Hitler, face to face. It was November 9, 1938—the day Ernst vom Rath died of his wounds.

Roosevelt said that he'd given thought to a meeting with Hitler in the Azores. But at the moment, he said, he was more concerned with building up a strong air force.

"I questioned in my innermost mind and heart whether one can with one hand prepare the instruments of war and with the other hand the instruments of peace," Pickett wrote. "It produces a split personality in our national life."

HERSCHEL GRYNZSPAN SAID: "Being a Jew is not a crime." He said: "I hoped President Roosevelt would take pity on us refugees." He said: "I am not a dog. I didn't mean to kill. I lost my head."

GOEBBELS AND HITLER had a conference about the Grynzspan agitation. "He decides: Let the demonstrations continue," Goebbels wrote. "Pull back the police. The Jews should for once feel the anger of the people."

Party leaders called their subordinates, and the Gestapo sent out, by Teletype, rules to guide the rioting throughout Germany that was to be the consequence of Ernst vom Rath's assassination. It was to be savage but orderly. The burning of synagogues was permitted "only if there is no danger of fires for the neighborhood." Jewish homes and businesses "may be destroyed but not looted." And foreigners "may not be molested even if they are Jews."

It began at 1:00 in the morning on November 10, 1938. Otto Tolischus reported on it for *The New York Times*. "There was scarcely a Jewish shop, cafe, office or synagogue that was not either wrecked, burned severely, or destroyed," he said. "Before synagogues, demonstrators stood with prayer books from which they tore leaves." The wealthy synagogue on Fasanenstrasse "was a furnace." Twenty-five thousand people were sent as hostages to concentration camps.

It was called Kristallnacht, Crystal Night, because it happened at night and a lot of plate glass was broken, and because the word "crystal" simultaneously distracted from, and raised a toast to, the ferociousness of the rioting—and perhaps finally also because the word echoed the title of one of Goebbels's favorite books on propaganda technique, Edward Bernays's *Crystallizing Public Opinion*. Goebbels had successfully used vom Rath's assassination to crystallize German anti-Semitism.

In Leipzig, the American consul, David Buffum, wrote up a report on the riots. "In one of the Jewish sections an eighteen year old boy was hurled from a three story window to land with both legs broken on a street littered with burning beds and other household furniture," Buffum said. "Three synagogues in Leipzig were fired simultaneously by incendiary bombs and all sacred objects and records desecrated or destroyed, in most instances hurled through the windows and burned in the streets." It was, he said, "a barrage of Nazi ferocity as had had no equal hitherto in Germany, or very likely anywhere else in the world since savagery, if ever."

Thomas E. Dewey, who had just run for governor of New York and lost, said: "The civilized world stands revolted by a bloody pogrom against a defenseless people." Herbert Hoover said: "These individuals are taking Germany back 450 years in civilization to Torquemada's expulsion of the Jews from Spain." But, as *Time* magazine observed, President Roosevelt and other heads of state did not speak out immediately against acts that "shocked an almost shockproof world with a display of deliberate and unprovoked mass cruelty."

The British consul-general in Cologne got an anonymous letter, quoting from the police orders to burn synagogues and loot shops. "The population of Cologne had absolutely nothing to do with this murderous arson and condemns it, as does the whole German nation," the resident wrote. "These actions were ordered by the government in Berlin." It was November 12, 1938.

CHARLES LINDBERGH was perplexed by the riots in Germany. "They have undoubtedly had a difficult Jewish problem," he wrote, "but why is it necessary to handle it so unreasonably? My admiration for the Germans is constantly being dashed against some rock such as this." It was November 13, 1938.

ROOSEVELT GAVE his five hundredth press conference. It was November 15, 1938, five days after Crystal Night. Roosevelt was asked about the new Washington airport and about cherry trees. Then he read a short statement announcing that he was recalling the German ambassador and that public opinion had been "deeply shocked." He did not use the word "Jews."

"I myself could scarcely believe that such things could occur in a twentieth century civilization," Roosevelt said.

A reporter asked if he felt that there was any place in the world that would be able to take a mass emigration of the Jews from Germany.

"I have given a great deal of thought to it," said the president.

"Can you tell us any place particularly desirable?" the reporter asked.

"No," the president answered, "the time is not ripe for that."

Another reporter asked the president if he would recommend a relaxation of the immigration restrictions so that Jewish refugees could come to the United States.

"That is not in contemplation," said Roosevelt. "We have the quota system."

A CORRESPONDENT for *The Manchester Guardian* wrote about the scene at the British and U.S. consulates in Berlin. Despairing Jews there were "begging for visas," he said. "I understand that neither Great Britain nor the United States are making any concessions, and that for the great majority of those applying there is little hope of getting what for them would be the only possible way of returning to a normal life." It was November 15, 1938.

RUFUS JONES had Clarence Pickett and twenty other Quakers over to his house in Haverford, Pennsylvania, to plan aid for German Jews. It was November 16, 1938.

The Jewish Joint Distribution Committee had called to ask whether the American Friends Service Committee could open feeding centers in Germany, which was something Jones knew how to do. Jones and Pickett founded the Refugee Service Committee, and the next day they sent a letter out to every Quaker meeting in the United States. "Cables from Germany indicate that American newspaper reports have not exaggerated the tragedy," the letter said. The refugees needed housing, money, and the affidavits of promised support required by the State Department.

A REPORTER asked a question: "On Tuesday, Mr. President, you intimated that you did not propose, or would not consider, lowering the immigration barriers for the benefit of German refugees. Since that time a good deal has been said in print that you might do so after all. Have you changed your mind?"

"No," said President Roosevelt. He said, however, that German visitors who were already in the United States under temporary visas could stay on. It wouldn't be right, "from the point of view of humanity," to put them on a boat and send them back.

Again a reporter asked if there would be any change to the quota laws.

"I think not," said the president. It was November 18, 1938.

PRIME MINISTER NEVILLE CHAMBERLAIN made a statement in the House of Commons about German Jewish refugees. He had been talking to Joseph P. Kennedy and Lord Halifax, and he had new possibilities to offer. It was November 21, 1938.

"His Majesty's government has been greatly impressed by the urgency of the problem," Chamberlain said. In the light of recent events, they had "again reviewed the situation." The British empire, though extensive and in places thinly populated, wasn't able to absorb large numbers of refugees, Chamberlain insisted. Even so, he had asked the governors of two colonies—Tanganyika and British Guiana—whether they might lease land to refugee organizations for the purpose of large-scale settlement.

The governor of British Guiana had replied that his country might have ten thousand acres to spare for German Jewish colonization. And the governor of Tanganyika—once a German colony, but since the Great War a British possession—had offered fifty thousand acres in the Western Province and the Southern Highlands. "He would welcome a mission from refugee organizations," Chamberlain told the House of Commons, "and would readily give them all facilities for inspecting the areas and forming an opinion on the possibilities."

LATER THAT DAY in Parliament, Sir Samuel Hoare, the home secretary, took up the question of accepting more Jewish refugees into England proper. Hoare was opposed to a quota, he said—some would think it too low, some too high. It would be better, in his estimation, to work with the Jewish, Quaker, and other relief organizations, treating individual cases on their merits.

"We are a thickly populated industrial community with, at present, a large number of unemployed," Hoare said. There were, he observed, undercurrents of suspicion and anxiety about large-scale immigration. "It is a fact—you had better face these facts frankly—that below the surface there is the making of a definite anti-Jewish movement. As Home Secretary I do my best to stamp upon evil of that kind."

THE NEW YORK TIMES liked Chamberlain's Tanganyika plan—assuming the colony was never returned to German control. "Tanganyika offers more hopeful possibilities for colonization than many of the territories mentioned as places of settlement for German refugees," a *Times* editorial said. The climate in the Southern Highlands was favorable for Europeans, the paper noted, and there were reportedly farmable valleys. It was November 24, 1938.

Time magazine said that Chamberlain's proposal was "a striking indication that under the impact of civilization's horror at Nazi pogroms the mills of diplomacy had at last begun to grind a useful grist."

Justice William Harman Black, of the New York State Supreme Court, was less enthusiastic. Tanganyika was too hot and too German, he said on the radio, and it might have plagues and tsetse flies.

Rabbi Stephen Wise, a Zionist, had the most extreme reaction to Tanganyika. "I would rather that my fellow Jews die in Germany," Wise wrote privately to Myron Taylor, "than live somehow, anyhow, in the lands which bear the imprint of yesterday's occupation by Germany."

GANDHI WROTE an article for *Harijan,* the weekly English-language paper he edited in Delhi. It was November 26, 1938.

Gandhi had, he wrote, received questions about the Jews and Arabs in Palestine and about the persecution of the Jews in Germany, and—not without hesitation—he had decided to offer his views.

"My sympathies are all with the Jews," Gandhi said. "If ever there could be a justifiable war in the name of and for humanity, a war against Germany, to prevent the wanton persecution of a whole race, would be completely justified." But no war was justifiable, Gandhi believed—only *satyagraha,* nonviolent resistance, and even *satyagraha* was justifiable only after attempts at negotiation had failed.

"If I were a Jew and were born in Germany and earned my livelihood there, I would claim Germany as my home even as the tallest gentile German may, and challenge him to shoot me or cast me in the dungeon," Gandhi wrote. "I would refuse to be expelled or to submit to discriminating treatment."

Even if the Allies were to go to war against Germany, Gandhi said, their action could bring to the Jews no inner joy or strength. Inner joy came from suffering voluntarily undergone.

"The calculated violence of Hitler may even result in a general massacre of the Jews by way of his first answer to the declaration of such hostilities," Gandhi wrote.

As for Palestine: "The cry for the national home for the Jews does not make much appeal to me," he said. "It is wrong and inhumane to impose the Jews on the Arabs." Palestine belonged to the Arabs just as England belonged to the English and France to the French, he said. "There are hundreds of ways of reasoning with the Arabs, if they"—the Jews—"will only discard the help of the British bayonet. As it is, they are co-sharers with the British in despoiling a people who have done no wrong to them."

ONE HUNDRED AND NINETY-SIX German refugee children stood in a line at the dock in Harwich, England. Many of them were orphans, without passports or visas—they were being allowed into the country under the provisions of a special act of Parliament. Some held toys, a few held violins. It was December 2, 1938.

Rufus Jones, the Haverford professor, went to Germany with two other men: Robert Yarnall, a Quaker businessman, and George Walton, the principal of a Quaker boarding school. They hoped to talk to someone in authority, perhaps Hitler, about the suffering of the Jews. Before he left, Jones wrote some names and addresses in his notebook, and he wrote: "We need the note of adventure, of the heroic and costly, not the twittering of birds over a volcano." He was seventy-five years old.

The three men got on the *Queen Mary* and began to sail across the Atlantic. A reporter for the Philadelphia *Record* called the boat and asked Jones what he planned to do in Germany. Jones said he would try to do whatever was possible, and that he was doing his best to avoid any publicity. The reporter wrote a front-page article saying that three leaders from the Society of Friends were on their way to "intervene personally with Chancellor Adolf Hitler on behalf of the persecuted Jewish and other minority groups in Germany." The visit was "shrouded in the greatest secrecy," the reporter helpfully added. Several more newspaper articles appeared in New York and London.

Dr. Goebbels, the propaganda minister, read the articles, and he wrote, in his newspaper, that the "three wise men" were on their way. "They are to investigate us, for bad things are told in Pennsylvania about Germans who relieve poor Jewish millionaires of a little of their swindled money," he said. "Don't expect us to take them seriously."

RUFUS JONES AND his two associates visited the office that the Quaker Center in Berlin had opened to give advice to Jewish and non-Aryan refugees. They heard stories of Dachau, Buchenwald, and Sachsenhausen. They talked with Wilfrid Israel, who owned a prominent firm of interior decorators; Israel said he expected to be shot within ten days. They talked to Hjalmar Schacht, who suggested that the United States and other countries take fifty thousand refugees immediately. They negotiated with the Intergovernmental Committee in London to make sure they weren't interfering with its rescue plans. At the central Jewish organization in Berlin, Cora Berliner, a former economics professor, pleaded for large transient camps in the United States, where Jews could live until they were able to come in under the yearly quota.

The three men took a taxi to the Gestapo offices. Six Blackshirts with helmets escorted them into the building. They walked down some corridors and up some flights of stairs, and they came to a room with a round glass-topped table and big modern chairs. They could hear Reinhard Heydrich talking in the next room. Two men, "hard-faced, iron-natured men," came in. Jones gave them a statement that they'd had translated into German.

The statement said that they had come to see if there was anything that American Quakers could do to help; that they had no interest in propaganda; and that they had always been opposed to the harsh conditions of the peace treaty. The statement further said that Quakers had fed German children during the time of the blockade, after the war—that the relief program had fed, at its peak, more than one million children a day. And that after the war they had brought coal to heat the hospitals. And that they had distributed food to any family who needed it, including Nazi families. "We do not ask who is to blame for the trouble which may exist or what has produced the sad situation," their statement said. "Our task is to support and save life and to suffer with those who are suffering."

THE TWO GESTAPO functionaries—Dr. Erlinger and Dr. Lischka—read the Quakers' statement. "We noted a softening effect on their faces," Rufus Jones later wrote, "which needed to be softened." Then they asked many questions. The Quakers and the Gestapo functionaries discussed transient camps, the possibility of speeding up emigration with the help of the Intergovernmental Committee in London and America, and relief through Jewish organizations. The functionaries left to talk to Heydrich. Jones, Yarnall, and Walton sat in silence, heads bowed, for twenty-five minutes. The two men reappeared.

"I shall telegraph tonight to every police station in Germany that the Quakers are given full permission to investigate the sufferings of Jews and to bring such relief as they see necessary," said Lischka.

Jones cabled a report back to Pickett in Philadelphia. "It is the settled purpose of the German government to drive out Jews," Jones wrote. "The events of November 10th were to hasten that purpose. Until a plan of rapid emigration, especially for young, effective persons is established, the authorities consider the problem unsolved, and further outrages are likely to occur, bringing greater suffering and injustice."

When they got back to the United States, Jones told reporters that they'd made some progress. But everywhere they went, Jones said, Jews were saying they needed to get out of the country: "They said, 'Don't put food and hunger first. We can stand hunger. We can stand anything, but get us out before something more awful happens.'"

At the Friends Center in Berlin, workers discovered that they had, briefly, an easier time making legal and financial arrangements for the emigration of Jewish households. "This short reprieve meant the difference between life and death to some families, at least," Clarence Pickett wrote.

CHARLES LINDBERGH was back in the Third Reich, target shooting with Ernst Udet and trying to convince Erhard Milch, the aviation minister, to sell German airplane engines to France. It was December 20, 1938.

If France bought German engines, the two countries would have friendlier feelings toward each other, Lindbergh believed. Milch sounded interested, but he said he would need to get Hitler's approval. As for the recent violence toward Jews, Milch told Lindbergh that Goering and Hitler had had nothing to do with it. "I suppose this means that Himmler and Goebbels are responsible," Lindbergh wrote in his journal.

On the train back to Paris, Lindbergh thought more about the "Jewish problem." "I did not talk to a single person who I felt was not ashamed of the lawlessness and disorder of the recent demonstrations," he wrote. "But neither did I talk to anyone who did not want the Jews to get out of Germany, even though they disagreed with the methods now being used."

The Jews, Lindbergh had been told, were responsible for Germany's collapse after the war. "At the time of the inflation the Jews are said to have obtained the ownership of a large percentage of property in Berlin and other cities—lived in the best houses, drove the best automobiles, and mixed with the prettiest German girls."

Rufus Jones and Clarence Pickett went to the State Department to talk to Assistant Secretary of State George Messersmith. It was December 1938.

Jones and Pickett had a proposal. They'd seen the long lines at the American consulates in Europe—thousands of visa applications from refugees awaited processing. The State Department was saying that it couldn't afford to add staff to handle the surge.

"I therefore offered to recruit a number of trustworthy young men who spoke German fluently," Pickett wrote, "and to see that their salaries and other expenses were taken care of while they worked in American consular offices in Europe to help clear up this bottleneck." Through appeals at Friends meetings, Pickett had already lined up student volunteers.

Messersmith, irritated, said that the State Department could handle its own affairs. If the department wanted to add staff, it would ask Congress for funding.

"It was an extremely unpleasant and unsatisfactory interview," wrote Pickett.

In Dachau, Walter Loeb, one of the thirty thousand men arrested after Kristallnacht, was ordered to take a medical examination. "I did not pass," he wrote later, "because I had visible frostbite on my hands, and they did not want the outside world to see scars or marks of maltreatments (such as beatings, etc.)." A German prisoner lent him gloves, and a week later, when the doctor examined him, he passed.

Most of the "November Jews" were released that winter, many after they had signed away their assets and promised to emigrate. "Because of the cold wave that began Sunday," *The New York Times* reported, "there were dozens of cases of men whose frozen limbs had been amputated."

It was December 1938.

GANDHI WROTE about Hitler again in *Harijan.* It was January 7, 1939.

Even the hardest metal melts under sufficient heat, Gandhi observed; the hardest heart must melt before the heat of nonviolence. "Herr Hitler is but one man enjoying no more than the average span of life," he continued. Without the German people, he was nothing, and the German people would in the end be touched by nonviolence.

"I must refuse to believe that the Germans as a nation have no heart or markedly less than the other nations of the earth. They will some day rebel against their own adored hero, even if he does not wake up betimes," he said.

LINDBERGH READ THE HEADLINE in the Paris *Herald Tribune*: "Lindbergh Reported Providing U.S. with Data on Reich Air Force." Lindbergh was troubled—would this news upset the Germans? He'd been passing on the alarmingly high airplane levels that the Germans gave him—inflated figures, as it later turned out.

"If we must arm, we should arm for the purpose of our own strength, just as a man trains his body to keep fit and for the purpose of health," Lindbergh wrote. "The thing that bothers me most of all is that our own northern peoples are now snarling at and arming against each other."

It was January 7, 1939.

BRITISH FASCISTS rioted and threw stink bombs, protesting the Lord Baldwin Fund for refugees. The *Sunday Pictorial* said: "European refugees are stealing jobs from Britons by the hundreds every week." It was January 15, 1939.

A British group called the National Unemployed Workers Movement struck a different note: "The unemployed are not enemies of refugees. Help them both."

REINHARD HEYDRICH set up a new department, called the Reich Bureau for Jewish Emigration, to rationalize and speed up the pace of extortional expulsion. It was January 24, 1939.

The same week, the state-controlled Jewish newspaper, the *Jüdisches Nachrichtenblatt,* printed a hope: "If the United States could decide to accept 100,000 Jews from Germany conditionally, they could remain in the thinly settled regions in the West of that country and would make a very valuable contribution to the solution of the emigration problem." Alaska was another possibility for Jewish settlement, said the *Nachrichtenblatt. The New York Times* republished their hope.

STEFAN ZWEIG was in a travel bureau in London. It was filled with fifty refugees, most of them Jewish. One gray, exhausted man said he thought Haiti and Santo Domingo were still accepting applications; another man had heard that Shanghai was a possibility. "Their transit visa having expired, they had to go on," Zweig wrote, "on with wife and child to new stars, to a new language-world, to folk whom they did not know and who did not want to receive them."

HITLER SHOOK his finger on the stage of the Reichstag. Behind him was Hermann Goering, Reichstag president, and various notables. Behind Goering was an enormous backlit eagle, its wings outspread, with fabric draping fan-wise, boudoir style, behind it. Two swastika emblems hung to the right and left of the stage. Hitler was wearing a double-breasted jacket and tie.

"Today I will once more be a prophet," Hitler said. "If the international Jewish financiers, inside and outside Europe, succeed in plunging the nations once more into a world war, then the result will not be the Bolshevisation of the earth, and thus the victory of Jewry, but the annihilation of the Jewish race in Europe!" There was a roar and frantic applause from the assembled delegates. It was January 30, 1939.

Time magazine, studying the speech shortly afterward, couldn't understand why journalists were calling it mild. It was, *Time* thought, "one of the most sensational and threatening talks ever made by the head of a State."

FRANKLIN ROOSEVELT called in the Senate Military Affairs Committee for a secret meeting. The Senate was voting on a bill that would authorize the purchase of thousands of airplanes for the use of the Army Air Corps. It was January 31, 1939.

Germany's aim was world domination, Roosevelt told the senators, and the gradual encirclement of the United States. France and England were the first line of defense against this menace. Hitler himself was a wild man, Roosevelt said, who apparently thought he was the reincarnation of Julius Caesar and Jesus Christ. "What can we do with a personality like that?" the president asked. "We would call him a nut. But there isn't any use calling him a nut because he is a power and we have to recognize that."

Hence the need for thousands of airplanes.

EDITH NOURSE ROGERS, a representative from Massachusetts, and Robert Wagner, a senator from New York, introduced a bill that would allow twenty thousand refugees under the age of fourteen to enter the United States, outside of the German quotas. England was allowing in ten thousand children under special permits, to be looked after by Jewish, Catholic, and Quaker relief groups and placed in foster homes; Clarence Pickett's American Friends Service Committee proposed to supervise a similar Kindertransport in the United States.

"Thousands of American families have already expressed ther willingness to take refugee children into their homes," said Senator Wagner. "I have every confidence that there will be prompt and wholehearted response throughout the country to this noble cause, whereby the American people will give expression to their innermost cravings for liberty, justice, and international peace." It was February 9, 1939.

ELEANOR ROOSEVELT, who had set aside her anti-Semitism, said that passing the Wagner-Rogers child-refugee bill was "the humanitarian thing to do." A week later, she asked her husband, who was on a cruise in the Caribbean, if it was all right for her to give her full support to the bill. President Roosevelt replied: "It is all right for you to support child refugee bill but it is best for me to say nothing till I get back." When he got back, he said nothing about the bill. It was February 1939.

Dozens of newspapers wrote editorials endorsing the measure. It was a small gesture, said the New York *Herald Tribune,* but well worth doing, "both for the portion of misery that it would end and as a gesture to the world of where American sympathies unmistakably lie."

The *New York Times* editorial said: "If we had a barbed-wire frontier, as have some less fortunate countries, and could see these children, whose parents are dead or in concentration camps, we would not hesitate. All we need is imagination. They cry out to us from their darkness."

The *Times Herald,* of Newport News, Virginia, wrote, "The call of humanity in distress is universal and there is little doubt that the Wagner and Rogers bills will be adopted."

THERE WERE MORE than 120,000 visa applications awaiting action at the American consulate in Vienna. It was March 1939.

THE PLANNERS in the U.S. Navy distributed a new revision to its most important war plan, called Basic War Plan ORANGE. It was March 8, 1939.

The navy had been working on variations of War Plan OR-ANGE for years; it filled many pages. "War with ORANGE will be precipitated without notice," the secret plan said; it would be "an offensive war of long duration." The National Mission of War Plan ORANGE was:

> To impose the will of the UNITED STATES upon ORANGE by destroying ORANGE Armed Forces and by disrupting ORANGE economic life, while protecting AMERICAN interests at home and abroad.

ORANGE stood for Japan.

THE UNITED PACIFIST COMMITTEE had a conference at the Labor Temple on East Fourteenth Street in New York. It was March 11, 1939.

Reverend Abraham J. Muste, the leader of the Fellowship of Reconciliation, said: "When you accept the idea of war you immediately strengthen the reactionaries in the country." Dorothy Detzer, executive secretary of the Women's International League for Peace and Freedom, urged people to support the Ludlow Amendment to the Constitution—the one that would require a national referendum before any declaration of war.

But Secretary of State Cordell Hull had already made clear the administration's fixed opposition to any war-referendum bill. Such a measure would infringe upon the representative form of government, Hull said, "handed down to us over a period of 150 years."

IT WAS ARMY DAY, April 8, 1939. Twenty-two thousand people watched tanks and troops with new M-1 rifles parade down Fifth Avenue in New York. Governor Lehman said: "I am convinced that adequate preparedness, instead of being an incentive toward war, is our greatest safeguard for peace."

The United Pacifist Committee, led by Reverend Muste, led a tiny counterdemonstration. Fifty-two people walked on the sidewalk holding signs and passing out handbills. MASS MURDER IS NO DEFENSE OF LIBERTY, one sign said.

CHRISTOPHER ISHERWOOD, the English writer, wanted to live near peaceable people. He planned a trip by Greyhound bus to California to see Gerald Heard and Aldous Huxley, the two best-known members of the British Peace Pledge Union. Before he left, he and a friend mailed off some questions to some other British pacifists. It was April 1939.

One of Isherwood's questions was: What was a pacifist to do in wartime, apart from merely refusing to fight? Another question was: Does one open all doors to the aggressor and let him take everything he wants?

Runham Brown replied to Isherwood that a pacifist should do relief work, but not for the government. To an aggressor, he should practice civil disobedience, regardless of consequences. Rudolf Messel thought that pacifists should demonstrate and said that he hoped the war would turn into a revolution. George Lansbury, Labor party leader and member of Parliament, agreed with Runham Brown. "Our way of passive resistance has never yet been tried out," Lansbury wrote, "but war has been tried through all the centuries and has absolutely failed."

Isherwood agreed with George Lansbury.

HELEN HAYES, the actress, testified in favor of the Wagner-Rogers child-refugee bill. "I come here with only one credential—as an American mother," Hayes said. "Whenever you open the newspapers these days you find mention of boatloads of refugees, including children, being shunted from one port to another because nobody wants them. To whom can these children turn if nations such as ours do not open their doors?" It was April 20, 1939.

Clarence Pickett testified. "A Jewish child cannot go to school, and cannot play in the parks," Pickett said. "There is the crashing of glass at any time of the day or night when the neighboring rowdies choose to throw stones through the window." Pickett went on:

> And beyond all this terror and insult, his parents have lost their means of livelihood, his family has been put out of their home and perhaps crowded into a small unheated room, wondering how they will eat when the last bit of furniture has been sold. This is the daily life of those children in Germany whom the present regime has elected to disinherit.

A member of the Daughters of the American Revolution, Carrie Sifton, testified. "My father's name was Solomon Ginsberg, and he was a Polish Jew," she said. "I feel that in all fairness to a great number of members of the D.A.R. I should speak in support of this bill."

The next day, Robert Yarnall told the immigration committee about his recent visit with Rufus Jones to Germany. There was a sense, over the whole population, of something "corroding and fearful," Yarnall said. "The misery of the Jews was quite beyond description."

The problem was not going to go away, he told the committee. "Hitler promised a Jew-free Germany and the Nazi party has assumed that obligation." He quoted what one German official had said to him: "If you don't take these people off our hands we shall continue our pressure until you do."

HERBERT HOOVER sent a telegram in favor of the refugee bill: "No harm, and only good, can come to a nation by such humane action." Pickett read it at the hearings. Dorothy Thompson, the famous radio columnist, testified on behalf of the bill. People sobbed as Rabbi Stephen Wise read from the Forty-sixth Psalm. Pickett said that the hearings had raised a larger issue: "That issue is whether the American people have lost their ability to respond to such tragic situations as this one. If it turns out that we have lost that ability, it will mean that much of the soul has gone out of America."

Then the opposition began. Someone from the Allied Patriotic Societies said: "This is just part of a drive to break down the whole quota system—to go back to the condition when we were flooded with foreigners who tried to run the country on different lines from those laid down by the old stock."

Colonel John Thomas Taylor, of the American Legion, said: "If this bill passes, there is no reason why we should not also bring in 20,000 Chinese children."

Someone from the Widows of War Veterans said that there were already seven million communists, "boring from within."

Sensing that the refugee bill was in trouble, Clarence Pickett tried to increase support for it among conservatives. He asked Louis Taber, isolationist spokesman for agriculture, for help.

Taber, an Ohio Republican, served on the national committee of the Boy Scouts. He was unmoved by Pickett's appeal. The sufferings that the refugee children had undergone could well have produced, Taber feared, "many distorted minds and warped economic viewpoints which may be serious in the future development of our democracy." The young Jewish émigrés might, in other words, grow up to be Bolshevists.

"I would rather give $10.00 to find places for those children in some other land," Taber wrote Pickett, "than to give 10 cents to bring them here." It was April 25, 1939.

MURIEL LESTER, the relief worker, arrived in Palestine. "Bare, arid spaces that I had seen in 1910 were now blossoming like the rose," she wrote. There were orange trees. She saw the new port at Tel Aviv. It was 1939.

Near the Jewish settlements lived Arabs. "Bedouin tents shielded the women at home, veils when they walked abroad. The men folk gazed with disgust at the sophisticated Jewesses in their shorts and skin-tight skirts," wrote Lester.

The British forces lived behind barbed wire. "This sort of war wears you out," one soldier told Lester. You're planning to see a movie, the soldier said, and then you find out your friend's gone missing. "Picked off by an Arab in one of the villages. Mistake, maybe. Got him instead of a Jew. But it makes us mad." Once he went out with some mates and "did a little violence on our own account," he told Lester. "Felt fine at the time, but it didn't last."

MURIEL LESTER was at a tea table at the Hebrew University in Jerusalem. She had given a talk, which wasn't well received. It was early in 1939.

"Your dislike of British imperialism doesn't appeal to us," said one of her listeners.

It wasn't just British imperialism, Lester answered. "I hate the Japanese and American type just as much, the economic cruelty and the racial pride."

"Yes," said her questioner, "but it's the British type that we know. It's infinitely preferable to any other. We want its protection."

"Does it protect in the long run?" Lester asked.

THE BRITISH GOVERNMENT promulgated new policies in Palestine. It was May 17, 1939. Jews should make up no more than one-third of the total population, according to a document that came to be called the White Paper. Ten thousand Jews could come in each year for the next five years. "After the period of five years, no further Jewish immigration will be permitted unless the Arabs of Palestine are prepared to acquiesce in it," said the paper.

Jews hated the White Paper, and Arabs hated it, too. "Any one aware of the position of the Jews in Eastern and Central Europe today will not for one moment believe that they will cease coming to their homeland because some law terms it illegal," said David Ben-Gurion, head of the Jewish Agency for Palestine. "Jews who must choose between utter extinction and immigration to Palestine under conditions called illegal naturally will not waver for a moment in their choice."

Palestinian Arabs hated the White Paper because they wanted the British and the Jews out of their country.

GANDHI ANSWERED a letter from Hayim Greenberg, who edited the *Jewish Frontier,* a liberal Zionist newspaper in New York. Greenberg pointed out that in Germany, a Jewish Gandhi would last about five minutes before he was executed.

"That will not disprove my case," Gandhi replied. "I can conceive the necessity of the immolation of hundreds, if not thousands, to appease the hunger of dictators." The discipline of nonviolence—*ahimsa*—worked most efficaciously in the face of terrible violence, Gandhi said: "Sufferers need not see the result in their lifetime."

It was May 22, 1939.

PRIME MINISTER CHAMBERLAIN spoke very quietly in the House of Commons. It was March 31, 1939.

His Majesty's government was of the belief that free negotiation was the right way to settle differences, Chamberlain said, and His Majesty's government believed that there was no question that couldn't be solved peacefully. Force, or the threat of force, was unjustified. But if the Polish government were compelled to defend itself from an attack, he went on to say, His Majesty's government would offer the Polish government "all support in their power."

Ferdinand Kuhn, reporting for *The New York Times,* was thunderstruck. "Mr. Chamberlain's pledge sounded so sweeping it took one's breath away," he said. Kuhn quoted Arthur Greenwood, deputy leader of the Labor party, who said that Chamberlain's guarantee of Polish independence "may prove to be the most momentous statement made in this House for a quarter of a century."

Poland's foreign minister, Józef Beck—the leader who had wanted to send Polish Jews to Madagascar—soon reciprocated with a pledge of military assistance to England.

THE DAY HAD COME, Hitler believed, to reclaim Poland. Secrecy was the precondition of success, he said in a room full of generals. If England comes to Poland's defense, then Germany must take over Holland with lightning speed. And Belgium. Germany needed the airfields of both countries. A conflict with England would be, he said, a life-and-death struggle.

It was May 23, 1939. Hitler's generals still didn't want to go to war.

Germany must burn its bridges! Hitler said. It was a question of the lives of eighty million people. The war might last ten or fifteen years. The English were "proud, courageous, tenacious, firm in resistance, and gifted as organizers." They had the love of adventure and the courage of the Nordic race, he said. They'd been a world power for three hundred years. But a surprise attack could lead to a quick decision. Surprise was the plan. And secrecy.

LOCKHEED STOPPED SELLING airplanes to Japan, at the request of Secretary of State Cordell Hull. Lockheed employees remained in Japan, however, assembling and testing the airplanes that were arriving in fulfillment of previous orders. It was May 1939.

A REFUGEE JOURNALIST named Manfred George addressed the American Writers' Congress in New York. It was June 4, 1939.

"Never before in history has a country lost practically all of its poets, novelists and essayists at the same time," George said. "Within one year Germany lost the overwhelming spiritual influence its famous thinkers and writers had exerted over the whole world. It was a kind of death—the body stayed where it was, the soul was spread all over the world."

FREDERICK WINTERBOTHAM, the English spy, bought a Lockheed 14 Super Electra airplane with a heated cabin and installed three Leica cameras under the floor. He hired a civilian pilot from Australia to fly over Germany, taking pictures of factories and aerodromes, so that the Royal Air Force could make target lists and maps. The warmth of the cabin kept the camera lenses from fogging over, allowing the pilot to fly very high. It was the summer of 1939.

A MEMBER OF THE HOUSE OF REPRESENTATIVES, Caroline O'Day, tried to reach President Roosevelt to ask him what he thought of the child-refugee bill, which was still alive in committee. It was June 2, 1939.

Roosevelt's secretary passed on O'Day's message. Roosevelt wrote "File No action FDR." Without his support, the bill—and the children—had no chance.

Clarence Pickett wrote: "The facts and the logic, the eloquence and the fervor, seemed to me all on the side of the bill, but those of us who supported it plugged away in vain. The bill never came out of committee."

HITLER ASKED two of his helpers—his personal physician, Karl Brandt, and his staff aide, Philip Bouhler—to set up a mechanism for registering children born with spina bifida, retardation, malformations of the head, and other congenital problems. Registration forms went out to hospitals. They were filled out and forwarded to 4 Tiergarten Street, Berlin, which was Bouhler's office. The house, soon known as the headquarters of the T-4 program, had been confiscated by the government from its Jewish owner. It was the summer of 1939.

NINE NEWSPAPER EDITORS and publishers got off the *Yankee Clipper* in New York after a trip to England. A reporter from *Life* magazine was there to talk to them. The publishers had met powerful people—including Lord Beaverbrook, publisher of the *Daily Express,* and Neville Chamberlain, the prime minister—and they were reassured. "Their virtually unanimous prediction," according to *Life* magazine: "There will be no war this year." It was July 13, 1939.

ONE HUNDRED BRITISH BOMBERS took off from English airfields and flew to Bordeaux, France, and back. It was July 19, 1939. A few days later another hundred planes flew to Marseille, France, and back; then, 240 planes flew to Marseille and Bordeaux and back. Never before had so many bombers flown at one time. England and Poland began discussing the possibility of "shuttle bombing"—taking off from England, bombing Germany, and landing in Poland, or taking off from Poland, bombing Germany, and landing in England. A British Air Ministry spokesman announced that Berlin was "within easy striking distance of London."

Prime Minister Neville Chamberlain didn't want the Royal Air Force bombing Germany, and he didn't want the Luftwaffe bombing England. He wanted to keep peace by demonstrating a stern, warlike resolve. The newspapers said that he should bring Winston Churchill, first lord of the admiralty, into his cabinet. Churchill was a warrior who knew about aerial bombardment—bring him in. Chamberlain didn't want Churchill in.

GENERAL EDMUND "TINY" IRONSIDE, inspector general of British Overseas Forces, stayed up until five in the morning talking to Winston Churchill. It was July 25, 1939. Ironside had just been to Poland, where he had visited military training centers and reviewed the war-readiness of Polish forces—one German newspaper called Ironside's visit a "secret council of war."

In his diary, Ironside wrote down some thoughts on Neville Chamberlain. "He is a pacifist at heart," Ironside wrote. "He is not against Winston, but he believes that chances may still arrive for averting war, and he thinks that Winston might be so strong in a Cabinet that he would be prevented from acting."

NEVILLE CHAMBERLAIN wrote a letter to his sister, as he often did to clarify his thoughts. The German people were jealous of the Jews, he said, because Jews were clever. "No doubt Jews aren't a lovable people," he wrote. "I don't care about them myself; but that is not sufficient to explain the Pogrom." It was July 30, 1939.

PRESIDENT ROOSEVELT wanted the world to know how much airpower the United States had. A brand-new B-17 Flying Fortress flew nonstop from Burbank, California, to Floyd Bennett Field in Brooklyn. There was a picture of the airplane in *The New York Times,* with a banner caption: "Huge United States Bomber after Crossing Continent in Less Than 10 Hours." It was August 1, 1939.

The next day, on a noontime signal from the president, 1,500 military planes took off from air bases around the country. They flew around for a while, and then they landed.

ADOLF HITLER invited his military commanders to his house in the mountains. It was August 22, 1939. Goering, the master of ceremonies, was wearing short pants, lace-up boots, a strap-on dagger in a red sheath, and a green jacket with yellow leather buttons. Hitler was in the usual Nazi brown, standing by the grand piano, on which stood a bust of Richard Wagner.

"I have called you together to give you a picture of the political situation," Hitler said, "in order that you may have insight into the individual elements on which I have based my decision to act and in order to strengthen your confidence." Now was the time for an attack on Poland, he said. War was inevitable, and he was the man to lead the country into it. There would never again be a man who carried more authority. He would not live forever. He could be eliminated at any time "by a criminal or an idiot." Germany must strike or be destroyed. "We can only hold out for a few more years," he said. There was risk in striking, yes. But England wasn't prepared for war yet. They had only 150 antiaircraft guns. They didn't really want to defend Poland, or even to lend Poland money. And now that Germany was working out a pact with Stalin, there was less of a worry about an English blockade. "Our enemies are *kleine Wurmchen*," Hitler said. "I saw them in Munich." *Kleine Wurmchen* means "little worms."

Goering thanked Hitler and said that the armed forces would do their duty. They broke for a bite to eat on the terrace.

Still, the commanders weren't convinced. Hitler talked to them again. No shrinking back, he said. Peace won't do us any good. "A manly bearing," he said. The goal was the destruction, the complete annihilation, of Poland. Poland first, then the western powers. "Close your hearts to pity," he said. "Act brutally."

No one said no. They returned to their posts, keeping their doubts to themselves. One general thought that the bragging in Hitler's speech was repulsive: "Here a man spoke who had lost all feeling of responsibility and any clear conception of what a victorious war signified," he wrote. Hitler was determined, he thought, "to leap into the dark."

HITLER WAS NOT WELL—his generals wondered whether he was in the midst of some sort of mental breakdown. It was the very end of August 1939. President Roosevelt had written Hitler an appeal: "Countless human lives can yet be saved," Roosevelt said, if Germany and Poland would just agree on a "pacific means of settlement." A rich Swede, Birger Dahlerus—managing director of Electrolux's British subsidiary—conveyed a last-minute message from London to his friend Goering, saying that Britain wanted to find some way to peace. Goering woke Hitler, and Hitler met with Dahlerus. Hitler paced, talking rapidly in a way that was, thought Dahlerus, "abnormal." At times he stared, at times he seemed to be addressing a political rally. "I will build U-boats, build U-boats, build U-boats," Hitler said. "I will build aircraft, build aircraft, build aircraft, and I will destroy my enemies." Then he settled down. He and Dahlerus worked out a proposal in which Germany got something, Poland got something, and Germany "pledged to defend the British empire."

England was not interested. Dahlerus was "a wasp at a picnic," wrote Alexander Cadogan, the permanent undersecretary, in his diary. "He spent most of Tues with Goering and Hitler, but their 'terms' were as to be expected: give us a free hand in Central and E. Europe and we will guarantee the British Empire."

Meanwhile, another intermediary, Nevile Henderson, was also in negotiations to avert a war. Hitler shouted at Henderson, Henderson shouted at Hitler. On August 29, one of Hitler's staff said that Hitler was "unimaginably nervy, edgy and sharp."

VICTOR KLEMPERER, a retired teacher in Dresden, was trying to make progress on his autobiography. It was August 29, 1939.

Klemperer wanted to write about studying in Paris at the Sorbonne in 1903, but he couldn't. "These last few days pulled and still pull too much at my nerves," he wrote. Would there be a bloody pogrom as soon as the war started? "Incalculable danger for all Jews here," he sensed. His friend Moral had just visited from Berlin: "He is expecting the outbreak of war and in that case being shot down, perhaps not in some wild pogrom, but properly rounded up and put up against a barracks wall."

NOBODY KNEW what Hitler would do next. He remained in solitary meditation after Nevile Henderson left, according to an informant for the New York *Herald Tribune*. "For almost two hours he remained absolutely alone, deciding on his future course," the reporter wrote. "Men in his entourage are nearly at the end of their strength, this informant said. Night after night since arriving at the Chancellery a week ago tonight, Hitler has been working till 4 a.m."

ULRICH VON HASSELL, the former German ambassador to Italy, wrote: "So far as I'm concerned, the one vital thing is to avoid a world war." It was August 31, 1939.

Hitler and Foreign Minister Ribbentrop had reached, von Hassell thought, a state of "criminal recklessness." They were fixating on the return of Danzig—the port city detached from Germany and annexed to Poland as a result of the Versailles Treaty. "Must we really be hurled into the abyss because of two madmen?" he asked.

Von Hassell made a last flurry of calls and visits—to Goering's sister, to Goering, to Nevile Henderson, to Secretary of State Ernest von Weizsäcker, then back to Henderson, and then to Bernardo Attolico, the Italian ambassador—trying to clear up misunderstandings and keep the parties from rupture. At one point, everything seemed to hinge on getting the Polish ambassador, Josef Lipski, to talk to Ribbentrop. But when the Polish ambassador finally put in an appearance, in the afternoon, the German side wasn't willing to receive him.

Attolico called Count Galeazzo Ciano, Mussolini's son-in-law, to say that the situation was desperate; without some new demarche, war was inevitable. Ciano called Lord Halifax to ask if the Germans could have Danzig back. Halifax checked with the cabinet and called Ciano back to say no. "The sky is becoming darker and darker," wrote Ciano.

William Shirer, the CBS correspondent in Berlin, was puzzled. "Everybody against the war," he wrote in his diary. "How can a country go into a major war with a population so dead against it?"

SOME OF HIMMLER'S SS MEN, pretending to be Polish partisans, entered a German radio station in the border town of Gleiwitz. They hustled the employees into the basement and interrupted the broadcast to say subversive things in Polish while firing their guns. For authenticity, they left some corpses behind. Germany had thus been attacked.

"To put an end to these insane incitations, nothing remains but for me to meet force with force from now on," Hitler told the army.

Goering said: "The German Air Force today stands ready to carry out every command of the Führer." He ordered a thousand planes into Poland. There were dive-bombers over Danzig. It was September 1, 1939.

William Bullit, the American ambassador to France, called President Roosevelt and told him that Polish cities were under attack. Roosevelt, looking at his clock and noticing that it was a little before three in the morning, had a strange feeling that he'd been through it all before. He recalled the days of his assistant secretaryship of the navy under President Wilson—those urgent telephone calls that came in at his bedside. "I had *in fact* been through it all before," Roosevelt realized. "It was not strange to me but more like picking up again an interrupted routine."

STEFAN ZWEIG, the bestselling writer, was in the registry office in Bath, England, filling out papers so that he could marry his second wife. An official burst in. "The Germans have invaded Poland," the man said. "This is war!"

Zweig said: "That doesn't have to mean war."

The man disagreed. "We've had enough! We can't let them start this sort of thing every six months! We've got to put a stop to it!"

ROOSEVELT SENT OUT a two-paragraph letter to the governments of Germany, Poland, Italy, France, and England. It was September 1, 1939.

> The ruthless bombing from the air of civilians in unfortified centers of population during the course of the hostilities which have raged in various quarters of the earth during the past few years, which has resulted in the maiming and in the death of thousands of defenseless men, women, and children, has sickened the hearts of every civilized man and woman, and has profoundly shocked the conscience of humanity.
>
> If resort is had to this form of inhuman barbarism during the period of the tragic conflagration with which the world is now confronted, hundreds of thousands of innocent human beings who have no responsibility for, and who are not even remotely participating in, the hostilities which have now broken out, will lose their lives. I am therefore addressing this urgent appeal to every government which may be engaged in hostilities publicly to affirm its determination that its armed forces shall in no event, and under no circumstances, undertake the bombardment from the air of civilian populations or of unfortified cities, upon the understanding that these same rules of warfare will be scrupulously observed by all of their opponents.

Roosevelt requested an immediate reply.

CHILDREN HAD TO GO AWAY, for their safety. "In London's crowded East End, in the heart of the Jewish quarter, the correspondent watched 180 sleepy-eyed children between the ages of three and thirteen gather at the Myrdle Street School prior to the evacuation," wrote the *Herald Tribune*. Each child had a gas mask, some clothes and food, and an address label hung around his or her neck. Parents and grandparents were there to say tearful goodbyes. "Among the children was a six-year-old girl who spoke no English. She had arrived in London yesterday as a refugee from Germany and twelve hours later was on the move again," said the paper.

Herbert Morrison, head of the air-raid precautions committee, said: "Pack up your troubles in your old kit bag and smile, smile, smile."

It was September 1, 1939.

AT THE KROLL OPERA HOUSE, where the Reichstag met, at ten o'clock in the morning, Hitler gave a war speech—or rather a war-as-suicide speech. He began by denouncing the Treaty of Versailles, which had now become "utterly intolerable." "Danzig was and is a German city!" he said. Germany was under Polish attack: "Since 5:45 A.M. we have been returning fire!" he claimed. "Whoever disregards the rules of humane warfare can but expect us to do the same."

Hitler was prepared to make the ultimate sacrifice for Germany, he told his deputies. His voice sounded odd. If something should happen to him, Goering would succeed him, and if something should happen to Goering, then Rudolf Hess would take charge. If Hess died—well, then the Senate would choose someone worthy.

He, the Führer, would never give up. Frederick the Great had confronted a strong alliance of nations. He had triumphed over them because he'd had faith.

It was a weak speech, wrote Ulrich von Hassell. Joe Barnes, the *Herald Tribune* correspondent, remarked on the "amazingly small" crowd that waited to watch Hitler return to the Chancellery afterward. "The younger Germans shouted, 'Sieg heil!' " Barnes wrote. "Others stood silent and expressionless."

After the speech, Hitler had another tête-à-tête with Dahlerus. He was going to wipe out the Poles, he said, but he was still willing to negotiate with the British if they cared to. Hitler's breath knocked Dahlerus back a step.

"At twilight," wrote Joe Barnes in Berlin, "the air raid sirens went off—a long, wailing sound, invented especially for the end of the world. Everyone ran for cover like ants whose anthill has been carelessly kicked." But no planes followed.

The planes would come eventually, William Shirer thought—and when they did, he would, he said, "be in the by no means pleasant predicament of hoping they bomb the hell out of this town without getting me."

It was September 1, 1939.

CHRISTOPHER ISHERWOOD was in his living room with his friend Vernon, listening to the radio. "It was as though neither of us were present. The living room seemed absolutely empty—with nothing in it but the announcer's voice. No fear, no despair, no sensation at all. Just hollowness."

ENGLAND AND FRANCE released their response to Roosevelt's bombardment appeal. It was September 2, 1939. They promised to "conduct hostilities with a firm desire to spare the civilian population and to preserve in every way possible those monuments of human achievement which are treasured in all civilised countries," the joint statement said.

There was a catch, though. If Germany bombed civilians or destroyed cultural treasures, the deal was off. England and France would then "take all such action as they may consider appropriate."

Hitler wrote Roosevelt: "I agree to your proposal—on condition, of course, that the enemy observes the same rules."

THAT DAY, near the beach at Tel Aviv, more than one thousand Jewish refugees were trying to get to shore. They had come on an old ship, the *Tiger Hill.* A British patrol boat, enforcing the prohibitions of the White Paper, fired on the refugees to force them back. Two were killed. Of the rest, some reached land and merged with the Jewish population, and some were held at a British detention camp.

NEVILLE CHAMBERLAIN told the House of Commons that England was officially at war with Germany. "It is a sad day for all of us, but for none is it sadder than for me," Chamberlain said. "Everything that I have worked for, everything that I have hoped for, everything that I have believed in during my public life has crashed in ruins." It was September 3, 1939.

Churchill's mood, as he listened, wasn't sad at all. He felt, he wrote later, a sense of uplifted serenity and a detachment from human affairs. "The glory of Old England, peace-loving and ill-prepared as she was, but instant and fearless at the call of honour, thrilled my being and seemed to lift our fate to those spheres far removed from earthly facts and physical sensation," he said.

In Berlin, a knot of listeners, grouped near loudspeakers on the Wilhelmplatz, took in the news in silence. "There was not a murmur," William Shirer wrote. "They just stood there as they were before. Stunned." It was a balmy, sunny day—the beginning of the Second World War.

Life magazine said: "Second Armageddon was on."

DUNCAN SANDYS, a conservative member of Parliament, wrote a long letter of congratulation to his father-in-law, Winston Churchill, who had just been made Lord of the Admiralty again. Small-minded, mediocre people had kept Churchill from power, Sandys said, and Europe had been muddled into a catastrophe. "You would have saved the world from all this, but you were not allowed to." It was September 3, 1939.

In the Admiralty office that evening, Churchill sat down in his old chair. In a wooden map case behind a sofa, he found the chart of the North Sea on which he had planned battles and blockades in the last war. A signal went out to the British fleet: WINSTON IS BACK.

THE BRITISH, having agreed not to bomb civilians and cultural monuments, immediately instituted a hunger blockade and dropped threatening propaganda leaflets. The Germans sunk a large passenger ship, the SS *Athenia.*

Hours after Chamberlain's declaration of war, a British warship, the *Ajax,* patrolling the waters near Uruguay, overtook the *Olinda,* a German freighter sailing out of Montivideo for the Hamburg-American Line. British officers boarded the *Olinda* and asked captain and crew to pack their things and get into lifeboats. Then the British fired on the German ship, which was filled with grain and canned meat, and sank it. Nobody was killed.

In the North Atlantic, a U-boat commander, Fritz-Julius Lemp, got an order: "Do not wait until attacked. Make war on merchant shipping in accordance with operational orders." At twilight, he saw a distant ship and wanted to destroy it. It was very big, it was blacked out, it was zig-zagging, and it looked like the enemy. He fired some torpedoes at it.

On the SS *Athenia,* a ship sailing from Liverpool to Montreal with fourteen hundred people crowded on board—Canadians, Americans, and German-Jewish refugees—there was a huge explosion. More than one hundred passengers and crew were blown up, crushed, or drowned.

THAT NIGHT, six million leaflets fluttered down over northern and western Germany:

A WARNING

GREAT BRITAIN TO THE GERMAN PEOPLE

"With cold deliberation the Government of the Reich has forced Great Britain into war," the leaflets said. "President Roosevelt offered you peace with honor." Instead, your government has "condemned you to mass murder, misery and privations of a war you cannot even hope to win." Censorship held the spirit of the German people imprisoned in a concentration camp, the leaflets said. Germany was on the brink of bankruptcy. "You, the German people, have the right to insist upon peace, at any and at all times. We, too, wish for peace and are ready to make it with any honestly peaceful German government." Some planes missed Germany and dropped the leaflets on Holland.

John Gunther, an American war correspondent, asked the British Ministry of Information what the leaflets said. "We are not allowed to disclose information which might be of value to the enemy," the information minister told him. Gunther observed that millions of the leaflets had fallen on Germany. The minister blinked. "Yes, something must be wrong there," he said.

THE NEXT DAY, the British sent twenty-nine airplanes out on a daylight bombing mission, in bad weather. Their target was German warships near the city of Wilhelmshaven, on the North Sea coast. "Our airmen *say* they bombed ships in Wilhelmshaven last night," Under-Secretary Cadogan wrote. "But how did they know they were there?"

In fact, some of the bombs meant for Germany fell on the Danish town of Esbjerg. One bomb went into the harbor, one blew up in a courtyard, one demolished an apartment house, and one landed in a field near the airport. In the apartment house, a woman was killed as she was making dinner. Fifteen people were injured. The Germans shot down seven planes.

The night after that, the Royal Air Force dropped three million more pieces of propaganda. And more fell the night after that. These said:

> Don't forget that England, when forced to fight, will end as victor. England's nerves are good and her resources are many.

The leaflet bombing was code-named Nickel. Arthur Harris, the RAF commander, observed that Nickel gave the Germans free toilet paper for the duration of the war.

Hundreds of thousands of leaflets fell in Denmark by mistake. The Danish were considering painting their flag on roofs and lighting the border.

THE FRENCH GOVERNMENT began rounding up German citizens. "Germans may not leave their residences except to go to concentration camps," the Associated Press reported from Paris, "taking food supplies for two days, knives, forks, and underwear." It was September 6, 1939.

About fifteen thousand Germans were sent to French concentration camps in the early weeks of the war, a relief worker later estimated. About nine thousand of these were Jewish refugees; most of the remainder were liberal enemies of the Hitler regime. Because there might be spies, saboteurs, or propagandists among them, they were all interned.

OTTO TOLISCHUS, the *New York Times* reporter, said that the Germans were "crushing Poland like a soft-boiled egg." Warsaw was resisting, however. The Germans leafleted the city, calling for surrender, promising that officers who gave themselves up would be allowed to keep their swords. Diplomats hurried out during a truce. When no white flags appeared, the Luftwaffe stepped up its activity. Bombs tore off the side of an apartment house. Streets were an inch deep in broken glass. Sonia Tomara, writing for the *Herald Tribune,* talked to an old man in a workers' settlement. "I lost my wife and two children," he said, weeping. The bombing appeared aimless, she wrote. In one field, she counted twenty-one bomb craters.

Warsaw's Old City Square, the Royal Castle, and the railway station were hit: "The great roof opened like the skin of a ripe melon," wrote an Italian journalist, "and out of it, launched into the air by the explosion, came fragments of iron and steel, pieces of locomotives and cars."

GENERAL HALDER told one of his subordinates, General Helmuth Groscurth, that Hitler and Goering intended to "destroy and exterminate the Polish people." Groscurth wrote this down in his diary on September 9, 1939.

HERMANN GOERING was in a factory, standing in a white jacket at a classically styled podium. The podium was surrounded by sprays of greenery; there were several enormous cannons off to one side. A crowd of munitions workers stood before him, their arms out like flak guns in the Hitler salute. It was September 9, 1939.

"You declared war on us, Mr. Chamberlain, not we on you," Goering said. Germany had a "deep will to peace," he claimed, but Germany would not give up the Führer, as the British were demanding. "Our love and veneration for the Führer is something that you cannot understand because it doesn't exist in your country."

Goering also took up the question of the British propaganda leaflets, which he called "laughable flyleaves." "Chamberlain may know something about umbrellas," he said, "but he knows nothing about German propaganda." True, the leaflets were written in good idiomatic German. He blamed their fluency on expatriates, Jews, and "other scoundrels."

EDWARD R. MURROW, the American radio newsman, had lunch at the Savoy Grill in London. It was September 9, 1939.

Murrow met the director-general of the Ministry of Economic Warfare, Sir Frederick Leith Ross. "It is his job to starve Germany by any known means, all of them, men, women, and children," Murrow told his audience that night. "His is an important ministry. He is expected to do a good job of it."

The minister of economic warfare was in charge of setting blockade policy, but Winston Churchill, as lord of the admiralty, was in charge of carrying that policy out. "Blockade was enforced with full rigour," he wrote later. "The Admiralty controlled its execution."

SOME PEOPLE BEGAN to feel disappointed with the war. Berlin and Londons both were still intact, still ungassed. Mollie Panter-Downs, *The New Yorker*'s correspondent in England, wrote: "The public at the moment is feeling like a little boy who stuffs his fingers in his ears on the Fourth of July only to discover that the cannon cracker has not gone off after all." It was September 10, 1939.

COUNT CIANO made another attempt at an intermediated peace. He talked to Percy Loraine, the British ambassador to Italy. Loraine sent a telegram to Lord Halifax, which Halifax mentioned in a war-cabinet meeting. Churchill, now a member of the war cabinet, put a stop to these negotiatory feelers. "Loraine does not seem to understand our resolve," he wrote Halifax; the Italian ambassador should be encouraged to display a "more robust mood." Whatever happened in Poland, England would see the war through to victory. "If Ciano realises our inflexible purpose he will be less likely to toy with the idea of an Italian mediation," he said. It was September 10, 1939.

MARY TAYLOR, a woman from Liverpool, walked to London, holding a banner. The banner said: FOR THE SAKE OF CHILDREN EVERY-WHERE, I APPEAL TO MEN TO STOP THIS WAR. It was September 1939.

HITLER WAS IN ONE of his rages. It was September 19, 1939. The English had repulsed what they called his "peace offensive"—no peace was possible until he was gone, they'd said—and the Poles were giving his army stiff resistance. He'd planned to give a victory speech in Warsaw, but Warsaw hadn't yet fallen, so he had to speak in the Guild Hall in Danzig instead, while guns still boomed in Gdynia. "I have neither toward England nor France any war claims, nor has the German nation since I assumed power," Hitler said. "I have had only in mind the great goal of attaining the sincere friendship of the British people." England was sacrificing the blessings of peace because of a "handful of fanatic warmongers," he said.

Leaving the hall, Hitler brushed against William Shirer; Himmler and the rest of the crew followed him out. They hadn't had time to shave, Shirer noticed, and they looked, he said, "like a pack of Chicago gangsters."

VICTOR KLEMPERER listened as a loudspeaker radiated Hitler's speech. "Some of it rhetorically very effective," he thought. But it pointed to a long war. At his library, all the English books were withdrawn.

Klemperer's heart was bothering him. "One of two things will happen," he predicted. "Either Hitler will conclude victorious peace in a week—then we shall perish. Or the war only really starts now and lasts for a long time—in that case we shall also perish."

HAROLD NICOLSON, the junior minister of information, was listening to Lloyd George, former prime minister of England, talk about Britain's chances of winning the war. Lloyd George was "frankly terrified," Nicolson wrote in his diary.

Later that day, in Parliament, Chamberlain gave his weekly statement. Nicolson counted ten members who were asleep. "He might have been the Secretary of a firm of undertakers reading the minutes of the last meeting," wrote Nicolson. That evening, Nicolson and Guy Burgess had dinner at the Savoy Grill with a Conservative backbencher, Ronald Cartland. Cartland was very pessimistic. "He says," Nicolson wrote, "that we are frightfully short of ammunition in every branch, that we have, in fact, no Army, Navy or Air Force and that we should make peace at once." It was September 20, 1939.

IN DANZIG, Hitler said, "All parts of the Reich are now complete." He again made a peace offer. William Shirer explained it on CBS Radio: "The peace that Hitler offers Britain and France," Shirer said, "is something like this: Stop fighting—you keep your empires—we won't bother you. As for Eastern Europe, all the little countries in what was once Poland, well, that's the affair of Germany and Russia. You keep away from there. Peace on that basis is possible. We want it, we hope you do, too. But if you don't, if you want to go on with the war, why then don't think we Germans are going to sit back and be starved and ruined by the blockade. No, we'll take to the offensive, and Russia will be back of us." It was September 29, 1939.

"There can be no peace with Hitler because there can be no peace with Hitler," said an editorial in *The Times* of London.

In the *Völkischer Beobachter* two days later, there was a front-page editorial: "The People Want Peace."

CHRISTOPHER ISHERWOOD wrote in his diary that it was one month since the war began. "One looks ahead to a war and imagines it as a single, final, absolute event," he said. "It is nothing of the kind. War is a condition, like peace, with good days and bad days, moods of optimism and despair."

Isherwood's radio was always on; it was driving him crazy. He especially hated the European correspondents, broadcasting local color: "The Paris sky is blue. The leaves in the Bois are turning yellow. A lark is singing over Montmartre." He said: "I feel about them the way some bums must feel about the Salvation Army worker who forces you to take hymns with your soup."

AT THE CARLTON GRILL, Harold Nicolson was talking to a dapper Swiss aristocrat who had known Hitler slightly. It was October 3, 1939. The aristocrat, Burckhardt, imitated Hitler's hand waggings. "He says that Hitler is the most profoundly feminine man he has ever met, and that there are moments when he becomes almost effeminate," wrote Nicolson. "He says that Hitler has a dual personality, the first being that of a rather gentle artist, and the second that of the homicidal maniac."

Burckhardt said he once heard Hitler say: "It is a great sorrow to me that I have never met an Englishman who speaks German well enough for me to feel at ease with him."

WARSAW GAVE UP FIGHTING. A church had been hit during mass; many were killed in prayer, said a radio announcer. A bombed hospital "became the grave for hundreds of wounded soldiers, women and children."

Hitler met reporters at the airport: "Gentlemen, you have seen the ruins of Warsaw," he said. "Let that be a warning to those statesmen in London and Paris who still think of continuing this war."

Millions of Jews lived in Poland, including many of Russian descent who had been sent beyond the Pale during czarist persecutions. "Beyond the Pale" meant Poland, Lithuania, and the Ukraine. The Third Reich, founded on Jew hatred, had just quintupled its Jewish population.

The arrests began. Adam Zamenhof, director of a Jewish hospital, disappeared. His father was the man who invented Esperanto. He, Adam, had developed a method of detecting blind spots in the human field of vision.

LLOYD GEORGE stood in the House of Commons. It was October 3, 1939.

"It is quite clear from what has appeared in the press," the former prime minister said, "that there has been a discussion between the parties concerned, Russia, Germany and Italy, of more detailed terms of peace." He wondered whether Parliament might not go into secret session to talk over any proposals; it was, he said, very important not to make a hurried rejection. "Let us take heed of what we are doing because we are entering on something which involves the whole life of this empire and the whole future of our people."

VERA BRITTAIN, a British novelist, mailed out the announcement of a weekly newsletter she was going to be writing called *Letter to Peace Lovers.* "I want repeatedly to examine those popular slogans and hate-images by means of which we work up one another's emotions," she said. She quoted a sentence from a Norwegian novelist, Johan Bojer, written during the First World War: "I went and sowed corn in my enemy's field that God might exist."

A thousand people subscribed to Brittain's letters. It was October 4, 1939.

HITLER WENT ON the radio at noon from the Kroll Opera House to set out his peace offer in more detail. He wanted the four powers to have a conference. He was willing to give back some of Poland—but not the German and Russian parts. He offered to attempt to reach, through discussion with the other powers, "a solution and settlement of the Jewish problem." But, he said, if the Churchillian faction prevailed in England, Germany would fight. "In the course of history," he said, "there have never been two victors, but very often only losers."

John Colville, Chamberlain's secretary, wrote about Hitler's proposal in his diary: "Rather surprisingly he did not threaten us with destruction in its most appalling form; but the terms he offered are, as was to be expected, unacceptable to all except a few intellectuals suffering from senility like Bernard Shaw."

In the *New Statesman,* Shaw had written: "What in the devil's name is it all about now that we have let Poland go?" Abolishing Hitlerism, Shaw said, was as nonsensical a war aim as that of abolishing Churchillism. "Though we can easily kill a hundred thousand quite innocent Germans, man, woman, and child, in our determination to get at Herr Hitler, we should not finally succeed in lynching him."

MILTON MAYER, assistant to the president of the University of Chicago, published an article in *The Saturday Evening Post.* It was October 7, 1939. The article was called "I Think I'll Sit This One Out."

All of Mayer's onetime peace-pledging friends had now become eager interventionists, he said; Mayer, on the other hand, had not. "I make my decision to oppose this war, to oppose it now and when America enters it," he said, "and I make that decision despite my horror of 'the Berchtesgaden maniac' and my disinclination to set myself up as a martyr to my ideals."

Who was this Hitler, anyway? Mayer asked.

> A man, like the rest of us, capable, like the rest of us, of acting like a man; but a man brutalized, as the rest of us may be, by war and the poverty of war and the animal degradation of war—a man, in short, behaving like an animal.

It wasn't Hitler we had to fight, but fascism, and we couldn't fight fascism by acting like animals—we could fight it only by trying to stay human. "War is at once the essence and apotheosis, the beginning and the triumph, of Fascism," Mayer wrote. "I take myself to be an ordinary man, and I wonder what will happen to my humanity when I am hired, as Swift puts it, to kill in cold blood as many of my own species, who have never offended me, as I possibly can."

Mayer remembered what President Wilson had said: We have no quarrel with the German people. "But it was the German people whom we shot," Mayer said, "and the forces with whom we really had a quarrel grew and festered, and festered and grew, until they flowered into Hitlerism. And now we're asked to shoot the German people again."

Mayer said: "I can't get it out of my head that if Hitler menaces America today, it is not because he won the last war, but because he lost it."

Joseph Goebbels talked to Hitler, who was waiting for a reply from Chamberlain. "The Führer still has no clear idea of what England intends to do," Goebbels wrote in his diary. "In any event, it is the English who must decide whether the war is to continue." It was October 11, 1939.

The next day, Goebbels read Hitler a translation of Bernard Shaw's recent article. Hitler "laughs until the tears come," wrote Goebbels.

Chamberlain's response finally came later that day. The German chancellor, Chamberlain said—standing stiffly in the House of Commons—was demanding that England recognize his conquests and ratify his methods: "It would be impossible for Great Britain to accept any such basis without forfeiting her honour and abandoning her claim that international disputes should be settled by discussion and not by force." Chamberlain's new note of defiance caused, said *The Times,* "deep and prolonged cheering." It was October 12, 1939.

George Lansbury, elderly Laborite leader of the British pacifists, rose to question Chamberlain's rejection of Hitler's offer. Lansbury was, he said, just as horrified as anyone by German aggression and slaughter, but he didn't see how more slaughter would undo the horrors already past. He hoped that President Roosevelt could convene a summit—something that Roosevelt had no interest in doing.

Hitler studied Chamberlain's speech for three hours, and then told Goebbels to rally the press for a sharp attack. "It is high time, too," said Goebbels. "We can no longer put up with his insolence."

VICTOR KLEMPERER WAS SHOPPING. "In the fishmongers', confectioners' etc. the goods are often replaced by the picture of the Führer with flag cloth and victory green," he wrote in his diary. But there were no real shortages yet, as there had been in 1917 and 1918. "On the other hand, England-France appear to believe in the prospects of a long war, since the peace offer seems to have been rejected." It was October 12, 1939.

VERA BRITTAIN mailed out her first *Letter to Peace Lovers*. In it, she wrote about an open letter that she and five other women writers had recently sent to the prime minister, asking him not to bomb German cities. "The Government's own avowed intention of winning the sympathy of the German people would be ruined by this terrible expedient," she wrote in her newsletter. Even if Germany bombed English cities, England must refuse to retaliate: "It would not help us that German women and children should join us in our agony." She sent copies of the letter to all the newspapers. *The Times,* the *Telegraph,* and other leading papers ignored it; *The Manchester Guardian* printed it. Prime Minister Chamberlain wrote Brittain that he was in sympathy with her aims. Brittain's letter enraged one woman reader: "There is no reason whatsoever why German women should be spared anything that our own people have previously experienced at the hands of their menfolk." If Germany bombed England, England should BOMB THEM, she capitalized, back.

It was October 18, 1939.

A LETTER WENT OUT on Hitler's personal letterhead, approving an expansion of the program of *gnadentod,* "mercy death." It was backdated September 1, 1939, the first day of the war. In September and October, soldiers from one SS Death's Head unit removed patients from the Owinska Mental Home in Poland, took them to a forest, and shot them. The building became a barracks for SS troops. Other mental institutions were similarly cleared.

At the same time, much of the intellectual class of Poland was gradually wiped out. "The little people we want to spare," said Reinhard Heydrich, "but the nobles, priests, and Jews must be killed."

ULRICH VON HASSELL, right-wing opponent of Hitler, wrote in his diary about the war in Poland. It was October 19, 1939.

"Among well-informed people in Berlin I noticed a good deal of despair," von Hassell wrote. Germany's good name was disgraced by the bombing of Warsaw and the anti-Semitic bestialities of the SS. "When people use their revolvers to shoot down a group of Jews herded into a synagogue," von Hassell said, "one is filled with shame."

Von Hassell believed, however, that the current government couldn't last forever: "It must gradually be converted into an organic state based on the rule of law and operating under popular controls." A coup d'état was the only hope, he and his fellow conspirators thought. "But how?"

CYRIL JOAD, a philosopher who was writing a book called *Journey Through the War Mind,* had a talk with his pacifist friend "D." Joad asked D. whether D. thought Chamberlain should have negotiated with Hitler after Hitler's peace offer. "Yes, of course," said D.: Wars should never be begun, and as soon as they were begun, they should be stopped. D. then listed off many war evils: the physical and moral mutilation, the intolerance, the public lying, the enthronement of the mob. He quoted from the text of Chamberlain's refusal—that by discussing peace with Hitler, Britain would forfeit her honor and abandon her claim that international disputes should be settled by discussion and not by force. "Our claim is, you see," D. told Joad, "that international disputes are not to be settled by force, and this claim we propose to make good by settling an international dispute by force. We are fighting to show that you cannot, or at least must not, impose your will upon other people by violence." Which made no sense.

Once a war has started, D. said, the only thing to do is to get it stopped as soon as possible. "Consequently I should negotiate with Hitler."

Joad said: Ah, but you couldn't negotiate with Hitler because you couldn't trust him—Hitler would break any agreement as soon as it benefited him to do so.

"Suppose you are right," D. said—suppose that Hitler violated the peace agreement and England had to go back to war. What had they lost? "If the worst comes to the worst, we can always begin the killing again." Even a day of peace was a day of peace. Joad found he had no ready answer to that.

CYRIL JOAD talked about the war with another acquaintance, "Mrs. C.," a vigorous Tory. War was natural and unavoidable, said Mrs. C. The Germans weren't human—they were brute blond "perverted morons."

Joad asked C. what she would do with Germany, and a light came into her eyes.

"I would make a real Carthaginian peace," she told Joad. "Raze their cities to the ground, plough up the land and sow it afterwards with salt; and I would kill off one out of every five German women, so that they stopped breeding so many little Huns."

Mrs. C.'s ideas were shared by others, Joad had noticed; he'd recently read a letter to the editor about Germany in London's *News Chronicle:* "Quite frankly," said the letter, "I would annihilate every living thing, man, woman, and child, beast, bird and insect; in fact, I would not leave a blade of grass growing even; Germany should be laid more desolate than the Sahara desert, if I could have my way."

The longer the war lasted, Joad believed, the more this kind of viciousness would multiply: "Already," Joad wrote, "Mr. Churchill was reviving the appellation 'Huns.'"

TWO THOUSAND VIENNESE JEWS were on their way to a "reservation" near Lublin, in Poland, said a small wire-service article in *The New York Times:* "They left here aboard special trains last night for their new and permanent homes in an area described as being similar to an American Indian reservation. It was understood that this was the first of a series of mass migrations that eventually may include all Austrian, or perhaps all German Jews." It was October 21, 1939.

A week later, according to the Associated Press, two thousand more Jews were sent to Lublin from Vienna. The second group included women and children over sixteen. The goal, the report said, was a "Jew free" Vienna by March 1, 1940.

GENERAL JOHANNES BLASKOWITZ, commander in chief of the German occupying army in Poland, began assembling an atrocity report. It was November 1939.

There were actually two German occupying armies in Poland, one superimposed on the other. There was the army army, the Wehrmacht, which had fought a traditional sort of war with the Polish army. And then there was the growing SS army—the race-purifying, IBM-card-sorting shadow empire of Himmler and Heydrich.

General Blaskowitz, of the army army, wasn't a nice or a gentle man—he had subdued Poland, and he viewed Jews and Poles as "our arch-enemies in the Eastern sphere"—but he didn't believe in torture, flogging, looting, rape, and the killing of families, and he was disgusted by the stories his men were telling him. The special-operations units of the SS were obviously out of control.

Blaskowitz sent his report of wrongdoing to his superiors in Berlin. He talked things over with General Groscurth, who distributed the report widely, and with Lieutenant Colonel Helmuth Stieff, who later plotted against Hitler. Stieff wrote his wife that there was no atrocity propaganda that could equal the murder and plunder going on in Poland. And it was going on "with supposed tolerance from the highest quarters." Whole families were being exterminated by "subhumans who do not deserve the name German," Stieff wrote. "I am ashamed to be a German."

Hitler read one of Blaskowitz's reports, which talked of "blood lust" and the failure to keep order, and he said: You can't fight a war with the Salvation Army.

Despite the cool reception in Berlin, Blaskowitz began work on another dossier of Polish and Jewish misery. He carried it around with him for a while, wondering whether to send it directly to Hitler or not. In the end, he submitted it to his superior officer, General Walther von Brauchitsch. General Brauchitsch had resisted Hitler for a while, but he was weakening—he had, with Hitler's advice and help, divorced his wife and married a rabid Nazi. Brauchitsch shelved the report.

"Every soldier feels disgusted and repelled by these crimes," Blaskowitz wrote. There were fearful consequences to the open tolerance of brutality: the depravity would "spread like an epidemic."

> Surprisingly quickly the like-minded and the deviant personalities come together, as is the case in Poland, in order to give full vent to their animalistic and pathological instincts.

Eventually, Blaskowitz said, "only the brutal will rule."

Prime Minister Neville Chamberlain wrote another letter to his sister. Hitler simply had to go before there could be any possibility of peace. "He must either die or go to St Helena or become a real public works architect, preferably in a 'home,' " Chamberlain wrote. "His entourage must also go, with the possible exception of Goering, who might have some ornamental position in a transitional government." It was November 5, 1939.

A man named Elser began building a time bomb. He stole dynamite from a quarry where he worked. He hollowed out a place for the bomb in a pillar of the Burgerbrau beer hall in Munich and set the timer for November 8, 1939, when Hitler would be there, giving a speech. He put his ear to the column. Yes, he could hear the ticking. He got on a train for Switzerland.

The bomb went off, killing eight people and injuring many more. Hitler had left ten minutes earlier. The *Völkischer Beobachter* called it "the miraculous salvation of the Führer."

GOERING HELD a press conference. It was November 1939. A reporter asked why the Luftwaffe was attacking British ships instead of British harbors. "Warships are important, too," Goering said. "Besides, they are good practice."

Someone else asked whether Goering was going to bring the Blitzkrieg to Britain.

"We are humane," Goering said. The reporters laughed. Goering said, "I am serious. I really am."

Was he going to remain humane?

"That depends on the others," Goering said. "And that is no joke either."

VERA BRITTAIN sent out a peace newsletter describing Hitler's bursts of fanatical rage. Psychiatrists had some experience with his variety of mental illness, Brittain observed. "Of the many methods of dealing with it which have been evolved," she said, "reciprocal violence is usually regarded as the least successful."

It was November 23, 1939.

VICTOR KLEMPERER WROTE: "The ever increasing food difficulties are getting on my nerves." But he didn't see how the British blockade could be conclusive: "This state of affairs—light harassing fire in the West, usually quiet—can, almost certainly will drag on for years yet, and it is just as difficult to see how England can deal with Hitler as how Hitler can deal with England." It was November 29, 1939.

GOERING BECAME vocally impatient with the British hunger blockade and wanted to attack London. His planes were ready, he told reporters—they had been photographing England's war preparations. "All that is needed is the Führer's command," he said, "for them to carry over their load of bombs instead of an insignificant load of cameras." It would be an attack "the like of which the world has never known." It was December 30, 1939.

A REPORT came in from the Jewish Telegraphic Agency about the Polish Jews in Lublin; it was reprinted in the New York *Herald Tribune*. "For more than three months, the city's Jews were the target of pogroms, systematic plunder, torture and expulsion," the report said. The Yeshiva Chachmei, the Jewish religious college of Lublin, had been turned into a "barracks for Nazi storm troopers and a torture chamber."

Deportations of Jews to Lublin had been suspended, however, "reportedly because of a sharp division of opinion on the matter between the German Gestapo (secret police) and the military authorities," the *Herald Tribune* reported. The deportations might resume soon: "It has been reliably learned that the Gestapo has succeeded in getting the upper hand in the controversy."

Another cable, also printed in the *Herald Tribune,* described freight cars filled with deported Jews. "Cars are sealed, unheated, windowless and without food. In one car, opened at a Warsaw station, eight infants were found dead from cold and starvation," the cable said. "So great is the fear of Lodz Jews of these sealed cars that thousands have run from the city on foot."

The United Jewish Appeal for Refugees and Overseas Needs made an announcement: In addition to their efforts on behalf of Jews, they were giving $250,000 to help refugees of other faiths. Half the money would go to the pope, for aid to Catholics, and half to Protestant agencies.

It was January 2, 1940.

HENRY MORGENTHAU, JR., the secretary of the treasury, got President Roosevelt's okay to divert twenty-five new P-40 fighter planes to France. France was desperate for fighter planes. It was January 1940. "I did a magician's trick for you," Morgenthau said to one of the Frenchmen. "Pulled twenty-five planes out of the hat."

CHRISTOPHER ISHERWOOD, who was writing a movie for MGM, went to a meeting of the Hollywood Antiwar League. He disliked the dishonesty and self-interest in the arguments that the pacifists were using. One of the speakers, a screenwriter named Dudley Nichols, announced that he was a militant pacifist; he said he was willing to get in a fistfight with anyone who wanted America in the war.

Antiwar agitation would achieve little, Isherwood thought, unless it was based on a genuine condemnation of violence. "How all these people fear the plain moral stand against killing!" he wrote in his diary. It was January 16, 1940.

A NEW "1940 WAR EDITION" of John Gunther's bestseller *Inside Europe,* published by Harper and Row, was in the stores. It was January 1940.

Hitler was not in top physical condition, Gunther reported; he often brooded on death. In recent years, said Gunther, Hitler had gained weight—"his neck and midriff show it"—and he had a notoriously sloppy salute. As for his attitude toward women: "He is totally uninterested in women from any personal sexual point of view," Gunther explained. "Nor, as is so widely believed, is he homosexual." Journalists who had made careful inquiries had concluded that Hitler was a virgin.

Inside Europe had a section on Winston Churchill, too. Churchill had very pale, very blue eyes, Gunther wrote; he looked ten years younger than his age. "For years—not now—it seemed that he stood always on the wrong side of great social issues." He had opposed the vote for women; he had opposed the mild socialism of the Labour Party; he had opposed a democratic government in India; and—disastrously—he had invaded Russia in 1919 to save it from bolshevism. When he was a boy, he'd had fifteen hundred toy soldiers; once he jumped off a bridge and spent months recovering. "Sometimes, when one inspects his leading political ideas," Gunther said, "one feels that they are the ideas of an incredibly talented, willful, badly educated child."

Nonetheless, he was a man of imagination and foresight, Gunther believed: He had helped create the tank, and he had successfully urged the remilitarization of Great Britain.

There was one other thing about Churchill: "He is the only top rank cabinet officer or leader on either side during the last war who survives to hold important office today."

HAROLD NICOLSON had dinner at the Carlton Club with some parliamentarians and a man from the Air Ministry. It was January 17, 1940.

The Air Ministry man told the others that the Chamberlain cabinet had forbidden the dropping of bombs on Germany. "The Group agrees that this is a very serious situation," Nicolson wrote in his diary.

There was a faction in the war cabinet, Nicolson learned, that was in negotiations with former German chancellor Heinrich Brüning. The aim was to make peace with the German high command on the condition that they "eliminate" Hitler. "We discuss the means by which this intrigue can be countered," Nicolson wrote.

THERE WAS A JEERING bit of verse going around London, about how Auden and Isherwood had abandoned London during wartime:

> The literary erstwhile Left-wellwisher would
> Seek vainly now for Auden or for Isherwood.

Isherwood was hurt by it. "Am I afraid of being bombed? Of course. Everybody is," he wrote in his diary. But that wasn't why he had gone to the United States. "If I fear anything," he said, "I fear the atmosphere of the war, the power which it gives to all the things I hate—the newspapers, the politicians, the puritans, the scoutmasters, the middle-aged merciless spinsters." Isherwood shrank, he said, from the duty of opposition: "I am afraid I should be reduced to a chattering, enraged monkey, screaming back hate at their hate." That's why he'd left. It was January 20, 1940.

DR. NAHUM GOLDMANN, of the World Jewish Congress, gave a speech in Chicago. "If the war in Europe goes on for another year," Goldmann said, "1,000,000 of the 2,000,000 Jews in Poland will be dead of starvation or killed by Nazi persecutors." It was January 21, 1940.

WINSTON CHURCHILL gave a speech in Manchester's Free Trade Hall. It was January 27, 1940. There was, he said, a question that he was always running over in his mind: Why had England not yet been attacked from the air? "Is it that they are saving up some orgy of frightfulness which will soon come upon us?" he wondered. "Is it because they feared the massive counterstroke which they would immediately receive from our powerful bombing force?" It was certainly not, Churchill said, any "false sense of delicacy" that had restrained them.

> We know from what they did in Poland that there is no brutality or bestial massacre of civilians by air bombing which they would not readily commit if they thought it were for their advantage.

Churchill then asked: "Ought we, instead of demonstrating the power of our Air Force by dropping leaflets all over Germany, to have dropped bombs?" No, on the whole not, he believed: "We have striven hard," he said, "to make the most of the time of preparation that has been gained, and there is no doubt that an enormous advance has been made both in the protection of the civil population and in the punishment which would be inflicted upon the raiders."

Churchill did not say that Britain shouldn't have dropped bombs all over Germany because the British government had pledged not to, or because the bombing of cities was wrong. He said that Britain shouldn't have bombed because the country had needed several more months to accumulate bombers, train crews, and set up anti-aircraft defenses.

GENERAL ALAN BROOKE, of the British Expeditionary Force, was bothered by talk in the war office of bombing the Ruhr Valley, where there were more factories—and more people—than anywhere else in Germany. Brooke wanted to use English airplanes against the German army within the war zone, not against German industry outside the war zone. The day after Churchill spoke in Manchester, Brooke wrote in his diary:

> To contemplate bombing the Ruhr at a time when the Germans are using their combined army and air force in one mighty uniform attempt to crush the French and British forces to clear the way into France, is in my mind sheer folly.

"Two 'wrongs' do not make a 'right' in this case," Brooke wrote. It was January 28, 1940.

MASS OBSERVATION, the British government's morale-sampling service, concluded that people in England found the war too dull. "A new restlessness is setting in," according to a Mass Observation report, "a desire for something to happen, however unpleasant." It was February 1940.

SOME JEWS escaped from the Lodz ghetto in Poland by hiding in coffins. Mary Berg, a fifteen-year-old girl living in the Warsaw ghetto, had heard about them. "The Jewish cemetery is outside the ghetto, and it is possible to carry dead persons there," she wrote. "Thus some people had themselves boarded up in caskets, which were carried off with the usual funeral ceremonies; before reaching the cemetery they rose from their coffins and escaped to Warsaw." One person died of heart failure, she said, while he was confined. It was March 2, 1940.

GERMAN BOMBERS flew across the North Sea to Scapa Flow, a harbor in the Orkney Islands where there were English warships. It was March 1940. The bombers dropped their bombs, and someone was killed—the first civilian to die from German bombs on British soil since the First World War.

"Was that deliberate?" asked Lord Strabolgi in the House of Lords.

"No, I should think not," replied Lord Halifax.

Yet it must be countered. Lord Boom Trenchard, the creator of the Royal Air Force, stood and said, "I do beg your Lordships to remember that the Air Force is an offensive and not a defensive weapon."

Fifty English planes flew to the German island of Sylt, in the North Sea, hoping to destroy an air base. Some airplanes overshot and dropped incendiaries and high explosives in Denmark, breaking windows.

"Peace Hope Dies," said *The New York Times*. "War Seen Entering New Phase of Violence." "One of the main ideas," reported the *Times*'s Raymond Daniell in London a day later, "was to drop two British bombs for every German one that landed in the Orkneys." Messenger boys, bus drivers, and members of Parliament all cheered the Sylt reprisal raid, Daniell wrote: "Unanimously they were applauding, shouting for more, although none were so blind they failed to realize that such reprisals invite counter-reprisals and that thus starts the holocaust the whole world has been praying may be averted somehow."

WINSTON CHURCHILL, lord of the admiralty, wrote a memo about mining Norwegian waters. Iron ore, which made steel, which made the tools of war, was getting through to Germany from Norwegian points of entry. Stopping the influx of iron ore through the remote port of Narvik, above the Arctic Circle, would cripple the enemy's industry, Churchill contended—and it also might "succeed in provoking Germany into an imprudent action which would open the door for us." The plan, code-named Wilfrid, was "minor and innocent," he told his admirals.

Hints of Churchill's plan appeared in the press, alerting the German high command, which made counterplans. Prime Minister Chamberlain didn't like the Narvik idea, partly because it was illegal. Norway was a neutral country, and sowing mines in neutral harbors was contrary to international law. It was also a war-widening provocation.

German admirals mused over the consequences of losing Norwegian ports. The war would be as good as lost, they said. Vidkun Quisling, the former war minister of Norway, began talks with Hitler about setting up a puppet government. There had been no plans in Berlin for an invasion of Norway; now there were. It was March 1940.

HAROLD NICOLSON noted in his diary that the British navy was laying mines in Norwegian waters. "This will create a rage," he said. It was April 8, 1940.

A Swedish foreign officer dropped by Under-Secretary Cadogan's office. "Says we have done the silliest thing in history—in our own interests," Cadogan wrote. "And I think he is right, but I had to argue with him."

"The Norwegian Government protests gravely and strongly against this open breach of international law," said Norway's foreign minister. German forces surged in. By April 9, 1940, they were in control of an unbombed Oslo. And of Narvik. "Germans seem to have got in to Narvik!" wrote Under-Secretary Cadogan. "How?!"

SUDDENLY, IT was a real war, on the ground. There were midnight landings on Norwegian soil of small English and French forces, which were set upon by German airplanes. The French had forgotten their mules. The English had no snowshoes. One group commandeered some horse-drawn sleds from local peasants and surged through the drifts. A squadron of RAF planes was sunk when it parked on a frozen lake and the Luftwaffe bombed the ice. The Royal Air Force began raiding Norwegian airports under German control, sometimes with delayed-action bombs.

Then British retreat, disaster—excoriation and leaping outrage in the press and Parliament. The outrage was aimed not at Churchill, who had conceived of the Norwegian campaign, but at Chamberlain.

"The first of our glorious evacuations," H. G. Wells said later—a debacle. Or not a debacle, if what you wanted was noble chaos, wounded struggle, a spotlight trained on Chamberlainian indecisiveness, and the image above all of a stoic England, beset but steadfast, carrying bravely on in a world everywhere enslaved and prostrate.

"Norway was Winston's adventure, and poor Neville blamed for it," Chips Cannon wrote in his diary.

CHARLES "PETER" PORTAL, the rising star of the Royal Air Force, was made head of Bomber Command. Portal was a chilly man who enjoyed killing birds and rabbits. As a boy at Winchester, he had raised hawks, keeping a detailed diary of how many larks, starlings, and pigeons they killed:

> The hawk poises herself for a decisive swoop, and makes a brilliant cut at the fast disappearing quarry. As we strain our eyes in the failing light we see a puff of feathers shoot from the pigeon's body, and the bird tumbles to earth, from which he will never rise again.

He hawked, beagled, and shot his way through Oxford. He skipped class and raced motorcycles, and then he learned to fly. In 1917, he began bombing German soldiers by night. After the war, he went back to keeping his hawking diaries. In the 1920–21 season his hawk force killed 105 larks, forty-six partridges, one pigeon, and a turtledove.

In the twenties, Portal began working for Boom Trenchard's Royal Air Force. He was given command of the Number 7 squadron at Worthy Down, where for several years running he was the winning bomb aimer during the annual bomb aiming competition. Finally, in 1934, in southern Yemen, Portal got his chance at combat, crushing the will of the Qutaibi tribe with weeks of bombing. He gave a lecture on the operation; it was thought to be a classic instance of the successful application of the principles of air control.

When Portal assumed control of Bomber Command, in April 1940, *The Times* of London wrote: "There is more than a streak of ruthlessness in his nature though he has suppressed it so far in this war."

A CAPTAIN in the French army drove Clare Boothe, the American journalist, to see a fort in Lorraine. The fort was part of the Maginot Line—"that vast row on row," Boothe wrote, "of cement catacombs, of sunken earth-bound battleships" that ran along France's border with Germany. The commandant of the fort showed her the huge guns, the racks of shells, the stocks of food and medicine, the fire-proof sliding doors, the fifty-foot pits, the "bewildering mazes of machinery."

It was obviously impregnable, Clare Boothe concluded. "Why," she asked, "should the Germans try to come this way?"

Because, answered the commandant, that's what two great armies are for, to hurl themselves at each other.

Couldn't the Germans get into France some other way? Boothe asked.

The commandant and his subordinates laughed. "What other way?"

"Holland? Belgium?"

They laughed some more. "The Germans are stupid—but not *that* stupid."

A GERMAN OFFICIAL, Hans Frank, was talking to some of his subordinates in his governmental palace in Cracow. It was April 12, 1940.

Cracow, Warsaw, and Lublin were now part of a large eastern territory in Poland that the Germans called the General Government. Hans Frank—a longtime Hitler worshipper—was the governor-general of the General Government. Millions of Jews lived in the General Government, and while Frank was prepared to tolerate that fact for the time being, he thought Cracow, his capital city, should become as Jew-free as possible. In Cracow, Frank said, housing was short, and "thousands and more thousands of Jews slink around and take up apartments." He ordered all but economically useful Jews to leave the city. If they left by August 15, they could take their possessions. Some left for smaller towns; thousands remained.

GERMANY ISSUED a warning to Britain about some bombs that had fallen on a railroad line at the Heiligenhafen station in Schleswig-Holstein, far from any war zone. It was April 12, 1940. The British Air Ministry denied the raid. On the night of April 22, the British bombed occupied Oslo, something the Germans had not done, for two and a half hours. The British hit, the Germans said, a civilian area.

Then, on April 25, the German high command issued its third, "final," warning. This time it was over an attack on the town of Heide, in northern Germany. "The enemy has opened aerial warfare against undefended places," the German high command said. Although the Luftwaffe remained under orders to avoid attacks on civilians, Germany would, if the British persisted in this pattern of attack, retaliate. "Bomb will be repaid with bomb if the British continue bombing nonmilitary targets," the warning said. The next response would be a "sad awakening" for England.

CHURCHILL WAS CONSUMED by the idea of recapturing Narvik. "Here it is we must fight and persevere on the largest scale possible," he wrote to one of his naval commanders. It was April 28, 1940.

"He wanted to divert troops there from all over the place," General Ironside noted in his diary. "He is so like a child in many ways. He tires of a thing, and then wants to hear no more of it." First he wanted Namsos, then he got bored with Namsos—now he wanted Narvik again. "It is most extraordinary how mercurial he is."

THE BRITISH AIR MINISTRY issued a denial: "No attack was made on the town of Heide." Which didn't mean that British bombs hadn't fallen on Heide. It was difficult, using dead reckoning and peering down at moonlit rivers and coastlines, for English fliers to know where they were going. They dropped their bombs in the dark, hoping they were where they thought they were. Later in the war, when the British had radio-beam navigation systems, called "Gee" and "Oboe," it would be easier. But for now, getting lost was not uncommon. "Normally it was not difficult to find the target area but almost impossible to be anywhere near a specific target," one flier recalled of that early period, "so we just dropped the bombs at an estimated position and hoped for the best. I very much doubt if we ever hit a specific target."

A PHOTOGRAPHER began taking pictures of people before they were killed. It was May 1940, in a medieval castle in Austria. The people in Hartheim Castle who were being killed were mentally and physically handicapped; their bodies were burned in a cremation oven. "Hitler felt that by exterminating these so-called useless eaters," one of the T-4 euthanasianists later testified, "it would be possible to relieve more doctors, male and female nurses, and other personnel, hospital beds, and other facilities for the use of the Armed Forces."

The smell of burning bothered the photographer. Hartheim's supervisor, a former police officer, said: Drink, you'll feel better. So the photographer drank and took the pictures. The assembly-line killings led to the brutalization of the staff, writes one historian: "Reports abounded of drunken orgies, numerous sexual liaisons, brawling and bullying." One eyewitness said that at the castle "almost all employees were intimate with each other." More than nine thousand people died at Hartheim in 1940.

SOME OF THE German generals began to feel more enthusiastic about Plan Yellow, the invasion of the Low Countries and France. Hitler was paying them monthly bonus checks—those who were compliant—out of a special Chancellery account. The army was corrupted, General Halder said later, by the distribution of "closed envelopes with extraordinary remunerations." In fact, Halder himself took Chancellery money. Hitler bribed his way westward.

CLARE BOOTHE, the American journalist, was asleep on the top floor of the American embassy building in Brussels, Belgium. A maid shook her: "The Germans are coming again!" It was May 10, 1940.

Boothe went to the window and looked out at the black trees across the park. She saw about twenty planes flying in formation, their underbellies agleam in the gold of dawn. "I heard a thin long, long whistle and a terrible round *bam!*" she wrote. A house across the square was hit. "The *bam* was the glut and vomit of glass and wood and stone that was hurled into the little green park before me." Antiaircraft guns started going, and she got dressed. "I was very careful to fill my purse with an extra supply of powder, lipstick, and cold-cream and to choose the only flat-heeled shoes in my suitcase."

PERMANENT UNDER-SECRETARY CADOGAN was awakened at 5:40 A.M. with the news that Holland and Belgium were under attack. "Germans have relieved us of a number of embarrassing questions by invading *both* countries," he wrote. It was May 10, 1940. The war cabinet met, discussed bombing Germany on behalf of the invaded countries, and postponed the decision. Hermann Goering's Luftwaffe began blowing up airdromes.

Neville Chamberlain came on the radio. "I sought an audience of the King this evening," he said, "and tendered to him my resignation, which his Majesty has been pleased to accept." Winston Churchill would be the new prime minister, he announced. "You and I must rally behind our new leader, and with our united strength, and with unshakeable courage, fight and work until this wild beast

that has sprung out of his lair upon us be finally disarmed and over-
thrown."

Harold Nicolson loved the speech. "All the hatred I have felt
for Chamberlain subsides as if a piece of bread were dropped into a
glass of champagne," he wrote.

WINSTON CHURCHILL, taking his office as prime minister and
minister of defence, offered blood, toil, tears, and sweat. What was
his policy going to be? Very simple: war—war against "a monstrous
tyranny, never surpassed in the dark, lamentable catalogue of human
crime." What was the aim of waging the war? To win. The House
gave him an ovation. Catching the eye of an aide as he walked out,
Churchill said: "That got the sods, didn't it?"

GERMAN PARATROOPERS landed in Rotterdam and on the roof of
the fort of Eben Emael in Belgium. People thought there were thousands of them, but there weren't—some were dummy paratroopers
dropped to create the illusion of a massive invasion. The Luftwaffe
targeted the airport at Nancy but missed. Fifteen civilians died, including a family sprinting for an air-raid dugout. Four elderly people were caught under collapsing masonry. Twenty miles from Paris,
German bombers, harried by antiaircraft fire, dropped incendiaries
on a terrified village. It was May 10, 1940.

LORD HALIFAX accepted Churchill's request that he carry on at the Foreign Office. It was May 11, 1940. "I have seldom met anybody with stranger gaps of knowledge, or whose mind worked in greater jerks," Halifax wrote of his new leader. "Will it be possible to make it work in orderly fashion? On this much depends."

With the shift of power, Neville Chamberlain's private secretary, John Colville, became Churchill's private secretary. Later, Colville wrote: "The mere thought of Churchill as Prime Minister sent a cold chill down the spines of the staff at 10 Downing Street." He said that Churchill's "verbosity and restlessness made unnecessary work, prevented real planning and caused friction." Chamberlain had been weak, Colville felt, in allowing Churchill "to assume responsibilities far in excess of his Departmental concerns." And: "Churchill's impetuosity had, we thought, contributed to the Norwegian fiasco." Their views were, said Colville, shared throughout Whitehall.

But within weeks, Churchill's energy and self-assurance had won their loyalty. He came out jabbing, pecking, growling. He was minister of defence and prime minister, both together. He worked very late, attended by advisers and generals—two, three, three-thirty in the morning—drinking and gnawing through cigars. His dress was casual: one-piece zippered teddy-bear rompers, blue, over which he sometimes wore a red robe with topsy-turvey golden dragons. He wasn't an alcoholic, someone said later—no alcoholic could drink that much. He knew Macaulay's *Lays of Ancient Rome* by heart.

He wrote innumerable notes to his staff, all phrased in his brilliant, anachronistic idiom, ready-made for quotation in any future history he might write. Everyone agreed that he was a maladroit administrator and a capricious military strategist. He had no sense of proportion. But he created, said Colville, a welcome sense of urgency: After only a few days, "very respectable civil servants were actually to be seen running along the corridors."

EIGHTEEN OF the Royal Air Force's Whitley bombers took to the air, intending to do harm to places within Germany. It was the second night of Churchill's prime ministership. "Bomber Command went to war on 11 May, 1940. It had only been fooling with war until then," wrote James Spaight, an air-power theorist, several years later. "We began to bomb objectives on the German mainland before the Germans began to bomb objectives on the British mainland."

In the town of Mönchen-Gladbach, in Westphalia, a little after midnight, four civilians—one, as it happened, an Englishwoman—were killed by English bombs. The Germans shot down three out of thirty-six planes. The next night, more random bombing by the RAF. The night after that, more still. English planes were meandering over Germany in the dark, as they'd done with bays full of leaflets. Now they carried bombs.

The early nights of air raids were not officially announced, although the Associated Press reported them, citing German sources: "A German radio broadcast heard here early today said Essen, where the great German Krupp arms works are situated, and two other German towns had been bombed by Allied planes," said one article. The British Air Ministry denied the bombing: "Essen was not among the objectives bombed by the R.A.F. last night or the night before."

The planes were out there somewhere, anyway.

TELEGRAMS WENT OUT to the chief constables of English counties where German paratroopers might land. It was May 11, 1940. Churchill wanted German and Austrian aliens locked up. Hundreds of people, then thousands, most of them Jewish refugees, were marched by soldiers with fixed bayonets to prison.

THE COMMANDER of the U.S. fleet, Admiral James O. Richardson, was puzzled and irritated. Why had President Roosevelt ordered him to keep his fleet so far west, concentrated at Pearl Harbor, after spring maneuvers? Why couldn't his ships just return as usual to their bases on the California coast, at San Diego, San Pedro, and Long Beach?

Admiral Richardson wrote a letter to his superior officer, Admiral Stark. "I feel that any move west means hostilities," he wrote. "I feel that at this time it would be a grave mistake to become involved in the west, where our interests, although important, are not vital." It was May 13, 1940.

A week later, still sitting at Pearl Harbor, Richardson wrote another letter to Stark. "Are we here primarily to influence the actions of other nations by our presence?" he asked. "Are we here as a stepping off place for belligerent activity?"

Admiral Stark sent a reply. "You are there because of the deterrent effect which it is thought your presence may have on the Japs going into the East Indies," Stark said. "You would naturally ask— suppose the Japs do go into the East Indies? What are we going to do about it? My answer to that is, I don't know and I think there is nobody on God's green earth who can tell you."

THE GERMANS sent the Dutch an ultimatum: Unless all resistance ended, Rotterdam would be visited with "complete destruction." It was May 14, 1940.

The Dutch delayed, asking for the rank and signature of the officer who sent the ultimatum. One of the German generals, General Schmidt, believing that a capitulation was imminent, radioed the high command to call off the air attack. Others above him—probably Goering and probably Hitler himself—authorized it anyway.

At 1:30 in the afternoon, the Luftwaffe flew in with more than fifty Heinkel bombers. Failing to notice, or ignoring, the red "do not bomb" flares that General Schmidt sent up, they burned and blasted the center of the city. Oil from a margarine factory fed fierce fires. Nine hundred died.

THE GERMAN GOVERNMENT's opinion-polling service, run by a studious SS man named Otto Ohlendorf—later hanged at Nuremberg for his part in Ukrainian atrocities—surveyed its regional bureaus in Aachen, Koblenz, Darmstadt, and Neustadt. It was May 14, 1940.

The polls reported that the British bomber attacks "carried out on open cities and villages have caused great disgust, but not any grave disquiet among the population."

ETTY HILLESUM, a Jewish woman who lived in Amsterdam, ran out the doors of the Skating Club. It was May 15, 1940.

Hillesum caught up with her former professor, Willem Bonger. People she knew had been talking about nothing except trying to get away to England. "Do you think it makes sense to escape?" she said.

"The young have to stay put," Professor Bonger said.

She asked him if he thought democracy could win.

"It's bound to win," Bonger said, "but it's going to cost us several generations."

He looked, she thought, suddenly broken and defenseless. She put her arm around him and walked with him for a little. Then she took one of his hands between hers. "He gently lowered his heavy head a little and looked at me through his blue glasses." They said goodbye.

He shot himself that night.

THE NEW BRITISH WAR CABINET—sixteen men sitting around a big table, with Churchill in the middle—met at eleven o'clock in the morning. It was May 15, 1940. Churchill called for a "very large round-up of enemy aliens and suspect persons." It would be better, he said, if these people were behind barbed wire—safer for them, if the Germans started bombing England and people got angry. The war-cabinet minutes record no mention that the majority of the aliens were Jewish refugees of recent arrival.

There was another important item of business—was it time, Churchill asked, to bomb the German industrial heartland—the Ruhr Valley? He thought it was. The bombing would, he said, "cut Germany at its tap root." This was the "psychological moment to strike Germany in her own country and convince the German people that England had the will and the power to hit them hard." It should begin immediately. There was no need to inform France.

The air marshal, Richard Peirse, said that his staff had been at work choosing suitable German railroad-marshaling yards as targets. (Railroad yards, which are often in the middle of cities, are easier to aim at from the air than specific blacked-out buildings or industrial neighborhoods.) Hugh Dowding, the head of Fighter Command, said that England should not be deterred by fear of return attacks. These were "bound to come sooner or later." Churchill agreed. "We must expect this country to be hit in return," he said.

There was another important consideration, Churchill said: "American sympathy had recently been veering very much in our favor." Would this contemplated bombing of targets located within German cities produce a "revulsion of feeling" in the United States? Or would it be accepted there as justifiable retaliation?

To shore up the case for England's retaliatory bombing of Germany—despite the fact that no English cities had yet been bombed—Churchill asked the new minister of information, Duff Cooper, to "arrange that discreet reference should be made in the press to the killing of civilians in France and the Low Countries, in the course of German air attacks." The press should not actually mention retaliation, however, Churchill thought.

Permanent Under-Secretary Cadogan wrote in his diary: "Cabinet this morning decided to start bombing Ruhr. Now the 'Total War' begins!"

THAT AFTERNOON—it was still May 15, 1940—Churchill wrote his first prime-ministerial letter to President Roosevelt. What England needed, Churchill wrote, was: forty or fifty destroyers, several hundred aircraft, antiaircraft guns and ammunition, and help in the Far East. "I am looking to you to keep that Japanese dog quiet in the Pacific, using Singapore in any way convenient," Churchill wrote.

THAT NIGHT—it was still May 15, 1940—one hundred British bombers took off and did their best to bomb whatever targets they could find in the dark. Otto Ohlendorf's survey people reported raids on Aachen, Düsseldorf, Cologne, Duisburg, Koblenz, and Munster.

The German high command said that English planes were bombing at random, killing civilians but failing to hit anything of military significance. A girls' boarding school in the town of Marienberg was damaged by incendiary bombs, said the high command. The girls were away, however, when the raid occurred.

A GROUP OF FRENCH SCIENTISTS went to talk to Lord Hankey, chairman of the Microbiological Warfare Committee. It was May 1940. The scientists worked at France's Commission de Prophylaxie, or Disease Control Commission, a biological-warfare establishment in Vert-le-Petit, near Paris. Since May 1939, the French had been investigating the possibility of air-dropping Colorado beetles onto German potato crops. They had also looked into infecting potatoes with *phytophthora infestans,* or potato blight—the disease that brought on famine in Ireland in the mid-nineteenth century. The aerial delivery of bovine plague was another of their research areas.

The potato-bug idea was not new—late in World War I, a Major Tiverton (later the earl of Halsbury), had proposed Colorado-beetle bombings over Germany. Although his plan was pronounced "well worth considering," it came to nothing because of the risk that the beetles would destroy French potatoes.

Now, however, France looked as if it was about to fall to the Germans. French potatoes would be German potatoes.

GOERING TOLD HIS PILOTS to be careful about attacking French cathedrals. "I strongly emphasized to my fliers that the magnificent Gothic cathedrals of the French cities were, under all circumstances, to be protected and not to be attacked, even if it were a question of troop concentrations in those places," he said later, "and that if attacks had to be made, precision bombing Stukas were to be used primarily." Amiens, Rouen, Chartres, and other monuments were deliberately saved, he said. "There was of course some broken glass in the cathedrals, caused by bomb detonations, but the most precious windows had been previously removed, thank God."

GERMAN TANK DIVISIONS moved through France. General Halder wrote: "Rather unpleasant day. The Führer is terribly nervous." The next day: "He rages and screams that we are on the best way to ruin the whole campaign." It was May 18, 1940.

Soon, however, with the British force backing toward the

towns of Dunkirk and Calais on the coast of France, Hitler was in an expansive mood again. Lord Gort, the commander of the British forces, had ordered a retreat. Blumentritt, a German military aide, wrote that Hitler said he thought the war would be done in six weeks. "After that he wished to conclude a reasonable peace with France, and then the way would be free for an agreement with Britain." Then, according to Blumentritt, Hitler launched into an admiring monologue on the greatness of the British empire. True, the British had often used harsh means—but if you use a plane, there will be shavings. "All he wanted from Britain," wrote Blumentritt, "was that she should acknowledge Germany's position on the Continent." Hitler's aim was to "make peace with Britain on a basis that she would regard as compatible with her honour to accept."

A BRITISH BOMBER CREW was ordered to bomb a railway station in Düsseldorf. They couldn't find it—the city was blacked out—so they performed something called a "square search." They flew in one direction, turned, flew in another direction—going around and around, hunting for the place they were supposed to blow up. Meanwhile, there was no flak and no German fighters. Eventually, they dropped the bombs and flew away. One crew member said that assigning targets like railroad stations was pointless. After all, many planes "found difficulty in even locating the cities in which they were situated."

On May 24, 1940, Hitler issued a directive. The Luftwaffe was now "authorised to attack the English homeland in the fullest manner, as soon as sufficient forces are available." The changed policy, when it came, was to be inaugurated with "an annihilating reprisal for English attacks on the Ruhr."

And yet still the attack didn't happen.

PRESIDENT ROOSEVELT, watching things go wrong in France, said, "I should like this nation geared up to the ability to turn out at least fifty thousand planes a year." It was May 24, 1940.

Henry Morgenthau was in *The New York Times* a week later: "Plans Mass Output of Plane Engines." The designs of the motors would be standardized in various horsepower classes, Morgenthau explained, and farmed out to subcontractors, big and small, so as to meet the fifty-thousand-a-year goal. Morgenthau had met with Alfred Sloan, head of General Motors, and talked with him for an hour about the liquid-cooled engine. Factories were going up around the country.

CHURCHILL, who had been flying back and forth to Paris, ordered the small British force left at Calais—rifle brigades and tanks—to fight to the death. No ships would rescue them. Their last stand would be a distraction to the Germans, allowing the masses at Dunkirk time to get away. "Have greatest possible admiration for your splendid stand," Churchill wrote to the Calais commander. "Evacuation will not (*repeat* not) take place, and craft required for above purpose are to return to Dover."

Churchill was, as they say of generals, a killer of men: "It was painful thus to sacrifice these splendid trained Regular troops, of which we had so few."

It was May 26, 1940.

PHILIPPE PÉTAIN, of the French war cabinet, was talking to an aide, Paul Baudouin, in Paris. Capitulation was imminent. "It is easy, but also stupid, to talk of fighting to the last man," Pétain said, with tears in his eyes. "It is also criminal in view of our losses in the last war."

Baudouin went off to confer with Maxime Weygand, commander of the French forces, who was at general headquarters, in a castle in Vincennes. Weygand agreed with Pétain: There was no point in fighting to the last cartridge. If the French army was destroyed, troubles could well ensue. Sometimes it was right to stop in order to "prevent a useless massacre," Weygand said. It was May 26, 1940.

GOERING PROMISED to blow up the British Expeditionary Force on the beach. Thirsty English soldiers stood in long lines reaching out into the water, waiting for boats to pick them up and carry them home. The German planes dove, and the bombs fell, but the explosions were muffled by the sand, and there wasn't much for incendiary weapons to set on fire.

Also the weather was overcast—mists hid what Churchill called the miracle at Dunkirk.

"It is perhaps fortunate that the B.E.F. is so good at retreating," wrote Harold Nicolson in his diary, "since that is what it mostly has to do."

THE BRITISH MILITARY CHIEFS OF STAFF, at Churchill's request, had already figured out how to win the war "in a certain eventuality"—that is, if France fell and agreed to a separate peace with Germany. It was late May 1940.

Three things would carry the day: (1) general starvation and a shortage of raw materials throughout Germany and the occupied countries; (2) the undermining of morale with long-range bombers; and (3) the incitement of subversion wherever it could be incited.

With America's help, the chiefs of staff theorized, a tight European blockade would result in a shortage of bread, essential fats, and fruit. "Life will be sustained for a period by the heavy slaughtering of immature animals," they predicted, recalling past famines. Before the winter of 1940 there would be "widespread starvation in many of the industrial areas." Meanwhile, there would be lowered stocks of cotton, wool, rubber, and gasoline. And if America was willing to furnish more planes, England would become "an advanced base for the operation of large long range bombers flown from production centres across the Atlantic." Finally, a special subversion group would everywhere plant "seeds of revolt" in the conquered territories.

Imposing these measures on an entire subcontinent—in other words, starving millions of people—might raise moral questions, the report conceded. On the other hand, "it is only by this pressure that we can ensure the defeat of Germany" and eventually rebuild European civilization.

A THOUSAND MEN from the Criminal Investigation Division of Scotland Yard went out knocking on doors where "enemy aliens" lived. They assembled several thousand German and Austrian women, many of whom had been working as servants, and sent them to the Isle of Man, in the Irish Sea. "A few, mainly those with young children, wept," reported *The New York Times*. It was May 27, 1940.

The British government now held eleven thousand people in its detention facilities, most of them Jews. Eventually, some refugees were shipped to Canada, where they were imprisoned for the duration of the war. One was Max Perutz, a German refugee who had been researching hemoglobin at Cambridge. He organized a school at a prison camp in Quebec and taught X-ray crystallography to fellow inmates. "To have been arrested, interned, and deported as an enemy alien by the English, whom I had regarded as my friends, made me more bitter than to have lost freedom itself," Perutz wrote.

At the Mooragh detention camp, on the Isle of Man, inmates published a camp newspaper. "Let the *Mooragh Times* be a witness of how a great nation thought it right—for the first time in the long centuries of its heroic history—to begin a war for the liberation of Western civilisation by imprisoning the most embittered enemies of its own enemies," wrote its editor, Robert Neumann, in German.

The newspaper was quickly suppressed.

Lord Halifax and Neville Chamberlain—no longer prime minister but still in the war cabinet—thought England should continue to try to make peace with the Germans, perhaps using Mussolini as an intermediary. It was May 27, 1940.

Churchill said no—no negotiation. England's prestige was very low, and the only way to get it back was by fighting on. "Let us therefore avoid being dragged down the slippery slope with France," he said to the cabinet.

They talked for hours around the big table. Churchill harangued; Halifax lost his temper and threatened to resign. "I thought Winston talked the most frightful rot, also Greenwood"—Arthur Greenwood, the war cabinet's minister without portfolio—"and after bearing it for some time I said exactly what I thought of them," Halifax wrote in his diary. Churchill then took a walk with Halifax in the garden of 10 Downing Street and was full of conciliatory affection and apology. But Halifax wasn't entirely won over. "It does drive me to despair when he works himself up into a passion of emotion when he ought to make his brain think and reason," Halifax wrote.

Churchill later recalled England's wish—that is, his own wish—to fight on: "There was a white glow, overpowering, sublime, which ran through our island from end to end."

HEINRICH HIMMLER, a schoolteacher's son with small, mobile eyes, wrote a memo describing his plans for alien populations. Out of the genetic "mush" of twenty-some million people living in the newly acquired territories, Himmler proposed to strain out the racially valuable elements. The Jews would go to a colony in Africa or elsewhere, he wrote:

> However cruel and tragic each individual case may be, this method is still the mildest and best, if one rejects the Bolshevik method of physical extermination of a people out of inner conviction as un-German and impossible.

Hitler read Himmler's memo and, according to Himmler, found it "good and correct." It was May 28, 1940.

CHURCHILL FLEW to Paris to talk with the French generals. It was May 31, 1940. Narvik was the first matter they took up—it had been retaken and held, at some cost, by the Allies. It must now be abandoned immediately, said Churchill. They also discussed what to do about Italy, if Italy were foolish enough to enter the war. "I proposed that we should strike by air-bombing at the northwestern industrial triangle enclosed by the three cities of Milan, Turin, and Genoa," Churchill said. "Many Italians were opposed to war, and all should be made to realise its severity."

Bombing was, to Churchill, a form of pedagogy—a way of enlightening city dwellers as to the hellishness of remote battlefields by killing them. The French were not keen on it, however; they wanted to avoid reprisals.

Churchill also assured the French that the United States had been "roused by recent events." A German invasion of England would have a profound effect on the United States, he said. The important thing was to continue the struggle. "It would be better far that the civilisation of Western Europe with all its achievements should come to a tragic but splendid end than that the two great democracies should linger on, stripped of all that made life worth living," he said.

DOROTHY DAY, the editor of the *Catholic Worker,* wrote an editorial called "Our Stand." "As in the Ethiopian war, the Spanish war, the Japanese and Chinese war, the Russian-Finnish war—so in the present war we stand unalterably opposed to the use of war as a means of saving 'Christianity,' 'civilization,' 'democracy.' " She urged a nonviolent opposition to injustice and servitude: She called it the Folly of the Cross.

"We are bidden to love God and to love one another," she wrote. "It is the whole law, it is all of life. Nothing else matters." It was June 1940.

NORMAN THOMAS, the leader of the Socialist party, addressed an antiwar meeting in Washington.

The United States must take responsibility for European refugees, Thomas said—and must protect civil liberties at home, "which already have suffered from war hysteria."

Senator Burton Wheeler also spoke. "A mad hysteria grips our people," said Wheeler. "I want to do everything to help the Allies stamp out the brutal forces which seek to dominate Europe and perhaps the world. But by setting the United States on fire we will not help put out the fire in Europe."

It was June 7, 1940.

A REFUGEE SCIENTIST, Rudolf Peierls, had a meeting with Professor Lindemann, Churchill's scientific adviser. Lindemann, dour, querulous, with a bowler hat, was a vigorous proponent of city bombing. Peierls and his colleague Otto Frisch had become convinced of the possibility of making a superbomb out of a concentrated isotope of uranium.

Peierls described to Lindemann how the bomb would work, and Lindemann listened. "I do not know him sufficiently well," Peierls wrote, "to translate his grunts correctly." But Peierls felt that he had convinced Lindemann that the notion of a chain reaction had at least to be taken seriously. It was early June 1940.

RONALD HEALISS, of the Royal Navy, was on an aircraft carrier headed home from the abandoned port of Narvik. Churchill had said go to Narvik, and the Navy had gone. Churchill now said come home, and they were coming home. It was June 9, 1940.

Two big German battleships, the *Scharnhorst* and the *Gneisenau,* blew holes in Ronald Healiss's ship. As it tipped and began to go down, Healiss jumped over the moving propeller into the North Sea, which was very cold. He found a boat, damaged and listing, and got in. There were twenty men there, all of them lashed down so as not to be washed away. "In the next four hours I saw all those men die," Healiss wrote. "I watched them go, one by one, sliding silently into death, glassy-eyed and motionless, except when the waves lifted them in their ropes and flopped them back into the boat."

Healiss left that boat and swam to a raft, where there were more dying people. He got in. One man suddenly screamed and hurled himself into the black water. Eventually, a Norwegian ship picked Healiss up. He was dropped off, frostbitten but safe, at the Faroe Islands—home from Narvik.

IN ENGLAND, the war-hysterical Home Office sent out a new, wider detention order. All enemy aliens between sixty and seventy years of age, men and women—again, mostly Jews—were to be imprisoned, in addition to those between sixteen and sixty. Not tortured or beaten, as in Dachau, where some had been held—just deprived of liberty for several years. It was June 10, 1940.

Churchill had prepared the way in the House of Commons. He knew, he said, that the Germans who were being imprisoned were, many of them, enemies of the Nazis. "I am very sorry for them," he said, "but we cannot, at the present time, and under the present stress, draw all the distinctions which we should like to do."

IN ITALY, everyone was told to gather in the main square of his or her town or city to hear Mussolini speak. It was June 10, 1940.

At six o'clock, Mussolini stood on the balcony of the Palazzo Venezia in Rome, wearing a black shirt. Count Ciano, his son-in-law, stood in flying uniform, near at hand. "We will conquer!" said Mussolini, declaring war on England.

"The news of the war does not surprise anyone and does not arouse very much enthusiasm," wrote Ciano in his diary. "I am sad, very sad. The adventure begins."

THE ENGLISH GOVERNMENT began rounding up Italian people—they were now also enemy aliens. Using lists supplied by MI-5, the government arrested the manager of the Picadilly Hotel, the head chef of the Cafe Royal, and two clowns in the Bertram Mills circus. "Collar the lot," Churchill reportedly said. *Hotel Review,* an English trade publication, was pleased: the "extensive Italianization of our hotels would now be checked."

Canadian mounted police arrested several hundred Italians, as well. During roundups in Toronto, anti-Italian demonstrators broke windows in Italian-owned fruit shops. The Italo-Canadians were assembled in Toronto's Exhibition Park; from there, they went to detention camps.

VICTOR KLEMPERER, in Dresden, heard a story. At one of the local hospitals, a woman came in to see her wounded husband, back from the front. He was in very bad shape. Half of his face and his arm were gone. The woman screamed, "It's the Jews' fault! It's the Jews' fault!"

Klemperer wrote down what someone else said: "We'll all be sent to Lublin." It was June 11, 1940.

HAROLD NICOLSON wrote a letter to his wife, Vita Sackville-West. "What makes me gnash my teeth is that Hitler said he would be in Paris by 15th June," he wrote, "and I think he will meet that date, thereby increasing his mystic legend." But Nicolson was enjoying himself nonetheless. He felt *embattled,* he said. "I did not know that I possessed such combative instincts. Darling, why is it that I should feel so *gay?*" It was June 12, 1940.

FIVE BRITISH BOMBS fell on a railroad station and a hotel in Renens, north of Lausanne, in the neutral country of Switzerland. "A woman in a wheelchair was killed, her husband's foot was torn off and a man asleep in the hotel was fatally injured," the Associated Press said. It was still June 12, 1940.

The British government offered its regrets, explaining that the airplanes had lost their way.

SIX MEMBERS of the Peace Pledge Union were arrested and tried for publishing a poster in London. The poster said: "War will cease when men refuse to fight. What are YOU going to do about it?" The Ministry of Information attacked the Peace Pledge Union's "pernicious propaganda." Eventually, the men were released, but people got the point: Pacifism was subversion. It was June 1940.

In Germany, Dr. Hermann Stöhr, secretary of the German Fellowship of Reconciliation, refused to join the army. He was shot.

GENERAL JOHN DILL, chief of staff and member of the war cabinet, weighed the merits of using poison gas in the defense of the British Isles. It was June 15, 1940.

There were two grave objections to the idea, Dill thought. First: "We have bound ourselves not to use gas except in retaliation. To break our word may tend to alienate American sympathy." And, second, the use would invite immediate retaliation by Germany against the English population.

Still, it was an attractive idea. "Enemy forces crowded on the beaches, with the confusion inevitable on first landing, would present a splendid target," Dill wrote. Airplanes might spray them as they came ashore—as Mussolini's planes had sprayed Ethiopians— and the shoreline might be slathered with thickened mustard. All in all, Dill said, the benefits outweighed the risks.

Other cabinet members dismissed Dill's proposal, and the idea languished. Then Winston Churchill took it up: "Let me have a report upon the amount of mustard or other variants we have in store," he wrote. "In my view there would be no need to wait for the enemy to adopt such methods."

The British began stockpiling mustard gas, manufactured by Imperial Chemical Industries.

PARIS GAVE UP. "Strange how lukewarm the reaction is here," wrote Marie Vassiltchikov, a young Russian émigré in Berlin. "There is absolutely no feeling of elation." Churchill drafted a letter to the leaders of Canada, Australia, and the other Commonwealth countries, reassuring them that England was going to see its "life-

and-death struggle" through to the end. There would be no peace. Germany might well mount an aerial attack and attempt a sea-born invasion, Churchill said, but England would wear them down by attacking the "congested and centralised war industry"—the cities—"in the Ruhr."

"I personally believe that the spectacle of the fierce struggle and carnage in our Island will draw the United States into the war," Churchill said. "I trust in conjunction with the United States, until the Hitler régime breaks under the strain."

He showed his letter to Air Marshal Newall, who was very moved. "I felt a glow of sober confidence," Churchill later said.

It was June 16, 1940.

AFTER A DISCURSIVE war-cabinet session, Lord Halifax tried again to make some sense of Churchill. "It is the most extraordinary brain, Winston's, to watch functioning that I have ever seen, a most curious mixture of a child's emotion and a man's reason," he said. It was June 19, 1940.

The next day, Churchill addressed the House of Commons in a secret session. England's throes would pull the United States into the war, Churchill—whose mother was American—told them. "Nothing will stir them like fighting in England," his notes for that speech say. "The heroic struggle of Britain best chance of bringing them in." Once Roosevelt gets reelected, America will do more, he promised: "All depends upon our resolute bearing and holding out until Election issues are settled there."

THE ROYAL AIR FORCE bombed Genoa and Milan. It was June 1940. They dropped bombs on Düsseldorf, flew away for a while, and then returned to drop more bombs while people were climbing out of shelters to put out the fires. In Munster and Wertheim, the RAF lit parts of the town and then flew low, machine-gunning fire brigades. "Strong hatred against England becomes heavily concentrated," Ohlendorf's SS polling service reported, "and calls time and again for revenge."

FRANKLIN ROOSEVELT fired his secretary of war, Harry Woodring. It was June 1940. Woodring liked having lots of airplanes in the United States—he didn't want them going to England. Morgenthau and Roosevelt had come up with a scheme in which some fairly new B-17s, each of which had cost a quarter of a million dollars, would be tagged as surplus and given back to Boeing so that Boeing could resell them to England. American neutrality would thus remain intact.

Woodring refused to support the scheme. Roosevelt fired him and offered him the governorship of Puerto Rico, the administration of which was "of the utmost importance to this country." Woodring said no, thank you, and wrote a letter saying that he thought that the release of the bombers "was not in the best interests of the defense of our country."

Roosevelt wrote a tart letter back saying that Woodring had a "slight misunderstanding of facts and dates." He, Roosevelt, had made no "request" that the bombers be released. "The simple fact is," he explained, "that on June seventeenth, in going over a list of Army and Navy equipment with the Secretary of the Treasury, there appeared a number of 'flying fortress bombers' which had been in service in the Army for quite a long time—in some cases between two and three years. It was suggested that if these bombers, because of their age, had become obsolete, it would be in the interest of national defense to turn them in to the builders in exchange for new bombers of the latest type." Roosevelt was, he said, quite sure that he, Woodring, had not meant to create an impression that was contrary to the factual record. He hoped there would be no appearances before congressional committees, no stirring up of "false issues." He closed with his sincere regards.

In Berlin, Marie Vassiltchikov, the Russian émigré, went to a party at the apartment of her new friend, C. C. von Pfuel. It was June 21, 1940. Von Pfuel, who had taken Vassiltchikov to the theater and seen her a few times, was pessimistic about the war—he thought it would not end soon. Vassiltchikov got home and was getting ready for bed when air-raid sirens went off. "We sat downstairs on the steps and chatted with the doorman, who is an air raid warden as well," she wrote in her diary. "Later we learnt that bombs were dropped near Potsdam, but none over Berlin."

THE ITALIANS took some foreign correspondents on a bus tour of bomb damage in Turin and Milan. Four British bombs had fallen in a square in a poor section of Turin, near an oil tank. "They caused the death of ten civilians, killed mostly in their rooms," wrote Allen Raymond in the New York *Herald Tribune.* In Milan, the reporters saw the Breda airplane factory, the Pirelli tire factory, and a steel mill. All were undamaged. Five bombs had, however, hit a building at a Catholic children's home. A man with a weak heart had been rushed to the hospital after the raid, the reporters learned, where it was discovered that the shock of the bombardment had cured him. "The parish priest and the people about the home are convinced that this was a miracle," wrote Raymond.

Residents pointed out a second miracle: "A terra-cotta statue of the Madonna, right between where two bombs fell, was untouched, whereas everything around it was devastated."

It was June 21, 1940.

PRESIDENT ROOSEVELT nominated Henry Stimson to be the new secretary of war, replacing Harry Woodring. The Chinese were pleased; the Japanese were not. "Mr. Stimson is disliked by the Japanese possibly more than any other American statesman," said the New York *Herald Tribune.* It was June 21, 1940.

CLEMENTINE CHURCHILL, sitting at Chequers, the Churchill country house, wrote her husband a letter. It June 23, 1940. She decided that she couldn't send it, and she tore it up. A few days later, at Downing Street, she was moved to write it again.

> One of the men in your entourage (a devoted friend) has been to me & told me that there is a danger of your being generally disliked by your colleagues & subordinates because of your rough sarcastic & overbearing manner.

She was astonished to hear this complaint, she said, but, "My Darling Winston—I must confess that I have noticed a deterioration in your manner; & you are not so kind as you used to be." She advised urbanity, kindness, and olympic calm. She drew a picture of a cat and closed with "Please forgive your loving devoted & watchful Clemmie."

HITLER AND ALBERT SPEER toured the empty but fully lit Paris Opera House. It was June 25, 1940. Hitler had never been there before—he'd never been to Paris before, in fact—but he'd studied the floor plans of the opera carefully. It was the first thing he wanted to see. With Hitler in the lead, they inspected every ornate component of the building. Hitler "went into ecstacies about its beauty," Speer recalled, "his eyes glittering with an excitement that struck me as uncanny." Near one of the boxes of the proscenium, Hitler noticed that a room was missing: The floor plans had indicated that a salon was there, yet there was no salon. Ah, yes, said the attendant—years ago, there had been renovations. "There, you see how I know my way about," said Hitler.

Later that day, Speer joined Hitler in a temporary headquarters in a Belgian border village, Brûly-de-Pesche. "Wasn't Paris beautiful?" Hitler said. He said that it was time, now, to resume work on Berlin—when they'd finished with the grand boulevard in Berlin, it would put even Paris in the shade.

Later, recalling his visit, Hitler said: "It was a great relief to me when we weren't obliged to destroy Paris."

CHURCHILL ISSUED instructions to the minister of information. It was June 26, 1940.

"The press and broadcast should be asked to handle air raids in a cool way and on a diminishing tone of public interest," Churchill said. No undue prominence, no headlines. "Everyone should learn to take air raids and air-raid alarms as if they were no more than thunderstorms. Pray try to impress this upon the newspaper authorities, and persuade them to help."

THE NEW YORK TIMES published a tally of how many Hudson bombers the United States had sold to England and France. The total, as of June 1940, was 1,860. They had been used for dropping leaflets, and they had "borne a heavy share of the North Sea patrol work and the long-range bombing activities of recent days."

Meanwhile, there was the other weapon: the hunger blockade. "An official British statement surveyed the famine possibilities, found the chances good if the war and blockade could be made to last until winter," said *Time* magazine. It was July 1, 1940.

General Raymond E. Lee, an American air attaché in London, went to a performance of *The Mikado* at the D'Oyly Carte. "They do it well and there are so many familiar tags and quotations recognizable that it is like listening to Shakespeare," he wrote in his journal. "The audience, in tweeds and gas masks, responded very well." It was July 1, 1940.

A Gestapo man in Warsaw told Adam Czerniakow, the head of the Jewish Council, that the war would be ending very soon, in a month. Afterward, all the Jews would go to Madagascar. "In this way the Zionist dream is to come true," Czerniakow wrote. It was July 1, 1940.

Work promptly stopped on the new Warsaw ghetto. The SS and the Foreign Office were abuzz with competing proposals. The Jews would all go to a huge island concentration camp, a "superghetto," as one memo called it, administered under an SS governor, with a Jewish mayor, police, and post offices. One hundred and twenty boats, each carrying fifteen hundred Jews, could, over a period of four years, transport four million Jews to Madagascar, thought Adolf Eichmann, Jewish emigration expert at the Central Security Office. France owned Madagascar, but France was Germany's now. As soon as ships could travel freely again—in other words, as soon as England made its peace with Germany and stopped blockading ocean traffic—the European Jews would go away, after being stripped of any wealth they might still have.

It was all contingent, though, on peace with Churchill.

COUNT CIANO, son-in-law of Mussolini, was talking to William Phillips, the American ambassador to Italy. It was July 3, 1940.

Ciano asked Phillips whether the United States was ready to enter the war. Phillips said no—for the moment, the United States didn't plan to be in the war. "We are arming on a very large scale, and are helping the British in every way," he told Ciano. "However, some new fact might decide our intervention, such as a bombardment of London with many victims among the civilian population."

Ciano wrote: "This is why Hitler is careful and thoughtful before launching the final adventure."

A BRITISH ADMIRAL, Lord Somerville, delivered an ultimatum to a squadron of French warships anchored in the port of Mers el Kebir, on the Algerian coast: Join the British navy or scuttle your ships. "We reckoned that Somerville found this pretty distasteful," Vernon Coles, a crewmember on the HMS *Faulknor,* recalled. Admiral Gensoul, the French commander, was affronted, and he refused to comply; the British, under Churchill's orders, opened fire. "It was a sad irony," said Coles. "We were not attacking the Germans or Italians, but the Royal Navy's oldest enemy and our twentieth-century ally." The *Dunkerque* was hit, also the *Bretagne,* the *Mogador,* and the *Provence.* "Admiral Gensoul then said, 'For God's sake, stop firing. You're murdering us!'" More than a thousand French sailors died. It was July 3, 1940.

In the House of Commons, Churchill gave a rousing speech about the destruction of the French fleet. "When he finished, the decorum of the Parliament vanished," wrote General Raymond Lee, who was watching from the Distinguished Strangers Gallery. "All were on their feet, shouting, cheering and waving order papers and handkerchiefs like mad."

MOHANDAS GANDHI wrote an open letter to the people of England. It was July 3, 1940. "Your soldiers are doing the same work of destruction as the Germans," Gandhi said. "I want you to fight Nazism without arms."

If Hitler and Mussolini chose to overrun England, he said, let them. "Let them take possession of your beautiful island, with your many beautiful buildings. You will give all these, but neither your souls, nor your minds."

> If these gentlemen choose to occupy your homes, you will vacate them. If they do not give you free passage out, you will allow yourself, man, woman and child, to be slaughtered, but you will refuse to owe allegiance to them.

This method, Gandhi said, had had considerable success in India.

OTTO OHLENDORF'S German opinion service wrote that the press and radio reports of bombings by the Royal Air Force had caused "a general rage against England and the wish for a 'real' retaliation by way of the bombardment of English cities." It was July 4, 1940.

Hitler still hesitated to give Goering the order. His armies had conquered half a dozen countries. The military campaigns had gone well—the English had been forced off the continent—but even so, thousands of soldiers had died. Fighter planes lay wrecked. Tanks were broken. Injuries needed to heal. Medals needed awarding; promotions needed conferral. Ammunition needed replenishing.

Hitler had a hundred million new subjects, including several million Jews. Slave-state eugenics called for further careful analysis. Hitler required time to take in the experience of being Führer of France.

But Churchill didn't give him time: He played the picador role, sending out squadrons night after night. Compared with the mass raids that began two years later, the damage that the Royal Air Force's bombers did was minuscule and unsustained, but it didn't feel that way to German civilians—and it was played up in the British and American press. A small raid on the docks of Hamburg became, in the Air Ministry's release, a strike on oil tanks accompanied by a "violent explosion which lit up the sky for many miles around."

VICTOR KLEMPERER recorded a new prohibition: No Jews allowed in Dresden's parks. It was July 6, 1940.

Meanwhile, the news was of air raids. "Day after day English aircraft cause 'insignificant damage to non-military targets' and kill only civilians, mostly women and children, and Germany will take terrible revenge for these crimes," he wrote, paraphrasing the official line.

"What will happen to us in the case of a German victory?" Klemperer wondered. "And what in the case of a German defeat?"

Katz, an old man at the Jews' House, told Klemperer: "In Berlin the Jews are praying for Hitler's victory."

The next day, Klemperer heard a rumor: The British government had resigned. "Now they'll make peace," his informant said, "and we'll be packed off to Madagascar."

CHURCHILL WROTE a memo to Max Beaverbrook, the minister of aircraft production and owner of the *Daily Express*. It was July 8, 1940. Fighters were what they needed right now, Churchill said. But in the future they'd need more bombers. "The blockade is broken," he wrote. Hitler had Asia and maybe Africa; he might be repulsed in England, or he might choose not to invade at all, Churchill speculated. He might move eastward, and England would have "no way of stopping him." What then? If Hitler moved east, England would have no war to fight.

"But there is one thing that will bring him back and bring him down," Churchill wrote, "and that is an absolutely devastating, exterminating attack by very heavy bombers from this country upon the Nazi homeland." Air mastery was the aim, he said to Beaverbrook. "When can it be obtained?"

PRESIDENT ROOSEVELT wanted to draft people into the U.S. Army even though the United States was not fighting a war, something that had never happened before. A group of several hundred writers and teachers—including Rufus Jones, Dorothy Detzer, Reverend Harry Fosdick, and Milton Mayer—signed a declaration against conscription.

Universal military service, said the declaration, had always been a way for dictators to suppress the conscience of a people and to indoctrinate them with the notion that brute force was superior to ideals. "The essential idea underlying military conscription is the major premise of every dictatorship and all totalitarianism," the signers said. "It is the assumption that the individual citizen is but a pawn in the hands of unlimited State power."

It was July 8, 1940.

CHRISTOPHER ISHERWOOD had lunch with Thomas and Katia Mann and their son Klaus, who was, like his father, a novelist. Isherwood and Klaus Mann got into a disagreement over the war. Mann said that Isherwood should make a public statement in support of the Allied cause—that his silence was being misinterpreted. Mann said that he himself was, of course, a pacifist—he couldn't kill anyone personally. But still, pacifism was no good now: "If you let the Nazis kill everyone, you allowed civilization to be destroyed."

Isherwood, in reply, used an argument that he had heard Aldous Huxley make: "Civilization dies anyhow of blood poisoning the moment it takes up its enemies' weapons and exchanges crime for crime."

Mann said that professions of pacifism merely helped the Nazis and the fifth columnists.

"That," answered Isherwood, "is why I keep my mouth shut." It was July 8, 1940.

"OUR ACTION against the French Fleet has made a tremendous effect throughout the world," Harold Nicolson wrote his wife. "I am as stiff as can be."

It was July 10, 1940.

THE VICEROY OF INDIA, Lord Linlithgow, politely rejected Gandhi's suggestion to the British people that they employ nonviolent methods in opposing Hitler. The British government, Linlithgow said, was "firmly resolved to prosecute the war to a victorious conclusion." It was July 10, 1940.

"I was grateful to H.E. the Viceroy for forwarding my offer to His Majesty's Government," Gandhi replied, in *Harijan.* "No doubt the determination is natural and worthy of the best British tradition. Nevertheless the awful slaughter that the determination involves should induce a search for a better and braver way to achieve the end."

THE SENATE MILITARY AFFAIRS COMMITTEE was having contentious hearings on the Compulsory Military Training and Service bill—the draft bill. It was July 1940. James Conant, president of Harvard, said: "The country is gravely threatened. It seems to me a law should be enacted as soon as possible providing for the building up at once of our armed forces." William J. "Wild Bill" Donovan—a lawyer who did spy work for Roosevelt—said: "If you want to fight you have got to be strong; but if you want to have peace you have got to be stronger; and it is because I believe in peace that I am for this bill."

Norman Thomas, the socialist leader, was opposed to the bill. It was, he said, false to claim that raising a conscript army would help the cause of freedom. "Military conscription is not freedom but serfdom; its equality is the equality of slaves," Thomas said. "Conscription, whatever may be the hopes and intentions of some of its present supporters, in a nation potentially as powerful and aggressive as ours, is a road leading straight to militarism, imperialism, and ultimately to American fascism and war." Thomas said that it was perhaps fitting that the bill's sponsor, Senator Edward R. Burke, had, on his return from a visit to Germany in 1938, announced that Hitler was "bringing about the well-being of the entire German people."

CATHERINE FITZGIBBON, of the Women's International League for Peace and Freedom, was also utterly against the draft bill. "I would just like to enumerate a few things that make us somewhat frightened," FitzGibbon said. "When the Jews sought refuge from Germany, this Government made no special effort to help them; the established immigration quotas stood exactly where they were." That failure, she said, "did honor to Hitler." Then, too, the country's overeager hunt for spies, foreign agents, and fifth columnists, she said, mimicked totalitarianism. And now, for the first time in American history, the U.S. government was proposing to turn men into vassals of the state when the state was not at war. Large conscript armies were what allowed Hitler, Mussolini, and Stalin to hold power. "The totalitarian pattern is practically complete," FitzGibbon said.

A judge from Philadelphia, William F. Clark, testified after Catherine FitzGibbon, in favor of the bill. His clothing caused comment: He wore a khaki shirt and a red, white, and blue armband. There was, Judge Clark said, "no analogy between selective compulsory military service and totalitarianism."

CHURCHILL'S VOICE boomed on the radio. "We await undismayed the impending assault," he said. "We shall seek no terms, we shall tolerate no parley. We may show mercy—we ask none." It was July 14, 1940.

Hitler issued Directive Number 16: "Since England, in spite of her hopeless military situation, shows no signs of being ready to come to an understanding, I have decided to prepare a landing operation against England, and, if necessary, to carry it out."

But he didn't carry it out. He began writing a speech.

GENERAL RAYMOND LEE looked at a bomb crater near a farmhouse in the English countryside. The crater was thirty-five feet wide and thirty feet deep. "On its edge was a barn containing a horse, a cow, and a bull, none hurt," he wrote. "A pig was transfixed by a flying splinter of wood and a rooster was killed. That is all." It was July 16, 1940.

HITLER GAVE A SPEECH to the Reichstag. His voice was under better control, thought William Shirer, and he was in unusually good oratorical form. He didn't shout or cry out, as he had in the past. It was July 19, 1940.

"Mr. Churchill has just declared again that he wants the war," Hitler said.

> A great world empire will be destroyed, a world empire which it was never my intention to destroy or damage. But I am fully aware that the continuation of this war will only end with the complete destruction of one of the two warring parties. Mr. Churchill may believe that this will be Germany. I know it will be England.

His conscience, he said, obligated him to make one final appeal to England: "I see no reason that should compel us to continue this war."

Count Ciano, who was there applauding, wrote that he heard an "unusually humane tone" in Hitler's speech. "I believe that his desire for peace is sincere," he said. "They are hoping and praying that this appeal will not be rejected."

At the same ceremony, Hitler bestowed promotions on his sparkle-chested generals. Goering was privileged to wear a splendid new jacket with silver embroidery on the collar tabs. He also got a raise and a specially minted medal in a box—he took a quick peek in the box onstage. "His boyish pride and satisfaction was almost touching, old murderer that he is," said Shirer.

AN HOUR AFTER the broadcast of Hitler's final appeal to reason, one of the BBC's German-language newsmen, Sefton Delmer, transmitted an unofficial response for German listeners: "Let me tell you what we here in Britain think of this appeal of yours to what you are pleased to call our reason and common sense," Delmer said in German. "Herr Führer and Reichskanzler, we hurl it right back at you, right in your evil-smelling teeth."

Count Ciano wrote: "Late in the evening, when the first cold English reactions to the speech arrive, a sense of ill-concealed disappointment spreads among the Germans."

Churchill himself was silent. "I do not propose to say anything in reply to Herr Hitler's speech," he said, "not being on speaking terms with him."

HAROLD NICOLSON WROTE: "The reaction to Hitler's speech yesterday is a good reaction. Yet I know well that we shall be exposed to horrible punishment." It was strange, Nicolson thought, how little hatred there was of Hitler or the Germans. "We flinch today from central enmity," he wrote. "If we are invaded we may become angry." It was July 20, 1940.

That night, Charles Portal, head of Bomber Command, stayed over with the Churchills at Chequers. "The Prime Minister asked what could be done about bombing Berlin, and gave the date 1 September," Portal noted afterward. He told the prime minister that, with twelve hours' notice, heavy bombers could be sent to Berlin any time after August 1.

FRANCES PARTRIDGE—who lived in Wiltshire with her husband, Ralph, a conscientious objector—heard that Hitler had begun another peace offensive. She was tempted to speculate as to what would happen if the British government took Hitler seriously. "But it's too tantalising, since there's no shadow of doubt we will reject any such suggestion," she wrote in her diary. "Now I suppose Churchill will again tell the world that we are going to die on the hills and on the sea, and then we shall proceed to do so." It was July 20, 1940.

LORD LOTHIAN, ambassador to the United States, had heard a summary of the current German peace terms from a Quaker intermediary. He thought they merited discussion. "We ought to find out what Hitler means before condemning the world to 1,000,000 casualties," Lothian told Lord Halifax.

"Philip Lothian telephones wildly from Washington in the evening begging Halifax not to say anything in his broadcast tonight which might close the door to peace," wrote Harold Nicolson in his diary. "I am glad to say that Halifax pays no attention to this and makes an extremely bad broadcast but one which is perfectly firm as far as it goes." It was July 22, 1940.

"Halifax Adamant," said *The New York Times*. A reporter for United Press filed a tiny addendum, however. Minutes before Halifax sat down at the microphone, someone had made cuts to his text. "Various sentences that might have been interpreted in some quarters as a bid for Chancellor Hitler to make a new and more generous offer were stricken out," said the United Press report. "As he spoke, Lord Halifax seemed to falter momentarily at these revised portions of his manuscript."

The German press bureau announced that in the period since Hitler's "Final Appeal" speech, the British had bombed civilian targets in Wismar, Bremen, Hamburg, Pinneberg, Paderborn, Hagen, Bochum, Schwerin, Wilhelmshaven, and Kassel. It was July 23, 1940.

Churchill's response to Hitler's peace offer—more air strikes— and the response in the British press were not representative of the actual state of British opinion, claimed the *Frankfurter Zeitung*. "The British Press is an iron curtain hiding the real opinions and feelings of the British people," the paper said, using a phrase that Churchill would later immortalize. "They have found no way to make their voice heard, nor can they speak their opinion publicly."

The Germans printed Hitler's peace offer and dropped it from airplanes all over England. Some of the leaflets fell into a sewage plant. "Magnetic attraction," said the Ministry of Information.

LORD HANKEY decided that it was time to begin a full-fledged biological-weapons program. It was to be housed at Porton Down, an isolated place not far from Stonehenge where chemical weapons were being tested. "I recently came to the conclusion," Hankey wrote in a memo, "that we ought to go a step further in the matter of bacteriological warfare so as to put ourselves in a position to retaliate if such abominable methods should be used against us." It was July 26, 1940. He began recruiting scientists.

CHRISTOPHER ISHERWOOD had tea in Palos Verdes, California, with his friend Wystan Auden, the poet. Auden had by now abandoned his antiwar position. He told Isherwood that he disliked Sanskrit words—the sort that Gandhi used. "The truth is," Auden said, "I want to kill people." It was August 3, 1940.

THE ROYAL AIR FORCE bombed Hamburg. Another night, Hanover. "Britain Loses Her Honor," said the headline in the Bremen *Zeitung*. The RAF attacked Munich, city of Hitler's triumphs. They dropped delayed-action bombs on Lippspringe. It was August 1940.

The description in English-speaking newspapers of the alleged pulverization of Hamburg irritated Joseph Goebbels: A group of journalists, including William Shirer, was given a tour of the city in order to show that the damage was, in a military sense, almost nonexistent. "I had expected that after two months of almost nightly bombings the English would have accomplished much more," wrote Shirer. The heading in the *Völkischer Beobachter* gave the moment a typical twist:

MAD BRITISH LIES BORN OUT OF ANXIETY
AMERICAN JEWS SUPPORT CRUDE
ENGLISH FRAUDULENT MANOEUVRE

A DUTCH CORRESPONDENT wrote Gandhi that Nazi youths had become machines. Nonviolent methods were hopeless against robots.

Gandhi disagreed. "No man can be turned into a permanent machine," he wrote in *Harijan*. "Immediately the dead weight of authority is lifted from his head, he begins to function normally." It was August 6, 1940.

WINSTON CHURCHILL went to a rifle range with his son, Randolph, and his secretary, John Colville. He shot a Mannlicher rifle and a revolver, smoking his cigar. His aim was pretty good.

"The whole time he talked of the best method of killing Huns," wrote Colville. "Soft-nose bullets were the thing to use and he must get some." Randolph pointed out that soft-nose bullets—which expand when they hit, making a bigger wound—weren't legal in war. Churchill said he didn't see why he should have any mercy on Germans when they would have none for him. It was August 11, 1940.

MURIEL LESTER, the Christian relief worker, was trying to figure out how to help the refugees in France. It was 1940. "A sort of nausea grips one when facing starving children," she wrote later. "They are so undemanding of sympathy or apology. They bear no resentment. They give one a straight level look and something quite beyond oneself, quite 'other' than the child, convicts one of sin and shame."

The leaders of nations, Lester said, don't have this direct experience of the hungry; women, parish workers, teachers, and doctors do. "If it's your job as a diplomatist to make a jeering speech at Italy, Germany, or Japan, you assume emotions of scorn and your carefully balanced threats protect you from facing the flesh-and-blood results of your policy."

The Fellowship of Reconciliation, the Quakers, and Herbert Hoover wanted to send ships full of food to Europe. They and others had formed something called the Committee for the Feeding of the Little Democracies. "But the British government declared against the plan," Lester wrote.

IN COLORADO SPRINGS, Herbert Hoover gave the press a statement about the food situation in Belgium, Holland, Poland, and Norway. "The obvious truth is that there will be wholesale starvation, death and disease in these little countries unless something is done about it," Hoover said. It was August 11, 1940.

Churchill was the chief obstacle, Hoover wrote later. "He was a militarist of the extreme school who held that the incidental starvation of women and children was justified if it contributed to the earlier ending of the war by victory."

Poland, as it happened, was particularly vulnerable. Hoover's Polish Relief Commission had set up canteens in Polish ghettos and poor districts, where they had been feeding two hundred thousand people per day—the Chamberlain government had allowed the food through the blockade. "When Churchill succeeded Chamberlain as Prime Minister in May, 1940," Hoover wrote, "he soon stopped all permits of food relief to Poland."

MURIEL LESTER WROTE a pamphlet, "Speed the Food Ships," for distribution in America. It was 1940. "A common-sense sort of war work awaits all women," she wrote. "This work is nothing less than the feeding of Europe." The American food surplus must cross the Atlantic: "It will be a new sort of invasion, an entering wedge into the old-fashioned unscientific surgery of Europe."

Of course, the British War Office might threaten to sink any ship that defies the blockade, Lester acknowledged. "In which case the U.S.A. would send ships regardless, for they would be manned by Americans, millions of whom would gladly risk death in the effort to save life."

> No political or military situation is likely to be able to hold
> back for long the great stream of generosity once it has burst
> its way through the obstructions that have so long impeded
> its life-bringing flow.

A counterleaflet, "Spiritual Issues of the War," attempted a rebuttal.

"I received a warning from friends in England to be careful," Lester said. "Behind the scenes opposition was gathering momentum."

CHARLES DE GAULLE was at Chequers. It was August 1940. Churchill was waiting for the German air attack, and, De Gaulle later recalled, he was finding the wait hard to bear. He raised both fists to the sky. "So they won't come!" he said.

"Are you in such a hurry," De Gaulle replied, "to see your towns smashed to bits?"

"You see," Churchill said, "the bombing of Oxford, Coventry, Canterbury, will cause such a wave of indignation in the United States that they'll come into the war!"

De Gaulle was doubtful. France's distress had not pulled America in. Ah, said Churchill, that's because France was collapsing. "Sooner or later the Americans will come, but on condition that we here don't flinch."

The attack on Coventry was three months away.

EDWARD R. MURROW of CBS Radio drove around the outskirts of London, where bombs had fallen. "From what I saw I am convinced that the Germans were after military objectives," he said. He wasn't allowed to visit the military areas. What he did see was a red sponge in a soap dish in a destroyed bathroom, the blown-out stained glass in a church, and one house in a row of houses that "appeared to have been jabbed with a huge, blunt stick." It was August 18, 1940.

IN MILAN, three English bombs hit a private building. More bombs, and leaflets as well, fell on Cuneo and Turin. Nobody was killed. It was August 19, 1940.

"Italians!" the English leaflets said. "Now the British bombers have brought war to your own firesides. It is Hitler and not England who points the sword at your heart. The responsibility for the victims of the air raids falls on Hitler and on his Italian satellites."

The *Giornale d'Italia* wrote an editorial in response. The leaflets existed, the editorial said, so that "Italians may have proof of the stupidity of those who are ruling England and leading the British Empire to a rapid collapse."

SEVERAL ANTIWAR ACTIVISTS got on the radio to argue against a peacetime draft in the United States. It was August 19, 1940.

"Combat service will fall most heavily upon the unemployed, unskilled workers and low-income groups," said John Nevin Sayre of the Fellowship of Reconciliation. Burton Rascoe, an editor and literary critic, said: "The truth is that the agitation for peacetime conscription is not what youth thinks it is at all. It is a ruse of warmongers and politicians to rush this country into war as soon as they can."

CHURCHILL, IN A SPEECH in the House of Commons, raised the topic of hunger. He had heard proposals "founded on the highest motives" for allowing food to pass the British naval blockade, he said. "I regret that we must refuse these requests." Fats make bombs, he explained, and potatoes make synthetic fuel. Then he said: "The plastic materials now so largely used in the construction of aircraft are made of milk." It was August 20, 1940.

Those who groaned beneath the Hitlerian yoke would, Churchill said, have food if and when they threw the yoke off.

"The notion," wrote Herbert Hoover later, "that the special type of food we needed for children (milk, chocolate, fats, and meat) would be used for munitions was sheer nonsense."

Hoover recalled the old adage—that truth was war's first fatality.

LORD LYTTON, the new chairman of the Advisory Council on the Welfare of Refugees, told newspaper reporters that conditions in the alien-internment camps in Britain were "disgraceful and deplorable." He blamed the problems on individual camp commandants, and on the chaos produced by the government's decision—Churchill's decision—to lock up every enemy alien between sixteen and seventy years of age. Lytton said he hoped conditions would rapidly improve. It was August 22, 1940.

THE DOORMAN banged a saucepan to wake up Marie Vassiltchikov in Berlin: air raid, down in the basement. It was August 26, 1940.

A few nights later, a pair of hundred-pound bombs fell on a Berlin street and blew the leg off a man standing in his doorway. A few nights after that, the RAF gave the city a "good strafing," wrote William Shirer. The next night, timed-release bombs fell in the Tiergarten; prisoners from concentration camps removed them.

Vassiltchikov described her air-raid cellar: "Small children lie in cots, sucking their thumbs. Tatiana and I usually play chess." When her sister had a slight fever, they decided to brave a raid above ground. The planes flew very low, and sudden flashes of light filled the bedroom. "Tatiana fears that if the house is hit I might be hurtled into space while she would remain suspended in mid-air, so I got into her bed and we lay hugging each other for two full hours. The noise was ghastly."

HARRY "BART" BARTHOLOMEW, editor of the London *Daily Mirror,* had dinner with a man named Heanley, a newspaper photographer who was now a rear gunner in a Royal Air Force bomber squadron. Bart Bartholomew told Cecil King, owner of the *Mirror* and the *Sunday Pictorial,* what they had talked about.

"Heanley revealed," King noted in his diary, "that his squadron were supplied with tanks to fit under the wings of their aeroplanes for spraying mustard gas. They had also done some work on spraying troops from the air with a pink powder to represent mustard gas." Heanley had said that he was under the impression that the English wouldn't use the gas unless the Germans did. It was August 31, 1940.

Meanwhile, Winston Churchill was keeping track of preparations. "I am very glad to know the chemical warfare stocks are piling up in this country," he wrote Herbert Morrison, minister of home security. "Press on."

CHURCHILL ASKED PORTAL to see if he could try something a little different, using some special weapons. They'd tried it before, back in the summer, just after France fell, but it hadn't worked all that well. Maybe they should give it another chance.

The weapons to be used weren't bombs exactly; they were leaflets without words. The British called them "calling cards." They were about the size of a playing card—maybe a little smaller—and they were made of a phosphorus wafer held between two layers of moist fabric. When the fabric dried out in the sun, the phosphorus caught fire. There were other shapes and configurations—sometimes they were coated with a plastic substance that cracked when it dried. When it cracked, the wafer burned.

What might these fire sandwiches set alight? Grain? They'd tried that already. Churchill's thoughts turned to the Black Forest. Hitler had storehouses and command headquarters hidden away there. In fact, why not burn down all the forests of Germany?

They began on a Monday night, September 2, 1940, but the Air Ministry held back the news for two days: "Woods Are Bombed" was the headline in *The New York Times*. "R.A.F. bombers have unleashed a devastating attack with incendiary bombs on the famous Black Forest, east of Baden, the dense woods of the Oberharz Mountains, the forest district of Grunewald, on the outskirts of Berlin, and forests in Thuringia," said the paper.

Fires were still burning in the Black Forest a day afterward. The pine trees of the Harz Mountains "blazed up like tinder." One returning pilot recognized one of the peaks in the Harz Mountains—he'd stayed near there once on a holiday. On this mountain, he remembered, lived a legendary giant. "I was telling the other chaps in my plane about it as we were flying over it," he said. Near the railway line that went up the giant's mountain, bombs started "a nice new little patch of fire about a mile square," the pilot added.

HITLER STOOD AMONG swastikas and storm troopers at the Sports Palace, the Madison Square Garden of Berlin. Before him was a large crowd of cheering, foot-stamping party members and workers for the Winter Relief Drive. Goebbels was up on the platform with him. It was September 4, 1940. "The English come in the night and drop their bombs, without choice of objectives and without plan," Hitler said, "on civilian residential sections, farms, farmhouses, and villages." They flew at night, he said, because they couldn't come by day. "Wherever they see a sign of light, a bomb is dropped on it."

> For three months past, I have not allowed an answer to be given because I was of the opinion that they would stop this nonsense. Churchill interpreted that as weakness on our part. You will understand that we are now nightly giving the answer—and in increasing measure.

He threatened to "wipe out" (*ausradieren*—"erase," "obliterate") British cities if the attacks didn't stop. "The people of England are very curious and ask: 'Why in the world don't you come?'" he said. "We are coming." He waited for the applause to die down. "People should not always be so curious," he said.

Two German prisoners, shot down from the sky, stood in the train station at Tonbridge, England. "Tiny little boys of 16 they are," wrote Harold Nicolson in his diary, "handcuffed together and guarded by three soldiers with fixed bayonets." One shuffled without boots, wearing only thick gray socks. It was September 7, 1940.

At five o'clock, the sirens came on. A writer named Virginia Cowles was staying at a country house thirty miles outside of London. She lay on the lawn, looking up at the sky. "The planes were so high it was difficult to spot them, but every now and then the sun caught their wings," she wrote. "The noise was appalling. It sounded like the roar of Niagara." She counted more than two hundred planes. "We knew this was the worst raid of the war." In all, there were about a thousand airplanes. Goering was in France now, directing the attack from his sumptuous private train.

"Several military targets appeared to be the raiders' chief objectives," wrote *The New York Times*—Thames docks and warehouses among them. Hundreds were killed by "screamer" bombs, collapsing buildings, and fire. The Blitz had begun. In an alley, one man was overheard to say, "After all, our chaps are doing this every night to the Germans."

A reporter visited an air-raid shelter. "There was a heavy smell inside, compounded of smoke and dust and unwashed clothing and bodies. A baby whimpered."

"We have not yet reached the top note of this crescendo of air attack," predicted an official at the Air Ministry.

BRITISH AIRPLANES returned to the Black Forest, where they saw many black, seared patches. "Skirting these blank spots," the *New York Times* reporter said, "they unloaded hundreds of incendiary bombs on green parts of the forest, starting many new fires which, according to the Air Ministry, spread rapidly and were accompanied by explosions, some of an extremely violent nature, indicating that munitions dumps had been touched off."

Goebbels called the reporters into the Propaganda Ministry to show them samples of the English fire wafers. The British had hoped to burn lots of grain, Shirer theorized. "Unfortunately," he said, "we had a very wet August and few of them got dry enough to ignite."

CECIL KING, the newspaper editor, walked out of Baker Street Station and looked around. It was September 10, 1940. "A large bomb had hit Madame Tussaud's and scooped the inside out," he noticed. The most recent bombs didn't scream or whistle, he wrote in his diary—they made a sort of whispering sound that increased in volume: "It sounded rather like the passing of wind through leafy trees."

A BRITISH PILOT saw the moon reflected in the lakes of blacked-out Berlin and knew that he had found his target: the Potsdam railroad station. It was the night of September 10, 1940. "Typical of present R.A.F. bombing operations, last night's raid was made by a force of bombers which delivered the attack with great precision," said an English communiqué. "One fire was particularly large and several smaller ones were seen." The BBC propaganda team took up the news, beaming it at Germany.

But the bombs had missed—the Potsdam railroad station was undamaged. What was damaged was the Reichstag building, the Brandenberg Gate, St. Hedwig's Catholic hospital, a Jewish hospital, the Charité hospital, and the Berlin Academy of Art—although the room of Hitler's models wasn't harmed. A bomb splinter made a hole in the double window of the American embassy and plunged into the wall in the office of one of the foreign secretaries; several incendiary bombs burned in the garden. Five civilians were killed, according to the official German communiqué. Afternoon headlines in Berlin were: "Reichstag Bombarded! Berlin Hospitals, Hotels, Residential Districts and Monuments Attacked According to Plan—Bombs Also on Brandenberg Gate." Also: "Mad Attacks on National Symbols."

"Now that our Reichstag building has been bombed, there is no reason why we should not bomb the British Parliament out of existence," said an anonymous source close to Hermann Goering to a reporter for the Associated Press. "I wouldn't give one farthing for the Houses of Parliament."

CHURCHILL TORE into Hitler over the radio. "This wicked man, the repository and embodiment of many forms of soul-destroying hatreds, this monstrous product of former wrongs and shame, has now resolved to try to break our famous Island race by a process of indiscriminate slaughter and destruction," he said. It was September 11, 1940.

VICTOR KLEMPERER heard rumors of things to come: yellow armbands; the confiscation of sewing machines and typewriters. "I am so far not suffering any privation despite all the taxes," he wrote. True, his need of clothing had become "grotesque." His carpet slippers were nearing their end, and "the situation with socks is very bad." But it could be worse, and, he said, he did not think about tomorrow.

Tomorrow, in fact, left him cold: "The Jews' House continually reckons on massacre in the case of German defeat," he wrote. It was September 12, 1940.

THE GERMANS claimed that British fliers had tossed bags of Colorado potato bugs out of their airplanes. The bugs were allegedly landing in fields in Germany, Luxembourg, Belgium, and Holland.

The British denied the charge. It was September 12, 1940.

A CANADIAN BOMBARDIER wrote home to his family about German air crews. It was September 12, 1940.

"Planes crashing near our station are manned by boys fifteen or sixteen years old," the bombardier wrote. "Some five man German planes have only two boys to handle them."

SOME REFUGEES from Wandsworth, a part of London, were staying with Frances Partridge in Wiltshire. "Our Wandsworth family believed that peace *must* come because Londoners couldn't stand this fearful strain and lack of sleep," Partridge wrote in her diary. "They were in a way the most pacific people we have lately seen. They have no bitterness against the German people, only sympathy for those we were bombing in Berlin." It was September 13, 1940.

GANDHI GAVE A SPEECH to the All India Congress Committee. "The thought of St. Paul's Cathedral being damaged hurts me as much as it would hurt me to see the temple of Kashi Vishwanath or the Jama Masjid damaged," Gandhi said. "I do not seek the defeat of the British. I want them to win. They are a brave nation. But I cannot bear that their rule over my country should be perpetuated and we for ever remain under their protection. So I shall not board their ship." It was September 15, 1940.

THE NEW SECRETARY of the U.S. Navy, Frank Knox, visited the fleet, which was still in Pearl Harbor, far from base. Knox played golf with Admiral Richardson, and Richardson gave him a memo requesting that the fleet return to the West Coast. It was September 15, 1940.

"Present policy appears to be headed towards forcing our will upon another Pacific Nation," Richardson wrote in the memo. "Have the objectives of such a war been formulated," he asked, "and its costs considered and compared with the value of victory?"

Admiral Richardson also told Secretary Knox something he'd learned from personal experience: "I told him that the President had two hobbies—stamp collecting and playing with the Navy."

CLARENCE PICKETT asked Eleanor Roosevelt to help him get an appointment with the president to talk about the compulsory military service bill—now called the Selective Training and Service Act. It was on the verge of passage in Congress. The president said he had no free time to talk to Pickett. The bill passed, forty-seven to twenty-five votes in the Senate, and 232 to 124 in the House of Representatives.

Henry Stimson, the new secretary of war, and George Marshall, the Army's chief of staff, stood behind President Roosevelt, watching him sign the bill into law. It was 3:08 in the afternoon on September 16, 1940.

The president made a proclamation: In one month's time, every male citizen and every male alien in the United States between the ages of twenty-one and thirty-six must submit to registration. "We cannot remain indifferent to the philosophy of force now rampant in the world," he said. "The terrible fate of nations whose weakness invited attack is too well known to us all."

The act was, the president asserted, bipartisan and fair, and it expressed the will of the people. It was a first step: "Our young men will come from the factories and the fields, the cities and the towns, to enroll their names on registration day."

Anyone who failed to enroll his name, and anyone who "knowingly counsels, aids, or abets another to evade registration or service in the land or naval forces," would be, according to the act, punished by jail or a ten-thousand-dollar fine or both.

CHAMBERLAIN WAS BACK in the House of Commons after his cancer operation. He'd aged, Harold Nicolson thought: His nose looked bigger and his head smaller. Churchill warned the House that the bombing was going to get worse. It was September 17, 1940.

"Everybody is worried about the feeling in the East End, where there is much bitterness," Nicolson wrote. "It is said that even the King and Queen were booed the other day when they visited the destroyed areas."

In the bomb shelters, British communists were passing around a peace petition to send to Churchill.

HITLER GAVE UP on Operation Sea Lion, the cross-channel invasion. The Royal Air Force wasn't destroyed, and therefore German landing boats filled with troops couldn't cross. And therefore the Madagascar Plan, in its several versions, went away—ships full of deported Jews wouldn't be able to pass the blockade. Hitler's hostility turned eastward. It was the middle of September 1940.

AFTER AN AIR RAID, Edward R. Murrow went around to watch buildings burn in a working-class district of London. With him was a bomber pilot who'd flown twenty-five missions over Germany. They saw a woman carrying a cooking pot and another woman holding a baby. The women were looking back over their shoulders at fires gusting through a housing block.

"I've seen enough of this," said the bomber pilot. "I hope we haven't been doing the same thing in the Ruhr and Rhineland for the last three months." It was September 25, 1940.

COUNT CIANO was on the train to Berlin to sign the Tripartite Pact between Japan, Germany, and Italy. Hitler called and had the train stopped. "Attacks by the Royal Air Force endanger the zone, and the Führer does not wish to expose me to the risk of a long stop in the open country," Ciano wrote in his diary. It was September 26, 1940.

He flew from Munich to Berlin, where he noticed a cooler mood than when he had signed the Pact of Steel—the agreement between Italy and Germany—in 1939. Food was scarce in Berlin now, and the sirens were wearing on people. "Every night the citizens spend from four to five hours in the cellar. They lack sleep, there is promiscuity between men and women, cold, and these things do not make for good humor." At ten o'clock, everyone would look at his watch, he said, and think about being home with loved ones. "Bomb damage is slight," Ciano thought, "nervousness is very great."

FAMILIES IN BERLIN and Hamburg signed their children up for the new rural evacuation program, called Kinderlandverschickung, or KLV. The program was organized, at Hitler's request, by Baldur von Schirach, the party leader of Vienna. Von Schirach was one of the old comrades—he'd written poetry in praise of Hitler's genius and had bought his art in Munich. His mother was American; von Schirach said that he'd discovered anti-Semitism when he was seventeen, reading a copy of Henry Ford's *The Eternal Jew.*

The KLV children were safe from British bombs, but they spent long periods away from their parents, living in camps, where they underwent incessant nationalist indoctrination, anti-Semitic harangues, military drills, sadistic bullying, and song singing. The program was run by the Hitler Youth, which Baldur von Schirach had directed since 1933.

CHURCHILL SENT A WORRIED NOTE to General Hastings Ismay, his chief of staff, about war gas. "The possibility of our having to retaliate on the German civil population must be studied, and on the largest possible scale," he wrote. "We should never begin, but we must be able to reply." It was September 28, 1940.

That night, there was a raid on Berlin. Marie Vassiltchikov stayed in bed again, rather than go down to the cellar. People were beginning to distrust cellars, she said. "A few nights ago a bomb landed on a house nearby, hitting it from the side. Though the house itself remained standing, in the cellar the pipes burst and all the inmates were drowned."

COLONEL HENRI SMITH-HUTTON, the American naval attaché in Tokyo, submitted a report to Washington about Japanese cities. It was September 30, 1940.

"Hoses are old, worn, and leaky," Smith-Hutton wrote. "Water mains are shut off at night. Little pressure is available. Fire hydrants are few and far between." There weren't many bomb shelters, the attaché continued—and, because transportation was overcrowded, evacuation would present tremendous difficulties. "Incendiary bombs sowed widely over an area of Japanese cities would result in the destruction of the major portions of these cities," Smith-Hutton said.

A list of important bombing objectives would follow, Smith-Hutton promised.

ALEXANDER S. LIPSETT, an economist who worked for Herbert Hoover's food-relief agency, wrote a letter to *The New York Times*. He wanted the British to lift the food blockade. "We are confronted with the appalling problem of mass starvation," Lipsett wrote. "Those who think that the Germans, severely pinched themselves, will not let these people starve and, if they riot, will not shoot them wholesale, are tragically mistaken. Perhaps they do not know the Germans. I do."

If the plan failed—if the Germans diverted food shipments—then we would have at least tried, Lipsett observed. "Those who condemn this or any other food relief plan should bear in mind that nothing is more destructive, more demoralizing and in the final analysis more advantageous to incipient Hitlers and the preachers of totalitarianism than acquiescence by word and deed in the death sentence that now hangs over the heads of millions of innocent people," he wrote. Lipsett was working on a book: *Famine Stalks Europe*.

It was October 2, 1940.

THE BRITISH PRESS SERVICE organized what it hoped would be a devastating reply to the blockade lifters, signed by fifteen prominent American leaders. "The American people are deeply sympathetic with the civilian populations of Europe in their sufferings and threatened sufferings," the statement said—but this was a total war. "Between the agony of empty stomachs for a time in one part of the world and the agony of stricken souls in every part of the world there can be but one choice." James Conant of Harvard, Harold Dodds of Princeton, Henry Sloane Coffin of Union Theological Seminary, and twelve others put their names to it. It was October 6, 1940.

A JAPANESE AIRPLANE dropped wheat, rice, and fleas on the island town of Chuhsien, on the China coast. It was October 4, 1940. People began dying of bubonic plague in Chuhsien. Japanese airplanes also dropped a cloud of grain on the city of Ningpo. A hundred people died of plague in Ningpo.

THE ROYAL AIR FORCE released a list to the press of some of the places that its planes had bombed through the first year of war. It was October 1940. Hamburg had been bombed thirty-six times, according to the list. Bremen had been bombed thirty-one times. The other places that had been bombed ten times or more were: Berlin (15 times), Dortmund (14 times), Dortmund-Ems Canal (11 times), Duisberg (12 times), Ehrang (10 times), Emden (19 times), Essen (16 times), Frankfurt (12 times), Hanover (19 times), Homburg (12 times), Kiel (12 times), Krefeld (13 times), Magdeburg (10 times), Mannheim (16 times), Nordeney (14 times), Osnabrück (22 times), Soest (29 times), and Wilhelmshaven (20 times).

The Black Forest had been bombed only five times; Dresden once.

Churchill gave a report on the war to the House of Commons: "Death and sorrow will be the companions of our journey," he said, "hardship our garment; constancy and valor our only shield."

PETER STAHL, pilot of a Ju-88 bomber, was flying on one of the first night raids on London. "The Luftwaffe has changed its tactics," he wrote in his diary. "The aim of wearing down the enemy is now to be achieved by raids of larger formations at night, in exactly the same manner as the British have already tried experimentally over Germany." His airplane had been sprayed with black paint: "It would seem that in this garb we are not visible to the searchlights."

They swerved to avoid flak and released their bombs, and then it was time to go home. One of Stahl's crewmates, Hein, asked for some music. They tuned into Radio Hilversum, the Dutch station. "Accompanied by cheerful entertaining sounds we cross the North Sea." It was October 7, 1940.

ADMIRAL RICHARDSON, commander of the U.S. fleet, had a confrontation with President Roosevelt. It was October 8, 1940. Richardson said what he'd said in his letter to Admiral Stark and his memo to Secretary Knox—that Pearl Harbor was the wrong place for his ships. Roosevelt said he thought that having the fleet in Hawaii had a "restraining influence" on Japan.

Was the United States going to war? Richardson asked the president. "He replied," in Richardson's account, "that if the Japanese attacked Thailand, or the Kra Peninsula, or the Dutch East Indies we would not enter the war, that if they even attacked the Philippines he doubted whether we would enter the war." But the Japanese couldn't always avoid making mistakes, the president said. "Sooner or later they would make a mistake and we would enter the war."

CECIL KING'S newspapers were in trouble. Hugh Cudlipp, the editor of the *Pictorial,* had written that Chamberlain's "paralyzing influence" remained in the cabinet. The *Daily Mirror* had a phrase about the "shifting or shunting of mediocrities." Cudlipp had quoted Churchill's book about the First World War. In peacetime, Churchill had said, leaders can proceed cautiously and vacillate, but in war you must make ruthless, clear-cut decisions. Cudlipp closed with: "Mr. Churchill, you have warned yourself."

Churchill, incensed, brought one of the articles into a cabinet meeting, and in the House he denounced the "vicious and malignant" attacks. It was October 8, 1940. Clement Attlee, the lord privy seal, called in the head of the Newspaper Proprietors' Association and threatened general censorship of editorials as well as news.

Cecil King went to see Attlee. Attlee had retired to a gas-proof bomb shelter nine feet square; he was sitting on a bed reading the

New Statesman. He said that King's papers showed "subversive influence" and that they might endanger the war effort. King said he thought Churchill didn't mind it when his papers kicked Chamberlain; he just "didn't like being hurt himself." Attlee insisted that the government had no objection to differences of opinion, only to "irresponsible" criticism.

"Obviously we shall pipe down for a few weeks," King wrote, "until the course of the war alters the whole situation."

THE MOON was almost full. The British attacked Berlin's electric-power station and the working-class Moabit district surrounding it. The next night, the Germans bombed Stoke Newington, a Jewish working-class neighborhood in London. It was October 14, 1940.

Vera, a typist, was in the Stoke Newington shelter with her family when the bomb exploded, breaking a water main. The lights went out, and water began pouring into the room. The door was blocked. In the darkness, someone said: "Don't panic! Remember you're British!" Vera and her family held hands and found their way to a second exit. "We were the last family," she said later. "By the time we reached the exit, the water was up to my armpits."

One hundred and sixty-four people died in the Stoke Newington bombing—fifty from drowning.

PRESIDENT ROOSEVELT announced on the radio the opening of registration for the draft. "Calmly, without fear and without hysteria, but with clear determination, we are building guns and planes and tanks and ships—and all the other tools which modern defense requires," he said. "Today's registration for training and service is the keystone in the arch of national defense." It was October 16, 1940.

John Haynes Holmes, national chairman of the War Resisters League, spoke to a small crowd at the Community Church in New York. "You must not hate or be bitter against those who will make it unpleasant for you," he said. Sixty sign-carrying people walked down Fifth Avenue, laughed at by pedestrians. One of the signs read: DOES ANYONE WIN AT WAR?

Four members of the Fellowship of Reconciliation, two members of the Young People's Socialist League, and eight students from the Union Theological Seminary—among whom were future civil-rights activists David Dellinger and George Houser—refused to register.

The divinity students came to be called the Union Eight.

CHURCHILL WAS SIPPING a glass of port in the House smoking room. Harold Nicolson was listening to him talk. A conservative member of Parliament told the prime minister that the British public was demanding the unrestricted bombing of Germany.

"You and others may desire to kill women and children," Churchill replied, but the British government's desire was to destroy military objectives. "My motto," the prime minister added, "is 'Business before Pleasure.' " It was October 17, 1940.

PRESIDENT ROOSEVELT gave a campaign speech in Philadelphia. He warned against a "blitzkrieg of verbal incendiary bombs" coming from his critics. One particularly outrageously false charge, the president said, was the charge that his administration wished to lead the country into war.

"To Republicans and Democrats, to every man, woman and child in the nation I say this: Your President and your Secretary of State are following the road to peace. We are arming ourselves not for any foreign war."

He then made a pledge—that the United States would not send troops to foreign lands except in case of attack.

"It is for peace that I have labored," he said, "and it is for peace that I shall labor all the days of my life."

It was October 23, 1940.

IN DRESDEN, air-raid sirens went off at three in the morning. It was the fourth time Victor Klemperer had heard sirens, but bombs never followed—the planes were flying somewhere else. He noted in his diary that there had been no coffee for Jews for a year. Aryans, such as his wife, Eva, got 1½ ounces per month—except in Cologne and Berlin, where they got 2½ ounces per month because they had more bombings. The butcher's wife told Klemperer that the English were bombing buildings that had a red cross on them because there were weapons factories under red-cross roofs. It was October 25, 1940.

THERE WAS A NEW NAZI decree: Jews and Aryans must be physically separated in air-raid shelters. It was October 1940.

THE BRITISH government in India made it illegal to publish anything that would "directly or indirectly foment opposition to the prosecution of the war to its successful conclusion." In response, Gandhi launched a campaign of civil disobedience. It was October 26, 1940.

A follower of Gandhi, Vinoba Bhave, was jailed for public pacifism. Then Jawaharlal Nehru, president of the Indian Congress, made a second pacifist speech, at Gandhi's request. Nehru was arrested and sentenced to four years in prison with hard labor.

LORD HALIFAX drew up a draft of peace terms to offer to Hitler. Someone at the Foreign Office showed the draft to Harold Nicolson, who thought it was pathetic—all about God. "I fear so much that we shall now have a peace offer from Hitler which will be difficult to explain away to our people," he wrote in his diary. It was October 26, 1940.

Halifax's peace terms, which granted Austria and parts of Poland and Czechoslovakia to Germany, found their way to Generals Halder, Beck, and Brauchitsch. One of Halifax's stipulations, however—so Halder recalled later—was that Hitler himself was to be assassinated. That was too far for the generals to go, and the offer died.

A RESIDENT of the Gurs concentration camp in southern France sent a letter to a member of the Women's International League for Peace and Freedom. "Yesterday news came calling us together to tell us that the barracks were to take in thousands of people just arriving," the letter said. "When I arrived at the door, I saw numberless shrivelled little old women climb down from trucks into pouring rain." It was dark and very muddy. Some women were blind, some deaf, some unable to walk. They were from old-age homes in Mannheim, and they said they were relieved not to be going to Lublin. They had brought a little luggage. Several from their party had died on the way there.

"To stand there and see this misery was the most terrible sight we had any of us ever witnessed," the woman wrote. "We were all so upset that we found ourselves crying." She and other residents found straw sleeping sacks and covers and walked the women to the outhouses.

"Do help us," the letter said. "Four thousand women have already been brought in." The French soldiers and officers were doing their best to assist, given the situation. But: "I have eight hundred people in my block alone."

VICTOR KLEMPERER wrote in his diary: "Much perturbed by brutal evacuation of Jews from Wurtemberg." It was November 7, 1940. *The New York Times* reported that ten thousand Jews, "in age from six months to 98 years," had been sent away from Germany. They'd been expelled from two areas: the Palatinate, near the Rhine

River; and Baden-Wurtemberg, where the Black Forest was. Mannheim was in Baden.

The Jews had ended up in concentration camps in southern France. They weren't quite penniless—they'd been allowed to take the equivalent of two dollars and fifty cents with them.

A German internal report said it was part of the Madagascar Plan: "Since there is a shortage of food and suitable accommodation for the deportees, who consist mainly of old men and women, it is believed here that the French government is intending to send them on to Madagascar as soon as the sea routes have been reopened."

Hitler didn't want them, the French government didn't want them, and Roosevelt didn't want them. Churchill wanted to starve them until they revolted against their oppressors.

"Relief work has been administered under the supervision of the Quakers," said the *Times*.

SECRETARY OF WAR HENRY STIMSON stood in an auditorium in the War Department. A blindfold—made from a strip of yellow cloth cut from a chair someone had sat on at the signing of the Declaration of Independence—was tied around his eyes. President Roosevelt, who had just made a speech, watched while Stimson reached into a ten-gallon glass fishbowl and pulled out a blue capsule with a number on it. He handed it to the president, who opened it, studied the slip of paper inside, and said: "The first number is one—five—eight." A woman screamed—her son was being drafted. It was October 29, 1940.

THE RED CROSS cut its staff in France. Since England was not allowing food to reach the country, there was nothing for the relief workers to do. Food supplies were exhausted; fifty trucks had nothing to truck. A skeleton force was to remain in Paris. It was November 8, 1940.

"Something deeply damaging to the human race was happening," wrote Muriel Lester.

In New York, John Haynes Holmes gave a sermon at the Community Church. "One of the reasons for fighting this war is to liberate these people," he said, "and the question now is are we going to let them starve in the process."

"If famine and plague sweep Europe," wrote *Commonweal* in an editorial, "we shall find it intolerable to reflect that we might have prevented them, and we shall find the aftermath of the war bitter with a terribly disruptive bitterness."

IN MUNICH, Hitler gave another big speech. It was November 8, 1940, the anniversary of the day that the Nazis had tried to overthrow the government in 1923. Hitler spoke in the grand Lowenbrau beerhall, which had a tower with the word LOWENBRAU curving around it and a chandelier inside. (The Burgerbrau beerhall, bombed a year earlier, was still unrestored.) Hitler wore the gray uniform, reports said, of the "Supreme Field Lord."

The speech was partly aimed at the United States, where Roosevelt had just been reelected. Hitler said he was "one of the hardest men Germany has had for decades, perhaps for centuries." He had never waged war against civilians in this war, he claimed. He had allowed bombing attacks only during the day, he said—

generally—because one couldn't target precisely at night. "Then it suddenly occurred to Mr. Churchill to attack the German civilian population at night."

> I watched for eight days. They dropped bombs on the people of the Rhine. They dropped bombs on the people of Westphalia. I watched for another fourteen days. I thought that the man was crazy. He was waging a war that could only destroy England. I waited over three months, but then I gave the order. I will take up the battle.

As for the United States, Hitler had heard the stories of massive airplane production, but he doubted the figures. And even if they were accurate, Germany would triumph. Germany would outproduce its enemies. The headline in *The New York Times* was "Adolf Tells the World He's One Tough Fellow."

Hitler's speech was supposed to go out on the radio—but then the Royal Air Force bombed Munich.

CHRISTOPHER ISHERWOOD was thinking about unhappiness, how much of it there was in the world. "No need to search for it in bombed London, or China, or Greece," he wrote in his diary. "The other evening, outside my window, a little boy cried to his mother: 'You don't want *anyone* to play with me!' Even the most trivial unkindness is heartbreaking, if one weren't so deaf and blind." He recalled running over a tin can in the parking lot. "I felt almost as bad as if I'd killed a cat," he wrote. " 'Oh God,' I said to myself, 'must we *always* keep smashing things?' "

ITALIAN NEWSPAPERS said that British pilots were cowards. They were afraid to go near places that were protected by antiaircraft defenses, the editorials said, and instead they bombed at random. According to one communiqué, recent bombs on Turin had hit a maternity hospital, a military hospital, a barracks, and a sanatorium. Churchill's pilots had insulted humanity in their attacks on the weak and the defenseless, said the *Fascist Worker,* and they would pay for it in blood a hundredfold.

"By betraying every rule of the code of honor, by trampling upon every humane consideration, the British authorize the enemy to have no scruples," said the editorial. It was November 9, 1940.

FRANK LLOYD WRIGHT, the architect, was at the Museum of Modern Art, showing off architectural models of houses and public buildings that were part of his vast, clean, decentralized, bomb-proof utopian metropolis, called Broadacre. "It is so spread out that scarcely any real damage could be done," Wright said to a *New York Times* reporter. "I would not say that the bombing of Europe is not a blessing, because at least it will give the architects there a chance to start all over again." It was November 10, 1940.

Which was architecturally the finest European city? the reporter asked. They were all bad, said Wright. Vienna was perhaps the most beautiful. "Moscow, though, has made the greatest strides in spreading out the population."

The London *News-Chronicle* later invited Wright to supply fifteen hundred words describing how he would rebuild England's ravaged capital. The new London could be a vast, clean, decentralized place, its nodes interconnected by highways—rather a lot like his Broadacre, in fact. "The bombing is not an unmixed evil," the architect said again. "Slums and ugliness that would have taken centuries to overcome have been blasted in a few days."

GENERAL RAYMOND LEE, the American air attaché, gave a farewell luncheon at Claridge's for Air Marshal Newall, whom Churchill was firing. He asked Portal, the new head of the Royal Air Force, if he wasn't perhaps trying to reach too far when he sent his bombers to Czechoslovakia. "Not at all," said Portal. Portal proposed to continue bombing eastern Europe, "if only for the effect it would have on the conquered peoples, whom it would greatly encourage." It was November 11, 1940.

ALEXANDER CADOGAN went to Neville Chamberlain's funeral at Westminster Abbey. It was noon on November 14, 1940.

All the windows in the chapel were gone, blown out. "Coldest thing I've ever known," Cadogan wrote. "Rather too long a service."

THE BRITISH INSTITUTE of Public Opinion asked a sample of citizens this question:

> In view of the indiscriminate bombing of this country, would you approve or disapprove if the R.A.F. adopted a similar policy of bombing the civilian population of Germany?

The results were that 46 percent would approve the bombing of the civilian population of Germany, 46 percent would disapprove the bombing of the civilian population of Germany, and 8 percent weren't sure. It was November 1940.

Eighty-nine percent of the sample thought Winston Churchill was doing a good job.

A NEWLY CAUGHT GERMAN PRISONER OF WAR had a conversation with his cellmate. The cellmate, who was an informant for British intelligence, wrote up a report: "He believes that riots have broken out in London and that Buckingham Palace has been stormed and that 'Hermann' "—Hermann Goering—"thinks the psychological moment has come for a colossal raid to take place between the 15th and the 20th of this month at the full moon and that Coventry and Birmingham will be the towns attacked." It was November 12, 1940.

That same day, another burst of information came in from cryptanalysts at Bletchley Park. An operation of "very considerable dimensions" was upcoming, the decoders reported, which was to use "all available aircraft." The commanding officer of a special unit of the Luftwaffe, the Kg100, which was trained to use radio-direction beams, would be personally leading the attack. Its code name was MOONLIGHT SONATA.

THE BRITISH AIR STAFF, collating the incoming intelligence, wrote a memo to the prime minister about MOONLIGHT SONATA. "It is probably a reprisal for our attack on Munich," the memo said. "We believe that the target areas will be those noted in paragraph 1 above, probably in the vicinity of London, but if further information indicates Coventry, Birmingham or elsewhere, we hope to get instructions out in time."

In response, Bomber Command proposed a "knock-for-knock policy": The commander in chief, Richard Peirse, would choose a German city—Berlin, Essen, or Munich, depending on the weather—and bomb it.

It was November 12, 1940.

THE UNION EIGHT stood before a judge for refusing to register for the draft. The students pled guilty and made a statement. "War consists of mass murder, deliberate starvation, vandalism, and similar evils," the students said. "Physical destruction and moral disintegration are the inevitable result. The war method perpetuates and compounds the evils it purports to overcome."

The urgent need, said the divinity students, was to build a group of people trained in techniques of nonviolent opposition to militarism and fascism. "We do not expect to stem the war forces today," they said in closing, "but we are helping to build the movement that will conquer in the future."

Judge Mandelbaum sentenced them each to a year and a day in prison. "This is a national emergency, where the very life, liberty and defense of our country are at stake," Mandelbaum said, "and I have no alternative but to enforce the law."

"Some of the girls and older women in the courtroom wept," the *New York Times* reporter wrote. An old man said, "Another triumph for Hitler."

It was November 14, 1940.

THE GERMAN SQUADRONS received the attack signal—"MOND," "moon"—and their directional radio beams angled so that they intersected over Coventry. It was November 14, 1940.

By one o'clock that afternoon, British signals watchers knew that Operation MOONLIGHT SONATA was on for that night. Two hours later, they knew where: "By three o'clock on the afternoon of the raid, No. 80 Wing was able to report that the X-Gereat beams were intersecting over Coventry," wrote an intelligence officer, Aileen Clayton, after the war. "All RAF commands were informed, as were Home Security and Home Forces."

The British counterplan, Operation COLD WATER, went into effect: Thirty airplanes took off for Berlin.

Churchill was in the car with one of his secretaries, on his way to Ditchly, the borrowed country house where he stayed on moonlit nights, when Chequers was overly visible from the air. He held a locked box marked "Only to be opened by the Prime Minister in person." He opened it. In it were deciphered messages, sorted for Churchill by Frederick Winterbotham, the spy who had helped to photograph Germany. Churchill read the messages and immediately told the driver to turn back to London. "False start for Ditchly," wrote the secretary, John Martin, in his diary. "'The moonlight sonata.'"

NOBODY CALLED UP COVENTRY to tell the people who lived there that an enormous attack, involving hundreds of airplanes, was coming their way in several hours' time. The Coventry Fire Brigade was not notified; the mayor was not notified; the ambulance service was not notified. Twenty minutes before bombs fell, a local antiaircraft team got a message: "Major raid expected on Coventry tonight."

At 7:10 p.m., German pathfinder planes arrived over the target. They dropped ten thousand incendiaries in the first half hour. The bombing continued until dawn.

Several hundred thousand people lived and worked in Coventry. Rolls-Royce made bomber engines there, and Armstrong Siddeley made the Whitley bomber. The city also held a fourteenth-century cathedral church—"one of the finest specimens of Perpendicular architecture in England," according to the 1911 *Encyclopaedia Britannica*. The central part of the city was destroyed; five hundred people died; fifty thousand houses were damaged. The tower and some of the walls of the cathedral were left standing amid the obliteration. "All the shops, Boots, Flinns the jewellers, Marks, Woolworths, all along and down Smithford Street, gone, not a shop standing," one inhabitant recalled.

A reporter for the German Propaganda Ministry flew in one of the bombers. He wrote that it was the greatest attack in the history of aerial warfare and that it had crippled Britain's aviation industry. "It looked as if the earth had broken open and spewed fiery masses of lava far over the land," he wrote. "The collapsed iron girders of great factory buildings were surrounded by gigantic columns of flames." The attack was, the German command explained, a reprisal for the attack on Munich while Hitler was giving his anniversary speech.

"Coventry as a production center for munitions has passed out for the time being," wrote Cecil King, the publisher, in his diary. It troubled King that there had apparently been no evacuation plan, even though Coventry "must be the most concentrated conglomeration of military objectives of an industrial nature in the whole country."

The German Propaganda Ministry later prepared a pamphlet for children about the raid. "In revenge for the attack on Munich, bombs have fallen on an important area of the English Midlands and have had their effect," the pamphlet said. "As the fall morning dawns over Coventry, this armaments center is badly damaged."

MARGARET COULING, returning to Coventry the day after the bombing, found that her office building was standing. She went up to the top floor and looked out at the remains of the cathedral, which were still smoking. "There was a little procession came from the back end of the cathedral and walked down Hay Lane," she said. It was the king and other notables. "They'd brought their own picnic basket," she said, "so that they could have lunch before they went on elsewhere."

The king wrote in his diary: "I think they liked my coming to see them in their adversity."

Winston Churchill asked for heavy publicity to be given to the Coventry raid. He didn't visit.

THE ROYAL AIR FORCE flew to Hamburg and bombed the city all night long, with—wrote Raymond Daniell in *The New York Times*—a break in the middle "just long enough to encourage the Reich's port's citizens to believe the attack had ended." The raid happened twenty-four hours after Coventry: "Hamburg Pounded in 'Reply' by R.A.F." was the *Times*'s page-one headline. It was November 17, 1940.

There were some observers in London, wrote Daniell, who thought that both sides were on the wrong track. Was this war of reciprocal extermination really the only way to go? Some were "demanding a re-examination of policy on this side." Daniell wrote:

> Each raid on human kind, whether carried out by the British, who insist they are not swerving from a policy of concentrating the attack on military objectives, or by the Nazis, who boast they are exacting an eye for an eye and a tooth

for a tooth, speeds the pace of the mass murder and intensifies the lust for blood.

The city of Coventry was still smoldering that day. "Sometimes small explosions spurted up little geysers from the hot ruins as canned goods generated enough steam to blow out their containers," a United Press reporter wrote. The reporter asked a fire warden how many had died in the bombing. The fire warden looked at him pityingly and took him to a collapsed air-raid shelter, where they had just managed to jack up the roof. "Look under there," the fire warden said. The reporter saw, under the layer of concrete, many bodies. "Some of them were not entire bodies."

Mass Observation, the British government's opinion service, wrote up a morale report. There were signs of hysteria, terror, and neurosis, the report said. "Women were seen to cry, to scream, to tremble all over, to faint in the street."

A sign went up at the mortuary:

IT IS GREATLY REGRETTED THAT THE PRESSURE
AT THE MORTUARY IS SUCH THAT IT IS NOT POSSIBLE
FOR RELATIVES TO VIEW ANY OF THE BODIES

In a common grave, 172 bodies, many of them burned or mutilated beyond recognition, were quickly buried.

RAYMOND DANIELL was at a mass burial ceremony in Coventry—the first of two. It was November 20, 1940.

Two hundred unnamed flag-draped coffins lay in a row, Daniell said—"a long, narrow, deep gash cut in the red earth by a steam shovel and shored up with rough boards so that it looked like an excavation for a water main." There was a pile of dirt with spades poking out of it, and there were shovelers waiting in rubber boots. The bishop, standing on a bare mound with the steam shovel behind him, asked people to remember that Hitler had killed their loved ones but could not kill the human spirit. Assistants sprinkled dust and ashes on the stacked coffins, and a thousand mourners moved past. There was no music. The king and queen weren't there. Winston Churchill was in London discussing Greece with his war cabinet and being photographed by Cecil Beaton.

Daniell's article was "heavily censored without explanation" by the British authorities, said an italicized note printed at the end.

CHURCHILL VISITED BIRMINGHAM, where eight hundred people had been killed in a raid a few days earlier. It was the end of November 1940. "A very pretty young girl ran up to the car and threw a box of cigars into it," Churchill later wrote. "I was very glad (in my official capacity) to give her a kiss. I then went on to see the long mass grave in which so many citizens and their children had been newly buried."

IN ANTWERP, JEWS were compelled to wear Star of David armbands. In solidarity, non-Jews in the city wore armbands, too. It was November 1940.

ULRICH VON HASSELL, part of the loose anti-Hitler coalition, talked with two of his co-conspirators about the food situation. "In Germany we can get along till August 1 if we made use of all reserves," he wrote. "In some of the occupied areas there will be acute food shortages pretty soon." It was November 23, 1940.

A GROUP of Jewish refugees from Germany and Austria were put on a boat in the harbor of Haifa, Palestine. With Churchill's approval, British forces were deporting the Jews from Palestine, where they'd arrived illegally after many hardships. The English planned to take them to Mauritius, a small island in the Indian Ocean not far from Madagascar. It was November 25, 1940.

Two saboteurs from Haganah, a Jewish paramilitary group, blew a hole in the boat with a mine, in order to keep it from leaving. The boat, which sunk, was called the *Patria,* and the disaster was called the Patria Disaster. More than 250 people died. The survivors were taken to a British prison.

THE FRENCH AMBASSADOR made a formal request for help from Secretary of State Cordell Hull. It was November 25, 1940.

Ambassador Gaston Henry-Haye described the recent arrival of several thousand "Israelites" expelled from Wurtemberg and Baden. They were but a part of a larger problem, Henry-Haye said, which was that in the free zone of France, there were now three and a half million aliens: Armenians, Assyrian-Chaldeans, Austrians, Czechs, Germans, Jews, Poles, Saarfolk, and Spaniards. "The problem of supplying them with food has," the ambassador noted, "become particularly difficult to solve." He hoped that France, the United States, and other countries could find a way to permit some of the refugees—principally the German Jews—to emigrate to the Americas. The ambassador closed with renewed assurances of his very high consideration.

The State Department sat on the letter for several weeks, weighing a formal response.

JAPAN CHOSE a new ambassador to the United States. "There are few—if any—Japanese who want war with the United States," Admiral Kichisaburo Nomura said before he left Tokyo. "The fate of the world hangs on American actions just now. If the United States becomes involved in a conflict either in Europe or in the Pacific, civilization will go up in flames." It was November 26, 1940.

ROOSEVELT ASKED HENRY MORGENTHAU to loan China one hundred million dollars, to help the nationalist government keep fighting against the Japanese. The money would go for airplanes.

Claire "Leatherface" Chennault ghost-wrote a four-page memo to Roosevelt from Chiang Kai-shek, proposing a Special Air Unit operated in China by pilots and crewmembers from the United States. Chiang Kai-shek's wealthy emissary and brother-in-law, T. V. Soong, delivered the memo to Morgenthau, who read it. It was November 30, 1940.

"There are 136 airfields available in China," Chiang Kai-shek's memo said, "more than half of which are in excellent condition, and all serviceable for both bombers and pursuits. Several of these airfields are within 650 miles from Japan." The new Special Air Unit could, Chiang said, work in concert with the Chinese army—or it could operate independently by striking "Japan proper." Maps showing the location of airfields might be provided.

Morgenthau thought about the airfields and their proximity to Japan. He sounded out Lord Lothian, the British ambassador. Morgenthau told Lothian he was going to try to get four-engine bombers and crews for the Chinese, "with the understanding that these bombers are to be used to bomb Tokyo and other big cities." Lothian seemed agreeable.

"It might change everything," Lothian said.

MILO PERKINS told the readers of *Harper's Magazine* what the United States should do with its food glut. Perkins, who supervised the U.S. government's new food-stamp program, said: "The invasion of Norway, the collapse of the Low Countries, and the closing of the Mediterranean shut off important markets." There were hundreds of millions of unsold bushels of wheat, he explained, forcing prices down.

What to do? Some people, Perkins wrote, believed that the United States should be able to sell its grain to Europe, but Perkins didn't think so. After the Great War, he pointed out, thousands of half-starved German boys were brought back to health in Dutch and Scandinavian homes, and then, twenty years later, they attacked the very countries that had saved their lives. "This is a new and an utterly different kind of world and parts of it are unbelievably brutal," Perkins believed. "Horrible as it is, some starvation in Europe now, under the British blockade, may be necessary to break the Hitler stranglehold on free men."

Food stamps for American consumers, not food sales to Europe, were the answer to the problem of the American surplus.

It was December 1940.

CHARLES PORTAL wrote a secret memo to Winston Churchill: "You instructed me two days ago to prepare a plan for the most destructive possible bombing attack against a selected German town," Portal wrote. He had complied. About one hundred airplanes would participate.

> The first attacks will be with incendiary bombs, and if weather permits it is intended to continue the bombing with HE and incendiary throughout the night.
>
> 1,000 lb and 500 lb bombs will be used in preference to 250 lb bombs, and a number of mines will also be dropped if conditions are suitable. All HE bombs will be fuzed for the best destructive effect against buildings, gas and water mains, and electric cables.

("HE" stands for "high-explosive bombs.") The possible cities were Hanover, Mannheim, Cologne, and Düsseldorf. "As soon as I receive your authority I will give your instructions for the operation to be done on the first suitable night," Portal wrote. The code name of the operation was "Abigail." Each city had a code name: Bremen was "Jezebel," Düsseldorf was "Delilah," and Mannheim was "Rachel." It was December 7, 1940.

The Air Ministry's orders to Portal had begun: "With object causing widespread uncontrollable fires suggest first ten sorties carry incendiary bombs only."

"The moral scruples of the Cabinet on this subject have been overcome," wrote secretary John Colville in his diary.

HENRY MORGENTHAU, the secretary of the treasury, had lunch with President Roosevelt. Then he had a talk with T. V. Soong. It was December 8, 1940.

Morgenthau swore Soong to secrecy and then brought up the equipping of China to bomb Tokyo and other cities.

"To say he was enthusiastic is putting it mildly," Morgenthau wrote in his diary.

> I told him that I had not discussed this with the President, but intimated it was the President's idea, which it is in part, because he has mentioned to me that it would be a nice thing if the Chinese would bomb Japan.

Morgenthau brought up the airfields—the ones that were within 650 miles of Tokyo. Could Soong furnish some information on them?

The next day, Soong sent a handwritten note. "In connection with General Chiang Kai-shek's secret memorandum to the president concerning China's air needs, I take the pleasure of enclosing a map of China, showing the location of the airfields now in the possession of our Air Force, which, I hope will prove of interest." There was a P.S.: "This map is of course very secret, and is for your personal information."

IN THE HOUSE OF COMMONS, Richard Stokes, a socialist and member of the Peace Pledge Union, put a question to the minister of home security. Why, he asked, were Sir Oswald Mosley, his wife, and several hundred other British fascists being held in prison without trial and without legal representation? Not that he had any sympathy with Mosley's fascists, Stokes said—but shouldn't they either be tried in a court for treason or released? It was December 10, 1940.

"The security of the State comes before anything else in time of war," said Herbert Morrison, the minister of home security. Morrison said he was getting fed up with this kind of objection.

Stokes pointed out that Morrison could imprison every member of Parliament if he wanted to.

Somebody wondered why, if the fascists were in prison, the communist *Daily Worker* was still allowed to appear on newsstands.

THE AMERICAN FRIENDS SERVICE COMMITTEE announced that it was going to attempt to carry on feeding people in Europe regardless of whether the British enforced their blockade or not. "At the moment, American Quaker workers in unoccupied France are feeding more than 30,000 children daily," Clarence Pickett said. "Orphaned and abandoned children, many of whom are in concentration camps, are wholly cared for by the committee's representatives." It was December 11, 1940.

"We can't build a workable peace on the dead bones of mothers and babies," Pickett said.

A FORCE OF WELLINGTON BOMBERS, filled with incendiaries and flown by the most experienced crews in the RAF's roster, reached Mannheim, Germany. It was December 16, 1940. The Wellingtons' task was to start fires that would then serve as the aiming points for the bombers that followed. The goal of the raid was to "concentrate the maximum amount of damage in the centre of the town," according to Commander in Chief Richard Peirse. It was Plan Abigail in action.

The center of the town was laid out like few in Europe, in a Manhattan-like grid. It looked like a chessboard, said one pilot—a brilliantly moonlit chessboard. Antiaircraft fire rose "like a golden fountain." And then the firebombs went down. German high command reported hits to a castle and a hospital.

Churchill used one of his favorite metaphors, the metaphor of the pugilist, the Thor hammerer: "We have struck very heavy blows—the blows at Mannheim appeared to have been of a very heavy character—and the enemy has not found any means to prevent that."

Actually, the raid was a disappointment to the Air Ministry. It had been meant as a retaliation for Coventry, but it hadn't reached the Coventry scale. The fires set by the Wellingtons had been off target, misguiding the bombardiers behind them. Commander Peirse said that the orders had been too rigidly worded—they should have said to aim at the target, not at the fires. The fires should illuminate the target, but the target itself was the important thing. In the future, Peirse said sternly, "I count on the great majority of bombs hitting within half a mile radius of it."

PRESIDENT ROOSEVELT got back from a Caribbean vacation and held a press conference. He had a bit of a tan; his cigarette holder tilted upward as he spoke. It was December 17, 1940.

Roosevelt's word for the day was "lend." Lord Lothian had announced that England was going broke buying weapons and needed military aid. But the United States was still officially neutral. Now, suppose my neighbor's home catches fire, Roosevelt said, and I lend him a hose to help him put out the fire. Afterward, he gives it back to me. If, as may happen, the hose gets torn or wrecked in the firefighting, he can furnish me with a new hose of the same length. The fire is out, the hose is restored, and everybody's happy. And that's what we'll do, he said. We'll lend England the planes and boats they need. If the planes and boats are wrecked, England can replace them after the war.

The reporters blinked, thought, scribbled—hose, lend.

Roosevelt wasn't proposing to lend anything like a garden hose to England—by December 1940, the English, having survived many fire raids, knew a thing or two about hoses, and they did not need more. What the English wanted, as they had said several times already, was heavy bombers. They wanted to set fires, not fight them.

FOREIGN AIRPLANES flew over Basel, Switzerland, and dropped bombs near the railroad station. It was December 18, 1940. Seventy railroad cars were damaged, and four women were killed. The bomb fragments were from British bombs. The town asked for permission to rescind the blackout regulations; it was being bombed because it was blacked out.

Mannheim was "blasted" again, according to *The New York Times,* officially for the thirty-fourth time. "On other nights also Mannheim has heard the crump of British bombs as incidental phases of R.A.F. raids elsewhere in Germany," the *Times* reported, "when the pilots either chose the city as an alternative objective or dropped spare bombs there on the route home from other targets."

MORGENTHAU CALLED up the president and told him he needed to have a meeting—he'd gotten a very secret message from Chiang Kai-shek saying that Chiang wanted to attack Japan. It was December 18, 1940.

"Is he still willing to fight?" asked President Roosevelt.

"That's what the message is about," said Morgenthau.

"Wonderful," said Roosevelt. "That's what I have been talking about for four years."

THE CHINESE GOVERNMENT charged that the Japanese had recently released plague germs over three cities. It was December 19, 1940.

A spokesman from imperial headquarters in Tokyo made an absolute denial of the charges. Japan didn't need to resort to such methods, the spokesman said. He countercharged that the Chinese had been putting cholera germs in the wells to infect occupation forces.

HAROLD NICOLSON gave a lecture to some members of the air force in Nether Wallop. Nicolson's subject was the German character. He sensed, though, that his audience wasn't with him. "They are all fascists at heart and rather like the Germans," he wrote in his diary. It was December 20, 1940.

DR. SOONG was in Henry Morgenthau's dining room with Claire Chennault, planning the firebombing of Japan. It was December 21, 1940.

Chennault said that each plane would need an American bombardier and an American pilot, plus five American mechanics. Morgenthau said he could arrange to have enlisted men released from active duty in the U.S. Army Air Corps—assuming the men would be paid a good salary. One thousand dollars per month, say? Soong and his aide said yes.

Chennault discoursed on the range of different bombers. The Hudson bomber could fly a thousand miles with a good load. Since it was twelve hundred miles to Tokyo and back, the Hudson couldn't bomb Tokyo. "However, Nagasaki, Kobe, and Osaka were within range of the Hudson bomber," he said. The Flying Fortresses could reach Tokyo—and there were two Chinese fields with the long runways that the Fortresses needed.

Could the planes fly at night? Morgenthau asked. Yes, said Chennault, they'd have to fly at night, because the fighter escorts they needed for daylight missions didn't have enough range to make it to Japan.

And what about incendiary bombs? Morgenthau asked—"inasmuch as the Japanese cities were all made of just wood and paper."

A lot of damage could be done that way, they all agreed. Then they said goodbye and went to bed.

UNDER-SECRETARY OF STATE Sumner Welles drafted a reply to the French ambassador's plea for help with Jewish emigration. He sent it to Roosevelt for approval. It was December 21, 1940.

The reply presented Secretary of State Cordell Hull's compliments to the French ambassador and acknowledged the receipt of the ambassador's note asking for assistance in the solution of the problem of refugees, particularly refugees of "German nationality and Jewish religion." It was true that France was now feeding and caring for these thousands of German Jewish refugees. It was true that the French wanted the United States government to help find homes for these refugees in the American hemisphere.

Politely, with great ceremony, the secretary of state found it necessary to refuse the French request. "The laws of the United States regarding immigration are quite explicit," he said, "and do not permit any further liberalization." The time would come when conditions of order and peace prevail, but for now, the United States "does not believe that any useful purpose can be served by discussing migration problems bilaterally with the French Government or multilaterally with the several Governments at this time."

IN A COVER LETTER, Under Secretary Welles offered the president his views on Ambassador's Henry-Haye's request. It was "totalitarian blackmail," he contended: the Germans were pressuring the French to pressure the United States. "Were we to yield to this pressure," he wrote, "the Germans would drive on the French the remaining Jews from Germany and the occupied territories, hundreds of thousands of persons, in the expectation that the French in turn would persuade this country and the other American countries to receive them."

All over Europe, Welles argued, the Germans would "inaugurate something approaching a 'reign of terror' against the Jewish people." The Jewish refugees in France must therefore stay where they were. "We must think above all of the tragic victims," he said.

Roosevelt wrote "OK" on the draft letter; Secretary of State Cordell Hull signed it; and it went out to the French ambassador a few days later.

FRANCES PARTRIDGE was writing in her diary about one of her friends. "Colin thinks the Germans ought all to be sterilized, that they aren't like other people—and this statement aroused no anger in me, only detached surprise," she wrote. "Yet he is a very intelligent man. How will this seem in the years after the war, if we survive it?"

It was December 21, 1940.

CHURCHILL WAS THINKING about the thousands of people, such as Jawaharlal Nehru and Oswald Mosley, whom he had ordered locked up as political prisoners. He had a gentle word for these men and women: *détenus.* The *détenus* were those who, said Churchill, had not committed any specific offense but who nonetheless had to be held in custody. "Naturally I feel distressed at having to be responsible for action so utterly at variance with all the fundamental principles of British liberty, *Habeas Corpus,* and the like," he said. "The public danger justifies the action taken, but the danger is now receding."

He requested that the "rigorous character" of Nehru's punishment be mitigated. But he didn't let Nehru out of jail. It was December 22, 1940.

THE ROYAL AIR FORCE bombed the cathedral in central Berlin. There was snow on the ground; it was a few days before Christmas 1940.

"Low-flying planes pumped machine gun bullets into searchlight gun batteries," said *The New York Times*. The Lustgarten—a place of early Nazi assembly—was hit, as was the Zeughaus, a museum of German military history where Hitler had given a speech the year before.

The next day, the *Völkischer Beobachter* said, "The attack on the largest church in the Reich capital proves the complete planlessness of the British Air Force." Germany was able to "practice retribution of the sort that Londoners, despite repeated experiences, cannot yet imagine," the article threatened. "There has been no lack of warnings."

GANDHI WROTE an open letter to Adolf Hitler. He used "Dear Friend" as the salutation. It was December 24, 1940.

"We have no doubt," Gandhi told Hitler, "about your bravery or devotion to your fatherland, nor do we believe you are the monster described by your opponents." But your actions, Gandhi said, were monstrous. Czechoslovakia, Denmark, "the rape of Poland"—these conquests degraded humanity.

Gandhi explained the technique of nonviolence to Hitler. "Ours is a unique position," Gandhi said:

> We resist British imperialism no less than Nazism. If there is a difference, it is one of degree. One-fifth of the human race has been brought under the British heel by means that will not bear scrutiny.

For the past half century, Gandhi went on, India has been trying to throw off British rule. "We have found in non-violence a force which, if organized, can without doubt match itself against all the most violent forces in the world."

Refer your dispute to an international tribunal, he advised Hitler. The successful use of a science of destruction does not prove the user right: "If not the British, some other power will certainly improve upon your method and beat you with your own weapon."

> You are leaving no legacy to your people of which they would feel proud. I, therefore, appeal to you in the name of humanity to stop the war.

Gandhi sent a telegram to Sir Gilbert Laithwaite, secretary to the governor-general of India: OPEN LETTER TO HERR HITLER BEING SENT TO PRESS. HOPE HIS EXCELLENCY COULD ALLOW IT QUICK PASSAGE TO THE WEST.

THE LUFTWAFFE started fifteen hundred fires in London. It was December 29, 1940. The medieval guildhall was destroyed. The bells were melted in the steeple of Christopher Wren's St. Bride's Church, built after the 1666 fire of London. The raid was called the Second Great Fire of London. Charles Portal, chief of the air staff, and Bomber Harris, deputy chief of the air staff, stood on the roof of the Air Ministry, looking at the dome of St. Paul's above the flames. "They are sowing the wind," said Bomber Harris.

The war cabinet met at noon the next day and discussed what to do. "Decided to advertise attack on City—quite rightly," Under-Secretary Cadogan wrote in his diary. "This may help us enormously in America at a most critical moment. Thank God—for all their cunning and industry and efficiency—the Germans are fools. Lunched at home."

Censorship was suddenly lifted for American reporters—they were free to tell the whole story, naming specific buildings and neighborhoods. "Buildings have been destroyed," wrote Robert Post in *The New York Times,* "in which men could feel the brush of the wings of centuries."

Portal checked in with Churchill. Then he let his head of Bomber Command know that he was "quite at liberty to have another 'Abigail' on any of the towns previously approved."

Louis MacNeice, the poet, watched a building in London burn and was struck by its beauty—"a large shop-building that seemed to be merely a facade of windows and these windows were filled to the brim with continuous yellow flame, uniform as a liquid but bubbling a little at the top of the windows like aerated tanks in an aquarium." The Germans were stage-lighting London, MacNeice said.

Sylvia Townswend Warner, the short-story writer, asked MacNeice to lend his support to a People's Convention organized by the socialists and communists. A six-point plan was in circulation:

1. Defense of the people's living standards.
2. Defense of the people's democratic and trade union rights.
3. Adequate air-raid precautions, deep bomb-proof shelters, rehousing and relief of victims.
4. Friendship with the Soviet Union.
5. A people's government truly representative of the whole people and able to inspire confidence in the working people of the world.
6. A people's peace that gets rid of the causes of war.

The convention was going to take place in January.

MacNeice asked Warner why he should support such a gathering. "Because the revolution is needed immediately," Warner said. MacNeice said he didn't think that the British communists could swing a revolution and, if they did, whether it would be the right kind. "Apart from that," he said, "if we had a revolution—however successful—to-day, Hitler would invade England—and probably successfully—tomorrow."

Senator Burton Wheeler, an isolationist, gave a speech on NBC Radio. "I firmly believe that the German people want peace just as any people prefer peace to war," he said, "and the offer of a just, reasonable and generous peace will more quickly and effectively crumble Hitlerism and break the morale of the German people than all the bombers that could be dispatched over Berlin." It was December 30, 1940.

Roosevelt wrote Churchill a cable about milk in France. It was New Year's Eve, 1940.

Clarence Pickett had asked Roosevelt to petition Churchill to allow a Red Cross food ship past the blockade. "If it did not sail," Pickett wrote, "we did not know how we should have milk after January 5."

The British blockade authorities, Roosevelt wrote Churchill, were refusing to let the Red Cross send even small amounts of milk to children in France, "on the ground that it would be difficult to make a distinction between occupied and unoccupied territories." Roosevelt felt that such a distinction could be made and that the milk should go through.

He had no intention, he said, of pursuing a policy that would weaken the efficacy of a British blockade: Germany must feed the territories under German occupation. But children in the *unoccupied* part of France needed milk, layettes, and vitamins. And Spain needed flour. If Spain got flour, it might stay out of the war, he said.

FIVE PACIFISTS, dressed as refugees, led a march to the Broadway Tabernacle on Fifty-sixth Street in New York. It was January 1, 1941. They had walked from Lancaster, Pennsylvania, pushing a handcart, to protest the British hunger blockade. KINDNESS BUILDS REAL PEACE, one of the marchers' signs said. Another said, STARVATION BREEDS ANARCHY, NOT PEACE AND DEMOCRACY. The marchers sang a song about the power of love.

Lee Stern, a student at the Case School of Applied Science, was one of the original five. He lived at a place called Ahimsa Farm, a commune in Aurora, Ohio; he said that the Food for Europe Pilgrimage to the Sea was inspired by Gandhi's walk to the sea for salt. Muriel Lester, author of "Speed the Food Ships," was also in the parade—she was the founder of Kingsley House, in the East End, where Gandhi had stayed when he visited England in 1931.

A woman pushed a baby stroller and carried a sign that said BREAK THE CHAINS OF STARVATION'S SLAVERY. Her husband, Angelo Mongiore, was in prison for refusing to register for the draft.

ELVIRA NIGGEMAN, Harold Nicolson's private secretary, went on a walk after a bombing raid in the West End. "All along there were little groups of people talking quietly but quite determinedly about revenge," she wrote Nicolson. "There is no doubt that the feeling is growing that similar treatment of the Germans is the only thing they will understand." It was January 2, 1941.

WINSTON CHURCHILL sent a reply to Roosevelt's letter about food to Europe. It was January 3, 1941.

Churchill agreed to admit one Red Cross ship, as long as every effort was made to keep the relief goods from getting into occupied France. "I feel sure that I can count upon your help to maintain this distinction," he said, "for otherwise the whole fabric of our blockade would be fatally undermined and I need not stress to you what this would mean in terms of final victory."

The goods that Churchill was allowing through were: tinned or powdered milk, vitamins, and medicine "in the strict sense." Cod and halibut oil he refused to allow in.

In granting this tiny, temporary opening in the blockade, Churchill made one further request. "We would like it stated that the relief goods are available only by good will of His Majesty's Government," Churchill wrote. "The impression which we should like to see created is that of Anglo-American cooperation for humanitarian ends."

THAT SAME DAY, Churchill also wrote a note to one of his aides about enemy aliens. More than fifty thousand German Jews had finally been released, with Churchill's consent—leaving more than two hundred thousand still in prison—and some of them would be serving in the Pioneer Corps, a branch of the military similar to the U.S. Army Corps of Engineers. Churchill wanted to be sure that the corps was "scrubbed and re-scrubbed" to keep it clear of Nazi cells. "I am very much in favor of recruiting friendly Germans and keeping them under strict discipline," Churchill wrote, "instead of remaining useless in concentration camps, but we must be doubly careful we do not get any of the wrong breed."

ROOSEVELT GAVE his annual speech to Congress. American security was under threat, he said. Great numbers of secret agents were already in Latin America. The United States was behind schedule in building airplanes. We must make sacrifices to meet the present emergency. We must furnish our friends with "ships, planes, tanks, guns."

But with all that, we had something to look forward to: four essential human freedoms.

Freedom of speech was one; freedom of religion was another; freedom from want was a third. And the fourth: "The fourth is freedom from fear—which, translated into world terms, means a worldwide reduction of armaments to such a point and in such a thorough fashion that no nation will be in a position to commit an act of physical aggression against any neighbor—anywhere in the world."

This commendable goal—the worldwide reduction of armaments—explained why the United States needed to manufacture, as fast as it could, more ships, more planes, more tanks, and more guns.

It was January 6, 1941.

WINSTON CHURCHILL was *Time* magazine's Man of the Year. It was January 1941.

ANOTHER DRAFT RESISTER was sent to jail. It was January 6, 1941.

"In registering I would have only dropped incense on the fire now burning on the altar of hate," said Ernest J. Kirkjian, a former student of divinity at Temple University. Judge Welsh said that Kirkjian was "thoroughly sincere" and sentenced him to a year and a day in federal prison.

CHURCHILL LEARNED from the White House that Harry Hopkins would like to visit England. "Who?" Churchill asked. His aides explained that Hopkins was the president's personal confidant and agent.

A state visit was arranged for Hopkins, including an audience with the king and queen, tours of air-raid damage, meetings with Bomber Command, and a trip by private train to see the war boats at Scapa Flow. It was January 1941.

Hopkins met Lord Beaverbrook, press lord and head of aircraft production, and he had a dinner with newspaper editors and publishers. He stayed up late while Churchill drank and took snuff from a little silver box. Churchill, who had struck Hopkins at first simply as a smiling, red-faced rotundity with a fat hand and a mushy voice, soon conquered Hopkins's affections. It was all new—the brilliant pugnacity, the Euphratean word stream, the memory for stirring bits of verse.

Hopkins wrote Roosevelt that Churchill was the one man he had to deal with—he didn't have to worry about anyone else. Churchill was the government, Hopkins explained: "The politicians and the upper crust pretend to like him." And he was doing a splendid job. "It has been emphasized more than ever in my mind that Churchill is leading this country magnificently in every respect and that the whole nation is behind him," Hopkins said.

Churchill believed, Hopkins reported, that "this war wouldn't be fought with great forces massed against one another." It was to be a war of bombers—bombers and blockades. At the moment, Churchill said, the German-to-English bomber ratio was two and a half to one, but that was coming down. "He looks forward with our help to mastery in the air and then Germany with all her armies will be finished." As for the blockade: "He expressed the hope that we would not go too far in feeding any of the dominated countries." Peoples who were dejected and despairing were harder for Hitler to control.

THE *DAILY WORKER* ran an ad in *The New York Times* for the People's Convention. "The British People Speak Up!" said the headline, written over the skyline of a bombed and burning London. It was January 11, 1941.

The next day, two thousand delegates met in London and heard speeches. Soldiers in uniform were there, as were clergymen, students, and union organizers. D. N. Pritt, socialist member of Parliament, was the convention treasurer. There was a big sign that said, FRIENDSHIP WITH THE MIGHTY SOVIET UNION. Theodore Dreiser and Paul Robeson sent messages of greeting, and so did Earl Browder, head of the American Communist Party.

The convention asked for better pay, better bomb shelters, housing and compensation for air-raid victims, and the restoration of union rights and civil liberties. It also asked for a "people's peace won by the working people of all countries and based on the right of all people to determine their own destiny."

Military police reportedly lurked outside. Herbert Morrison, minister of home security, had threatened to ban the meeting, but in the end he allowed it to proceed.

THAT SAME DAY, Winston Churchill sent a short note to Herbert Morrison about D. N. Pritt and the communists, enclosing one of their recent flyers.

The flyer oughtn't to be allowed, Churchill said. It was contrary to the will of Parliament, and it hampered the government's ability to resist the enemy. Why, Churchill asked, if the fascist Oswald Mosley was in prison, weren't Communists like Pritt also locked up? "The law and regulations ought to be enforced against those who hamper our war effort, whether from the extreme Right or the extreme Left," he said. "Sauce for the goose is sauce for the gander!"

THE FRENCH were calling Winston Churchill the "famisher." "In many respects," wrote Lucien Romero in *Le Figaro,* "totalitarian doctrines are the products of the blockade of 1918." The new blockade, too, Romero said, "kills liberalism." It was January 13, 1941.

CATHOLIC PRIESTS gathered photos of some churches and a monastery filled with historical relics that had been bombed in Düsseldorf. They forwarded the photographs to the Vatican.

THE *JAPAN ADVERTISER* carried an editorial about Pearl Harbor. "Huge overseas naval concentrations are equivalent to extension of national boundaries," the newspaper said. "In America's case, they suggest a dictatorship over the parallels of latitude below Pearl Harbor, an invitation to others to keep away, therefore a challenge and threat, preliminaries to hostilities, hence a contradiction of America's announced policy of keeping its fighting sons at home." It was January 17, 1941.

The sixteenth annual Conference on the Cause and Cure of War was not held that January. It was canceled for lack of funds.

CHURCHILL AND HIS CABINET were tired of the *Daily Worker.* The wide coverage of the People's Convention, with its demand for a negotiated peace of the masses, was the last straw. It was January 18, 1941.

A government source told a *New York Times* reporter that the cabinet was about to suppress the *Daily Worker,* as it had earlier suppressed Oswald Mosley's Fascist party and its newspaper, *Action.* The necessary legislation was all ready to go. "While fun is fun, matters have gone far enough," said the source.

Three days later, police from Scotland Yard raided the *Daily Worker* offices. It was now illegal to print, distribute, or in any way assist in the publication of either the *Daily Worker* or a tiny mimeographed publication called *The Week.*

Herbert Morrison, minister of home security, said in Parliament that the government could not allow newspapers to be published that would "weaken the will of our people." The *Daily Worker,* Morrison said, had suggested that "our people have nothing to gain from victory, and that the hardships and sufferings of warfare are unnecessary and imposed by a callous government carrying on a selfish conflict in the interest of privileged classes."

No force that consciously or unconsciously impeded the war effort or helped the enemy could be tolerated, Morrison said. He was cheered.

The Communist party was not banned, just its paper. Cecil King, editor of the *Daily Mail,* was bothered by the action. "It is not in the interest of any paper that any other paper should be suppressed," he said. "It gives the Communists wonderful publicity and is of inestimable value to them."

IN DRESDEN, Victor Klemperer wrote down his impossible wish: to drive around the United States for a year in his own car, speaking English, reading newspapers and magazines, and going to movies. "Then study and write about American literature in my own house on the American East Coast," he wrote. "But I am going to be sixty and my heart rebels every day."

His wife, Eva, was prone to melancholy, too. And of course with the immigration quota it was very difficult to get into the States. But even if he could, what would he do there? His English wasn't good. Who would have him? It was January 21, 1941.

IN TOKYO, the American ambassador to Japan heard something about a possible surprise attack. "There is a lot of talk around town to the effect that the Japanese, in case of a break with the United States, are planning to go all out in a surprise mass attack at Pearl Harbor," the ambassador, Joseph Grew, wrote in his diary. "Of course I informed my government." It was January 24, 1941.

HOPKINS ASKED ROOSEVELT if he could stay in England a little longer. Roosevelt said yes but told him to keep sending reports. The Lend-Lease Bill would probably go to vote around the end of February, Roosevelt told him, and things looked encouraging. "Do get some sleep."

It was January 29, 1941.

HITLER BEGAN PAYING more attention to Roosevelt's idea of lending weapons to England. He warned 13,000 cheerers in the Sports Palace that America should stay out of the war. Germany had novel weapons coming—"blue wonders." He had nothing against the American people; he had no claims against the United States at all, he said.

Hitler then repeated his prewar threat: If international Jewry pushed Germany into a world war, the Jews would be finished in Europe.

It was January 30, 1941.

ADMIRAL RICHARDSON greeted Admiral Kichisaburo Nomura, who was passing through Honolulu on his way to San Francisco and from there to Washington to take up his duties as ambassador. It was January 31, 1941.

Richardson liked Nomura—"an intelligent and friendly person"—and put on a lunch party for him. "Admiral Nomura, I speak for the officers of the United States Navy when I express the professional gratitude which we feel in having a Japanese Naval Officer appointed to such a high diplomatic post," Richardson said at the lunch. "We hope that your mission to the United States will be fully successful."

It was Richardson's last day on the job; Roosevelt had relieved him of his command a few weeks earlier.

THE BRITISH INFORMATION MINISTRY turned out leaflets describing Harry Hopkins's visit and dropped them on Germany. And the Royal Air Force made some daring raids while Hopkins was there, too. It was January 1941.

One raid was a 3:00 A.M. flight to Padua and Mestre, the industrial port near Venice. "Over Venice we circled 'round to draw their fire," said a wing commander. He and his crew swooped past the chimneys of Mestre, shot two sentries standing at a fort, and rose up again to drop the bombload. "We were carrying one of our heaviest bombs and when it burst it nearly blew us out of the air," the wing commander said. It landed on or near a building "with a lot of pipes around it." Then they dropped down again, flying around the spires of Padua. They strafed the airport, showering leaflets as they went. At last it was time to turn for the Alps and home.

In Germany, the RAF created what was described as a "lake of fire" at Wilhelmshaven.

TOGETHER, WINSTON CHURCHILL and Harry Hopkins came up with a list of what England needed in the way of "hoses" from the United States. They needed so many ships, so many aircraft engines, so many guns, and so much ammunition—twenty million rounds of .50-caliber ammunition, "and as many extra fifty caliber gun barrels as are available." The need was for big planes, middle-size planes, and little planes—but especially big planes:

> The maximum number of B-17, BS C's or D's in addition to
> the 20 already agreed upon to be sent to England immedi-

ately. Planes should be sent completely ready for immediate operation, including spare parts, bombs and ammunition. Crews urgently needed.

Hopkins and Churchill wanted the two countries to work out a plan to ferry the bombers to England using American crews. "This would release nearly 800 British R.A.F. personnel." And they wanted eighty trained observers, half from the airplane manufacturers and half from the army and navy, to go to England to teach British crews how to use the planes.

Churchill got on the radio and said to Roosevelt, "Give us the tools and we'll finish the job." It was February 9, 1941.

HARRY HOPKINS flew back to the United States. There was something big waiting for him at the airport: a new Consolidated B-24 bomber, the first of twenty-six that were going from San Diego to England. "The giant bomber bore the insignia of the Royal Air Force and was camouflaged in mottled gray-green," said *The New York Times*. "Greatest secrecy was maintained when the plane landed. Either by accident or design, it appeared over the field when the Yankee Clipper bearing Harry L. Hopkins, President Roosevelt's adviser, was arriving at the marine terminal." The airplane could deliver more than four tons of bombs to any place in Europe, the article said. It was February 17, 1941.

American factories would eventually manufacture 18,482 B-24 Liberators.

JAMES CONANT, the president of Harvard University, attended a conference sponsored by the Chemical Warfare Service in Washington. The purpose was: "To consider the possibility of providing for additional development space and facilities for the Chemical Warfare Service in order that any new ideas, devices, or processes developed on the laboratory basis by the National Defense Research Committee might be tested out on a large scale to determine their probable application for military purposes." The committee recommended setting up a large laboratory at MIT. It was February 1941.

During the First World War, James Conant had been in charge of manufacturing lewisite, a war gas that smelled like geraniums. He had set up a large lewisite factory near Cleveland, for which service he won a medal. A boatload of lewisite had been on its way to Europe in 1918 when Germany capitulated. The gas bombs went into the sea.

In peacetime, James Conant was the president of a university— and a good president, too, although he imposed limits on the number of Jews hired and admitted. During wartime, he was the president of a university, and he was also in charge of Division B of the National Defense Research Committee. Division B covered bombs, fuels, gases, and chemical problems. Conant's group was interested in perfecting new ways to stun, frighten, blind, sicken, or kill people—chemical weapons, germ weapons, and new kinds of incendiary weapons: blue wonders from the United States.

Testifying before the Senate Foreign Relations Committee in favor of the Lend-Lease Bill, Conant said: "We must bravely do the things that we know ought to be done. And we must lay the moral, intellectual and spiritual foundations for the kind of world we want our children to inherit."

AT AUSCHWITZ, a large prison camp in Poland, two Polish prisoners wearing underpants and gas masks filled a room with dirty clothes. "There were very many lice in the clothes," one prisoner, Andrzej Rablin, testified later; the lice fell onto the floor. They threw pea-size crystals of a substance called Zyklon Blausaure—"Cyclone Blue-acid," a powerful insecticidal fumigant and rat poison—onto the lice. "After throwing the crystals we went out, closed the door and stuck strips of paper over the gaps." The lice died.

It was early 1941.

A DRAFT RESISTER, Albert Herling, said to a judge: "I do not have any right to take part in any legislation the result of which would be a sacrifice of life. One of the things I do not want to see is for the United States of America to become a totalitarian country." The judge sentenced Herling to two years in prison.

SENATOR BURTON WHEELER, a Democrat from Montana, made a long speech against Roosevelt's Lend-Lease Bill. The bill was supported, he said, by "international bankers"—Rothschilds, Warburgs, Sassoons—who were using their influence to bring the United States into the war. It was February 14, 1941.

George Gordon Battle, head of the Council Against Intolerance in America, said that Burton was playing the Nazis' game. By referring to international bankers, he had injected "a deplorable note of bigotry" into his argument.

TEN THOUSAND JEWS were deported from Vienna to Poland, on the urging of party leader Baldur von Schirach, patron of the Hitler Youth. There were still about fifty thousand Orthodox Jews there, *The New York Times* said. "Most of them are very old or very young." It was February 19, 1941.

JOSEPH GOEBBELS was working on a long article for *Das Reich* about Winston Churchill. It was February 1941. Goebbels went through some of Churchill's old Boer War pieces in the *Morning Post,* quoting extracts. Then he seems to have taken a moment to look searchingly at a photograph of the prime minister. "His face is devoid of one single kindly feature," Goebbels wrote. "This man walks over dead bodies to satisfy his blind and presumptuous personal ambition. The end of a cigar stuck between his lips is the last vestige of a voluptuous life coming to a close."

ROBERT MENZIES, the prime minister of Australia, went to Chequers to visit the Churchills. It was February 22, 1941.

Mary Churchill, Winston's seventeen-year-old daughter, was, Menzies said, "the freshest and best looking girl I have seen for years." Churchill himself, though, was a holy terror and not a good listener. "Oratorical even in conversation. The master of the mordant phrase and yet, I would think, almost without real humour. Enjoys hatred."

VICTOR KLEMPERER had to sell his car to a salvage dealer. A compulsory-sale ordinance was in force. Two small boys watched the dealer tie Klemperer's car to his own. "The Jew's car, the Jew's car," they chanted. But the dealer, Meincke, was a decent man, Klemperer thought—anti-Nazi, though a party member of many years. It was February 25, 1941.

That night, Victor and Eva went to out to dinner: "We arrived at the Monopol as Hitler was raving the last few sentences into the radio in his paranoid, screaming voice." They stood outside until he was finished with his speech and the singing was over. Then they went in.

MARY BERG, who lived in the Warsaw ghetto, drew a portrait of a girl in her drawing class. It was February 27, 1941; the ghetto was slowly starving. "Many of our students come to class without having eaten anything, and every day we organize a bread collection for them," she wrote in her diary. But the situation of the models was worse. They waited in line to earn money by posing.

> Yesterday our model was an eleven-year-old girl with beautiful black eyes. All the time we were working the child shook with fever and we found it hard to draw her.

They gave her food. "The little girl tremblingly swallowed only part of the bread we collected for her, and carefully wrapped the rest in a piece of newspaper. 'This will be for my little brother,' she said." Then the girl sat quietly as they drew her.

CHURCHILL WROTE a brief secret memo to his air minister. It was about the bombing of Rome. "If we should decide later on to do it," Churchill said, "I hope we shall not confine ourselves to the targets shown in (b), but let them have a good dose where it will hurt them most." It was February 28, 1941.

MENZIES, PRIME MINISTER OF AUSTRALIA, noticed the little bag of sand in every London doorway, ready to be used on incendiary bombs. He had lunch with some judges at Gray's Inn. These old men were having a bad time, Menzies wrote in his diary. "Apart from the dreadful loss of life, it is hard to see mangled or destroyed things of ancient beauty which you have grown up to love."

Menzies then drove to Chequers. Churchill talked about U-boats. The light of battle was in his eyes, Menzies wrote: "In every conversation he ultimately reaches a point where he positively enjoys the war." It was March 1, 1941.

The next day was Sunday. Young Mary Churchill took Menzies and the dog on a grand walk in the morning. "A marvel (she is, not the dog) of vitality and complete naturalness."

Churchill was growing on him, Menzies wrote—the man had an astonishing grasp of detail: "His real tyrant is the glittering phrase—so attractive to his mind that awkward facts may have to give way."

ULRICH VON HASSELL, the anti-Nazi conspirator, talked to yet another German general about a coup—whether and when. "Salient points in the situation," wrote von Hassell. "Rapidly developing food crisis, which will be absolutely threatening if Hitler really attacks Russia in the spring."

An invasion of Russia would be insanity, von Hassell believed; it was being justified on the grounds that Germany needed the wheat fields of the Ukraine and that Russia was a potential ally of England. The result would be complete encirclement.

Germany wasn't going to succeed, the Brazilian ambassador told von Hassell—"a view," wrote von Hassell, "which is spreading rapidly." It was March 2, 1941.

MENZIES WAS OUT walking again in London. It was March 5, 1941. Lincoln Inn's Fields, the large square designed by Inigo Jones, stood in a blue-gray mist with a touch of sunlight. Every so often, Menzies came across a house or a shop destroyed. "It is a bedlamite world," he wrote, "and the hardest thing in it is to discuss and decide (as we do in War Cabinet) policies which, even if successful, must bring the angel of death into many homes."

THE EDITOR OF THE *SUNDAY DISPATCH,* Charles Eade, had lunch with Winston and Clementine Churchill in the basement of 10 Downing Street.

Mrs. Churchill was wearing a scarf with patriotic slogans on it: LEND TO DEFEND and GO TO IT. The guests had sherry, fish patties, white wine, tournedos with mushrooms, peaches, cheese, port, brandy, and cigars. Churchill lit his cigar ten times. James Conant, the president of Harvard, was there, as was Professor Lindemann. It was March 6, 1941.

"We talked about the huge bomb which was dropped about three weeks ago at Hendon," Eade wrote afterward. "Mr Churchill said it weighed about 4,000 lbs and killed about 80 people."

Somebody brought up the absurdity of Englishwomen who offered tea and cigarettes to downed German airmen. Clementine Churchill said that English people cannot hate their enemies. Churchill said: Before the war is over, we shall be hating our enemies all right.

There was, said Eade, a great desire that ordinary German citizens should suffer the effects of British bombing.

Churchill repeated his quip: "Duty must come before pleasure."

Clementine Churchill laughed immoderately. "You are bloodthirsty," she said.

THE BRITISH AIR STAFF distributed a memo, "Chemical Board Crop Subcommittee: First Report." It discussed the possibility of dropping weed seeds, bugs, and plant diseases on Axis crops. Such attacks might have a "moral effect" on the German population, it was contended. It was March 6, 1941.

Another idea was to kill crops or stunt their growth using substances developed by Imperial Chemical Industries, the English company that made bombs and Runcol-brand sprayable mustard gas. ICI's chemical 1313 acted on wheat and other grains, while chemical 1414 ravaged root crops. "In 1941, their use by aerial distribution over Germany was envisaged," a later memo said. "The size of such an operation was, however, in terms of our resources at the time rather formidable and for this reason and because of the early extension of the war into the corn growing areas of South Eastern Europe, active development was discontinued."

ONE NIGHT, ROBERT MENZIES was again at Chequers. Charles De Gaulle was there, and so was Churchill's son-in-law, Duncan Sandys. Sandys was a "whole-hogger," Menzies wrote: "hang Hitler and wipe out 40 millions of Germans." To which Churchill had a fine-sounding retort:

> In war—fury
> In defeat—defiance
> In victory—magnanimity
> In peace—good will.

It was March 8, 1941.

IN LONDON, the Café de Paris nightclub, below the Rialto theater, was hit by a powerful bomb. It had a dance floor that was supposed to be safe but wasn't. The bandleader, Ken "Snakehips" Johnson, was decapitated. "Gentle, magnetic Snakehips Johnson with his thin elegant face and his joyous rhythm," wrote a teenage diarist named Joan Wyndham. "They were dancing 'Oh, Johnny' when the bomb fell. The couples on the floor, killed by the blast, stood for some seconds as if they were still dancing, just leaning a little—then fell, heaped on top of each other."

Afterward, looters moved among the corpses, feeling for pockets and necklaces, cutting off ringed fingers. Some of the corpses went to Charing Cross Hospital, which had a small elevator. Each dead person, tied to a gurney, was tipped upward to fit in the elevator to go down to the morgue, accompanied by a living person. "That, in the dark, with the body tending to fall on you, was a very disagreeable task," one doctor recalled. It was March 8, 1941.

EDWARD R. MURROW watched a farmer trying to fill a bomb crater in his field. It was March 9, 1941. "The bombs this spring will be bigger and there'll be more of them," he said on the radio. "Berlin and London will continue to claim that their bombs hit the military targets while the enemy's strike mainly churches, schools, hospitals, and private dwellings."

Murrow believed that the United States must send more weapons to England and enter the war.

GENERAL DE GAULLE was asleep at Chequers. "Mr. Churchill came and woke me up to tell me, literally dancing with joy, that the American Congress had passed the Lend-Lease bill."

Hitler said he wished he had a long-range bomber to attack American cities—that would teach the American Jews a lesson. He gave the Propaganda Ministry permission to assail the United States. "Now we shall let rip," said Goebbels.

"Reprisals on Jews Hinted," was a subhead in *The New York Times* just after the passage of the Lend-Lease Bill.

> Political circles in Berlin allege further that the connection of names like Frankfurter, Cohen and Baruch with the lease-lend bill demonstrated for whose interest the United States was embarking upon this lethal step.

"The Jew Frankfurter did them no service by getting around and undermining American neutrality," said Berlin's *Borsen Zeitung*. European Jews were now burdened with a "heavy responsibility," the paper said.

"We now know for what and against whom we are standing," said the *Völkischer Beobachter.* "The final battle begins." It was March 12, 1941.

A BRITISH NAVIGATOR named George Carter was in a Whitley airplane flying to Berlin. "I hope we knock the blazes out of the target (which incidentally is the post office in the centre of the city)," Carter wrote his girlfriend as he flew. He had brought along a brick and a piece of concrete and some "personal messages to the. Hun" to drop from the plane.

Over Berlin, he got smoke in his eyes from the terrifyingly heavy flak. "I let our bombs go in the middle of the city. I hope they helped our war effort. I could not see where they landed."

It was full moon, March 1941.

CHURCHILL GAVE a progress report to Anthony Eden, his foreign secretary, who was out of the country: "Everything is going quite nicely here, and we have begun to claw the Huns down in the moonlight to some purpose. God bless you all." It was March 14, 1941.

ETTY HILLESUM, in Amsterdam, wrote in her diary: "It is the problem of our age: hatred of Germans poisons everyone's mind." She'd had, she remembered, a thought a few weeks earlier that "surfaced in me like a hesitant, tender young blade of grass thrusting its way through a wilderness of weeds."

The thought was: Suppose that there were only one decent German in all of Germany. That decent German should be cherished. "And because of that one decent German it is wrong to pour hatred over an entire people," she wrote. "Indiscriminate hatred is the worst thing there is. It is a sickness of the soul."

It was March 15, 1941.

ULRICH VON HASSELL wrote in his diary that he had all but given up on Generals Halder and Brauchitsch. No coup or uprising could come from them—they were weak, he thought, no more than Hitler's caddies.

"An indescribable hatred is piling up against us," von Hassell wrote. It was March 16, 1941.

GOEBBELS HEARD about the recent deportations. "Vienna will soon be entirely Jew-free," he noted in his diary. "And now it is Berlin's turn. I am already discussing the question with the Führer and Dr. Frank." It was March 18, 1941. One of Goebbels's assistants had a talk with Adolf Eichmann and one of Albert Speer's assistants. Speer's assistant agreed that the Berlin Jews should go, pointing out that the Jews used twenty thousand apartments in Berlin at a time when Berlin had a housing shortage.

But several days later, Goebbels found out that the Jews couldn't go. They were doing essential work, and dangerous work, in weapons factories. The Jews were necessary to the success of the war effort.

AN EDITOR AT *TIME* MAGAZINE got a small black coffin in the mail. Inside a note said: "Read GERMANY MUST PERISH! Tomorrow you will receive your copy." It was March 1941. *Germany Must Perish* was a self-published book by Theodore Kaufman, a ticket seller from Brooklyn. It argued that twenty thousand surgeons performing twenty-five operations every day would take about a month to render the German army sterile. The rest of the male population would take another three months. Women would take longer, perhaps three years.

The editor at *Time* thought this would make an interesting story, which it did. Back in 1939, Sterilizer Kaufman, as *Time* called him, had appointed himself chairman of a group called the American Federation of Peace and had urged that the populace of the United States stay out of European wars or submit to sterilization. Now, in 1941, in the middle of a war, Kaufman was going after Germany. The program would be easy to administer, he said: "Just like registering for social security." Soon, the German race would be extinct.

Goebbels pounced on this crank effusion. "Had he written this book for us, he could not have made it any better," he said in his diary. He published extracts and an analysis of it in pamphlet form, playing up its danger. Passages were read on the radio. Women's magazines published scornful articles. Kaufman was transformed into a powerful shadowy figure—a member of the Roosevelt brain trust, "one of the closest advisors to the New York Jew Samuel Rosenman, who as is well known provides advice and assistance in speechwriting to the current President of the United States."

THOMAS MANN, the expatriate writer, recorded a message to the German people. It was broadcast by the BBC. Mann said: "Have you heard that the so-called Lend-Lease Bill, the law which authorizes the most all-embracing help for England, has now been approved by the Senate of the United States by a great majority?" Germany, he said, was now at war not only with the British empire but with America, too—and the situation grew more oppressive every day. "What shall become of you?" Mann asked. "If you are defeated, the vindictiveness of the whole world will break loose against you."

It was March 1941.

MENZIES WALKED AROUND LONDON after a bad raid. "Street after street afire," he wrote, "poor old people shocked & dazed are led along to shelter." He was grimly glad to have seen it, he said. "I am all for peace when it comes, but it will be a tragedy for humanity if it comes before these beasts have had their own cities ravaged. The Hun must be made to learn through his hide."

It was March 21, 1941.

HEINRICH HIMMLER, head of the SS, asked Viktor Brack to investigate something. Brack, who was Philip Bouhler's assistant, had supervised the T-4 euthanasia program. Brack was told to see about using X-rays to secretly sterilize deported Jews. A blending of the western strain of Jewry with the eastern strain, Himmler thought, in his race-fetishistic way, might be an even greater danger to Germany than either one of the two strains separately. He'd talked this problem over with the Führer; sterilization might be the answer. It was March 1941.

Brack looked into the question with some care and wrote a top-secret report, signed "Heil HITLER! Brack." "One practical way of proceeding," wrote Brack, "would be, for instance, to let the persons to be treated approach a counter, where they could be asked to answer some questions and fill in forms, which would take them two or three minutes." During that time, their gonads or their ovaries would be subjected to a high-radiation dose emanating from two hidden X-ray sources.

The disadvantage to this method was that "other tissues of the body will be injured," Brack pointed out. "If the X-ray intensity is too high, those parts of the skin which the rays have reached will exhibit symptoms of burns—varying in severity in individual cases—in the course of the following days or weeks." Thus, although mass sterilization could be carried out without difficulty, Brack said, it was impossible to do it without the persons concerned knowing it was done.

Himmler's aide sent a reply: Himmler was in Greece, but he thanked Brack very much for his report on X-ray castration. "He has read the report with interest and will discuss this question with you at the first opportunity."

THE YUGOSLAVIAN PRIME MINISTER, Dragisha Cvetkovitch, was tilting toward Hitler. Alerted, Churchill threatened Cvetkovitch: The British empire had unchallengeable command of the seas, and with help from the Americans it would soon rule the air as well, he wrote. If Yugoslavia joined the Axis, "her ruin will be certain and irreparable." It was March 22, 1941. Cvetkovitch, unswayed, signed a pact with Germany.

Within forty-eight hours, a military coup, encouraged and funded by the British Special Operations Executive, was in motion in Belgrade. It was bloodless and fast. The Serbian head of the Yugoslavian air force took over the radio station and the telephone company. Artillery and machine-gun units imposed order. The royal palace was sealed. Prince Paul was forced to abdicate and sent to Greece with his family; a new teenage king, Peter II, was sworn in at the Belgrade cathedral. English and French flags came out; crowds filled the capital singing the Serbian anthem. "Few revolutions have gone more smoothly," Churchill recalled with satisfaction. On the radio he announced that he had great news: "Early this morning the Yugoslav Nation found its soul."

HITLER HEARD of the revolution in Yugoslavia and at first thought it was a joke. Then he began to plan furiously—Churchill described his state of mind as that of a "boa constrictor who had already covered his prey with his foul saliva and then had it suddenly wrested from his coils." Hitler called in Goering and other military leaders and told them to "destroy Yugoslavia militarily and as a national unit." No diplomatic messages, no ultimatums. The blow was to be carried out with lightning speed and "unmerciful harshness."

CHURCHILL WAS in the smoking room of the House of Commons again, drinking his sherry. England had a real army now, he said. "We have tanks—good tanks. We have guns." It was April 1, 1941.

Harold Nicolson thought he looked better than he had in years. "All that puffy effect has gone and his face is almost lean, with the underlip pouting defiance all the time."

LYLE WILSON, a United Press reporter, reported on air-raid precautions in Germany. It was April 2, 1941.

There were two exits out of most shelters now, Wilson reported: "Some grim things happened last autumn in Germany when direct hits set fire to buildings above sheltered tenants and roasted them down below, or when bombs burst water pipes and blocked single exits, leaving refugees below stairs to drown." Yellow signs saying TO THE AIR RAID SHELTER, with red arrows, were to be seen all over Germany. In Bremen and Hamburg, shelters for two thousand people had gone up, but in Berlin most people still just used their basements.

"Hardest hit are the Jews," wrote Wilson. "I was told that they no longer were permitted to share the Aryan shelter but were compelled to find such safety as they could unless the building basement was large enough to provide a special shelter for them."

The next day, the German government issued a new punitive rule: Jews would receive no pay for time spent in air-raid shelters.

IN MANCHESTER, ENGLAND, six thousand apprentice engineers went on strike for higher pay. Ernest Bevin, the minister of labor, had six of them arrested, and the strike was over.

It was April 4, 1941.

CHURCHILL SENT A letter to General Dusan Simovitch, head of the Yugoslavian air force, to warn him of intelligence reports that German bombers were converging on his country and to urge him to fire the first shot. This was the ideal moment to attack Albania, Churchill said, and collect the "masses of equipment" there. He closed by sending Simovitch his heartiest good wishes.

The Germans, in Operation Strafgericht ("retribution"), took off from Romanian airfields and bombed Belgrade for three days. The railroad station, the opera house, the power plant, and much else were destroyed; the palace of King Peter was damaged. "Stupefied inhabitants did not venture from their cellars for days on end," a United Press reporter wrote. The American vice-consul said Belgrade was "a city of dead."

Churchill then broadcast a message in Serbo-Croatian, offering his heartfelt sympathy for the murdered women and children and urging the country to fight on against the furious onslaught. British cities, too, had suffered, Churchill pointed out. British women and children had been murdered. Yugoslavian peasants, he exorted, rise and defend the rights of man as you did in the sixteenth century! Your reward would come—your courage would "shine in the pages of history."

The resistance collapsed almost immediately.

Later, in his war memoirs, Churchill took a moment to describe the agony of the animals in the Belgrade zoo.

"A stricken stork hobbled past the main hotel, which was a mass of flames," he wrote. "A bear, dazed and uncomprehending, shuffled through the inferno with slow and awkward gait down towards the Danube."

THE KEEP AMERICA OUT of War Congress met at Town Hall in New York. Jeannette Rankin said: "You cannot have war and democracy; you cannot have war and liberty." Rabbi Sidney Goldstein, chairman of the War Resisters League, said: "Democracy was never in greater danger than it is today." Norman Thomas said the country should have a national vote before going to war. Oswald Garrison Villard said that Roosevelt's Four Freedoms "cannot sustain the shock of our entering and pursuing this war."

It was April 6, 1941.

TIME MAGAZINE visited some of the refugee camps in France. "All the refugees now dream of escaping to the U.S.," said *Time,* "but it is only a dream. Most of them have sunk into the apathy of boredom, have lost all hope of ever again leading civilized lives." It was April 7, 1941.

THE CENTER OF BERLIN, the area around the Unter den Linden, where Goebbels and his students had burned books nine years earlier, was burning again. It was April 9, 1941.

The State Library, the university, and the crown prince's palace were hit. Thirty firebombs ignited the Berlin State Opera House, where Wilhelm Furtwangler conducted Wagner operas. Its walls still stood, but the stage was a roofless ruin. Hitler ordered Albert Speer to rebuild it immediately. Then he left the city. He spent two weeks living in a train parked in the mouth of an alpine tunnel, talking to his commanders. The train was named *Amerika.*

Churchill had some good news to report to the House of Commons. "The sorties which we are now accustomed to make upon German harbors and cities are increasing both in the number of aircraft employed and in the weight of the discharge with every month that passes," he said. "In some cases we have already in our raids exceeded in severity anything which a single town has in a single night experienced over here."

He looked forward, he said, to moonlight.

POPE PIUS XII, the former Cardinal Pacelli, made an Easter broadcast. "We must lament the fact that the limits of legitimate warfare have been repeatedly exceeded," the pope said. "May all belligerents, who also have human hearts molded by mothers' love, show some feeling of charity for the suffering of civilian populations." It was April 13, 1941.

VICTOR KLEMPERER WROTE: "I dread the thought of the USA." It was April 14, 1941. Klemperer thought of the intellectual sterility of having to study English grammar. "I often say to myself now: After all I have a long, interesting, not even so unsuccessful life behind me, and, whatever happens, only a remnant before me— why does it matter so much?" He was accumulating notes on the vocabulary of National Socialism, gathering evidence of the means by which a military dictatorship deformed the language it used.

PLANES FROM THE ROYAL AIR FORCE dropped some big bombs on the harbors of Lorient and Brest, on the coast of France. It was April 14, 1941, a cloudy night. This was the forty-ninth bombing of Lorient and the fifty-fourth bombing of Brest. The *Scharnhorst* and the *Gneisenau* were docked at Brest; at Lorient were pens where German U-boats returned for refueling and repair. The U-boats were sinking merchant ships that were going back and forth in convoys between the United States and England. The ships were filled with food and weapons.

It was practically impossible, with the bombs that the RAF had, to destroy ships or U-boats by night. But it was possible to devastate the inhabited area near the U-boats and ships. If the British firebombed the general vicinity of Brest and Lorient, fewer people would be willing to work there—the bombing would thus amount to a kind of reverse blockade, similar to the one Portal had imposed on the tribesmen in Yemen.

Shortly after the April 14 raid, an angry representative of the Vichy government held a press conference. The raid was "savage," he said. Brest had been bombed for seven hours; sixty-four people had died when a bomb hit a civil hospital. "It is impossible," the Vichy spokesman said, "to accept without protest the repeated bombardments, chiefly affecting the civilian French population, and the ravaging of great French ports without military objectives or importance so far as the war is concerned."

THE PRIME MINISTER wrote Sir Archibald Sinclair about chemical weapons. "I remain far from satisfied with the state of our preparations for offensive chemical warfare," he wrote, "should this be forced upon us by the actions of the enemy."

Five-and-a-half-inch and six-inch gas shells were in short supply, he wrote Sinclair. Production of the thirty-pound light-case gas bomb, the Mark I, which could hold either gas or leaflets, was lagging. And the output of phosgene gas was inadequate. "I propose to examine this whole position at an early meeting of the Defence Committee," he wrote. It was April 15, 1941.

TWO RED CROSS SHIPS were getting ready to leave for Marseilles from a pier on Staten Island. They were operated by the French Line, and they held flour and dried milk. The Red Cross asked that some machine guns and antiaircraft guns stored in their holds be removed—they didn't want to give the British "any excuse for stopping the ships."

A passenger got off a boat arriving from Martinique and said to a reporter: "They should not send the stuff. I believe it may never get to the French people. The Germans and Italians have a commission which checks everything that comes in and goes out." It was April 16, 1941.

Herbert Hoover, in a letter to *The Times* of London, again pointed out that the food distribution was to be monitored at every step by observers. If the Germans appropriated the milk and flour, the world would know, and the shipments would stop.

GENERAL RAYMOND E. LEE, the American air attaché, was back in England, sizing up the situation. "The people strike me as being much more solemn than they were in January." He went to a theater in London where they showed four propaganda films. One was of British soldiers in training, shouting, "Kill, kill, kill." Lee had talked to his friend Ted. "Ted tells me that the people in the Air Force have given up the sporting idea now and are grimly determined to kill as many Germans as they can by any means possible," Lee wrote. It was April 16, 1941.

GENERAL HAP ARNOLD, chief of the U.S. Army Air Corps, was in England on that day, too, watching planes get ready for trips to Germany. Harry Hopkins had written Churchill about Arnold in advance: President Roosevelt was anxious for Arnold to be "exposed to the actual warfare," Hopkins said. The general had been, Hopkins confided, resistant to giving aid to England; he hoped that Churchill would introduce him around and give him the full treatment—win him over to the necessity for Lend-Lease, in other words.

The raid that night was scheduled to drop 24,000 pounds of bombs on Berlin. Then, at the last minute, the target city was switched to Bremen. Two hundred planes were going. At Bomber Command's underground headquarters, Arnold listened to a description of the new British four-thousand-pound bomb, with a thin riveted shell. "Explodes above ground so that results are obtained by blast rather than fragments," Arnold noted in his diary. "We must have some at once."

He was flown to a wing station where men wheeled six cases of incendiaries and five five-hundred-pound bombs out to each Vickers Wellington bomber and loaded them in. Two of the planes carried four-thousand-pound bombs. They took off, one every two minutes, flying to the shipyards at Bremen.

HAP ARNOLD returned to his London hotel, where he was sharing a suite with Pete Quesada, one of his flying buddies. There had been a bad raid in the city while he had been away, the worst yet of the war. Selfridge's, the department store, was burning. A land mine had blown out the glass at the Savoy Hotel, where Arnold had had lunch with the secretary of state for air: "Drafty," he noted. Six hundred people were reportedly dead. "Clean up the city and then wait for another one," Arnold wrote. "Back of it all a determination not to be wiped off the map."

He went up to Ditchly and talked to Churchill until two in the morning. Russia, Churchill told him, was "an immoral crocodile waiting in the depths for whatever prey may come his way." But Churchill's main message was: England needed long-range bombers, as fast as the United States could send them over.

Arnold's valet opened his curtains for him the next morning and brought him tea in bed. Arnold went downstairs and inspected the deer heads mounted on the walls. "Some of the oldest deer heads known," he wrote. "They were shot back in the 1600s by various people." There was a grand lunch with the Churchills, Averell Harriman, and the president-in-exile of Czechoslovakia.

After some chat about the new British air base in Iraq and about the need for a proper propaganda program in the United States, Churchill took Arnold on a drive around the countryside. When they got back, Charles Portal of the Royal Air Force, Arnold's counterpart, was waiting for them. The two air-power enthusiasts talked and talked. Portal told Arnold about a possible six-thousand-pound bomb. "Portal is a brilliant man who does things, is capable and knows his job. Prime Minister a huge personality and has a most wonderful mind. On to bed at 2 A.M."

GEORGE BELL, the bishop of Chichester, wrote a letter to *The Times* of London. It was April 17, 1941.

The bishop had been moved by what the pope had said on Easter about the suffering of civilian populations. It was barbarous, Bell maintained, for any belligerent nation to attack and terrorize unarmed women and children. "If Europe is civilized at all," he asked, "what can excuse the bombing of towns by night?" He offered a proposal. What if the British government solemnly declared that it would not bomb at night, provided that the German government promised to do the same? "If this single limitation were achieved it would at least make a halt in the world's rushing down to ever-deeper baseness and confusion," he said. Gilbert Murray, a classicist at Oxford, wrote in support of Bell's idea, as did Bernard Shaw. The British government made no response.

GERMAN RADIO VOICES explained that the recent fire raid on central London—the one that burned Selfridge's and destroyed part of St. Paul's cathedral—was in answer to the British fire raid on central Berlin: the one that wrecked the opera house. "In the future," said the German high command, "every British air attack on residential districts in Germany will be retaliated in increasingly intense measure." It was April 17, 1941.

THE PRESIDENT OF GENERAL MOTORS, Charles E. Wilson, announced in Detroit that his company had begun production of sixty-one million dollars' worth of machine guns. Long rows of machine-gun barrels lay awaiting assembly at the AC Spark Plug Division in Flint, Michigan. The company's Saginaw Steering Gear division had built a new factory, with glass walls. It was making machine guns, too. It was April 17, 1941.

WINSTON CHURCHILL asked the Defence Committee of the war cabinet to approve a warning to Rome, to be broadcast by the BBC. It was April 18, 1941.

The warning was: If the Axis powers were to bomb Athens or Cairo, "we should begin the systematic bombing of Rome." After talking it over, the committee agreed to say that England would endeavor to spare Vatican City. The press statement went out, and it added a fillip: The English had heard, it said, that Italian planes were prepared to bomb the Vatican using captured English bombs if the British attacked Rome. "It is, therefore, necessary to expose this characteristic trick beforehand," said the statement.

GENERAL RAYMOND LEE eyed the damage after the recent raid. Fortnum and Mason, Dunhills, and Hoby and Gullick, Lee's boot-makers, had "gone west," he noted in his journal. "The more I think about it the more silly it seems to me for the British to keep on bombing Berlin," he wrote. The Germans had only the cross-channel distance from France to cover, after all, and they had more planes. The British should wait until they had more bombers, Lee concluded. "That will probably not be till next year, as most of them will have to come from the United States." It was April 19, 1941.

A NEW AMERICAN PRO-WAR, pro-blockade group released a manifesto. It was April 19, 1941.

The group, quartered in the RKO building on Sixth Avenue in New York, was called Fight for Freedom, Inc. Henry Hobson, an Episcopal bishop from Cincinnati, was its titular head; a venerable senator, Carter Glass, was its honorary chairman; and an advertising executive at Young and Rubicam, Peter Cusick, was its executive secretary. On its committee were William Donovan, President Roosevelt's wide-traveling spy—soon to become the founder and head of the Office of Strategic Services—and Allen W. Dulles, lawyer and future leader of the Central Intelligence Agency. The group received funding from British Security Co-ordination, a covert propaganda agency run by British spy William Stephenson.

The American people must accept the fact that they were already at war, said Fight for Freedom—"whether declared or undeclared." Once we accept that fact, according to the manifesto, "we shall at last find peace within ourselves which can never come as long as we seek safety at the cost of others' sacrifices."

LORD HANKEY became discouraged about Winston Churchill. "The war is going badly," he wrote in his diary. "It always does in the second year. The Greeks are collapsing. Our small supporting force is faced with evacuation. It is Norway all over again. Just the same mistakes." It was April 22, 1941.

The root trouble, Hankey thought, was that everyone in the war cabinet was a yes-man, bemused and under Churchill's spell. "Churchill is running the war as a Dictator," he wrote.

HOWARD SCHOENFELD, in prison in Danbury, Connecticut, for refusing to register for the draft, wanted to skip lunch with sixteen other prisoners to hold a demonstration in support of Student Peace Day. The warden said no to the demonstration. The prisoners said they were sorry, but it was something they had to do. Schoenfeld gave Warden Gerlach a note: "As an expression of solidarity with the student peace strike outside, the majority of people of the United States, and countless millions throughout the world, I intend to refuse to work on April 23, 1941. I am not striking against the U.S. government or the Bureau of Prisons, but against war, which I believe to be the greatest evil known to man."

The warden placed Schoenfeld and the others in solitary confinement, which he called "constructive meditation." He sent a report, along with transcripts of his covertly taped conversations with the resisters, to Washington.

Days went by. The walls and floor of Schoenfeld's cell were bare cement; the door was metal. Schoenfeld wrote novels in his head and braided his beard. "One day I began screaming mad parodies of patriotic music at the top of my lungs," he recalled in a memoir. A guard appeared. Schoenfeld explained that he'd been bitten by a patriot and that he had a case of patriotic fever. The guard told him to shut up. "I fell on my cot and laughed at my own joke."

Another day, one of the protesters, Ernest Kirkjian, sang "Ave Maria." "The holy music sounded incredibly beautiful after the awful days of silence," wrote Schoenfeld, "and it seemed to me I was hearing, really hearing and feeling, the human voice in its true splendor for the first time." In response, others said the Lord's prayer, and then Schoenfeld, Al Herling, and Stan Rappaport said a prayer in Hebrew. "It was a good day."

Weeks went by.

THE BRITISH AIR MINISTRY produced a new, more pragmatic paper on bombing policy. It was April 24, 1941.

Without moonlight, it was impossible to attack a specific target successfully, the Air Ministry paper observed. For three-fourths of the month, therefore, blitz bombing was the only option: "It is only possible to obtain satisfactory results by the 'Blitz' attack of large working class and industrial areas in the towns." Even hitting the towns, the paper went on to say, was a matter of great difficulty unless the towns were near a body of water.

The report's appendix listed some city targets near water, suitable for moonless attacks: Düsseldorf, Duisburg, and the east and west banks of Cologne. They were rail centers and "congested industrial towns, where the psychological effect will be greatest."

The appendix ended with a recommendation that delayed-action bombs make up 10 percent of the tonnage dropped, "so as to prevent or seriously interfere with fire fighting, repair and general traffic organization."

CHARLES LINDBERGH, who had been speaking out against Lend-Lease, was trying to decide whether he should resign from the army. Roosevelt had obliquely charged him with treason. "Here I am stumping the country with pacifists and considering resigning as a colonel in the Army Air Corps, when there is no philosophy I disagree with more than that of the pacifist, and nothing I would rather be doing than flying in the Air Corps," he wrote in his diary. "If only the United States could be on the right side of an intelligent war!" It was April 25, 1941.

CHURCHILL NOTED some uneasiness. His generals had warned him not to invade Greece, but he had insisted on it, and it was another Narvik. Yugoslavia was lost. And the air war was taking a toll. There was widespread looting now and homelessness, as well as constant numbing death and ugliness and waste. The rat population had surged. As a tonic, Churchill went on a tour of destroyed places in London, Liverpool, Cardiff, Swansea, and Bristol. Then he went on the radio. Yes, he knew of the uneasiness. Yes, he had seen fine buildings "blasted into rubble-heaps of ruin." Yes, people had died. But morale was, he claimed, most high and splendid. "This ordeal by fire has, in a certain sense, even exhilarated the manhood and the womanhood of Britain," he said. It had lifted them above material facts "into that joyous serenity we think belongs to a better world than this."

And the unwhimpering stoicism would bear fruit soon: "During the last year we have gained by our bearing and conduct a potent hold upon the sentiments of the people of the United States," Churchill said. "They have turned a large part of their gigantic industry to making the munitions which we need. They have even given us or lent us valuable weapons of their own." England and America were closely bound up with each other now.

"There are less than seventy million malignant Huns—some of whom are curable and others killable," Churchill said. The population of the British empire and the United States together amounted to some two hundred million. The Allies had more people and made more steel, he said. The Allies would win. It was April 27, 1941.

CHURCHILL WROTE a "Most Secret" directive to the war cabinet. "It may be taken as almost certain that the entry of Japan into the war would be followed by the immediate entry of the United States on our side," he wrote; British plans must be guided by that fact.

He also ordered staff officers who were considering surrender to keep fighting until half their men were killed or wounded, and to use hand pistols if necessary. "The honour of a wounded man is safe," he said. "Anyone who can kill a Hun or even an Italian has rendered good service." It was April 28, 1941.

SOME IRAQI TROOPS gathered on a plateau near Fallujah, Iraq. It was May 1941. Churchill, in his bombproof map room, had his eyes now on the Middle East. Yugoslavia and Greece, set ablaze and then left in Nazi hands, were lost—but Axis forces might yet swarm over from somewhere and capture Iraq's oil.

"Troops should be sent to Basra as fast as possible," Churchill wrote to General Ismay of the Chiefs of Staff. The Iraqi prime minister, Rashid Ali, sent word that he could not allow any more disembarkations of British troops until the troops already in Basra had moved on. Churchill ordered the landings to proceed. British civilians left Baghdad, seeking protection at the Royal Air Force training base at Lake Habbaniya. They got on flying boats and flew to safety.

CHURCHILL TOLD General Wavell to mount a general offensive in Iraq. General Wavell contested the order—there weren't enough troops, he said, and there were other countries to consider. He advised negotiations with Rashid Ali. Churchill countermanded him, whereupon Wavell sent a warning. "I consider the prolongation of fighting in Iraq will seriously endanger the defense of Palestine and Egypt," Wavell said. "The political repercussions will be incalculable." He asked again to be allowed to negotiate.

"I am deeply disturbed at General Wavell's attitude," Churchill wrote Ismay. To Wavell he said, "You do not need to bother too much about the long future in Iraq." Wavell's job was to "break into Baghdad, even with quite small forces." Trounce Rashid Ali and get a friendly government set up there, that was Wavell's assignment.

IRAQI TROOPS threatened the British flying school at Habbaniya. Rashid Ali was appealing to Berlin for help. It was time for air control.

Churchill told Wavell to tell the commander of the flying school that it was his duty to "defend Habbaniya to the last." The commander, a man named Smart, rose to the occasion. On May 2, 1941, RAF flight instructors and their cadets made almost two hundred flights over the Iraqis on the plateau, some of them flying out seven times, dropping wing-mounted bombs, and returning. Twenty-two out of sixty-four airplanes were wrecked, and ten pilots lay dead or so badly wounded they couldn't fly. Iraqi airplanes, including American-made Northrop-Douglas attack bombers with Wright Cyclone engines and semiretractable bombsights, arrived on the scene; they began strafing and bombing the flight school and its polo field.

"Iraq situation pretty bad," wrote Under-Secretary Cadogan. "Are we really going to be beaten by Iraquis?!" Cadogan authorized the Air Committee to say that if Habbaniya fell, the Royal Air Force would bomb Baghdad.

HITLER WAS STANDING at a microphone in front of the Reichstag. It was May 4, 1941. He talked about the Jewish-Democratic capitalists and the profits they were making on their war holdings. They wanted a long war, he said. They wanted a return on all the milliards in armaments they had invested. And now Churchill and his accomplices were trying to get help from across the sea.

"My peace offer was alleged to be a sign of fear and cowardice," Hitler said. And Churchill—what did Churchill care for culture or for architecture? "When war broke out he stated clearly that he wanted to have his war, even though the cities of England might be reduced to ruins. So now he has got his war."

Count Ciano, listening in Rome, thought the speech was excellent. "I like the oratory of this man more and more. It is strong and persuasive," he wrote.

ROOSEVELT RELEASED a letter to his secretary of war, Henry Stimson. "The effective defense of this country and the vital defense of other democratic nations requires that there be a substantial increase in heavy bomber production," Roosevelt said. It had to be done: "Command of the air by the democracies must and can be achieved," he said. It was May 5, 1941.

There was a new number in circulation: five hundred heavy bombers per month. The goal was achievable if the automobile industry underwent a gigantic retooling and built planes. Henry Ford was breaking ground for a mile-long plant at Willow Run, Michigan, where sixty thousand people would produce the four-engine B-24 Liberator.

William Knudsen, formerly head of General Motors—now the head of the Office of Production Management—and admirer of the German economic miracle, showed reporters a bottleneck-breaking letter that he'd sent to leaders of the machine-tool industry. "Let's get going and keep going," Knudsen said. "Let's forget everything except the welfare of our country."

THE BRITISH FLIGHT instructors won their great battle. Retreating from the plateau, Iraqi troops made their way down the road toward Fallujah, where they met late-arriving reinforcements. The two groups stopped and began to compare notes. RAF planes spotted this troop concentration and turned the site into a highway of death: "A reinforcing column from Falluja was caught on the road and destroyed by forty of our aircraft dispatched from Habbaniya for the purpose," Churchill wrote. When the "seige of Habbaniya," as he called it, was over on May 7, 1941, fifty-two British airmen were dead or critically wounded; four were in a state of mental collapse. The number of Iraqi dead was not known.

Then, for the last push to Baghdad, new equipment arrived. C. L. Sulzberger, the *New York Times* correspondent, reported that the Royal Air Force was using American-made Curtiss Tomahawk fighters and Glenn Martin 157 bombers to "harass" Rashid Ali's forces. There was word that Rashid had applied for a transit visa to Turkey. In the end, though, the Iraqi prime minister found his way to Persia, and British-friendly royals were reinstalled in the capital. Commander Smart, the overtaxed director of the flying school, had a breakdown; he was flown out, sedated, in a Douglas DC-2.

A GUARD UNLOCKED a metal door on Howard Schoenfeld's cell block. One of the solitary confinees, Donald Benedict, was a very good pitcher; Warden Gerlach needed him for a crucial prison-league softball game. Benedict said he wouldn't play unless everyone in solitary confinement—not just him and not just the pacifists but everybody—was released.

Warden Gerlach pondered for an hour and then ordered everyone's release from solitary. Benedict pitched a no-hitter. The prison erupted in celebration. "It was a mass catharsis of human misery," Schoenfeld wrote. "Some of the men were weeping, others were laughing like madmen. It was like nothing I had ever seen before, and nothing I expect to see again."

A RUMOR BEGAN circulating among Whitehall civil servants and reporters. Eventually the rumor reached *Time* magazine, which called it "eminently credible."

The rumor was that Rudolf Hess, the deputy Führer, had flown to Spain to discuss a peace agreement with Sir Samuel Hoare. Hoare was a possible prime-ministerial successor to Churchill; Churchill had muted his power in London by making him ambassador to Spain. Hess's approach to Hoare, if the rumor was true, raised in some minds the possibility of a double coup: What if the top Nazis deposed Hitler at the same time that Churchill was forced to resign? Was a negotiated peace possible then?

Churchill's doubters were at work in the House of Commons, too. The British army, having retreated from Greece, was now being bombed on the island of Crete; Lord Hankey's notion, that Churchill was acting like a dictator and had nobody around him strong enough to resist his military whims, was gaining whispered currency.

Churchill's response to the doubters was, as always, to write a brilliant fighting speech. I don't need people to say no to me, said Churchill; I need people to say yes to me. "I am the one whose head should be cut off if we do not win the war," he said. "Most of the Members of the House would probably experience an even more unpleasant fate at the hands of the triumphant Hun." Help from the United States was on its way, he promised.

In the end, 447 members of the House of Commons voted their confidence in the prime minister. Three MPs voted no—a socialist lawyer, a Quaker doctor, and a communist. It was May 7, 1941.

AN ARMADA of three hundred planes, including some supplied by the United States, reached Hamburg, Bremen, Emden, and Berlin on a single night. It was May 8, 1941, the day after the vote of confidence in Winston Churchill.

This was a "big show," said the Air Ministry, the biggest yet: "Many great fires were seen raging." One plane overshot Berlin and found Posen, in occupied Poland; a bomb fell near the recently Aryanized Anatomical Institute in the university there, breaking windows and killing people. In the basement of the Anatomical Institute was an oven that the Gestapo used for people they had murdered.

At Hamburg, there were clear skies and a bomber's moon: a stick of explosives split open a row of buildings; oil tanks burned; smoke rose ten thousand feet. Berlin reported victims in apartment houses.

It was the sixty-eighth time Hamburg had been bombed. The next night, the RAF went back to Hamburg. Ninety-four people died in the attack that night, some at a labor camp.

HANS JESCHONNEK, the Luftwaffe's chief of staff, got a telephone call from Hitler at eight o'clock in the morning. "We are staging a reprisal raid on London," Hitler said. It was to be big—all available planes—and it was to be that night. It was May 10, 1941.

Jeschonnek called Hugo Sperrle at the Hotel Luxembourg in Paris and relayed the orders: everything we've got on London. Sperrle, a tall man with a bull's neck and a lizard's mouth, had supervised the bombing of Guernica; he was now in charge of the Luftwaffe's Air Fleet Three. Sperrle called his commanders; his commanders called their crews; the fuel and the weaponry went into the planes.

It wasn't a long flight across the channel. Chandelier flares, their fall slowed by parachutes, lit up the docks, the curve of the Thames, and central London. The planes swooped and released, hundreds of them, and the fires began—like diamonds glittering on velvet, according to one policeman. There were hoses, but there wasn't enough water: The Thames was at low tide. The roof blew off the House of Commons—perhaps this was Hitler's answer to the House's overwhelming vote of confidence in Churchill. More than one hundred thousand books burned in the British Museum; the Coins and Medals Room, the Roman Britain Room, and the Prehistoric Life Room were destroyed. At Queen's Hall, flames swept over instruments owned by the London Symphony Orchestra. Westminster Abbey and St. Paul's cathedral suffered major damage. The northwest wing of the Old Bailey was ruined. More Christopher Wren churches suffered or succumbed—St. Stephen's Walbrook, St. Mildred's, St. Nicholas Cole Abbey, St. Mary-le-Bow. Streetlamps drooped, half melted by the heat. Reverend Pennington-Bickford, of St. Clement Danes church, stood crying with his wife as the bells of his fiercely burning tower—another Wren design—crashed to earth. Hundreds died in air-raid shelters.

"Our eyes were blinded by the glow of the fire raging below us," said one German flier-reporter. "One could recognize a great warehouse here, a large apartment complex there, glowing like a mountain of hot cinders." Hugo Sperrle lost ten planes.

"All that day I sensed a new and intensified hatred of Germany in the people of London," wrote an American journalist, Quentin Reynolds. A woman named Moyra MacLeon wrote in her diary: "I hate Germans and hope we blow the whole bastard lot of them to pieces with their Berlin around their ears."

WHILE THE GERMAN AIR FLEET was leaving for London, Rudolf Hess, the deputy Führer, took off in a Messerschmitt night fighter, wearing his handsome leather boots. He had some food, a fancy camera, and a blue-penciled map. He flew to Scotland and parachuted out of his plane. A farmer came at him with a pitchfork. Hess calmly said he wanted to see the duke of Hamilton. The farmer called the Home Guard. "I have no bombs on my plane, so you need not worry," said Hess. One of the guardsmen offered Hess some milk. Hess brightened. "Have you got milk?"

Churchill was at Chequers with some advisers. He called to ask about the raid. The news was not good. Then he went into the hall to watch *The Marx Brothers Go West*. One of his secretaries, Mary Shearburn, took a call from Downing Street. She called Churchill out of the movie and told him that Rudolf Hess had arrived in Scotland. Churchill's face "puckered with incredulous joy," according to one account. "The worm is in the apple," he said.

But what to do? Hess was on some kind of peace mission, independent of Hitler. The secretary heard Churchill say: "No, he'll be put inside—he'll be interned. The audacity of the man! He'll be interned like anyone else."

Hitler read Hess's farewell letter. "Oh, my God, my God!" he said, stricken. "He has flown to England!"

ROBERT MENZIES, prime minister of Australia, was in Washington, D.C., talking to President Roosevelt. The president was in bed that day with a touch of gastritis. It was May 11, 1941, a Sunday.

"R. is a little jealous of Winston's place in the centre of the picture," Menzies judged. He wondered how and when the United States would join the fight in earnest: Roosevelt's cabinet all wanted it. "But the President, trained under Woodrow Wilson in the last war, waits for an incident, which would in one blow get the USA into war and get R. out of his foolish election pledges that 'I will keep you out of war.' "

Menzies met Senator Claude Pepper—"an ugly fellow, but a real 'smash & grab' supporter of war," he wrote. "Has a dangerous wife, but agreeable."

DR. TOYOHIKO KAGAWA, the writer and Christian reformer, was in Rockefeller Center with Japanese bishop Yoshimune Abé, talking to a *New York Times* reporter. It was May 14, 1941.

Kagawa, a missionary-educated orphan who had lived in the slums of Kobe, had been briefly imprisoned by the Japanese government in 1940 for avowals of pacifism. Some referred to him as

Japan's Gandhi; one writer called him "a Gorki in literature, a Saint Francis in piety, and a Tolstoi in loving sympathy with the poor." Christopher Isherwood, who met him around this time, wrote that Kagawa was "very pale, in his heavy black frock coat, with thick glasses covering his weak, trachoma-inflamed eyes. Because of the trachoma, he wasn't allowed to shake hands: he offered each of us his forearm to grasp in greeting."

To the reporter, Kagawa said that there wasn't nearly as much talk about war among the people of Japan as he had encountered in the United States. The purpose of their trip, Kagawa and Abé explained, was religious, not political or economic or diplomatic. It was prayer—prayer for the preservation of peace between Japan and the United States. "We were thinking what we could contribute," said Abé, "to keep up this good friendship which has endured for eighty years."

IN FRANCE, police woke up several thousand Jews—mostly Polish, Czech, and Austrian men—and put them on locked trains to Lorient, on the coast. From Lorient, the men were sent to three concentration camps, where, said the authorities, they were to work on projects in the region. It was May 15, 1941.

The following night, the Royal Air Force again bombed Lorient and other coastal points. It was, said *The New York Times,* "one of the hardest attacks yet made on that area." Wakeful residents of English towns on the Channel heard the rumble of distant explosions.

MR. AND MRS. OTTO SUESSER and their daughter Hilga arrived at Pier Two in Brooklyn. It was May 17, 1941. Suesser had been in the optical-glass business in Berlin. In October 1940, he and his family had fled to Moscow. From Moscow, they'd taken the Trans-Siberian Railroad to Kobe, Japan. From Kobe, they'd gone to Yokohama, where the Jewish Joint Committee got them a visa for Costa Rica. They got on a freighter bound for Panama. At Panama, the port authorities wouldn't let them land and travel across Panama to Costa Rica. So they continued on to Valparaiso, Chile. In Chile, they were refused admittance. Ecuador and Peru wouldn't have them. They returned by freighter to Panama. Meanwhile, the Jewish Joint Committee had managed to get visas to the United States for the three of them. They got on a different freighter, the *Dona Nati,* which was bringing manganese from the Philippines, and they sailed to Brooklyn. Soon, Otto Suesser said, they would be leaving for San Francisco. San Francisco was where they'd been trying to get to all along.

LORD BOOM TRENCHARD asked himself what should happen next. For a year, the RAF had been unloading everything it had on cities from Schwerte to Kiel to Mannheim to Berlin, and it hadn't worked—no collapse of civilian morale, no revolutionary unrest, no industrial taproot cut. Trenchard's beloved RAF had lost many good airplanes and good men, and the men who made it home, interviewed after their flights, claimed that they'd blasted various objectives. Obviously, they hadn't. All they'd succeeded in doing was to make the Boche mad. And now here was the House of Commons, roofless to the sky. It was the end of May 1941. What next?

Trenchard's answer was: *more*. More bombing. Relentless nightly bombing—heavier bombers, more bombers. No distractions. The English could take it, he wrote in a long memo. "History has proved that we have always been able to stand our Casualties better than other Nations," he wrote. And the Germans couldn't take it. "The German nation is peculiarly susceptible to air bombing." Yes, it was true that "the percentage of bombs which hit the military Target at which they are aimed is not more than one per cent." That was only a problem if the military target was out in the middle of nowhere, like a battleship or an oil field. Ignore those targets. Ignore the French and Belgian coast. Ignore tactical operations in the Mediterranean. Drop more tonnage smack in the midst of Germany, where people live and where no bombs will go to waste: "The 99 per cent. which miss the military target all help to kill, damage, frighten or interfere with Germans in Germany and the whole 100 per cent. of the bomber organisation is doing useful work, and not merely 1 per cent. of it." Any town with more than five thousand inhabitants and some sort of military objective—which would not, of course, be hit 99 percent of the time—was fair game. "Not a single day or night should pass without a visit from our machines," Trenchard wrote. The object was to break them—to make the "civil population of Germany realise what war means."

Portal, head of the Royal Air Force, concurred.

THE HIGH COMMAND of the German army issued a directive. The invasion of Russia was to take place soon, and the military forces that did the invading would need guidance on how to behave. Bolshevism, said the directive, was the enemy of the National Socialist German people, and Germany's struggle was directed against this subversive ideology. "This struggle requires ruthless and energetic action against Bolshevik agitators, guerillas, saboteurs, and Jews, and the total elimination of all active and passive resistance." The directive was dated May 19, 1941.

The army would be doing the SS's work now.

IN WARSAW, Adam Czerniakow, the head of the Jewish Council, went to Gestapo headquarters and told a man there that 1,700 Jewish men and women had died in the first half of May. "I explained that this was due to the insufficient food allocation," Czerniakow wrote in his diary. It was May 19, 1941.

The next day, the Nazi commissioner of Warsaw, Heinz Auerswald, wrote a report on the ghetto. "The situation in the Jewish quarter is catastrophic," Auerswald said. "The corpses of those who have died of starvation lie in the streets. The death rate, 80% from malnutrition, has tripled since February." The bread ration was tiny, and a potato delivery, for which the Jewish community had prepaid, had not yet come, Auerswald said.

Czerniakow had a meeting with Auerswald. "He pointed out that the corpses lying in the streets create a very bad impression," Czerniakow wrote. "Indeed, the corpses do lie unattended (with their faces covered by newspaper and brick)." The ghetto needed food; the ghetto was dying.

Auerswald said he wanted to give the ghetto five hundred tons of oats. Czerniakow, carrying on as best he could, set about trying to find a mill that could grind oats.

REGINALD SORENSEN, a member of the House of Commons, raised Bishop Bell's idea. Mightn't Britain propose to Germany the possibility of a mutually agreed-upon end to bombing at night?

Clement Attlee, the lord privy seal, brusquely rejected Sorensen's suggestion.

Sorensen then pointed out that, in addition to Gilbert Murray, George Bernard Shaw, and two bishops of the Church of England, a considerable number of residents from London's most heavily blitzed areas favored such a proposal.

Attlee replied: "It is not practicable to think you can come to any agreement with people who do not keep their agreements." He was cheered.

Another member of parliament said: "There is a considerable body of opinion in the country which feels that we ought to bomb the Germans much harder than we are doing." More cheering.

It was May 21, 1941.

GANDHI WROTE a letter to one of his closest English associates, Madeleine Mirabehn. "The news about the destruction in England is heart-rending," Gandhi said. "The Houses of Parliament, the Abbey, the Cathedral seemed to be immortal. And yet there is no end. Nevertheless pride rules the English will." He asked: "Is it still bravery?" It was May 22, 1941.

That month Lord Linlithgow, viceroy of India, held about 14,000 of Gandhi's nonviolent resisters in jails.

SEFTON DELMER, the BBC broadcaster, got an order to begin writing covert radio propaganda for German consumption. His first assigned subject was the mysterious flight of Rudolf Hess. To spread anxiety and confusion, Delmer created a character named Der Chef—the Chief. The Chief was supposed to be a fanatical Hitlerian, broadcasting his disgust with the behavior of the Nazi elite.

In his first transmission, Delmer had the Chief—who was in reality an émigré named Peter Seckelmann—say of Rudolf Hess: "As soon as he learns a little of the darker side of the developments that lie ahead, what happens? He loses his head completely, packs himself a satchel full of hormone pills and a white flag, and flies off to throw himself and us on the mercy of that flat-footed bastard of a drunken old Jew Churchill."

Delmer listened to the recording of the broadcast. "The bit I liked best," he said, "was the denunciation of Churchill as a 'flat-footed bastard of a drunken old Jew.'" No German, thought Delmer, would ever believe that British propagandists could refer to their prime minister that way. "This was a phrase, I decided, which was well worth repeating in other broadcasts."

It was May 23, 1941.

SIDNEY GOLDSTEIN, associate rabbi of the Free Synagogue, decided not to speak at the Second National Anti-War Congress. Rabbi Goldstein, a member of John Haynes Holmes's War Resisters League, was opposed to America's entry into the war, but he objected to Senator Burton Wheeler's presence on the program.

"In view of the anti-Jewish statements Senator Wheeler has made privately and publicly," Rabbi Goldstein said, "I can not as a matter of self-respect appear upon the same platform with him."

DAWID SIERAKOWIAK, a seventeen-year-old boy in the Lodz ghetto, was famished. "When I receive my ration of bread," he wrote in his diary, "I can hardly control myself and sometimes suffer so much from exhaustion that I have to eat whatever food I have, and then my small loaf of bread disappears before the next ration is issued, and my torture grows." What could he do? "Our grave will apparently be here." It was May 24, 1941.

SEMI-SECRET, purposely leaked news about the American-trained Chinese air force appeared on page three of *The New York Times*. It was May 24, 1941.

"Chinese aviators have been trained under foreign instructors and now are reported ready to engage Japanese air fighters," said the anonymous author. "China has obtained numerous fighting and bombing planes from the United States and Britain and it is expected these will figure in the proposed retaliation against Japan." The Chinese communists were reportedly involved now, too; they'd asked Chungking for "immediate delivery of American-made bombers and fighters."

The subheadline was: "Bombing of Japanese Cities Is Expected to Result from New View at Chungking."

WALTER DURANTY, a reporter, was back in Honolulu after a trip to Japan, and he had a prediction. "Every day that I stayed in Tokyo my conviction deepened that Japan would not fight unless she was compelled to by the cutting off of her oil supply," Duranty wrote in *The New York Times*. A war carried grave risks, after all: "The flimsy wood and paper cities of Japan would be shockingly exposed to incendiary bombs," he said.

It was May 26, 1941.

GEORGE BELL, the bishop of Chichester, spoke before the other assembled bishops at the Canterbury Convocation. The archbishop had warned him not to bring up the subject of night bombing, but Bishop Bell brought it up anyway. It was May 27, 1941.

The bishop began summarizing the history of attack and reprisal from the outset of the war, pointing out that English night raids on German soil had preceded German night raids on English soil. There was a clamor; the bishop of Winchester said that Bishop Bell was out of order, and the archbishop asked him to end his speech. Bishop Bell ended his speech.

The next day, the archbishop scolded him: "I do not think you can complain of the concern which so many of your brother bishops showed when you turned from the motion which you were making to what seemed to them a tendentious history of night-bombing," he said. "I thought you had quite definitely agreed that you would be content, though reluctantly, with your motion of sympathy with the bombed peoples; and I was rather surprised that you went back upon that in order to bring in what you would have said if you had adhered to your original motion about night-bombing." Fortunately, the archbishop said, nothing about this ecclesiastical disturbance had made it into the papers. "So I hope no further trouble will occur."

DAWID SIERAKOWIAK, in Lodz, listened to President Roosevelt's speech declaring a state of "unlimited national emergency." Sierakowiak was disappointed; he was expecting an American declaration of war. "Listening to this disgusting blabber drives you crazy," he wrote in his diary. The hearse, he said, was busy in the ghetto. "Meanwhile, over there they wait. Damn them!" It was May 27, 1941.

THE VICHY GOVERNMENT raised the bread ration slightly. The danger of famine wasn't over, but the shortage of flour for bread had been to some extent countered by the use of flour substitutes. The potato crop was under some threat, however; schoolchildren were working a few days a week plucking Colorado beetles from the leaves of potato plants. It was May 28, 1941.

WILLIAM HENRY CHAMBERLIN, a writer, spoke at the Keep America out of War Congress. It was May 31, 1941. "A total economic boycott of Japan, the stoppage of oil shipments for instance, would push Japan into the arms of the Axis," Chamberlain warned. "Economic war would be a prelude to naval and military war."

THE UNITED STATES sent its first Lend-Lease boatload of food to England. Lord Woolton, minister of food, was waiting for it on the dock. "Cheese!" he said. He ate some Wisconsin cheddar from an opened crate. "And very good cheese, too," he added.

There were four million eggs on the boat, as well, and one thousand tons of flour. It was May 31, 1941.

THE NEW YORK *HERALD TRIBUNE* published an official statistic: Nearly twice as many British civilians had died in bombing raids—35,756—as British troops had died in combat. It was June 1, 1941.

The next day, the *Herald Tribune* ran photographs of the devastation wrought by the British bombing of Hamburg. "Reports from within Germany describe Hamburg as a tragic picture," said the article. "Among houses near important industrial objectives there has been widespread destruction."

AT THE ANNUAL CONVENTION of the British Labor party, fewer than 1 percent of the votes were in favor of a negotiated peace with Germany and Italy. Rhys Davies, a pacifist and member of Parliament, was one of the few public critics of the conduct of the war. "Prime Minister Winston Churchill's declaration in a recent speech that there were millions of Germans who were curable and others who were killable was comparable to Herr Hitler's attitude toward Jews," Davies said. Bombs settled nothing, he contended.

Another member of Parliament, Fred Watkins, said: "I would rather see every church in this country blasted to ruins than to remain as a pulpit from which to preach the doctrine of Hitlerism."

It was June 3, 1941.

MICHAEL EDELSTEIN, a congressman from New York, had a heart attack after giving a speech on the floor of the U.S. House of Representatives. It was June 4, 1941.

John Rankin, a Mississippi isolationist, had just said: "Wall Street and a little group of our international Jewish brethren are still attempting to harass the President and the Congress of the United States into plunging us into the European war unprepared."

Edelstein was angry. "Hitler started out by speaking about 'Jewish brethren,'" he said in reply. "I deplore the idea that any time anything happens, whether it be for a war policy or against a war policy, men in this House and outside this House attempt to use the Jews as their scapegoat. I say it is unfair and I say it is un-American."

Sidney Hertzberg, Edelstein pointed out, had served as publicist for the America First Committee; and he listed other prominent Jews opposed to war: Lessing Rosenwald, Rabbi Sidney Goldstein, Rabbi Isadore B. Hoffman, and Rabbi De Sola Poole.

After making the speech, Representative Edelstein slumped to the floor and died.

ELEVEN THOUSAND WORKERS went on strike at an airplane factory in Los Angeles, near the airport. It was June 5, 1941. The factory made fighters, bombers, and trainer aircraft; it was operated by North American Aviation. The workers wanted a 10 percent wage increase, and they wanted the minimum wage to go from fifty to seventy-five cents per hour. The company had about two hundred million dollars in pending orders from the American and British governments.

"Our sole desire is to resume production at the earliest possible moment and deliver the bombers which this country needs so badly at this crucial period," said James Kindelberger, the president of North American Aviation.

JOHN CUDAHY, an American reporter, went to Berchtesgaden and sat in Hitler's large living room. Swastikas and paintings of nudes hung on the walls; there was a garnet-colored carpet on the floor. Cudahy noticed a bowl of hydrangeas and a vase of calla lilies. The bust of Wagner was still on the piano.

Cudahy said, through a translator, that people in the United States were worried that "the next logical field for German military adventure was the two American continents."

Hitler laughed. "He said," wrote Cudahy, "the idea of a Western Hemisphere invasion was about as fantastic as an invasion of the moon."

It might seem fantastic, the reporter countered, but people in the United States thought it was true. Hitler replied that the invasion idea was put out by warmongers; an attack over 2,500 miles of open water was unthinkable. "The combined shipping tonnage of Britain, the United States and Germany would be hopelessly inadequate, he insisted, to transport an army of millions, which would be required for a successful conquest of the Western Hemisphere."

Hitler also claimed that he was "not interested in slaves or in the enslavement of any people." Somewhere, a clock chimed loudly.

As Cudahy rose to go, Hitler told him that he'd tried to answer all the questions as truthfully as he could, but he was skeptical that anything good would come from the interview. Cudahy wrote: "He said that time after time he had tried to emphasize that the position of Germany and his plans were not inimical to the United States, and his efforts had proved futile."

The interview was published on June 6, 1941.

RUFUS JONES, the Quaker professor, wrote a pamphlet. It was published by the American Friends Service Committee, and it was called "A Call to Persons of Good Will."

"It is a distinct disadvantage for any nation or people to use military force for its own ends," the pamphlet said, and it offered six principles. One was that "national armed forces be reduced with a view to universal disarmament." Another was that "all peoples shall be free to develop their own cultures; and that each nation shall be free to develop the form of government which its people desire." Peace was not a static condition, Jones contended, attained after the defeat of an enemy: "Peace is a dynamic method, by which to remove injustices, to accomplish necessary readjustments, and to remedy instead of aggravating the evils that have been inflicted on the world by military aggression." The remedy for war was not war, he said, but dynamic peace. And he asked: "Is there no one in any government at the moment enough detached and above the issues of strife to call for cessation and mediation?"

Newspapers ran excerpts from Jones's pamphlet. "Quakers Offer Roosevelt Plan to End the War" was the headline in the New York *Herald Tribune*. Jones sent copies to members of Congress, to the State Department, and to President Roosevelt. It was June 1941.

THE LEAGUE OF AMERICAN WRITERS had its annual congress at the Hotel Commodore in New York. Dashiell Hammett was elected president. Richard Wright's *Native Son* was chosen as the finest American novel of the year. Theodore Dreiser was given a peace award. Lillian Hellman, Clifford Odets, and Orson Welles were sponsors. It was June 6, 7, and 8, 1941.

The league opposed American involvement in the war. "Today, we must ask whether the present policy of the Administration and the program of big business are not leading us toward war and Fascism in the name of resistance to war and Fascism," the league's statement said. League members pledged support of the strike at North American Aviation's airplane factory; they denounced the America First Committee as fascists; they agreed to send people to join the American Peace Mobilization's picketers in front of the White House.

"There is ample evidence at hand," said Richard Wright, "that the current war is nakedly and inescapably an imperialist war, directed against the Negro people and working people everywhere in the world."

PRESIDENT ROOSEVELT, invoking emergency powers as commander in chief, ordered the War Department to take over the North American Aviation plant. "Our country is in danger," Roosevelt said, "and the men and women who are now making airplanes play an indispensable part in its defense." It was June 9, 1941.

There were about one thousand strikers outside the main gate of the plant that morning. Somebody said, "Here comes the army." Soldiers, who had previously served in China, jumped from trucks and formed a line. "Slowly they moved along, the hot early morning sun glinting on their bayonets," said *The New York Times*. One striker got a bayonet gash in the thigh.

After the strikers were subdued, a lieutenant colonel went to a microphone and announced that the Army Air Corps had taken over the factory in the name of the government of the United States.

Frank Knox, secretary of the navy, was pleased. The breaking of the strike "has had a profound psychological effect," he said in a letter to a friend. "From now on I think our troubles from that source will grow less."

Eleanor Roosevelt was asked about her husband's action. "I always grieve when there is need for anything of this kind," she said.

IN THE WARSAW GHETTO, resident Mary Berg went to a community home, where the poorest refugees lived. "On the floor I saw half-naked, unwashed children lying listlessly. In one corner an exquisite little girl of four or five sat crying. I could not refrain from stroking her disheveled blond hair. The child looked at me with her big blue eyes, and said: 'I'm hungry.' " Mary Berg was overcome by shame; she had eaten that day and had no bread to offer the girl. "I did not dare look in her eyes, and went away." Three hundred people per week were dying of starvation.

It was June 12, 1941.

TWO OF JOSEPH STALIN'S GENERALS were alarmed over the possibility of a German invasion. General Zhukov and General Timoshenko asked Stalin if they could put troops on alert and move them forward in readiness for a German attack. Stalin said no. "Germany is busy up to her ears with the war in the West, and I am certain that Hitler will not risk creating a second front by attacking the Soviet Union," Stalin said. "Hitler is not such an idiot." It was June 12, 1941.

HERMANN VOSS, a new instructor at the Institute of Anatomy in Posen, went to the basement to see the cremation oven. It was June 14, 1941.

"This oven was built to eliminate parts of bodies left over from dissection exercises," Voss wrote in his diary. "Now it serves to incinerate executed Poles. The gray car with the gray men—that is, SS men from the Gestapo—comes almost daily with material for the oven." Voss looked inside. "The Poles are quite impudent at the moment, and thus our oven has a great deal to do. How nice it would be if we could drive the whole pack through such ovens."

A BIG "FIGHT FOR FREEDOM" AD appeared in *The New York Times*. Its headline was WHAT ARE WE WAITING FOR, MR. PRESIDENT? The ad called for the repeal of the Neutrality Act and the "shooting of any Axis U-boat or raider which the American Navy sights."

The list of sponsors included writer Dorothy Parker, playwright George S. Kaufman, James Conant of Harvard, and assorted heads of colleges and prep schools.

"Why not, for once, get the jump on Hitler, Mr. President?" the ad asked. And it quoted Senator Glass: "I think we ought to go over there and shoot hell out of every U-boat." It was June 15, 1941.

IN NEW YORK, another draft resister went before a judge. His name was Lowell Naeve. "If everybody did what I did," he said, "there would be no wars." The judge sent him to jail for a year. It was June 16, 1941.

MIHAIL SEBASTIAN, a Jewish writer in Bucharest, was beginning to think that the Germans were going to attack Russia soon. "If Hitler realizes that he won't finish the British off this year," Sebastian wrote in his journal, "and if he resigns himself to this fact, then what is there left for him to do with such a huge army?" It was June 17, 1941.

THE STATE DEPARTMENT announced that it was worried that refugees might become spies once they arrived in the United States. It was June 17, 1941. If the refugees had left family members behind in Europe, the State Department contended, the Nazis might compel them to spy on America by threatening their families with torture. The United States was therefore no longer going to grant visas to refugees who had family members in occupied Europe.

The ruling covered Germany, Holland, Belgium, Norway, France, Poland, and the Balkans.

An increasingly discouraged Clarence Pickett told *The New York Times* that the decision would have "far reaching effects" on all efforts to help refugees.

The governing committee of the Keep America out of War Congress wrote a letter to Secretary of State Cordell Hull: "Is our government so destitute of facilities for detecting true spies that it must close the last door of hope to thousands of Jews, Spaniards, Poles, and Czechs who hate fascism and love democracy?"

A UNION ORGANIZER AND SOCIALIST, Philip Randolph, was in President Roosevelt's office to talk about jobs for Negroes in defense plants. It was June 18, 1941.

Randolph had announced a huge march on Washington. "Our people are being turned away at factory gates because they are colored," he said to the president. "They can't live with this thing. Now, what are you going to do about it?"

Roosevelt said he would call up the heads of defense plants and see that Negro citizens were given equality of opportunity. Randolph said he wanted more: He wanted an executive order that would compel the plants to hire Negroes.

"Well, Phil, you know I can't do that," Roosevelt said. "In any event, I couldn't do anything unless you called off this march of yours."

Randolph said the march couldn't be called off.

Roosevelt turned to Walter White of the NAACP. "How many people do you plan to bring?" he asked.

"One hundred thousand, Mr. President," said White.

"You can't bring 100,000 Negroes to Washington," said Roosevelt. "Somebody might get killed."

In the end, Roosevelt issued Executive Order 8802, declaring that "there shall be no discrimination in the employment of workers in defense industries because of race, creed, color, or national origin." Philip Randolph called off the march.

H. G. WELLS wrote a letter to Winston Churchill, enclosing a book and suggesting that England firebomb crops and forests in Germany. It was June 20, 1941. Churchill thanked him by telegram.

HITLER'S ARMY invaded Russia. At four o'clock in the morning, Adam Grolsch, a German radio operator, crossed the Meml River into Soviet-controlled Lithuania with an advance armored unit of the German army. It was June 22, 1941.

When Grolsch reached the far side of the river, he saw bodies hanging from the trees. A Lithuanian local explained that people had already "taken care of things": All the Jews in the town had been robbed and hung by fellow Lithuanians. "They had exploited the situation," Grolsch saw. "'Hitler is against the Jews anyway. We'll kill them and then we'll take all of their stuff.'" There were about twenty dead. "It was a small town."

CHURCHILL'S SECRETARY let him know of the German invasion of Russia at his bedside at eight o'clock in the morning. "Tell the BBC I will broadcast at nine tonight," Churchill said, and he went back to sleep for two hours. He spent the day on his speech: "So now this bloodthirsty guttersnipe must launch his mechanized armies upon new fields of slaughter, pillage, and devastation," he said.

> Poor as are the Russian peasants, workmen and soldiers, he must steal from them their daily bread; he must devour their harvests; he must rob them of the oil which drives their ploughs; and thus produce a famine without example in human history.

This invasion was merely a prelude to another full-scale attack on England, Churchill asserted, and to the general subjugation of the western hemisphere. But the English would bring down these "Hun raiders": "In another six months the weight of the help we are receiving from the United States in war materials of all kinds, especially in heavy bombers, will begin to tell."

England would, he said, bomb Germany by day as well as by night, "making the German people taste and gulp each month a sharper dose of the miseries they have showered upon mankind."

The speech was broadcast on five hundred stations in the United States; it went out from shortwave transmitters around the world.

TOWARD EVENING—it was still June 22, 1941—twenty-four German airplanes flew low over an airfield near the town of Vilnius in Soviet-occupied Lithuania. Ivan Ivanovich Konovalov, a student pilot, jumped under the left wing of one of the planes parked in rows on the airfield. There was a huge noise of exploding bombs, and everything caught on fire. "We buried 48 people that first night, student pilots," Konovalov said. "We put their bodies in the craters and filled them in."

THE SOVIET FOREIGN MINISTER, Vyacheslav Molotov, addressed the Russian people: "This unheard of attack upon our country is perfidy unparalleled in the history of civilized nations," he said.

Stalin listened and went to Molotov's office. "Well, you sounded a bit flustered," he said, "but the speech went well."

Toward evening, General Timoshenko brought report of the ruin of the Soviet air force. Stalin began pacing the office. "Surely the German air force didn't manage to reach every single airfield?"

"Unfortunately it did," said Timoshenko. The estimate was that seven hundred planes were already destroyed.

"This is a monstrous crime," Stalin said. He ordered the director of his secret police, Lavrentii Beria, to find out which of his officers had erred. "Those responsible must lose their heads."

THE FIGHT FOR FREEDOM COMMITTEE rushed an invasion-of-Russia ad into the paper. NOW IS THE TIME! it said. "The danger is that Quislings and Nazi stooges in this country will now try to lull us with the bedtime story that Hitler is saving the world from Communism, which all Americans abhor," the ad said. "The danger is that we may delay while Hitler secures his rear for the final assault upon Great Britain and the Western hemisphere."

But there was a supreme opportunity as well, said Fight for Freedom: "At last Hitler has exposed his back." The ad finished with a sort of poem in boldface:

> Let's go, then, America.
> Let us strike with all the mighty force which this
>   free and bounteous land holds.
> Let us strike by air and sea and if possible by land.
> Let there be no lagging hands.
> It is war—war to the death.

It was June 23, 1941.

CHURCHILL WROTE a secret memo to Charles Portal, the chief of the air staff. It was June 23, 1941—the day after the invasion of Russia, and the day after he had called Hitler a bloodthirsty guttersnipe.

"What is the position about the bombing of the Black Forest this year?" Churchill asked Portal. "It ought to be possible to produce very fine results."

"Crops will not burn, but forests will," Portal answered. "Bomber Command will therefore go for the forests." What the Royal Air Force needed, Portal said, was a better incendiary bomb—one more like a Molotov cocktail, which would "scatter an inflammable mixture on the trees themselves."

SENATOR HARRY TRUMAN gave his reaction to the news that Germany and Russia were at war. "If we see that Germany is winning we ought to help Russia and if Russia is winning we ought to help Germany, and that way let them kill as many as possible, although I don't want to see Hitler victorious under any circumstances," he said. It was June 23, 1941.

SEVERAL OF THE GROUPS most fiercely opposed to war—the ones aligned with Russia and the Communist party—reversed their stand and became militant. It was late June 1941. Dashiell Hammett's League of American Writers now called for the "military defeat of the fascist aggressors." The American Peace Mobilization, which had been picketing the White House, changed its name to the American People's Mobilization and stopped picketing. "The essential pre-requisite for achieving a people's peace has now become the military defeat of Germany," the group said.

There were now two kinds of antiwar groups left—one on the left, and one on the right. One was made up of genuine pacifists—people from the Fellowship of Reconciliation, the Keep America out of War Congress, the Quakers, the peace ministers and rabbis, John Haynes Holmes and the Gandhians, and the Women's International League for Peace and Freedom. And one was made up of isolationists who, like Lindbergh and his crowds of America Firsters, liked big armies and fleets of warplanes, and who held—some of them—quasi-paranoid theories about Judeo-Bolshevik influence. They wanted the United States to lay off Germany because Germany was the bulwark that held back Stalin.

GERMAN PLANES firebombed Minsk, a city in Russia. There were no air-raid shelters in the city; the water mains broke, the fires merged, and many died. It was June 24, 1941.

The Luftwaffe bombed England, too, but much less so now than before: Most of its strength was directed at the eastern front.

In Bucharest, Romania, new anti-Semitic posters appeared. In one, a Jew loomed in skullcap and side curls, holding a hammer and sickle. Soviet soldiers hid under his coat.

FRANCES PARTRIDGE's husband, Ralph, got a letter from his old friend Gerald Brenan, a writer. For some reason, Brenan irritably observed, pacifists were bad at math—they couldn't even do simple addition. As for the war: "Every German woman and child killed is a contribution to the future safety and happiness of Europe," Brenan wrote. When the war was over, he said, then there would be time for friendship. "Today, death to every German. This will shock you. I see your pained clergyman's expression." It was June 25, 1941.

THE LEADER OF ROMANIA, Ion Antonescu, called a commander in Iasi, a town near the Russian border where there were more than a hundred synagogues. It was June 27, 1941.

Antonescu told the commander to rid Iasi of Jews. Policemen and soldiers began killing. Thousands of Jews were put on sealed trains and pulled around the countryside for days. Most of them died of suffocation and thirst.

THERE WAS A HEAT WAVE in Berlin. "The city is like an oven," wrote Joseph Goebbels in his diary. It was June 28, 1941.

He drove out on a Saturday to his forest villa at Lanke to catch up on work. "The food supply situation in Berlin is very bad," he wrote. "No potatoes, very few vegetables." And it was worse in the occupied countries: "In some areas there is real starvation."

Hungary had declared war on Russia, he noted, which was a psychological boost. The entire continent was "undergoing an awakening," he said. "In the end, Churchill will be completely alone with his Bolsheviks."

WINSTON CHURCHILL pictured to himself an aerial invasion of England. It was June 29, 1941. A quarter of a million troops might parachute in, or crash-land, or arrive in gliders. The English must be able to respond, he wrote to his chief of staff and secretary of state for war:

> Everyone in uniform, and anyone else who likes, must fall upon these wherever they find them and attack them with the utmost alacrity—
>
> > 'Let every one
> > Kill a Hun'
>
> This spirit must be inculcated ceaselessly into all ranks of HM forces.

Every man was to have a weapon—even if only a mace or a pike. "Let me also see some patterns of maces and pikes," Churchill instructed his staff. He was also keeping a close watch, still, on stocks of poison gas.

THE U.S. GOVERNMENT arrested some people in Minneapolis and charged them, under the new Alien and Sedition Act, with seeking an "armed revolution against the Government of the United States." The people were members of the Socialist Workers Party, a small Trotskyist group that was opposed to American participation in the war. I. F. Stone, an independent-minded, interventionist journalist, went to Attorney General Biddle's office and asked, "What did these people *do*? What were they about to do? In what way did they menace Minneapolis?" It was July 1941.

Attorney General Biddle said he wasn't familiar with the specifics of the case, but he did his best to explain. "If I understood Mr. Biddle rightly," Stone wrote afterward in *The Nation,* "he thinks a government need not wait for an overt act but can punish men for the probable consequences which would result if they tried to put their ideas into action. This reasoning is no different from that on which Trotskyists are jailed in the Third Reich or the Soviet Union. On this basis Thoreau could have been kept in jail for life."

Another lawyer at the Department of Justice furnished Stone with the particulars of the case. The Trotskyists had distributed pamphlets and made speeches in which they said that they were against the war and that they didn't subscribe to democratic processes. They had gotten involved in union politics in Minneapolis. Their "defense guard," numbering between two hundred and five hundred people, owned between ten and fifty guns. They did calisthenics together. Once, as a test, the defense guard mobilized—everyone was at headquarters within an hour.

"What did they do when they got there?" Stone asked the lawyer from the Justice Department. They arrived, Stone was told, and then adjourned to visit the Gaiety, a burlesque club.

Eighteen Trotskyite Socialist Workers Party members, including the national secretary, spent more than a year in jail.

A GERMAN ÉMIGRÉ, Willy Ley, was hired to write about weaponry at a new newspaper called *PM,* published in New York City. *PM* published Ley's book *Bombs and Bombing,* which had a line drawing of the B-17 Long Range Heavy Bomber, courtesy of Boeing Aircraft Company, as its frontispiece. It was July 1941.

Ley used a metaphor from natural science to explain firebombing. There are two kinds of reproduction, he said. One method is when the parent animals give birth to a few carefully tended young. The other method, he said, is the oyster method, which involves producing two million eggs per season and hoping some of them will grow up. That was the idea behind the small bombs used in firebombing. You scatter many of them "in the hopes that some of the baby fires produced will survive the adversity of the air raid precaution's firemen."

At the end of the First World War, Ley explained, the Germans were making stocks of incendiary bombs that each weighed about two pounds. They looked like "tall and narrow tin cans, with fins attached to one end." They were made of a magnesium alloy called "electron," and they were filled with thermite, which was a mixture of iron oxide and powdered aluminum.

It was hard to look at burning thermite, Ley said. It looked like a piece of the sun.

C. L. SULZBERGER, the *New York Times* reporter in Turkey, wrote about hunger in Greece. It was July 1, 1941. Fish were scarce because the British had commandeered the fishing boats, Sulzberger reported. Children, dogs, cats, and horses were dying. On the island of Santorini, there had been no bread for thirty days.

Sulzberger interviewed a traveler who had recently returned from Greece. "The Greek people face an unprecedented famine as the result of their fight for freedom," the traveler said. "It is necessary for the British to scrap previous blockade restrictions to avoid responsibility for this situation."

REINHARD HEYDRICH issued killing instructions to the leaders of the SS's special motorized units, the Einsatzgruppen. It was July 2, 1941. Within Russia, certain classes of people were subject to execution: politicians, Jews in the service of the Communist party or the Soviet state, and all saboteurs, propagandists, snipers, assassins, and agitators, unless they were necessary for intelligence purposes. "Special care must be taken in regard to the shooting of doctors and others engaged in medical practice," Heydrich wrote.

GOEBBELS WAS in his misty forest villa at Lanke again: "Heavy English air raids on North and West Germany," he wrote. "Considerable damage." He noted a new term, *bombenfrischler* ("bomb tramps"): "idlers of both sexes who have cleared out of the areas threatened by bombing and are living in the open during this summer." The police, he felt, should be set on them. "They are wreaking havoc with public morals and ruining the good name of North and North-West Germany."

But the war in Russia was better: "Our panzers are moving forward beyond Minsk," he said. "The noose at Novogrodok is tightening."

It was July 3, 1941.

ALL OF BRITAIN celebrated a Lend-Lease Fourth of July. American flags hung in the railroad stations of London. At movie theaters, audiences stood and sang "My Country 'Tis of Thee" while the lyrics appeared on the screen, along with photographs of Franklin Roosevelt. Restaurants served dishes with names of American cities: Philadelphia Pepper Pot, Baltimore Fried Chicken.

At bomb-damaged St. Paul's cathedral, the secretary of war for air, Sir Archibald Sinclair, spoke at a memorial service for an American pilot who had died while flying as a volunteer for the RAF's new American Eagle Squadron. "Under no kind of compulsion he came and fought for Britain and, fighting, died," said Sinclair.

There were words of prayer for the king of England and the president of the United States and their subjects—a hope that they may "obtain at last the blessings of victory and a righteous and abiding peace." Then the Royal Air Force band played both national anthems.

MIHAIL SEBASTIAN, the Romanian playwright, stopped following the war. He couldn't afford to buy newspapers, and he had no radio. "To read the papers is like an exercise in textual decoding for which you do not have the code," he wrote. "And yet it is so interesting! For the first time it occurs to me that truth is definitely something that can never be camouflaged. Beneath all the fakes and lies and all the mental aberrations, however deeply hidden or wildly deformed, the truth still breaks through, still glitters, still breathes." It was July 5, 1941.

THE ROYAL AIR FORCE began using a star system of air-raid severity. On July 5, 1941, as part of a summer offensive, the city of Munster received a "three-star blasting," according to *The New York Times.* It was raided again the next night and the next and the next— and then the raid on July 9 got four stars, "the works."

The head of Bomber Command, Richard Peirse, gave these orders: "You will direct the main effort of the bomber force, until further instructions, toward dislocating the German transportation system, and to destroying the morale of the civil population as a whole, and of the industrial workers in particular."

During the offensive, Churchill wrote a most secret message to Charles Portal. "One of our great aims is the delivery on German towns of the largest possible quantity of bombs per night," he said. In order to keep up the pace of the attack, he proposed using what he called "less-qualified" crews. They would fly very high, "aiming simply at large built-up areas" over, say, the Ruhr Valley. "Regular trained pilots" would be used for more important missions.

U.S. MARINES moved into Iceland, a neutral country, at England's invitation and with Iceland's reluctant consent. They unloaded guns and began setting up Nissen huts. It was July 7, 1941. The German newspapers said that Roosevelt was "running after the war in order to catch up with it." Surely, thought Victor Klemperer, the fact that the United States was occupying Iceland meant that the United States was in the war.

PRESIDENT ROOOSEVELT asked for a new war plan—one that would estimate the "over-all production requirements required to defeat our potential enemies." It was July 9, 1941. The plan would soon have a name: the Victory Program.

The secretary of war forwarded Roosevelt's request to the army chief of staff, and the chief of staff sent it on to the head of the War Plans Division, and the head of the War Plans Division told Major Albert C. Wedemeyer—the man who had spent two years at the War College in Berlin—to get to work.

"Although the procedure was normal," Wedemeyer wrote, "the task was more than usually challenging, since a war plan of global dimensions had never before been attempted." Wedemeyer was himself opposed to any war with Germany—he had cordial contacts with several members of the America First Committee, and he agreed with much of what Charles Lindbergh said. Bolshevism, Wedemeyer thought, was the real menace to the United States, not fascism.

But Wedemeyer obeyed orders: "Thus I became the Victory Program planner of a war I did not want."

MARY BERG, the girl in the Warsaw ghetto, started having night-mares. "I saw Warsaw drowning in blood," she wrote. "Together with my sisters and my parents, I walked over prostrate corpses." It was July 10, 1941.

She heard Russian airplanes flying over the city—the sound of their bombs made the air tremble. But they spared the ghetto: "For that reason we no longer go to the cellar so often when we hear the alarm."

MAYOR FIORELLO LAGUARDIA offered a warning. It was July 14, 1941. Hitler might soon try to trick people into thinking that he wanted peace, LaGuardia said, when what he really wanted was to take over the world. LaGuardia told his audience—a group of South American teachers—that only a few days earlier a representative of the German government had tendered Nazi peace proposals to rep-resentatives of an unnamed peace organization. "Hitler is now and at this very moment, through his agents, seeking to exploit well-meaning, well-intentioned, peace-loving citizens in our country and in Central and South America as tools to get across what may be announced very shortly as the Hitler Peace Proposals," LaGuardia said.

Sumner Welles at the State Department seconded LaGuardia's warning.

WINSTON CHURCHILL stood under an awning in Hyde Park, London, and reviewed six thousand civil-defense troops. It was July 14, 1941. There were air-raid wardens, stretcher parties, women's voluntary services, and decontamination squads. "All these people we have seen on a lovely English summer morning, marching past," Churchill said on the radio. The Royal Air Force had frustrated Hitler's invasion plans, he said, and therefore in September Hitler had tried to raze the cities of England. Had London collapsed? No. Even with twenty thousand dead and whole districts ravaged by fire, Londoners were unconquered. "London is so vast and so strong she is like a prehistoric monster into whose armored hide showers of arrows can be shot in vain," he said.

He addressed Hitler directly at one point: "Where you have been the least resisted, there you have been the most brutal," he said. "It was you who began the indiscriminate bombing" in Warsaw, Rotterdam, Belgrade, and Russia. "We will have no truce or parley with you, or the grisly gang who work your wicked will. You do your worst—and we will do our best."

Then came another of Churchill's announcements of aerial retribution. "It is time," Churchill said, "that the Germans should be made to suffer in their own homeland and cities something of the torments they have let loose upon their neighbors and upon the world."

> Every month as the great bombers are finished in our factories or sweep hither across the Atlantic Ocean we shall continue the remorseless discharge of high explosive upon Germany.

In the past few weeks alone, he said, this remorseless discharge amounted to half of what the Germans had dropped on England during the whole course of the war. But this was only the beginning.

The bombing would continue, Churchill said, "month after month, year after year, until the Nazi regime is either extirpated by us or, better still, torn to pieces by the German people themselves."

That night, Sir Alexander Cadogan was working late at the Foreign Office. "About 7 we got Japanese intercepts showing the monkeys have decided to seize bases in Indo-China—by the 20th," he wrote.

THE NEW YORK TIMES published an editorial that tried to soften slightly Churchill's speech of the day before: "This is no sadistic desire for revenge manifesting itself; it is rather a sincere conviction that bombing Berlin will hasten the victory and speed the peace," the editorialist said.

THE PRIME MINISTER began thinking about the thickness of bomb casings. It was July 16, 1941.

He wrote a memo on the subject to Sir Archibald Sinclair, the secretary of state for air. Churchill noted that British bombs have relatively thick metal casings, amounting to about 70 percent of their weight, whereas German bombs have thinner casings, allowing them to carry more explosives inside and therefore to radiate a more powerfully destructive air blast when they blew. Thick bomb casings made for lots of shrapnel—Churchill called them "splinters"—but "splinters find very few useful targets, especially at night when most people are under cover," Churchill said. The thinner-shelled, stronger-blasting German bombs had a charge-to-weight ratio of fifty-fifty. "These are not only more efficient for destroying cities," he wrote, "they are also cheaper." Perhaps, the prime minister suggested, the charge-to-weight ratio of British bombs ought to be reconsidered—"especially now that the Air Ministry have asked for such a large increase in output."

Archibald Sinclair replied in a way that suggested to Churchill that his point had not been fully appreciated. Churchill restated his arguments about blast versus splinters and demanded lists of various bombs that would be in production soon. "I am pleased to note that the American bombs have a high charge-weight ratio," he said.

CHARLES DARWIN, grandson of Charles Darwin the naturalist, was in Washington, D.C., reading something called the Maud Report. It was July 16, 1941. Darwin, a physicist, was the director of the British Central Scientific Office, which coordinated British weapons research with the research going forward under the supervision of MIT's Vannevar Bush and Harvard's James Conant. The Maud Report, in typescript, was a brief, lucid, and enthusiastic description of the possibility of a bomb made from enriched uranium.

"We should like to emphasize that we entered the project with more scepticism than belief," the authors of the Maud Report had written. "As we proceeded we became more and more convinced that release of atomic energy on a large scale is possible and that conditions can be chosen which would make it a very powerful weapon of war." The authors believed that a bomb filled with a mere twenty-five pounds of enriched uranium would explode with the force of 1,800 tons of TNT. It would also release "large quantities of radioactive substances, which would make places near to where the bomb exploded dangerous to human life for a long period."

They wanted to build this bomb very much, and Imperial Chemical Industries was willing to help them. "Although the cost per lb of this explosive is so great," the Maud Report authors wrote, "it compares very favorably with ordinary explosives when reckoned in terms of energy released and damage done." But the cost savings was not the main point—the main point, the authors said, was "the concentrated destruction which it would produce, the large moral effect, and the saving in air effort the use of this substance would allow, as compared with bombing with ordinary explosives." Every effort should be made to produce these bombs, the authors urged.

Darwin, reading the report, pictured to himself the detonation of such a huge bomb. Then he wrote a letter to Lord Hankey. If this bomb was made, he wondered, would it actually be used? "Are our own Prime Minister and the American President and the respective general staffs," he wrote, "willing to sanction the total destruction of Berlin and the country round, when, if ever, they are told it could be accomplished in a single blow?"

ROLF-HEINZ HÖPPNER, an SS administrator in Posen, sent a memo to Adolf Eichmann about the Jews in Poland. "There is an imminent danger that not all the Jews can be supplied with food in the coming winter," he wrote. "We must seriously consider if it would not be more humane to finish off the Jews, insofar as they are not fit for labor mobilization, with some quick-acting means." That would be, Höppner said, "more agreeable than to let them die of hunger." It was July 16, 1941.

The next day, Hitler told a Croatian leader that the Lithuanians and the Estonians were taking their revenge on the Jews. When the Jews were gone, Hitler said, nothing would stand in the way of European unification. But if even one country allowed one Jewish family to survive in its midst, that family would constitute "a source of bacilli touching off new infection." He, Hitler, would demand that every country become free of Jews. "It makes no difference whether Jews are sent to Siberia or to Madagascar," he said. It was July 17, 1941.

LORD HALIFAX, once viceroy of India, now British ambassador to the United States, was at the Lockheed factory in Burbank, California. It was July 17, 1941. Halifax and Lady Halifax were there to celebrate the completion of the one-thousandth Hudson bomber bound for England.

This thousandth airplane, Halifax said, would do its bit to swell the stream of war material that had begun to flow eastward. "All you give us will be used in the defense of freedom of speech, thought and religion, and personal liberties, which things the English-speaking people, the world over, value more highly than life itself." The Hudson airplane was a household word in the coastal command, he said—it could take a beating and still limp home.

There were other great warplanes, too, Halifax went on: "Side by side with Lockheeds, we are hearing every day of the products of other great factories—Tomahawks from the Curtiss plant at Buffalo, Marylands turned out by the Glenn Martin plant at Baltimore; Martlets and Buffaloes from the Grumman and Brewster plants on Long Island; Liberators and Catalinas from the Consolidated plant at San Diego; Bostons and Havocs from the great Douglas factory at Santa Monica; Fortresses from the Boeing factory at Seattle; the Harvard trainers from the North American plant at Englewood; and Vanguards from the Vultee factory at Downey."

He closed by thanking the company for "the bomber you gave my people as a Christmas present last year." The Hudson bomber's pilot, Jimmy Mattern, was in the cockpit and ready to fly. Before he revved the engines, Lady Halifax said: "And now your labor takes wings. Go, Jimmy Mattern, and God bless you."

SOME FOREIGN MILITARY EXPERTS talked to *New York Times* reporter Ray Brock. It was July 17, 1941.

"Duesseldorf is little more than a charred ruin," the experts told Brock. "Royal Air Force pilots flying American-built 'flying fortresses' and dropping American-made 1,000-pound and 4,000-pound bombs, have made Duesseldorf a shambles," one of the experts said. Morale there was shaky. "Countless families are seeking permission of civil and Gestapo authorities to move into the countryside to escape heavier bombings."

Hanover was also in bad shape, a diplomat said. Flying Fortresses had reportedly dropped four four-thousand-pound bombs on the railroad station; the station and the neighborhood around it was now a "smoking furnace."

HAROLD NICOLSON, at the Ministry of Information, was once again worried about a possible peace offer from Hitler. If Russia collapsed, then Hitler could proclaim himself master of Europe. "He may then start a great peace drive," Nicolson wrote in his diary, "representing himself as the crusader against Bolshevism and offering us the most flattering terms." When England refused, Hitler could then say to the United States that England had lost a chance for an honorable peace.

"The best thing to do," Nicolson believed, "is to forestall this by warning America of the peace offensive."

That night, Nicolson got a black box from the prime minister, with a curt letter inside it. The letter asked him to resign from the Ministry of Information—no explanation given. "I am hurt and sad and sorry," Nicolson wrote. It was July 18, 1941.

HARRY HOPKINS was back in England, on his way to talk to Joseph Stalin about what the United States was going to give Russia under Lend-Lease. It was late July 1941. Hopkins intimated to Churchill that there was some unhappiness back home about the fact that the twenty big Boeing B-17 Flying Fortresses that the United States had sent to Britain that spring were underused, when they were the ideal plane to use on Berlin.

Churchill took the hint. "I think on the widest grounds it would be a very good thing if these bombers were used against Germany in bombing raids," he wrote Charles Portal.

Portal's difficulty was that this particular model of Boeing Flying Fortress—the B-17C—wasn't any good. The aerodynamic design of the plane was excellent—and improved models would, by the thousands, contribute to the ruination of German cities, beginning in 1943—but the B-17C Fortresses were more like prototypes than production planes.

They lacked power turrets and tail guns, and when they flew

during the day, even at thirty thousand feet, German fighters were able to reach them and shoot them full of holes. Their guns froze, their windshields iced over, their propellers stopped spinning, and their Sperry bombsights had no success in putting bombs near targets from high altitudes. Pilots called them Flying Targets; Goebbels called them Flying Coffins.

Even so, Churchill wanted these Fortresses used, and celebrated, on bombing missions.

The Joint Army-Navy Board of the United States approved a plan called JB 355. JB 355 proposed an expansion of the air force in China so that it would be able to carry out, among other things, the "incendiary bombing of Japan." The plan was drawn up by Roosevelt's economist and China expert, Lauchlin Currie. A front corporation, China Defense Supplies, formed by T. V. Soong and run by Roosevelt's former aide Thomas Corcoran, was to buy the planes from American manufacturers; Claire Chennault would hire and train American volunteer pilots to fly the planes. The pilots were to be paid through another front corporation, Central Aircraft Manufacturing Corp., or CAMCO.

Roosevelt read the Joint Board plan and okayed it. Lauchlin Currie wired Madame Chiang Kai-shek and Claire Chennault a letter that fairly begged for interception by Japanese spies: "I am very happy to be able to report that today the President directed that sixty-six bombers be made available to China this year with twenty-four to be delivered immediately. He also approved a Chinese pilot training program here. Details through normal channels. Warm regards." It was July 23, 1941.

Japanese intelligence agents relayed detailed reports of the airplane sale and training program back to Tokyo. American intelligence agents then intercepted and decoded these Japanese reports—tracking the progress of their provocations.

PRESIDENT ROOSEVELT was in the White House, talking to the Volunteer Coordination Committee, a war-preparedness group. It was July 24, 1941.

Sandbags may be necessary in certain parts of the country, he said. And we need to get the right information out. "There are a lot of things that people don't quite understand," he said. For example: "Why am I asked to curtail my consumption of gasoline when I read in the papers that thousands of tons of gasoline are going out from Los Angeles—West Coast—to Japan?"

The answer was very simple, said the president. "If we cut the oil off, they probably would have gone down to the Dutch East Indies a year ago, and you would have had war," he explained. "It was very essential from our own selfish point of view of defense to prevent a war from starting in the South Pacific. So our foreign policy was—trying to stop a war from breaking out there."

"Our foreign policy *was*"—Roosevelt had used the past tense, reporters noticed.

THE BRITISH AIR MINISTRY began an energetic campaign of news briefings on behalf of their twenty all-but-useless Flying Fortresses. It was July 1941. News bureaus on both sides of the Atlantic cooperated fully. The Associated Press said:

> Big four-motored American-made Boeing Flying Fortresses bombed the German battleship Gneisenau in port at Brest, France, yesterday, from a height so "fantastic" that the scream of their bombs was probably the first inkling the Germans had of their attack, the British Air Ministry news service reported today.

A *New York Times* dispatch said: "The raids were built around the participation of the American-made Flying Fortresses that are capable, because of a special supercharger and the world's most accurate bomb sight, of doing destructive work with a high degree of competence from the highest levels yet attempted in the war."

A British pilot read one of the many newspaper accounts aloud to his colleagues: "From altitudes of seven miles," he read, "the crews of these big Boeings unload their heavy bombs with uncanny accuracy, unbothered by squadrons of Messerschmitts far below."

Another pilot, who'd flown a mission in one of the "big Boeings," said, "I think I'm going to be sick."

COLONEL ENRIQUE ZANETTI, a chemistry professor at Columbia University, reported for active duty at the Chemical Warfare Service of the U.S. Army. It was July 1941.

Zanetti was America's expert in fire warfare. His interest in incendiary weapons, which began during World War I, had quickened with the Italian invasion of Ethiopia—a reporter for the New York *Herald Tribune* had sent him a partly burned Italian firebomb, which he inspected and handed over to the Chemical Warfare Service. In 1936, Zanetti wrote that fire was the "forgotten enemy"—more dangerous to a large city than poison gas. "Gas *dissipates* while fire *propagates*," he wrote. Each diminutive firebomb holds within itself "the devastating possibilities of Mrs. O'Leary's cow." Slums were particularly vulnerable, he noted; slum clearance ought to be a component of any national defense program.

Now, in the summer of 1941, Zanetti was put in charge of the new Incendiaries Branch of the Chemical Warfare Service. He went to London to meet bomb designers, and he brought back blueprints, manufacturing techniques, and recipes for the British four-pound magnesium-thermate bomb, which had especially good roof-piercing properties.

AN EXECUTIVE ORDER emanated from Hyde Park, New York. It was July 25, 1941.

"In view of the unlimited national emergency declared by the President, he has today issued an Executive Order freezing Japanese assets in the same manner in which assets of various European countries were frozen on June 14, 1941."

A joint Anglo-American oil embargo followed.

THE BRITISH MINISTRY OF INFORMATION made a policy decision. It was July 25, 1941. They decided to be sparing in their use of atrocity material in propaganda directed at the home front. A certain amount of horror was necessary, but the stories "must always deal with the treatment of indisputably innocent people," the propagandists felt. "Not with violent political opponents. And not with the Jews."

That day, Churchill sent one of his "Most Secret" notes to Portal: "This spell of dry weather brings the forest of Nieppe into importance," he said. "It would be good to have an experiment in forest burning, the results of which could be observed close at hand." Nieppe was in French Flanders.

MIHAIL SEBASTIAN was talking with his friend Camil Petrescu, a Nazi sympathizer. "The war with the Russians is hard, very hard," Petrescu said, but in the end, he believed, Hitler would save the world from the Bolshevists. As for the Jews, Petrescu said, "It can't go on quite like this." The Jews would get a state of their own somewhere in Russia. Perhaps it would be Birobidzhan, Petrescu thought— Birobidzhan being the marshy area in eastern Siberia that Stalin had set aside for Jewish colonization in the twenties. It was July 26, 1941.

HARRY HOPKINS gave a speech on the BBC, broadcast from Churchill's personal microphone at Chequers. It was July 27, 1941.

The speech was written for Hopkins by Quentin Reynolds, the American journalist, while Hopkins took a nap. "I did not come from America alone," Hopkins said. "I came in a bomber plane, and with me were twenty other bombers made in America." The BBC's propaganda bureaus broadcast the speech in several languages, and the Royal Air Force dropped copies of it from the sky onto enemy lands, spreading the idea that America was already in the war.

WINSTON CHURCHILL wrote Joseph Stalin a letter. It was July 28, 1941. Harry Hopkins was leaving for Moscow that night, Churchill told Stalin. He, Stalin, could place absolute trust in Hopkins. "A little while ago when I asked him for a quarter of a million rifles they came at once," he said.

Churchill assured Stalin that England would do all it could to help Russia. "A terrible winter of bombing lies before Germany," he said. "No one has yet had what they are going to get."

ALAN BROOKE, commander of the Home Guard, wrote in his diary that Churchill had said something very wise to him when he'd stayed at Chequers recently. Churchill had told him that the human mind was like the six-inch pipe that runs under a culvert—it could take only a certain amount of water. In times of flood, water simply overflows the culvert. "During the last two years I have frequently felt that my mind was unable to fully realize the volume and magnitude of events I was living through," Brooke wrote. It was July 29, 1941.

"JAPAN SMOLDERS OVER OIL THREAT" WAS the headline on page one of *The New York Times*. It was July 30, 1941. At a cabinet meeting with Roosevelt, Harold Ickes, the secretary of the interior, suggested an air strike. "I would like to see one of our latest models go to Siberia by way of Japan," Ickes said. "It could set fire to Tokyo en route by dropping a few incendiary bombs."

VERA BRITTAIN lay in bed at twilight, listening to the British bombers flying out to sea. It took an hour for the sound to pass. "How many children in Germany would be dead by morning?" she wondered. She wrote a peace letter: "To realise that one's own people are suffering damage is grievous, but to know that they are about to inflict it is detestable." It was July 31, 1941.

REINHARD HEYNRICH had a meeting with Hermann Goering in Berlin. It was July 31, 1941. Heydrich, who administered Jewish matters at the SS, had with him a draft order that he wanted Goering to sign. The order employed the word "solution" (*lösung*) three times—and the last time, the word "final" (*end*) was attached to it:

> Complementing the task already assigned to you in the decree of January 24, 1939, to undertake, by emigration or evacuation, a solution of the Jewish question as advantageous as possible under the conditions at the time, I hereby charge you with making all necessary organizational, functional, and material preparations for a complete solution of the Jewish question in the German sphere of influence in Europe. In so far as the jurisdiction of other central agencies may be touched thereby, they are to be involved. I charge you furthermore with submitting to me in the near future an overall plan of the organizational, functional, and material measures to be taken in preparing for the implementation of the aspired final solution of the Jewish question.

Years later, a historian, Richard Breitman, wrote: "The Final Solution was and was not a resettlement plan." One of Himmler's SS leaders, Hans-Adolf Prutzmann, was once asked where some "criminal elements" were being resettled to. To the next world, answered Prutzmann.

NINETY JEWISH CHILDREN and infants were locked in a house under Ukrainian guard. It was August 1941. Their parents had been shot, and they'd been given no food or water. Some German soldiers alerted two chaplains, who got in touch with a staff officer, Helmuth Groscurth. Groscurth, the son of a Lutheran minister, was the man who had tried to stop the SS's atrocities in Poland by distributing General Blaskowitz's reports among members of the high command. He'd been banished to the front for doing so.

Groscurth went to the house immediately. There was a terrible smell. Children were licking the walls. One was unconscious. He made inquiries: The children were to be killed soon, he was told, under orders from the SS. He asked for a delay, and he got the children water and bread. He requested a reconsideration. There was a meeting and a decision: Groscurth was overruled. The children were killed by Ukrainian militiamen, who trembled as they shot them.

THE ROYAL AIR FORCE resumed its flights to Berlin. One returning air crew reported three explosions and a fire that "heaved like a volcano." A pilot of one of the new four-engine British bombers, the Stirlings, described a big detonation and a shower of incendiaries: "I think we gave the Berliners their money's worth, all right." It was August 2, 1941.

Now the Soviet Union was bombing Berlin, as well: "The vast British air attack appeared to be part of a joint offensive with Russian fliers," *The New York Times* reported. And America was nominally present, too, at least in press reports—there was more talk in the press of "the R.A.F.'s latest pride, the American-built Flying Fortresses."

CARDINAL CLEMENS VON GALEN delivered a sermon in the cathedral in Munster, Germany. It was August 3, 1941. "For some months we have been hearing reports that, on the orders of Berlin, patients from mental asylums who have been ill for a long time and may appear incurable, are being compulsorily removed," the cardinal said. "Then, after a short time, the relatives are regularly informed that the corpse has been burnt and the ashes can be delivered."

The cardinal asked a question. "Have you, have I the right to live only so long as we are productive, so long as we are recognized by others as productive?"

The bishop of Limburg wrote a letter to the minister of justice in Berlin. "Children call each other names and say, 'You're crazy; you'll be sent to the baking oven in Hadamar,'" the bishop wrote. He humbly begged the minister to prevent futher transgressions of the Fifth Commandment.

Hitler suspended the T-4 program soon after; some of its staff moved east to Lublin, to work for SS leader Otto Globocnik.

ALEXANDER CADOGAN was on the train to Scotland with Lord Cherwell, Lord Beaverbrook, Harry Hopkins, and the prime minister of England. They were on their way to Scapa Flow, where they were going to get on a battleship and sail west to confer with the president of the United States. It was August 3, 1941.

On the train, they had tomato soup, sirloin of beef—"in unlimited quantities and quite excellent," Cadogan said—and a raspberry-and-currant tart. Churchill announced to the group that he'd drunk, on average, half a bottle of champagne every day for the past forty-eight years. "Got the 'Prof' to work out this in figures," wrote Cadogan, "and in tons, which was impressive."

IN BUCHAREST, police went from house to house, announcing that Jews between the ages of twenty and fifty must soon report to headquarters. It was August 4, 1941.

Was it for work camps, Mihail Sebastian wondered, or was it another massacre, as at Iasi? "When I went out at ten, the city had a strange air: a strange kind of nervous animation," he wrote in his journal. "Looks that wordlessly question one another, with the mute despair that has become a kind of Jewish greeting."

The next day, Sebastian remembered something a Gentile friend said to him recently: "Whenever I see a Jew, I feel an urge to go up and greet him and to say, 'Please believe me, sir, I have nothing to do with all this.'"

"Everyone disapproves and feels indignant," wrote Sebastian, "but at the same time everyone is a cog in the huge anti-Semitic factory that is the Romanian state, with all its offices, authorities, press, institutions, laws, and procedures."

FRANKLIN ROOSEVELT and Henry Morgenthau were talking about bombing strategy. "The way to lick Hitler is the way I have been telling the English, but they won't listen to me," Roosevelt said. The right way, he believed, was to bomb smaller towns that had up to then been safe from attack—a sort of WPA program in reverse. "There must be some kind of factory in every town," he said. "That is the only way to break German morale."

THE JAPANESE believed that they were being encircled. It was August 7, 1941. "First there was the creation of a superbase at Singapore, heavily reinforced by British and Empire troops," said the *Japan Times Advertiser.* "From this hub a great wheel was built up and linked with American bases to form a great ring sweeping in a great area southwards and westwards from the Philippines through Malaya and Burma, with the link broken only in the Thailand peninsula. Now it is proposed to include the narrows in the encirclement, which proceeds to Rangoon."

There was no justification, the newspaper said, for Roosevelt's "wall of Pacific bases," or for the joint British-American encirclement.

Cordell Hull, the secretary of state, said he knew nothing about encirclement. If Japan said she'd been encircled, well, she'd encircled herself.

PRESIDENT ROOSEVELT wanted even more of a food surplus in the United States. He wanted more dairy and poultry products, more tomatoes, and more pork. He wrote a letter to the secretary of agriculture. "Food is a weapon against Hitlerism just as much as munitions," the president said. "We need not only abundant production for ourselves and for other nations resisting aggression, but we need reserves to meet emergencies which can as yet be only dimly foreseen." It was August 1941.

CHURCHILL AND ROOSEVELT met secretly on the Atlantic Ocean. It was August 9, 1941. Churchill, sailing out of Scapa Flow in the *Prince of Wales*—one of Britain's newest warships—read *Captain Hornblower,* which he found "vastly entertaining." Franklin Roosevelt was waiting for him off the coast of Newfoundland, on the USS *Augusta.* On the quarterdeck of the *Prince of Wales,* two chaplains conducted a prayer service from a pulpit draped with British and American flags. Churchill found it deeply moving. He and Roosevelt ate apple pie together, and Roosevelt's crew distributed gift boxes to British sailors, each box containing two hundred cigarettes, some apples, an orange, and a half-pound of cheese. Roosevelt described his plan to grow Christmas trees at Hyde Park and sell them. They talked for several days, trading compliments, while their associates—Cadogan, Beaverbrook, Cherwell, Hap Arnold, and Acting Secretary of State Sumner Welles—commingled. And then, when it was over, they passed an incongruous document out to reporters.

The document was called the Atlantic Charter. It had eight principles, and it included the phrase "peace-loving peoples." Cadogan drafted it, Churchill worked it over, and Roosevelt's people added a few things. Oddly enough, though, the eight principles of the Atlantic Charter seem almost to have been prompted by the six principles of Rufus Jones's "dynamic peace" pamphlet.

Rufus Jones had called for all nations to have "equitable access to essential raw materials"; the Atlantic Charter called for access "on equal terms, to the trade and to the raw materials of the world." Jones said that "each nation shall be free to develop the form of government which its people desire"; the Atlantic Charter talked about "the right of all peoples to choose the form of government under which they will live." (That clause in particular Gandhi and Nehru read with attention.) Jones said that no nation should use "military force for its own ends"; the Atlantic Charter said that "all of the nations of the world, for realistic as well as spiritual reasons, must come to the abandonment of the use of force."

Peaceable words aside, what Churchill wanted out of the ocean rendezvous was hard language from the United States toward Japan—perhaps even a parallel British and American declaration that further southerly moves by Japan would lead to war—and the assurance of no letup in the deliveries of weapons to England. The question of weaponry was one reason why Churchill had asked along Max Beaverbrook, the former minister of aircraft production: He wanted to be sure that Stalin didn't divert Britain's Lend-Lease flow just because Russia was under savage attack. Heavy bombers were again at the top of the list: "British want 6,000 more than we are producing," wrote Arnold.

Churchill was successful. He cabled back to London that Russia was "a welcome guest at a hungry table" and that Roosevelt was going to be asking for five billion dollars more in Lend-Lease funding to pay for enough war hardware for everyone. "They are sending us immediately 150,000 more rifles, and I look for improved allocations of heavy bombers and tanks," Churchill wrote. "I trust my colleagues will feel that my mission has been fruitful."

Robert Sherwood, one of Roosevelt's speechwriters, wrote: "There could be little doubt that the cigarette-in-holder and the long cigar were at last being lit from the same match."

THE BRITISH AIR MINISTRY said that Royal Air Force pilots hovered over Berlin for two hours, setting "vast fires." It was August 12, 1941. *The New York Times* published a front-page map showing two lightning bolts striking the city, one from England, one from Russia. "British and Russian planes have been taking turns in bombing the Reich capital by night," the map's caption said.

In another raid, three hundred British bombers flew to the German cities of Hanover, Brunswick, and Magdeburg. "The first wave to reach Hanover lit big fires that guided later squadrons to the scene," the *Times* said. "Vivid explosions were seen by the plane crews among various buildings."

These bombings immediately followed the endorsement of the peace-loving language of the Atlantic Charter.

A TANKER filled with aviation fuel left Los Angeles. It was August 14, 1941.

The tanker was headed past Japan to Vladivostok, Russia. Harold Ickes, Roosevelt cabinet member and petroleum coordinator—the man who'd talked about flying an airplane to Siberia to drop a bomb on Tokyo—made the announcement. More oil tankers were scheduled to depart, as well—some American, some Russian. Vladivostok, directly across the Sea of Japan from Japan, was getting aviation fuel, while Japan itself got nothing. The Japanese government made formal protests to the American government.

THE ROYAL AIR FORCE turned the eight-point Atlantic Charter into a leaflet and dropped it on Germany and Italy. Secret agents in continental cities were asked to spread word of its existence. BBC broadcasters read the text of the charter in forty languages. It was the biggest propaganda campaign of the war, the British government declared.

HEINRICH HIMMLER asked to watch a shooting near Minsk, the newly captured city in Russia, home of fifty thousand Jews. The local commander had chosen for execution one hundred Jews, mostly men, who had been jailed after a roundup in the ghetto. Himmler noticed a blond, Germanic-looking boy among the group. Himmler asked, Are your parents Jews? The boy said yes. Himmler asked, Do you have any ancestors who weren't Jews? The boy said no. Himmler said, Then I can't help you.

Some of the Jews were told to jump into a ditch. They were shot and covered with earth. Then another group jumped down onto the first group and were shot. "Himmler had never seen dead people before," one of his aides later recalled, "and in his curiosity he stood right up at the edge of this open grave—a sort of triangular hole—and was looking in."

Then something from someone's head splashed onto Himmler's coat. He went pale and turned away. The commander pointed to the executioners. "Look at the eyes of the men in this Kommando," he said to Himmler. "What kind of followers are we training here? Either neurotics or savages!" Himmler told them to do their duty, however hard it may seem. It was August 15, 1941.

JOSEPH GOEBBELS released his thoughts about the Atlantic Charter to the German press. "Seldom has history seen such a stupid, unimaginative document as the two big guns of world plutocracy framed on the Potomac," he said, mistaking the location:

> These war and inflation profiteers, these fat capitalists and devoted Jewish servants, these perjurers of their own election promises, deserve only that the German people contemptuously spit at them and return again to its work: thus do we want to work and fight until humanity is freed from this scourge of God.

Goebbels was especially severe on the question of disarmament. "Whoever wants to disarm us will have to go to the little trouble of taking our weapons from us," he said. It was August 16, 1941.

IN THE MAGAZINE SECTION of *The New York Times,* there was a picture of two airplanes in flight. The caption said:

> THE B & B COCKTAIL. The newest concoction of the R.A.F. is a potent mixture dubbed the "B & B cocktail." It combines the bombs of the American-built Flying Fortress with the bullets of the British-built Beaufighter.

On the facing page was a picture of Churchill in profile, lighting his cigar in front of a four-engine bomber while an air crew in formal dress stood stiffly at attention behind him. "Concocter of the 'B & B,'" the caption said. It was August 17, 1941.

The next day, the Atlantic Charter team was riding the train back to London. Churchill drank a Benedictine and then shortly afterward asked for a brandy. The waiter remarked that the prime minister had just had a Benedictine. Churchill said, "I know: I want some brandy to clean it up."

Back at the big table at 10 Downing Street, Churchill told his cabinet that Roosevelt was definitely in. "The President had said he would wage war but not declare it," the war-cabinet minutes record. Roosevelt was expected to become "more and more provocative."

Churchill told his ministers: "Everything was to be done to force an incident."

LORD CHERWELL's personal secretary looked at 650 reconnaissance photographs of places the Royal Air Force had bombed earlier that summer. The secretary's conclusions were that, on average, one in five airplanes that took off from England to bomb Germany or the coast of France successfully placed its bombs somewhere within seventy-five square miles of its assigned target. When there was no moon or heavy flak, the miss rate was even higher.

The secretary's name was David Benusson-Butt, and his report, dated August 18, 1941, achieved fame as the Butt Report. It caused soul-searching at the Air Ministry. Churchill began to doubt that bombing alone would win the war. But the bombing continued. Churchill's slogan was "Keep buggering on."

A PRISON WARDEN said that things were going very well in the federal penitentiary in Atlanta. The prisoners were doing war work now. "We have 1,000 of them at work on two shifts, making such things as cases for TNT charges, clothing for aviators, shell covers, tents, pack sacks and mattresses," the warden said. Disciplinary problems had disappeared. It was August 18, 1941.

A warden in an Ohio prison said, "This national defense boom has really been a godsend."

MURIEL LESTER, author of "Speed the Food Ships," became one of England's political *détenus*. It was August 19, 1941.

Lester was on a boat in Trinidad, on her way to the Far East, where she planned to visit Gandhi. A British official said to her, "I am afraid I shall have to ask you to come ashore."

"Are you arresting me?" said Lester.

"Oh, no!" said the official.

"Then, supposing I say I won't come," said Lester. "What happens?"

"I'm afraid—er—we would have to find means to induce you to do so."

Lester's passport was revoked, and she was held in a barbed-wire prison camp for a month and a half, without charges. Later, she was transferred to Holloway jail in London and then, after friends made calls to the Home Office, freed.

GOEBBELS AND HITLER had another talk about the many Jews who were still in Berlin, and Hitler made him a promise. It was August 20, 1941.

"Immediately after the conclusion of the campaign in the East, I can deport the Jews of Berlin to the East," Goebbels recorded in his diary. "It is revolting and scandalous to think that seventy thousand Jews, most of them parasites, can still loiter in the capital of the German Reich." The situation, he said, must be approached without sentimentality.

A GERMAN POLICE BATTALION arrived at the shtetl of Sudilkov, in the Ukraine. The policemen led several hundred people to a bomb crater outside the town and shot them. The victims fell into the crater. A woman, unharmed, climbed out and sat on the edge, crying. A soldier shot her, and she fell back in. It was August 21, 1941.

IN PARIS, a German colonel was stabbed in the subway. It was August 22, 1941.

Six thousand Jews were arrested. A decree said: "In case of a new criminal act, a number of hostages corresponding to the gravity of the act committed will be shot." It was signed "Von Schaumburg, General Commanding, German Forces of Occupation."

CHURCHILL GAVE a speech about the meeting he had had with President Roosevelt, whom he called his great friend. It was August 25, 1941.

Churchill also talked about Hitler for a while, and then he turned to Japan. President Roosevelt was laboring with infinite patience to arrive at a fair settlement between Japan and the United States, Churchill asserted. "We earnestly hope these negotiations will succeed," he said. "But this I must say: That if these hopes should fail we shall, of course, range ourselves unhesitatingly at the side of the United States."

The Japanese newspaper *Nichi Nichi* said, "What Churchill said about peaceful settlement is nothing but a big lie."

GENERAL LEE, the American air attaché in London, analyzed twenty-three German raids on England and sent a report back to the United States. It was August 26, 1941.

"I find that it takes about forty bombers to knock out one key point," Lee wrote in his journal, "and one bomber will on the average kill three-quarters of a citizen and wound one and a quarter citizens."

Those figures were heartening for Great Britain, Lee felt, but worrying if one was hoping to paralyze Germany by air attacks alone. "My own theory is that you cannot beat a totalitarian at war by using only one weapon," he wrote. "This is going to create a great rumpus at home, I think, because Arnold and the Air Force are completely sold on the idea of bombing Germany to bits."

ENRIQUE ZANETTI's Incendiaries Branch, Chemical Warfare Service, U.S. Army, got its first assignment. It was supposed to find a way to make twenty-five million four-pound firebombs: one hundred million pounds of fire. It was August 28, 1941.

Zanetti knew he would need a lot of powdered magnesium. And fortunately for him, a new, federally financed, sixty-three-million-dollar magnesium plant, powered by Boulder Dam, was going up near Las Vegas. Las Vegas was destined to grow in the desert, fed in part by money from the men and women who made the raw materials for firebombs.

HALF OF GREAT BRITAIN's industrial capacity was being used to make bombs and bombers. "Mr. Churchill was, of course, responsible for deciding the allocation of manpower and industrial production of the three Services," the director of military operations wrote later. "We in the General Staff were quite sure that the decisions he gave at this time were dangerously wrong."

LORD CHERWELL told Churchill that the uranium weapon held promise. Churchill then wrote a memo for the chiefs of staff. It was August 30, 1941.

"Although personally I am quite content with the existing explosives," he said, "I feel we must not stand in the path of improvement." The chiefs of staff recommended immediate action, top priority.

SIR RICHARD PEIRSE, head of Bomber Command, got a letter ordering him to attack small railway towns in Germany. The small-town program had two aims. First, bombing a number of locations on the same rail line on the same night might disrupt train traffic. And second: "From the morale standpoint, by extending our attacks to the smaller towns, it is felt that the more widespread experience of the direct effect of our offensive may have considerable value." The theater of war—the grief, the fear, the witnessed ruin—was now to reach the hinterlands. President Roosevelt's advice had been heeded.

It was August 30, 1941.

A GROUP OF BRITISH AVIATION authorities flew to New York on the *Atlantic Clipper.* One of them, William Courtenay, an aeronautics correspondent for Allied Newspapers in England, answered reporters' questions at La Guardia Field. The Royal Air Force, Courtenay said, had already undertaken to "level" German cities such as Aachen and Cologne. In the coming winter, when it got dark earlier and planes could take off at four o'clock in the afternoon, they would continue to damage Berlin.

The next day, a former Australian sheep farmer flew one of the RAF's Flying Fortresses over Bremen at very high altitude, in broad daylight, and dropped thousand-pound bombs. Bremen was where Focke Wulfe made fighter planes, although there was little chance that one airplane's bombs would hit the factory from five or six miles in the air. "There wasn't any fire from anti-aircraft guns and we saw no fighters," said the sheep farmer. "Our bombs fell in the middle of the port."

It was August 31, 1941. The Germans ordered a heavy reprisal on a port city in England.

AN EYEWITNESS left Bremen for Stockholm. "The Germans cannot take it, particularly the really heavy raids," the eyewitness told *The New York Times*'s Stockholm correspondent, Bernard Valery. "I heard a worker who was standing by his whimpering wife in an air-raid shelter called Goering 'a damned fat liar.' "

Trainloads of wounded were now returning from Russia, Valery wrote. Women mail carriers in Vienna had gone on strike because they had to deliver so many death letters—they "were made too nervous to work by the painful scenes the delivery of these letters provoked among the recipients." If the Russians held out for a while and the British kept bombing, Valery thought, a collapse of Germany could come "with dramatic suddenness." It was September 1941.

THE JAPANESE PRESS was angry over the ships filled with oil and aviation fuel that were on their way to Russia. One newspaper, *Yomiuru,* said that the United States was "flaunting this oil in Japan's face by sending it past our shores to Vladivostok."

Colonel Hayto Mabuchi, chief of the press section of the Japanese army, gave a speech on the radio. Britain and the United States were engaged in an economic war with Japan, and Japan was faced with "slow death," Colonel Mabuchi said. "If Japan cannot reach a peaceful settlement through diplomatic negotiations Japan must break through the encirclement fronts by force." It was September 2, 1941.

COLOGNE, GERMANY, had been raided more than a hundred times. The mayor of the city was designated a "Führer of Immediate Measures." He began using French prisoners of war to clean up bomb damage. The POWs lived in a concentration camp on the Cologne fairgrounds, across the river from the cathedral. It was September 2, 1941.

AN INTELLIGENCE OFFICER published a book called *The War in the Air*. The officer, David Garnett, was also a novelist and publisher—he was part of the Bloomsbury group. Now, however, he was doing war work.

Garnett wasn't, he said, an advocate of terror bombing—not because it was wrong but because England didn't yet have enough airplanes to terror-bomb properly. "For bombing to be effective against civilians it must inspire abject terror and despair," Garnett wrote.

> I can conceive that in 1943, when Britain has achieved a tremendous air superiority, the ruthless bombing of the war-weary population of Germany on a far more gigantic scale than has been experienced by any British city may well be the most effective way to bring about a German revolution. By butchering the German population indiscriminately it might be possible to goad them into a desperate rising in which every member of the Nazi party would have his throat cut.

Garnett said that he'd had the pleasure of examining a Boeing Flying Fortress: "We need two or three thousand such aircraft," he said. It was September 1941.

PAUL JONES, the former Episcopal bishop of Utah, died. It was September 4, 1941.

Bishop Jones had lost his post in 1917, during the First World War, because he had preached against it. Jones had once said: "A pacifist between wars is like a prohibitionist between drinks."

AN AMERICAN BOAT, the *L. P. St. Clair,* arrived safely at Vladivostok with ninety-five thousand barrels of aviation fuel. Japanese protests to the United States had gone unanswered. The Japanese navy, however, ignored the provocation. It was September 5, 1941.

In Tokyo, citizens were ordered to be ready for air raids at any time.

A COUPLE, Hans Hirschfeld and Inge Korach, were to be married in Berlin. It was fall 1941. They picked up their mothers early in order to get to the marriage office on time: The small room reserved for Jewish weddings was open only from eight to nine o'clock in the morning. The civil servant moved some flowers from the Aryan room to the Jewish room to make things look more festive.

Later, at the temple, the Hirschfelds had a religious wedding, with Rabbi Leo Baeck presiding. The service was, however, marred by the sound of hammering. In a different part of the temple, workmen were knocking out pews. The building was soon to serve as a point of assembly and deportation.

In Bucharest, the courtyard of the Great Synagogue was filled with beds, pillows, mattresses, sheets, and blankets. It was September 5, 1941.

The city authorities told the Jews that if they didn't bring the bedding in themselves, the army would go around and confiscate it. "Crestfallen people keep arriving with things on their backs—resigned, mournful, not rebellious, almost not surprised," Mihail Sebastian wrote. "No one is surprised any more at anything."

Reinhard Heydrich issued an order. All Jews in Germany over the age of six must wear a star:

> The star consists of a six-pointed star, outlined in black on yellow cloth the size of the palm of one's hand, with a black superscription: "Jew." It must be worn visibly and firmly sewed to the left breast of clothing.

It was September 6, 1941.

Rita Kuhn, a Berlin teenager, baptized but half Jewish, went for a walk alone, wearing the star. "People looked pained and embarrassed and looked away," she said.

Her mother, who was Aryan, sewed a lining on the star's back. The lining made it easier to wash, and easier to pin on and take off.

IN PARIS, the occupation government arrested one hundred prominent Jews: lawyers, a former deputy, a former undersecretary of state, and an owner of racehorses. It was September 8, 1941.

"Today's was the first instance of systematic selection of the well-to-do," said *The New York Times*. "They are being held responsible for the maintenance of order, which seems to mean that they are being held as hostages."

IN HANOVER, GERMANY, the mayor began rounding up Jews. It was September 8, 1941.

About one hundred people, "of all ages and both sexes," were taken into the mortuary hall of the Jewish cemetery, according to the Associated Press. And from there they went—where? To the east.

The mayor of Hanover gave two justifications for his action. One was the self-published book by Theodore Kaufman, the Brooklyn ticket seller who advocated the forced sterilization of twenty million German men. The other was the bombing, in a war "forced upon Germany by the Jewry of other countries."

"The enemy air force attacks open towns and unloads explosive and incendiary bombs indiscriminately," the mayor said.

> In order to relieve the distressed situation caused by the war,
> I see myself compelled immediately to narrow down the
> space available to Jews in this city. I therefore demand that
> you quit your present abode immediately. You must leave
> your house keys with your police precinct headquarters.

Proceeds from the sale of Jewish property would be released, said the eviction orders, "at a given time."

"The bombing offensive," historian Shlomo Aaronson wrote years later, "fed Hitler's wrath, in direct connection with his concept of the 'Jew's war' against him, and helped unite his nation behind him and justify further Nazi atrocities against the remaining Jews."

It was September 9, 1941, the first anniversary of the London Blitz. The Royal Air Force marked the date with a series of record-setting raids on Berlin. "Capital Is Seared" was the *New York Times* headline. "It was bright moonlight as the bombers went in," the reporter said. "They flew so low the fliers could see by the light of the blazes they set fire engines scuttling about in the streets."

"Berliners crept out of shelters white, shaken, subdued and terrified at dawn this morning to find their city still ablaze and destruction everywhere," reported the *Herald Tribune*. "Many hundreds were homeless and schools and hospitals were filled with refugees."

German newspapers ran accounts of the heroic crews who manned flak guns around the capital, and they raged at England. "In the list of criminal attacks that the Royal Air Force has directed against the civilian population in the Reich's capital," one Berlin paper wrote, "that which it committed last night will for all future stand out as an especially base and disgusting one." And yet, said the article, the RAF's objective, the "terrorization of the Berlin population," had not been achieved. "This objective will remain a wish, for it collapses against the disciplined conduct of the people of Berlin."

An order went out in Bucharest: Jews there also had to wear the yellow star. Then the chairman of the Federation of the Union of Jewish Communities met with Prime Minister Antonescu. The order was rescinded.

Mihail Sebastian had gotten used to the idea of wearing the star. "I saw it as a kind of medal," he said, "an insignia certifying my lack of sympathy for the vile deeds around us, my lack of responsibility for them, my innocence." It was September 9, 1941.

DURING AN AIR RAID in Berlin, Rita Kuhn went with her family to the basement of their four-story apartment building. A woman from the Gestapo, Frau Burger—a new neighbor—was already there. Frau Burger saw the stars and ordered the Jews to leave, while bombs were dropping. "I panicked," said Kuhn. "I started crying."

Another woman—an Aryan, the wife of a doctor—put her arm around Kuhn's shoulders and led her to a smaller room and comforted her. "It was okay in the small room," Kuhn said. "I felt safe there." It was fall 1941.

Soon, though, the Kuhns and Frau Burger became friends. They had tea together. Frau Burger hadn't known Jews personally before—they were, Kuhn said, just an abstraction to her.

GENERAL PORTER, director of the Chemical Warfare Service, delivered the annual address at the fall meeting of the American Chemical Society. "To overcome the enemy, we must take the offensive," Porter said. All the belligerents were well equipped now with chemical agents, and the Nazis could lay on an overwhelming use of gas at any moment. There had been improvements since the First World War—fleets of airplanes could "spray large areas with vesicant liquids not only on military personnel but upon the civilian population as well." (Vesicants, such as mustard gas, cause injury or death through blistering, external and internal.)

One thousand reserve officers had been called up, said Porter, and—thanks to James Conant's National Defense Research Committee—the finest chemical talent in the country was in readiness.

The word "defense" was a weasel word, Porter said. "Wars are not won by gas masks."

It was September 10, 1941.

Franklin Roosevelt's mother died. Roosevelt drove around Hyde Park in his car with his head of security, saying nothing. Eight men from the Hyde Park estate carried Mrs. Roosevelt's coffin to the local church. No press was allowed.

The next day, Roosevelt gave what came to be known as his "shoot on sight" speech. An American flush-deck destroyer, the *Greer,* had shadowed a German U-boat while a British plane dropped depth charges. The U-boat fired torpedoes at the *Greer*; the *Greer* depth-charged back. Nobody was hit. "Roosevelt," said a German communiqué, "is endeavoring with all the means at his disposal to provoke incidents for the purpose of baiting the American people into the war."

In his speech, Roosevelt said that Hitler was trying to take over the world. "To be ultimately successful in world mastery Hitler knows that he must get control of the seas," he said. "He must first destroy the bridge of ships which we are building across the Atlantic, over which we shall continue to roll the implements of war to help destroy him and all his works in the end."

German U-boats were the rattlesnakes of the Atlantic, said Roosevelt. "When you see a rattlesnake poised to strike you do not wait until he has struck before you crush him." It was September 11, 1941.

CHARLES LINDBERGH gave a speech in Des Moines, at an America First rally. It was September 11, 1941.

Lindbergh said that agitators had worked together to involve the United States in the war in Europe. "They planned: First, to prepare the United States for foreign war under the guise of American defense; second, to involve us in the war, step by step, without our realization; third, to create a series of incidents which would force us into the actual conflict."

There were, Lindbergh said, three groups of war agitators: "the British, the Jewish, and the Roosevelt administration."

He could understand, he said, why the Jews wanted the Nazi government defeated:

> No person with a sense of dignity can condone the persecution of the Jewish race in Germany. But no person of honesty and vision can look on their pro-war policy here today without seeing the dangers involved in such a policy both for us and for them. Instead of agitating for war, the Jewish groups in this country should be opposing it in every possible way for they will be among the first to feel its consequences.
>
> Tolerance is a virtue that depends upon peace and strength. History shows that it cannot survive war and devastations. A few far-sighted Jewish people realize this and stand opposed to intervention. But the majority still do not.

And then Lindbergh said: "Their greatest danger to this country lies in their large ownership and influence in our motion pictures, our press, our radio and our government."

Lindbergh was booed and cheered by turns. Someone in the balcony threw a package of America First handouts at him as he spoke. It missed and knocked over a plant in a vase.

STEPHEN EARLY, Roosevelt's press secretary, said, "You have seen the outpourings of Berlin in the last few days. You saw Lindbergh's statement last night. I think there is a striking similarity between the two."

Peter Cusick, executive secretary of Fight for Freedom, said, "Mr. Lindbergh's prestige has descended even more quickly than the dive-bombers which he talks about so admiringly."

The American Jewish Committee and the Jewish Labor Committee issued a statement: "Each one of us has a right to his views, whether for or against isolationism, without fear that Mr. Lindbergh can intimidate any of us with the low and baseless charge that there are other 'interests' which we place ahead of loyalty to our country."

Norman Thomas, pacifist and head of the Socialist party, said: "Many groups and elements in this country are attempting to drive us into war. This issue cuts across all racial lines. No one race is responsible. The Socialist party has many Jews in its ranks and these take their stand with the party against American involvement. No race or people can be made a scapegoat for this crime."

DR. HENRY SZOSZKIES distributed a report to American newspapers about the Jews in Poland. It was September 13, 1941.

In the Warsaw ghetto, there were eighty-eight soup kitchens, Dr. Szoszkies said. Until recently, 115,420 people got a bowl of soup every day, paid for by a small tax on the entire community. Now there was only enough money to keep the kitchens open four days out of seven. The bread ration had dropped to three ounces a day, occasionally supplemented with potatoes and saccharine. "A large proportion of the deaths in the Warsaw ghetto," Szoszkies said, "is now of young children between the age of 1 and 5 who are no longer allowed a daily ration of milk." In Radom, he said, most of the seven thousand Jews who lived in the ghetto were destitute and starving.

Roosevelt's money blockade, which made it difficult to buy food for people living in German-controlled countries, was contributing to the problem, according to Szoszkies. "The latest restrictions imposed by the United States Treasury on the sending of remittances abroad," he said, "have increased the plight of many Jewish families who were receiving regularly—via Portugal and other neutral countries—food parcels through the generosity of their relatives in the United States."

James Reston, *The New York Times*'s Washington correspondent, wrote: "It is clear that the new Anglo-American blockade is going to give Germany its worst winter since the days of famine during the last great war."

JOSEPH STALIN sent four hundred thousand Volga Germans east, to Siberia. Volga Germans were people of German descent who lived near the Volga River in Russia. It was September 13, 1941.

Alfred Rosenberg thought that Hitler should retaliate by deporting all central European Jews. They must go east. He wrote up a plan.

HITLER'S HATE MANIA was at full flood. St. Petersburg was an Asiatic "nest of poison," he said to the German ambassador to France—now that the city was surrounded, he said, he would bomb it and shell it until it disappeared from the earth.

Hitler also talked to the party leader of Hamburg, Karl Kaufmann. Kaufmann wanted to expel Jews from Hamburg so that he could offer their houses to bombed-out Germans. Hitler approved the deportations. It was September 1941.

It wasn't yet time, though, apparently, to carry out a "reprisal" on the enormous scale that Rosenberg had suggested, by sending all German Jews east. One of Rosenberg's staff wrote: "The Führer is considering taking this step in the event of the possible involvement of America in the war."

IN MOGILEV, a city in Byelorussia near the Soviet border, two men tried a new way to kill people. Himmler had been asking his SS subordinates to find methods that were less traumatic—for the killers—than shooting was.

Albert Widmann, a forensic chemist, and Arthur Nebe, the commander of an SS squad, went to an insane asylum and put two pipes through a bricked-in window. When the room was full of patients, they connected an idling car to one of the pipes. The patients didn't die. "Nebe and I came to the conclusion that the car was not powerful enough," Widmann later testified. "So Nebe had the second hose fitted onto a transport vehicle which belonged to the regular police. It then took only another few minutes before the people were unconscious. Both vehicles were left running for about another ten minutes."

It was the middle of September 1941.

RUDOLPH HÖSS, the commander of Auschwitz Concentration Camp in Poland, walked to the mortuary and killed nine hundred naked Russian prisoners. The prisoners entered the chamber thinking they were being deloused. Höss used gas from crystals of Zyklon B pesticide.

"When the gas was thrown in some people shouted: 'gas' and then there was a lot of shouting and they pressed against both the doors," Höss recalled. "But they withstood the pressure."

Höss wrote later that he was relieved that Zyklon B was so effective. "I must even admit that this gassing set my mind at rest," he said, "for the mass extermination of the Jews was to start soon, and at the time neither Eichmann nor I was certain as to how these mass killings were to be carried out." It was September 15, 1941.

BRITISH HEADQUARTERS in the Far East sent General Douglas MacArthur a how-to memo: "The Problem of Defeating Japan." It was September 19, 1941.

The memo called for the creation of "subversion organizations" in China and French Indochina. These would carry out propaganda, terrorism, and sabotage, "creating discontent amongst the population, culminating in open rebellion." In Thailand, a subversive organization must "spread its tentacles," said the memo. "Assassination of individual Japanese should also be considered." And Vladivostock's air bases were within range of Japan's "vitals," too.

Should political methods fail, the memo said, "we must be prepared to fight."

MIHAIL SEBASTIAN went to temple for Rosh Hashanah and listened to some of Rabbi Safran's address. "Stupid, pretentious, essayistic, journalistic, shallow, and unserious," Sebastian wrote. "But people were crying—and I myself had tears in my eyes." It was September 22, 1941.

Mr. and Mrs. Churchill's private train stopped at the platform at Coventry. It was September 26, 1941.

The mayor of Coventry took them to what was left of the cathedral and the center of town, and then they visited airplane factories, which were back in production. At the Armstrong Siddeley factory, the men clanged their hammers deafeningly in greeting.

"The Whitley bomber factory is a hotbed of Communism and there was some doubt of the reception the P.M. would get," wrote John Colville, Churchill's secretary. "But his appearance with cigar and semi-top-hat quite captivated the workers who gave him vociferous applause." Colville noted with some disgust that their production tempo had quickened after Germany invaded Russia.

They also visited the Coventry cemetery, where they looked at the mass grave of air-raid dead, and then they got back on the train. They had lunch on their way to Birmingham to see a tank factory.

Elena Efimovna Borodyanska-Knysh and her daughter were led to Babi Yar, a ravine near Kiev, in the Ukraine, where many thousands of people were being shot. It was September 27, 1941.

"I didn't wait for the next command but immediately tossed my little girl into the pit and then fell in after her. A second later, bodies started falling on top of me. Then it grew quiet." Fifteen minutes later, there was more shooting. Then arguing. Elena carried her daughter away and hid in the basement of a brick factory. She and her daughter lived.

THE OCTOBER 1941 ISSUE of *Fortune* magazine went out to subscribers. Its feature article was entitled "A Tool for Mr. Churchill: The Heavy Bomber." The text began as an inset into a double-page color spread showing the B-17 Fortress and the B-24 Liberator flying side by side, high over grain fields; there were charts of bomb sizes and shapes, diagrams of bomb trajectories and fuzes, subassembly flowcharts, and blast-survivability circles.

"The four-engine heavy bomber is a peculiarly American weapon," *Fortune* said. "It was the logical development of a nation of high mountains and vast distances." The article, which went on for many pages, was surrounded by ads for roller bearings, needle bearings, drive chains, industrial paints, lathes, and grinding wheels; it described the production programs at Boeing, at Consolidated, at General Electric, at Nash Kelvinator, at Allis Chalmers, and at Henry Ford's vast factory at Willow Run. "Out of this protoplasm has come the blueprint for what amounts to a whole new industry with half again as many workers as U.S. Steel," *Fortune* said. The article quoted Boeing's Philip Johnson: "The public ought to wake up and see how big this bull is we've got by the tail."

There were challenges to flying at near-substratospheric altitudes, however, *Fortune* noted. And the basic assumption of the heavy bomber's effect on an enemy country—that, as *Fortune* put it, "used in force against factories and civilians, it would destroy his power to produce and eventually his will to resist, thus exacting a surrender, even though his armies remained undefeated"—was still, two years into the war, unproved.

"Yet, even after discounting the propaganda elements, an immense and spectacular portent remains," the article said. "What is under way now is so big as to leave even its architects breathless." And we, in the United States of America, had done it: "We Americans have thrown the heavy bomber into the wavering balance of human affairs. For good and for evil we have thrust it into the world."

In Lublin, Poland, fifteen German policemen got in fifteen trucks and drove to a camp where many Jews were imprisoned. Thirty people—men, women, and children—were ordered into each truck. They were driven out to an airfield and told to dig trenches. After they'd dug, they were told to take off their clothes, which they did. The policemen handed out long shirts made of a kind of corrugated paper. The people put the long shirts on. Straw was sprinkled over the bottom of the ditches. Ten people were ordered to get in one of the ditches and lie down. They were told to lie in opposing directions—head, feet, head, feet.

And then the policemen threw in grenades, which exploded. Pieces of bodies flew up. Anyone who was still alive after the grenades was shot. The men sprinkled lime and more straw, and the next group was made to lie down on the first layer of dead, blown-up people. More grenades exploded.

In Lublin, Poland, that was how 450 Jews died—bombed by grenades at close range. It was October 1941.

Winston Churchill gave a speech in the House of Commons. He took up a charge that he thought was "a little unfair." The charge was that the British government was "held back by excessive scruples and inhibitions."

> The people ask, for instance, "Why don't you bomb Rome?
> What is holding you back? Didn't you say you would bomb
> Rome if Cairo were bombed? What is the answer?"

The answer was, said Churchill, that only the outskirts of Cairo had been bombed. He said: "We should not hesitate to bomb Rome to the best of our ability and as heavily as possible if the course of the war should render such action convenient and helpful." It was October 1, 1941.

HENRY STIMSON, the secretary of war, wrote a letter to Dr. Frank Jewett, president of the National Academy of Sciences. "Because of the dangers that might confront this country from potential enemies employing what may be broadly described as biological warfare," he wrote, "it seems advisable that investigations be initiated to survey the present situation and the future possibilities." It was October 1, 1941.

Jewett recruited Dr. Edwin B. Fred, a homey bacteriologist from the University of Wisconsin, later to become its president. Dr. Fred recruited others, and they hired others, and soon dozens, and then hundreds, and then thousands of people were working at universities and research centers around the country on fevers, plagues, growth disorders, and pestilences of various kinds—how to cure them, and how to cause them.

THE *STUTTGART COURIER* published an article attacking "cases of unsuitable compassion for Jews." These cases were not unusual, the newspaper said. For instance, women from the Jewish old-peoples' home, wearing the star, would get on a tramcar, and passengers would stand to give them their seats.

Once, according to the newspaper, a German said to a Jew, "It really requires more courage to wear the star than to go to war." It was October 4, 1941.

THE FIGHT FOR FREEDOM COMMITTEE sponsored a big rally at Madison Square Garden—the theme was "It's Fun to Be Free." It was October 5, 1941.

Seventeen thousand people watched Bill "Bojangles" Robinson tap-dance in gold pants on Hitler's coffin, to the tune of "While That Man Is Dead and Gone." Eddie Cantor wore a hoopskirt. Carmen Miranda, Jack Benny, and Ethel Merman all showed off their talents. William Knudsen of the Office of War Production said that the country had to sweat hard for the next year or so; Wendell Willkie censured Lindbergh's racism; and President Roosevelt's face appeared on-screen while the sound system played an excerpt of his shoot-on-sight speech. Herbert Agar, editor of the Louisville *Courier-Journal,* quoted Ecclesiastes and said, "Today is a time for war."

At the end of the pageant, the theater went dark. Mock radio voices announced that bomber armadas were approaching Los Angeles, New York, and Laredo. There was a sound of propellers and explosions—and then thousands of five-inch-high cardboard parachutists fell from the ceiling through crisscrossing spotlights. "My God, I thought it was real!" said a woman in the audience.

VANNEVAR BUSH, the war scientist, talked over the uranium bomb one afternoon with President Roosevelt and Vice President Wallace. It was October 9, 1941. Roosevelt liked the idea and sent Churchill a note soon afterward: "My Dear Winston," Roosevelt said, "It appears desirable that we should correspond or converse concerning the subject which is under study by your MAUD committee, and by Dr. Bush's organization in this country, in order that any extended efforts may be coordinated or even jointly conducted." The Manhattan Project moved forward.

WALTER MATTNER, a police secretary from Vienna, wrote a letter to his wife. It was October 10, 1941.

Mattner had just taken part in a massacre in Mogilev. His hand was shaking slightly, he wrote, when he shot the first truckload, but by the tenth he was aiming more calmly. He had "shot securely many women, children, and infants"—and then he supplied further horrible details. All this he did, he said, with the understanding that he had infants at home, "with whom these hordes would do the same if not ten times worse."

He said: "Many say here that after our return home then it will be the turn of our own Jews. Well, I'm not allowed to tell you enough."

EIGHTY-TWO WELLINGTON BOMBERS, fifty-four Whitley bombers, nine Halifax bombers, and seven Stirling bombers flew in the direction of Nuremberg, six hundred miles away. Nuremberg was hard to find: The crews were still navigating by star position and wind speed, and a few planes ended up over Stuttgart, ninety-five miles to the southwest.

Nuremberg was the city where the Nazi Party held its annual congress. It was also a very old, very Gothic, very lovely city, where Jews and non-Jews had lived, with several eruptions and expulsions, for seven hundred years. In the Renaissance, it had been a city of handicrafts; it was known for pocket watches, dolls, astrolabes, and Albrecht Dürer. Copernicus's *Revolutions of the Heavenly Spheres* was first published in Nuremberg. It was part of German history, and Jewish history, and German-Jewish history, and world history.

"British Bombers Sear Nuremberg" was the headline in *The New York Times.* "Factories there that made dolls in peace time now produce tanks and airplane parts, guns and shells," said the paper. The targets were aircraft plants and machine-tool works. "Fires spread over a wide area," the *Times* reported, "raging so fiercely their red glow tinged the wings of the bombers soaring far above." The subsequent German communiqué said: "The civilian population suffered dead and wounded."

This wasn't the big raid on Nuremberg—the one that books have been written about, in which almost eight hundred airplanes incinerated the *Altstadt,* the city's old quarter. That came three years later. This was just the biggest raid on Nuremberg to that point. It happened on the night of October 12, 1941.

MOHANDAS GANDHI gave a speech in Savagram, the village where he lived. "A barbaric war is being fought in Europe with large-scale massacres," Gandhi said. "Young, old, even invalids, are being annihilated." There was only one correct response to this war: *ahimsa,* principled nonviolence, even at risk of imprisonment, starvation, and death. "Hitlerism and Churchillism are in fact the same thing," he said. "The difference is only one of degree." On the other hand, India must not embarrass Britain, either—not help, but not embarrass. India must love her enemies. It was October 12, 1941.

That same day, Gandhi told a reporter for the Associated Press that the United States should demand "guarantees of human liberties" before she continued helping England. "She should say what Abraham Lincoln would say," he said. "She should ask what will happen to India, Asia, and African possessions."

FREDERICK J. LIBBY, executive secretary of the National Council for the Prevention of War, testified at a congressional hearing on a modification of the Neutrality Act. It was October 14, 1941. Libby said that the United States should not allow the mounting of guns on merchant ships—not antisubmarine guns and not antiaircraft guns.

Britain should negotiate with Germany now, Libby held, while its empire was intact, and with the support of the United States. Jews and other oppressed minorities, Libby said, "stand a better chance of winning their rights at the conference table with Great Britain and the United States as their champions than they do on the battlefield."

IN BERLIN, things got suddenly worse. It was October 1941.

The Kulturbund, or Jewish Culture Association—where Jews, long since banned from Aryan events, were able to see plays and movies and hear concerts—was disbanded. Musicians and performers had been sent to work, said *The New York Times,* "in munitions factories, on road building projects and similar chores." Jews were forbidden to buy fruits and vegetables. The few remaining synagogues were closed to worship and filled with straw sleeping sacks.

Two thousand Jews received eviction notices. They were told not to look for other apartments.

CHRISTOPHER ISHERWOOD arrived at the train station in Haverford, Pennsylvania, to teach English to Jewish refugees at a Quaker hostel. It was October 15, 1941.

He stayed at the house of an elderly couple, Mr. and Mrs. Yarnall. Also living at the Yarnalls' house was a former lawyer from Lake Constance—"an aristocratic Jewish Dante," Isherwood called him in his diary—and a Berlin judge. The judge, said Isherwood, "spoke English well, carefully choosing his words, and expressing himself with a genuine, touching humility. He worried terribly about his wife and two little girls, who were in occupied Belgium." He was, said Isherwood, "a permanently saddened man."

Isherwood gave five or six English lessons per day. On Sunday, he went to a Friends meeting, where he listened to Rufus Jones, whom he called the uncrowned Quaker pope. Soon he was talking like a Quaker: "Caroline, is thee driving to Haverford this morning?"

MIHAIL SEBASTIAN learned that a ship filled with 750 Jews was leaving soon. It was October 16, 1941.

The ship was the *Struma.* "To get on there I'd need a sense of adventure, and above all I'd have to be younger, healthier, less ground down by life," Sebastian wrote in his journal. He quoted Dante Gabriel Rossetti: "Look in my face: my name is Might-have-been."

THERE WERE TERRORS and commotions at night—house searchings, confiscations, arrests. "Jews were being evicted from apartments in Berlin and other cities," *The New York Times* said, "reportedly to make room for 'Aryan' families whose homes were destroyed by air raids." It was October 16, 1941.

Viscount Trenchard, marshal of the Royal Air Force, told an audience at Leeds what his motto was: "Keep the Germans out of bed, and keep the sirens blowing." It was October 17, 1941.

President Roosevelt began gradually leaking the news of his new war plan, the Victory Program. One hundred billion dollars would go toward the building of 125,000 airplanes; half of the entire productive capacity of the United States would be devoted to the production of arms. "Tanks in what are described as unbelievable numbers are planned," *The New York Times* reported. It was October 18, 1941.

Eugene Duffield, the head of *The Wall Street Journal*'s Washington bureau, pondered the meaning of that many tanks, and he wrote a long story the next day. "By its emphasis on tanks and ordnance, the 'Victory Program' reveals that long-range bombing and ocean blockade no longer are counted on to subdue Germany," Duffield wrote. The program, he said, envisioned an American army composed of "one of every three men between the ages of 18 and 45."

At Imperial Chemical's large Runcol mustard-gas factory in Rhydymwyn, Wales, twenty-one people were injured, some severely, as they replaced a corroded effluent-pit pump. It was October 1941. The effluent was sent into the River Dee.

ALL JEWISH EMIGRATION from Germany was officially shut off, by edict. It was October 18, 1941.

HERBERT HOOVER gave a speech on the radio. There were about forty million children in the German-invaded democracies, he said, and the blockade was killing them: "Their pleas for food ascend hourly to the free democracies of the west." It was October 19, 1941.

Hoover cited two recent reports. One was about hunger in Belgium, and one was the report by Dr. Szoszkies about hunger in the Jewish ghetto in Warsaw. In Warsaw, Hoover said, the death rate among children was ten times the birth rate, and corpses lay in the street. America was now, by failing to compel England to change its policy, a moral participant in the blockade.

"Is the Allied cause any further advanced today as a consequence of this starvation of children?" Hoover asked. "Are Hitler's armies any less victorious than if these children had been saved? Are Britain's children better fed today because these millions of former allied children have been hungry or died? Can you point to one benefit that has been gained from this holocaust?"

IN NANTES, a city on the Loire River in France, the local commander of German forces started to cross the street. Two men rushed up and shot him in the head. It was October 20, 1941.

The Germans shot fifty French hostages in reprisal.

THE UNITED PRESS sent out a small story on deportations from Berlin. "55,000 of an estimated 65,000 Jews in the German capital would be deported to Russia and Poland," the article said. "The dispatches said each deportee would be allowed to take along an extra suit, several shirts and six handkerchiefs." It was October 21, 1941.

Special transports were leaving nightly for Poland, *The New York Times* reported. "When the eviction started it was said the Jews were being moved to make room for 'Aryans' whose homes had been destroyed in air raids." There were ads in the *Völkischer Beobachter* for auctions of possessions left behind.

Victor Klemperer wrote: "Ever more shocking reports about deportations of Jews to Poland. They have to leave almost naked and penniless. Thousands from Berlin to Lodz."

A source in the German government was asked by a reporter whether the Jews were going to concentration camps. No, the source said: "Their energies will be diverted to useful purposes." And there was a new term in use: "catastrophe apartment." A catastrophe apartment was an apartment "suitable for Aryan refugees from cities subject to bombings," *The New York Times* explained.

Albert Speer, Hitler's architect, was in charge of clearing the catastrophe apartments in Berlin: He tried to use the bomb damage to further his, and Hitler's, plans for a modern city, with a grand boulevard running through it. In a chronicle of progress on the grand boulevard, one of Speer's assistants wrote: "According to a Speer directive a further action for the clearing of some five thousand Jewish flats is being started."

HELMUTH JAMES VON MOLTKE, a lawyer, wrote an anguished letter to his wife. The news was gruesome everywhere, he said: hostage shootings in France, villages in Serbia reduced to ashes—and now the Berlin Jews. "Since Saturday the Berlin Jews are being rounded up," he wrote. "They are picked up at 9.15 in the evening and locked into a synagogue overnight." From there, they were sent to Lodz and Smolensk, he said, where they would starve or freeze. He asked: "How can anyone know these things and still walk around free?"

It was October 21, 1941.

IN THE LODZ GHETTO, Dawid Sierakowiak wrote, "The German Jews keep arriving: from Frankfurt am Main, Cologne, and also from Vienna and Prague (they live near us). Almost all are 'big fish.' At least so they look."

The price of bread had doubled. It was October 22, 1941.

IN BORDEAUX, FRANCE, a German officer was walking down the Boulevard St. Georges. Four assailants shot him dead. It was October 22, 1941.

That evening, a bomb blew up Romanian army headquarters in the city of Odessa. A commander, sixteen officers, and four German officers died.

In reprisal, the German army shot fifty French hostages, and the Romanian army shot and burned alive more than thirty thousand Jews.

ULRICH VON HASSELL, Hitler resister, had been hearing accounts of the nighttime evictions of Jewish Berliners: "terrible scenes," he'd been told, and the orders had come from Hitler himself. "The populace in part was so disgusted," von Hassell wrote, "that the Nazis found it necessary to distribute handbills saying the Jews were to blame for everything."

These handbills said: "Every Jew is your enemy. Every German who aids a Jew for reasons of false sentiment—even by only showing a friendly attitude toward Jews—commits treason against his own people." The evictions were justified on the grounds that Aryans whose houses were destroyed by bombing needed a place to live.

The Gestapo sent out bulletins to all branches: "It has repeatedly come to our notice recently that persons of German blood continue to maintain friendly relations with Jews and appear with them in public in a blatant fashion." The Gestapo's orders were to take a Jew-friendly person into "protective custody for educational purposes." Serious cases of friendship went to a Grade 1 concentration camp. The Jewish person to whom the friendly act was tendered also went to a concentration camp. It was October 1941.

THE CITY OF TOKYO, the third-largest city in the world, where six and a half million people lived, had a practice air-raid blackout. It was October 22, 1941.

"Japan does not go to America or any nation with hat in hand but stands conscious of its power for peace or war," said an editorial in the *Japan Times Advertiser.* Peace was still possible, though. "The trouble so far has been with malign propaganda," said the editorial; British and American newspapers had catered to the public's appetite for sensation. "The public mind has been steered to mistrust, suspicion, and downright hate."

EDGAR MOWRER, the journalist, was in a bar in Manila, having a drink with a man who worked for the Maritime Commission. It was late October 1941, and Mowrer was on a spy mission for Colonel Donovan.

"You will pass as a newspaper correspondent," Donovan had told Mowrer. Mowrer had already been to Singapore, Java, Thailand, Burma, Chunking, and Hong Kong. Now he was in the capital of the Philippines.

The maritime man in the bar, Ernest Johnson, said he had a daughter in San Francisco. He didn't expect ever to see her again. "The Japs will take Manila before I can get out," Johnson said.

"Take Manila?" said Mowrer. "That would mean a war with us."

Johnson nodded. "Didn't you know the Jap fleet has moved eastward, presumably to attack our fleet at Pearl Harbor?"

REVEREND BERNHARD LICHTENBERG, the dean of St. Hedwig's cathedral in Berlin, was arrested by the Gestapo. He had been offering daily prayers for the Jews. It was October 23, 1941.

Lichtenberg had also been praying for all prisoners in concentration camps, for stateless refugees, for wounded soldiers on both sides, and for bombed cities in friendly and enemy lands.

The Gestapo searched his house and found a declaration that Lichtenberg had intended to read from the pulpit. It concerned the propaganda handbill that said "Every Jew is your enemy." "Let us not be misled by this unchristian way of thinking," Lichtenberg wrote, "but follow the strict command of Jesus Christ: 'You shall love your neighbor as you love yourself.'"

Under interrogation, Reverend Lichtenberg said he was opposed to *Mein Kampf,* opposed to the killing of life unworthy of life, and opposed to the persecution and deportation of the Jews. He was asked whether he had prayed for the Bolsheviks. No, the Reverend said, he hadn't prayed for the Bolsheviks, but he would have no objection to including a daily prayer for them, too, "to heal their madness."

His interrogators threatened to send Lichtenberg to Lodz to join his "dear Jews." He answered: "That is the very thing I was going to ask: for what more beautiful task could there be for an old clergyman than to assist these Jewish Christians who are destined to die."

Lichtenberg was imprisoned. Two years later, after ordeals and humiliations, he died on the way to Dachau.

PRESIDENT ROOSEVELT talked about the tank-production program at a press conference, and then he made a joke. A reporter asked about the report of a sailor in Honolulu who said that his ship was bombed by the Germans while it was crossing the Red Sea. Was the president aware of that attack?

"No," said Roosevelt, "the only thing I heard on that was that Hitler had been going to one of the few prominent Jews left in Germany, and told him that he could stay, if he would explain to him how Moses managed to get the waters to stand aside and let the Children of Israel across."

The reporters laughed. It was October 24, 1941.

PRESIDENT ROOSEVELT AND WINSTON CHURCHILL condemned the killing of French hostages. It was October 25, 1941. "Civilized peoples long ago adopted the basic principle that no man should be punished for the deed of another," Roosevelt said. "Frightfulness can never bring peace to Europe. It only sows the seeds of hatred which will one day bring fearful retribution."

Churchill said: "Retribution for these crimes must henceforward take its place among the major purposes of the war."

THE *NEW YORK TIMES* magazine section carried an article about the "fanatic, gloomy Japanese." Tokyo was grim and thought controlled, said the paper. Dance clubs were closed. Spies, secret police, and German officers were everywhere. The elevators and lights were off to save power. Taxis ran on charcoal gas.

There were some pictures accompanying the article. One showed a row of women passing a bucket of water while their drill leader talked to them through a megaphone. The caption was: "Bucket brigade—Japanese women are trained in fire fighting." Another picture was of a group of men operating a hose. "Air Raid drill in Tokyo," said the caption.

It was October 26, 1941.

AT HITLER'S REQUEST, Heinrich Himmler went hunting with Count Ciano and Foreign Minister Ribbentrop. It was October 26, 1941.

Himmler, who had painful stomach cramps, brought along his Finnish masseur and confidant, Felix Kersten. Four hundred soldiers worked as beaters, flushing the game. "They all took their task seriously," wrote Count Ciano, "as if it were a question of ejecting the Russians from the forests of Wiesma or Briansck."

Kersten kept count of the birds. Ciano shot 620 pheasants. Ribbentrop shot 410 pheasants. Himmler shot only 95 pheasants. "Look what luck that Ciano has," Himmler said irritably to Kersten. "I wish the Italians in Africa had been such good shots."

Ribbentrop was in a buoyant mood. "Isn't this shoot symbolic?" he said. "As we combine to shoot down the pheasants, so we'll also combine to down the enemies of Germany!"

ALAN BROOKE, commander of the British Home Forces, was invited to Chequers to have dinner with Churchill and Lord Cherwell, the war scientist. It was October 26, 1941.

Dinner, including snuff taking, ended at eleven. Churchill led his two compatriots upstairs, where they watched some movies from Russia and Germany. Then they went back downstairs, and Brooke described Plan Bumper, which was a large anti-invasion exercise. Churchill sent Cherwell away, and he and Brooke talked over North Africa and the Mediterranean.

"I told him of the fears I had of being very short of tanks if we went on sending them to Russia as proposed," wrote Brooke in his diary. A little after 2 A.M., Churchill wanted a sandwich. "I hoped that this might at least mean bed!" Brooke wrote. "But no!! He had the gramophone turned on and in his many coloured dressing gown, with a sandwich in one hand and water cress in the other, he trotted round and round the hall giving occasional little skips to the time of the gramophone. On each lap near the fireplace he stopped to release some priceless quotation or thought."

One of Churchill's thoughts was this: A man's life is like a walk down a long passageway with windows on either side. "As you near each window an unknown hand opens it and the light it lets in only increases by contrast the darkness at the end of the passage."

Brooke got to bed a little before three.

President Roosevelt said in a speech that the United States had been attacked. There had been another U-boat incident; eleven navy men had died on the USS *Kearny* when a torpedo hit its boiler room as it escorted a convoy of merchant ships. "We have wished to avoid shooting," Roosevelt said. "But the shooting has started. And history has recorded who fired the first shot." It was Navy Day, at the Mayflower Hotel, October 27, 1941.

Hitler often claimed, said Roosevelt, that he had no designs on the Americas. But Roosevelt had evidence to the contrary. "I have in my possession a secret map made in Germany by Hitler's government," he said. The map showed existing boundaries obliterated, the Panama Canal absorbed, and Latin American countries turned into "vassal states" of Germany. "This map makes clear the Nazi design not only against South America but against the United States itself." He did not show the map.

The German reaction was extreme. The map was a product of "workshops of Jewish forgers," said a spokesman at the Propaganda Ministry. "Perhaps somebody put into Roosevelt's pocket a map showing the American bases and aviation lines in Latin America which he mistook for a German document," the spokesman said. Roosevelt was either "criminally insane or else just a criminal."

Goebbels's newspaper, *Der Angriff,* had this headline: "Roosevelt, the Viceroy of Jewry—Arch-Liars Double Swindle."

A REPORTER asked President Roosevelt what he thought about being called a liar and a faker by the Germans. It was October 28, 1941. Roosevelt said it was a "scream." A reporter asked to see the secret German map. Roosevelt said he couldn't show it, for fear of compromising his source. A reporter asked where the map was. Roosevelt said it was in some basket on his desk.

The map did not, in fact, show Hitler's plan to partition South America and conquer the western hemisphere. It showed routes in South America flown by American airplanes, with notations in German describing the distribution of aviation fuel. It was a British forgery.

FOUR PEACE GROUPS dropped a petition off at the White House. The Women's International League for Peace and Freedom, the Keep America out of War Congress, the National Council for the Prevention of War, and the Fellowship of Reconciliation had together gathered twenty-five thousand signatures. Reverend John Haynes Holmes wrote the cover letter. "We urge the President of the United States to use the influence which he possesses as elected representative of the American people for the cessation of hostilities and the achievement of a just peace," he wrote. It was October 28, 1941.

MIHAIL SEBASTIAN's friend Lena said, "Let's try not to think of the Jews in Ukraine."

"Maybe she is right," wrote Sebastian—yet he couldn't detach himself from the nightmare. "And the nightmare is also ours," he wrote, "even if it is not yet dragging us under."

The local massacres were part of a larger "European event," Sebastian suspected: "Everything is too calculated for effect, too obviously stage-managed, not to have a political significance." What would follow? he wondered. "Our straightforward extermination?" It was October 29, 1941.

CHARLES LINDBERGH gave a speech at an America First rally in Madison Square Garden. It was October 30, 1941.

Buses were routed off Eighth Avenue, and crowds outside gathered to listen on loudspeakers. "The entire block in front of Madison Square Garden was jammed with people—both street and sidewalks," Lindbergh wrote in his diary. "And the next block west was jammed as far as I could see!" A group from Fight for Freedom handed out contrary literature. "Read the facts about America's No. 1 Nazi," they called.

Inside, twenty thousand people cheered and rang cowbells for six minutes when Lindbergh rose to speak. He pointed at his watch and tried to begin, but they kept cheering. Finally, the band played "Marching Through Georgia" and the crowd went quiet.

"The war we are asked to enter would be the most devastating conflict of all history," he said. "Do you believe that civilized ideals can spring from death and disease and starvation all over the world?"

Lindbergh wrote afterward that while he sat on the platform, he had been carefully studying the faces in the audience. "The thing that I think pleased me most about the meeting was the quality of the people who attended," he said. "They were *far* above the average of New York. Those people are worth fighting for."

PROFESSOR VOSS'S anatomical institute in Posen, Poland, was getting its first bodies for student dissection. "Eleven Poles are being executed," he wrote. "I will take five of them, the others will be cremated." It was October 31, 1941.

UNITED STATES NEWS, a magazine, published a map of the Far East. Long red arrows and tiny red bombers converged on a bull's-eye in the middle of the map. The tiny red bombers were shown flying in from Guam, Singapore, Hong Kong, and the Philippines. The bull's-eye was Tokyo. It was October 31, 1941.

VICTOR KLEMPERER'S typewriter was taken from him. "That hit me hard, it is virtually irreplaceable." It was October 31, 1941. Someone told him urgently that he must renew his visa application to the United States. But there was no point now. "We heard from several sources that a complete ban on all emigration has just been decreed on the German side. Besides a year and a day would pass before the new American conditions were fulfilled. No, we must wait here and see what our fate will be."

THREE SS MEN arrived at a place called Belzec, Poland, where there was a railroad siding. It was November 1, 1941.

The SS men asked for twenty Poles to help with a building project. Stanislaw Kozak was one of them. The Poles built huts with thick walls filled with sand, Kozak said later, and lined them on the inside with zinc. "The doors were very strongly built of three-inch thick planks and were secured against pressure from inside by a wooden bolt that was pushed inside two iron hooks specially fitted for this purpose." The doors had rubber seals. Old truck motors would supply the exhaust to kill prisoners in these huts.

This was the Belzec extermination camp. It would begin killing people in January 1942.

ONE OF ALBERT SPEER's city planners in Berlin made a note in the logbook of progress on the grand boulevard: "During the period from 18 October to 2 November roughly 4,500 Jews were evacuated," he wrote. "As a result, a further 1,000 flats were vacated for bomb damaged tenants."

LORD HALIFAX, the British ambassador, was in Detroit to give a speech at the Economic Club. Two womens' groups—one called Mothers of the U.S.A. and one called American Mothers—picketed his appearance with signs and banners. They said things like HALIFAX IS A WAR MONGER and REMEMBER THE BURNING OF THE CAPITOL IN THE WAR OF 1812. Somebody threw an egg and a tomato at him, and the egg hit him. Halifax checked into the Henry Ford Hospital briefly to have his eye treated, but the British consul said it was not in connection with the egg-throwing incident.

"This is a war of the workshops," Halifax told the Economic Club. "I am told that at the moment something between 40 and 50 per cent of the armament contracts placed by the United States Government in connection with the defense program have been entrusted to manufacturing firms in and around Detroit." He recounted some of Hitler's crimes, and then he said: "The cry for retribution rings out from all those done to death by this modern Juggernaut." It was November 3, 1941.

IN TOKYO, Ambassador Joseph Grew sent a long telegram to the State Department, hoping someone there would heed it. Washington's imposition of severe economic sanctions might force Japan to risk "national hara-kiri," Grew warned. "An armed conflict with the United States may come with dangerous and dramatic suddenness." It was November 3, 1941.

In his diary the next day, Grew wrote: "If war should occur, I hope that history will not overlook that telegram."

AIR-RAID SIRENS went off in Changteh, China, early in the morning. A Japanese airplane flew low several times over Kwan-miao Street, dropping wheat, rice, bits of paper, and fluffs of cotton. It was November 4, 1941.

A week later, a resident of Kwan-miao Street died of bubonic plague. She was eleven years old.

LORD HALIFAX was in Cleveland. A reporter asked him about the egg-and-tomato incident. "My only feeling was one of envy that the people over here have eggs and tomatoes to throw around," he said. It was November 5, 1941.

There were picketers in Cleveland, too. HALIFAX PUT 400,000 INDIANS IN CONCENTRATION CAMPS, said one sign. Another, alluding to the blockade, said: HALIFAX BELIEVES IN FREEDOM OF THE SEIZE. Halifax read the signs and smiled politely.

HELMUTH JAMES VON MOLTKE received a poppy-seed cake in the mail from his wife. He ate some—it was an especially good cake—and then he decided to give some to a friend, Walther Unger. Unger had lost weight, and Moltke was worried about him. "He is, after all, the last Jew I know," he wrote his wife, "and I somehow regard this as the purchase of indulgences and am convinced that you approve."

Besides the cake, Moltke thought he would give Unger some bacon, some apples, and some eggs. It was November 5, 1941.

A NEW MESH of barbed wire went up in the Lodz ghetto. Transports of Gypsies were arriving from Burgenland, a part of Austria. It was November 5, 1941.

A typhus epidemic immediately broke out in the Gypsy camp. Every morning, a hearse arrived to take away bodies. The ghetto's newspaper said, "The overwhelming majority of the bodies removed from the camp were those of children."

WINSTON CHURCHILL submitted a war-cabinet paper recommending that all men over eighteen and a half and under fifty-one should perform compulsory military service. It was November 6, 1941. "The campaign for directing women into the munitions industries should be pressed forward," Churchill also recommended. A month later, Parliament passed the National Service Act, which included conscription for unmarried women between twenty and thirty. Women had a choice of joining the armed services or working in a government factory, such as the Royal Ordinance Factory at Bridgend, which employed thirty thousand people.

At the Bridgend factory, where workers made incendiary and high-explosive bombs, TNT powder dyed a person's skin, hair, and teeth yellow—as a result, the women who filled bombs with it were sometimes called "canaries." "Accidents were frequent and were mainly in the detonator assembly shops," according to a history of Bridgend. "The main casualties were the young women workers with the unfortunate ones losing fingers or suffering more serious injuries." Once, on an icy morning, a woman was carrying a tray of detonators from one building to another. She slipped and shook the tray, "causing the detonators to explode and blow her breasts off."

MIRIAM KORBER and her family, who were Romanian-Jewish refugees, reached the border town of Atachi, where many Jews had been killed. "During the first night in Atachi I saw what human misery really means," she wrote. "I saw children with swollen eyes, frozen feet, helpless little hands; mothers with dead children in their arms, old people and young ones wrapped in rags." It was November 7, 1941.

She and her family survived the inspection, and they crossed the river to Mogilev.

HELMUTH VON MOLTKE was at a meeting at the Foreign Ministry in Berlin with twenty-four men. They discussed a legal decree that would expropriate the property of deported Jews. Twenty-four of the twenty-five wanted to approve the decree; Moltke opposed it.

The men were chameleons, Moltke wrote his wife: "In a healthy society, they look healthy, in a sick one, like ours, they look sick. And really they are neither one nor the other. They are mere filler."

It was November 8, 1941.

DAVID "BUNNY" GARNETT, the novelist who wrote *The War in the Air,* arrived at Frances Partridge's house for a weekend visit. Garnett's son had joined a rescue squad in the Royal Air Force; he would be going out in boats to pick up floating airmen. "Bunny frankly desires to keep his sons out of danger, yet he is behind the war effort in every other way," Partridge wrote in her diary.

She talked this inconsistency over with her husband. "The primary fact is that wanting other people's sons to be killed to get the sort of life you want and believe desirable is horrible," she felt.

That evening, they turned on the radio and listened to Churchill's speech. "He rattled the sword very noisily in the direction of Japan," Partridge noticed: If the United States got into a war with Japan, Churchill said, the British war declaration would follow within the hour. He also warned of another "peace offensive" from Germany:

> The guilty men who have let Hell loose upon the world are
> hoping to escape with their fleeting triumphs and ill-gotten
> plunders, from the closing net of doom.

Peace talks would not happen, he said: There would never be any negotiation with Hitler or with "any party in Germany which represents the Nazi regime." There would, in other words, be no negotiation with anybody in Germany who was actually in a position to order an end to the fighting.

"Thunders of applause from the Mansion House or wherever the speech was made," Frances Partridge wrote.

A river of blood was flowing, Churchill said in the speech—the blood of Jews and communists. "We must regard them just as if they were brave soldiers who die for their country on the field of battle," he said.

It was November 10, 1941.

FELIX KERSTEN massaged Himmler's cramped stomach. It was November 11, 1941.

Himmler was depressed. "After much pressure and questions as to what's the matter with him he told me that the destruction of the Jews is being planned," Kersten recorded in his diary. "I was horrified and replied that it was fearful cruelty to want to destroy men simply because they were Jews." Himmler said that the Jews created "rottenness" and dominated the world through news, the press, movies, and art. He, Himmler, had tried to set up an emigration bureau that would force the Jews out without having to resort to extermination, but that hadn't worked—other countries hadn't been willing to take them. Now Hitler wanted them destroyed.

"It will be a great burden for me to bear," said Himmler. Then he said: "Retaliation strides remorseless through the history of the world."

Kersten had some influence over Himmler, because his massages offered the only relief for Himmler's cramps. "Since I labour in vain against the atrocious principle to which Himmler is committed," Kersten wrote, "I have promised myself that I will undertake as many special interventions as possible to rescue Jews, hoping that Himmler will grant a number of exceptions."

UNDER-SECRETARY CADOGAN was upset: Thirty-seven bombers had failed to return from a recent set of raids. "Our catastrophic losses over the weekend due to hopeless ignorance about weather conditions," Cadogan wrote. "*Bombing does NOT affect German morale:* let's get that into our heads and not waste our bombers on these raids." It was November 11, 1941.

AT MIT, the Radiation Lab began working on a new kind of aerial targeting system. It employed radar beamed down from a bomber onto the earth. The waves bounced back in different ways depending on what was below—water, farmland, or buildings. The prototype system was called EHIB, which stood for "Every House In Berlin." It was November 1941.

WINSTON CHURCHILL wrote a secret letter to Lord Linlithgow, viceroy of India. It was November 12, 1941.

Churchill was startled, he informed the viceroy, at the imminent release of Nehru and the other prisoners—the Indian *détenus*. "Undoubtedly a release of the prisoners as an act of clemency will be proclaimed as a victory for Gandhi's party," Churchill said. "Nehru will commit new offenses"—meaning, make more statements in opposition to war—"requiring the whole process to be gone through again."

ROOSEVELT'S ARMY CHIEF OF STAFF, George Marshall, had some reporters—from *Time, Newsweek,* the *Times,* the *Herald Tribune,* and three wire services—into his office for a briefing. "We are preparing an offensive war against Japan," Marshall said. He told the reporters about the Chinese air bases, and he said that there were thirty-five B-17s in the Philippines, with more on the way. Shuttle bombing from the Philippines to Vladivostok was under consideration. The aim was to "blanket the whole area with air power." Keep it a secret, he said. It was November 15, 1941.

ERNST UDET, the German flying ace, was wearing a red bathrobe. He went to his gun room and put a bullet into a Colt revolver. Dive-bombing in Stukas didn't work anymore; the new models of Heinkel and Messerschmitt airplanes that he had designed were no good; the Luftwaffe was a failure.

He drank a glass of brandy and lay down on the bed, and then he shot himself. It was November 17, 1941.

Goebbels immediately concocted a different story: Udet had died a hero's death, testing a secret weapon. He was given a state funeral, with drawn swords and a speech by his old flying companion Goering. Musicians from the Berlin Philharmonic played the Funeral March from Wagner's *Twilight of the Gods.*

A GERMAN AIRPLANE dropped leaflets on Moscow. "Your allies aren't helping you in any way," the leaflets said. An American-built fighter plane, flown by a member of the Russian air force, shot the plane down. It was November 1941.

THE GESTAPO in Bremen announced a roundup of Jews. Catholics, Evangelicals, and businessmen protested on various grounds—some to the mayor. They were punished. The transport left Bremen on November 18, 1941.

ALFRED ROSENBERG invited German press representatives to a secret briefing on the Jewish question. It was November 18, 1941.

Rosenberg invoked Crystal Night, three years before. "November 9 was a day of decision and destiny for us," he said. "On that day Jewry showed us that it stood for the annihilation of Germany." There were six million Jews in Russia, and Russia was part of Europe. "The Jewish question will only be resolved for Germany when the last Jew has left German soil, and for Europe when no Jew remains on the European continent this side of the Urals," he said. On the other side of the Ural Mountains is Siberia.

Germany's actions, Rosenberg said, must spring not from personal hatred but from clearheaded historical insight: The Jews must be kept out of Europe forever. "That is why it is necessary to drive them to the other side of the Urals or to eliminate them in some other way," he said.

Rosenberg told the journalists not to speak or write of what he had said. "It would be extremely harmful if the public got to know about these things," he said.

HENRY STIMSON was writing in his diary. He, Knox, Stark, Hull, and Marshall had been in the Oval Office with the president, batting around a problem that Roosevelt had brought up. The Japanese were likely to attack soon, perhaps next Monday, the president said. "The question was how we should maneuver them into the position of firing the first shot without allowing too much danger to ourselves," Stimson wrote. "It was a difficult proposition." It was November 25, 1941.

TWO STUDENTS sat in a crowded courtroom in Philadelphia. Arnold Satterthwait, a student at Haverford College, and Frederick Richards, a student at Swarthmore College, pled guilty when they were charged with refusing to register for the draft. Richards said: "For a man eager to work towards the alleviation of human suffering, conscription leaves no freedom of conscience." Satterthwait argued that kindness and forgiveness were supple enough to cope with man's mistakes, whereas violence was not. "I cannot understand how a life such as all of us desire can possibly be attained by spreading hate, death, chaos throughout the world," he said.

The judge sentenced them to a year and a day in federal prison. It was November 26, 1941.

GENERAL RAYMOND LEE, the air attaché, was talking over British strategy with some other air attachés before he returned to the United States. Should the British keep bombing when it obviously wasn't working? Lee used to think it was a mistake, but now he didn't: It was the only available method of attack. "The morale of the British people requires that the Germans be attacked in some way," he thought, "and if the bombing stopped, their spirit would immediately suffer." It was November 28, 1941.

THE HEINKEL COMPANY, in Berlin, began using slave laborers to build airplanes. The laborers came from the concentration camp at Sachsenhausen-Oranienburg. It was November 1941.

Adolf Eichmann, Heydrich's assistant, sent out invitations to a meeting and buffet. The meeting was an important one, about "a comprehensive solution to the Jewish question." It was to take place on December 9, 1941, in Wannsee, the wealthy suburb where the Lindberghs had almost rented a house.

A MEMBER OF THE JAPANESE PARLIAMENT, Jiuji Kasai, said, "There are no problems between the United States and Japan that cannot be settled by peaceful diplomacy." It was November 28, 1941.

The next day, Rabbi Herbert S. Goldstein, of New York's West Side Institutional Synagogue, offered a prayer for the political representatives of the United States and Japan. "May they be conscious," Rabbi Goldstein said, "of the awful sacrifice in life, blood and security that must be offered if hostilities between the two nations ensue."

Royal Leonard left China to hire American bomber pilots. It was the first days of December 1941. "Chennault and I had our own plans for the prosecution of the war against Japan already set," he wrote. "The United States government had promised us at least twenty-seven new light Hudson bombers with a 2000-mile range under an effective bomb load." But then something happened in Hawaii. "Our fondest dream, the bombing of Nagasaki, was not then to come true," Leonard wrote.

A load of potatoes arrived in the Warsaw ghetto. It had been on the way to the soldiers at the front, but then it froze, so it was given to the Jews instead. Fried in hemp oil, the potatoes made excellent pancakes, wrote Mary Berg. "Everwhere you go, the smell of fried potato pancakes assails your nostrils." It was December 1, 1941.

In Japan, Dr. Toyohiko Kagawa, the Japanese Christian pacifist, got a cable from Stanley Jones, a Methodist theologian and student of Gandhi. Jones said he was praying to avert a catastrophe in the Pacific and suggested that Kagawa do the same. Kagawa and two hundred followers began praying continuously, day and night. It was December 1, 1941.

DR. SAMUEL HARDEN CHURCH, president of the Carnegie Institute, called for a Jewish army. It was December 4, 1941. Church thought it should be made up of two hundred thousand American Jews, who would be exempted from the draft, trained in Canada, and supplied with Lend-Lease weaponry. Church said, in his address: "Jews will fight with grim determination to inflict a retribution so terrible that history will provide no parallel for its consummate execution." And when the Jews were done fighting Hitler, they would go to Jerusalem, "reclaiming into that ancient fold all the stricken refugees, inspired to a new existence where King David and those mighty men of Israel for many centuries held their state."

NEHRU WAS RELEASED from prison, along with five hundred other members of the Indian Congress Party. "The only meaning I can attach to their release," Gandhi said to a reporter, "is that the government of India expects the prisoners to have changed their opinion regarding their self-invited solitude. I am hoping that the government will soon be disillusioned." It was December 4, 1941.

SOMEONE LEAKED the full text of the Victory Program to a reporter for the *Chicago Tribune.* In the *Tribune* and its sister paper, the Washington *Times-Herald*—both anti-Roosevelt and isolationist— huge headlines appeared:

F.D.R.'S WAR PLANS!
GOAL IS 10 MILLION ARMED
MEN; HALF TO FIGHT IN AEF

"AEF" meant American Expeditionary Force.

"One of the few existing copies of this astounding document," wrote the *Tribune* reporter, "which represents decisions and commitments affecting the destinies of peoples thruout the civilized world, became available to The Tribune today. It is a blueprint for total war on a scale unprecedented in at least two oceans and three continents, Europe, Africa, and Asia." The news made the late edition on December 4, 1941.

Albert Wedermeyer, who had drafted much of the document, was dismayed. "As I read on, it became all too clear that the Chicago *Tribune* correspondent had published an exact reproduction of the most important parts of the Victory Program, on which I had been working day and night for the past several months," he later wrote.

The plan was for a long, slow war, in which the first land attack would not come until 1943. And it was a war against the German people, by hunger, by bombs, and also by words: "Popular support of the war effort by the peoples of the Axis Powers must be weakened, and their confidence shattered by subversive activies, propaganda, deprivation, and the destruction wrought." Against Japan, the United States would use "strategic methods."

A REPORTER asked Roosevelt about the alleged war plans. "I don't think I have any news on that," Roosevelt replied. Later, he ordered an investigation into the leak, and FBI agents questioned Wedemeyer closely about his pro-German leanings. But Wedemeyer wasn't the culprit—Senator Burton Wheeler later said that Hap Arnold, head of the Army Air Forces, had given the plans to him, and that he had passed them on to the *Chicago Tribune*.

Wedemeyer, though, suspected that President Roosevelt himself wanted the war plans made public. "I have no hard evidence," he told historian Thomas Fleming years afterward, "but I have always been convinced, on some sort of intuitional level, that President Roosevelt authorized it."

Whoever leaked the Victory Program, it functioned as a further provocation. A headline in a Japanese paper said: "Secret United States Plans Against Japan and Germany are Exposed."

JOHN DANAHER, a Republican from Connecticut, gave a speech on the floor of the Senate. "Current opinion is that the United States cannot begin an effective military offensive for at least two years," Danaher said—how many of the hungry in Europe would be alive by then? Starvation, he contended, was not a legitimate weapon. "So true is this that even if feeding the helpless Belgians, Poles, Frenchmen, Greeks, and others proved to be of some help to Germany, it would still be the duty of the United States, with huge surpluses and available carriers, to carry out this work." It was December 4, 1941.

IN HOLLYWOOD, Thomas Mann recorded a propaganda message. It went out to German listeners from the BBC. "You know the unspeakable crimes which have been and are being committed in Russia, against the Poles and the Jews," Mann said, "but you prefer not to know them because of your justified horror of the equally unspeakable, the gigantic hatred which some day must engulf you when the strength of your men and machines gives out."

It was December 6, 1941.

LORD HANKEY wrote Churchill about a way to kill a lot of animals—and people, too—in Germany. It was December 6, 1941.

"The only method technically feasible at the moment is the use of anthrax against cattle by means of infected cakes dropped from aircraft," Hankey informed the prime minister. "The experiments which have been made," he said, "give good ground for supposing that considerable numbers of animals might be killed by this method if it were used on a sufficient scale at the time of year when cattle are in the open."

To kill cattle, Hankey said, you would need a lot of anthrax bacteria, plus two million cattle cakes, plus people and machines to squirt the anthrax germs into the cakes.

Churchill approved the plan. Thus began Operation Vegetarian: the creation of millions of diseased cakes, which sat in storage, awaiting the prime minister's word of command. In the end, the Russian army, and years of round-the-clock firebombing, proved sufficient to compel an unconditional surrender.

THE CHINESE AMBASSADOR, Dr. Hu Shih, visited President Roosevelt in his study. It was Sunday, December 7, 1941. Roosevelt, dosed by his doctor with his morning squirt of nose drops, read aloud to Hu Shih the letter to the emperor of Japan that he had sent at nine o'clock the night before. Every so often, as Hu Shih listened, Roosevelt stopped reading and praised his own handiwork. "I got him there; that was a fine, telling phrase," Roosevelt said.

The letter to Emperor Hirohito talked sonorously about a long period of unbroken peace, and about new developments and their "tragic possibilities." It ended with this:

> I address myself to Your Majesty at this moment in the fervent hope that Your Majesty may, as I am doing, give thought in this definite emergency to ways of dispelling the dark clouds. I am confident that both of us, for the sake of the peoples not only of our own great countries but for the sake of humanity in neighboring territories, have a sacred duty to restore traditional amity and prevent further death and destruction in the world.

Roosevelt paused at one point. "That will be fine for the record," he said.

Ambassador Hu Shih took his leave, and the president worked on his stamp collection, sorting through the weekly envelope of philatelic novelties sent him by the Department of State.

JAPANESE PILOTS took off from six aircraft carriers and flew to Pearl Harbor, a naval base near Honolulu. It was December 7, 1941.

Their bombs sank eighteen American ships and killed more than two thousand people. One Japanese pilot who was shot down carried with him a bottle of whiskey, chopsticks, hardtack, tooth powder, and a hand-drawn good-luck sheet.

The pilot's sheet had drawings of exploding and sinking American ships. It said, in English, "You damned! Go to the devil!" In Japanese, it said, "Listen to the voice of doom! Open your eyes, blind fools!"

Dozens of Honolulu civilians died, too—killed by misfiring American antiaircraft shells.

CHURCHILL SAT, morose and uncommunicative, after dinner at Chequers. With him were his bodyguard, his private secretary, and two Americans: Averell Harriman, Roosevelt's envoy to Europe, and the U.S. ambassador, John Winant. Churchill's valet, Sawyers, brought in a flip-top portable radio—a gift from Harry Hopkins—so that they could all listen to the news. It was December 7, 1941.

A BBC announcer said something about a Japanese air raid. Harriman thought he'd heard that it was a raid on Pearl Harbor; the bodyguard, Thompson, said no, it was a raid on Pearl River.

"The Prime Minister," Harriman later recalled, "recovering from his lethargy, slammed the top of the radio down and got up from the chair." He told his secretary to call the president. "Mr. President, what's this about Japan?" Churchill said.

"They have attacked us at Pearl Harbor," said Roosevelt. "We are all in the same boat now." Ambassador Winant took the phone; Churchill overheard him saying something like "This certainly simplifies things." Martin, the secretary, recalled: "Winant's dominant reaction was one of elation at the certainty that the USA was now definitely in the war." Both Americans, Churchill observed, took the news "with admirable fortitude. In fact, one might almost have thought they had been delivered from a long pain."

Churchill began planning a trip to America.

JAMES ROOSEVELT walked into his father's office that afternoon. The president was very calm. "He had out his stamp collection he loved so much and was thumbing over some of the stamps when I came in," his son recalled.

Without looking up, the president said: "It's bad, it's pretty bad."

REVEREND HARRY FOSDICK, the war opponent, was sitting in his study in the tower of Riverside Church, with a microphone in front of him. He was making his weekly religious broadcast on NBC Radio, *National Vespers*. The choir had just sung "O Come, O Come, Emmanuel." It was still December 7, 1941.

"This radio audience is full of people who feel like trees in a high wind," Reverend Fosdick said. "Today the winds are terrific."

An announcer broke in to say that President Roosevelt had called a cabinet meeting following the attack on Hawaii. Then a newsman hooked up live from the roof of KGU in Honolulu. "It is no joke, it is the real war," the KGU man said. The announcer switched over to the White House Press Room, where correspondent H. R. Baukhage said that a powerful ship had been torpedoed thirteen hundred miles from San Francisco and that the Japanese were "busy with submarines within our own waters."

Only the day before, Baukhage said, he'd talked to Saburo Kurusu, the special envoy from Japan, who told him that 90 percent of the Japanese were opposed to war—but that the majority of them were willing to fight over China. Baukhage recalled sitting two years earlier in the Berlin broadcasting center, transmitting the news that Hitler had attacked Poland. "I must say that exactly the same feeling existed there, among the populace at least," said Baukhage. "It came as a terrific blow to the people as a whole."

National Vespers returned, with "Break Thou the Bread of Life." Then Baukhage came back on to announce that Stephen Early, the president's press secretary, had just handed out copies of Roosevelt's letter to the emperor of Japan—the one in which he expressed a fervent hope that there were still ways of dispelling the dark clouds.

Baukhage read into the microphone long passages from Roosevelt's letter, in a gentle, singsong voice. It sounded like a sermon.

HENRY MORGENTHAU was with the secretary of the navy, Frank Knox, when he got a damage report on Pearl Harbor. "Knox feels something terrible," Morgenthau wrote in his diary. "They have the whole fleet in one place—the whole fleet was in this little Pearl Harbor base. They will never be able to explain it."

IN WASHINGTON THAT NIGHT, Edgar Mowrer couldn't sleep. He thought, The man in the bar in Manila was right! "And if a member of the Maritime Commission knew the destination of the Japanese fleet, why had the President, why had Knox and Stimson and Hull who were expecting war, not known it and taken the necessary precautions?"

And then Mowrer realized: "Nothing but *a direct attack could have brought the United States into the War!* Here was the 'break' for which both Churchill and T. V. Soong had been waiting."

The Japanese warlords, Mowrer concluded, had saved the free world.

JAPANESE PLANES flew to Clark Field, the U.S. air base in Luzon, in the Philippines. The pilots looked down and saw rows of fighter planes and B-17 Flying Fortresses parked on the ground. Bombs destroyed half of them. It was December 8, 1941.

ELEANOR ROOSEVELT wrote her "My Day" newspaper column. "Finally, the blow had fallen, and we had been attacked," she said. "Because our nation has lived up to the rules of civilization, it will probably take us a few days to catch up with our enemy, but no one in this country will doubt the ultimate outcome." It was December 8, 1941.

THE POLICE went to all Japanese restaurants in the five boroughs of New York. It was December 8, 1941. They allowed patrons to finish eating, and then they escorted the staff and owners home. The FBI began arresting people on a list. One Japanese detainee was a banker, two imported silk, one exported pearls, and one was a doctor who had graduated from New York University in 1922. He was taken into custody at his home on Park Avenue, where he lived with his wife and daughter. "This is an unfortunate situation," he said. An FBI special agent told reporters, "We are at war and a censorship has been placed in Washington. I have received instructions to make no comments to the press."

By the end of the day, hundreds of Japanese nationals were in custody around the country, said Attorney General Biddle, with more arrests expected. Biddle said that the detainees would probably go to two abandoned army posts, where the government was already holding Italians and Germans: Fort Missoula held a thousand Italians, and Fort Lincoln, in North Dakota, held three hundred Germans. "A great man hunt was underway," wrote the *Los Angeles Times*.

WINSTON AND CLEMENTINE CHURCHILL went to a hurriedly summoned meeting of the House of Commons. It was December 8, 1941.

Chips Channon listened as Churchill declared war on Japan, beating Roosevelt to it, although Roosevelt had asked him to wait. While Churchill was speaking, someone whispered to Channon how lucky Churchill was: "Russia saved the government in July; now Japan will do likewise."

Churchill wrote: "Being saturated and satiated with emotion and sensation, I went to bed and slept the sleep of the saved and thankful."

PRESIDENT ROOSEVELT, wearing a cape and a black armband, arrived with Eleanor at the Capitol to give a speech. Army soldiers and marines with bayonets guarded the entranceways. The president asked Congress to declare war on the Japanese empire, in response to its "unprovoked and dastardly attack." Very many lives had been lost, he said. At the end of his speech, he smiled and waved. It was December 8, 1941.

Before the floor vote, there were denunciatory orations and readings of patriotic poetry. "The Japanese, like murderous imps from Hell, are clutching at our throats," said Congressman Homer Angell of Oregon. Japan had struck like a serpent, said Representative John Gibson of Georgia, and it would perish: "Yes, perish by the might and power of the people she so unjustly attacked."

At the same time, Representative Jeannette Rankin, the Montana pacifist, wanted to make a statement. "Mr. Speaker, I would like to be heard," she said. The speaker, Sam Rayburn, ignored her. She said, "Mr. Speaker, a point of order." She was still ignored. "Sit down, sister," someone called. A congressmen said to her, "They really did bomb Pearl Harbor."

"Killing more people won't help matters," said Rankin.

When she heard her name in the roll call, she stood. "As a woman I can't go to war," she said, "and I refuse to send anyone else."

Hers was the only no vote, and it was hissed and booed. In the cloakroom, some army officers shouted abuse at her. "You've been drinking!" Rankin said, and she took refuge in a phone booth.

Later, she told a colleague that the representatives had pressured her to make the vote unanimous—and yet it was that insistence on uniformity, that intolerance of dissent, that was just what was wrong with the other side in the war. No, Rankin thought, I'm going to vote one vote for democracy.

IN A MANOR HOUSE on a river in Chelmno, near Lodz, in Poland, soldiers ordered naked prisoners into a gray van parked at the end of a ramp. The soldiers locked the doors, and the driver turned on the engine, which was modified so that its exhaust fumes flowed into the space where the prisoners were trapped. "After a few minutes the cries and groans of the people gradually died away," the van driver later said. He drove to a grave in a forest clearing nearby. By the time he arrived, the prisoners were dead.

The first Nazi killing factory was now in operation. It was December 8, 1941.

FREDA KIRCHWEY, the editor of *The Nation,* wrote a post-Pearl-Harbor column: "The fruits of appeasement have burst," she said. "The horror has made America one. Today we love each other and our country. We feel a happy sense of union swelling in our hearts; hatred and contempt for our enemy runs warmly in our blood."

"THE WAR IS SPREADING to the whole planet," wrote Mihail Sebastian in Bucharest. "Everything is more serious, more complex, and more obscure." It was December 8, 1941.

FREDERICK LIBBY, the director of the National Council for the Prevention of War, made an announcement. The group would not obstruct the war effort, he said, but would "continue to support the method of negotiation, to take place at the earliest moment when negotiation becomes feasible." It was December 8, 1941.

REINHARD HEYDRICH hastily got word out to the invitees to the conference at Wannsee—the one scheduled for December 9 to discuss the Jewish question. It was postponed till January.

ONE MILLION CHILDREN and forty thousand teachers left their classes and stood in the streets of New York. Air-raid gongs had gone off all over the city. It was December 9, 1941.

"Swiftly and quietly the schools of the world's largest system were emptied in fifteen minutes," wrote *The New York Times*. "Not a trace of panic was evident." The parochial schools hadn't known about the drill, though. Sisters from the Church of the Lady of Pity school walked out to a police officer in the street and asked if a real air raid was going on.

An eight-year-old boy told his classmate that a million Hitler planes were coming. "But the cops are going to pop them all off."

MARY BERG, in Warsaw, heard that the Germans had gone through the ghetto at Lodz, confiscating all furs, warm underwear, and woolen clothes. Warsaw was next, she was told.

But America's entry into the war had inspired her ghetto with new hope. "Most people believe that the war will not last long now and the Allies' victory is certain," she wrote. The guards at the gates looked glum, and some were less insolent. "On others," she noticed, "the effect has been exactly opposite and they are more unbearable than ever." It was December 9, 1941.

IN LONDON, Chips Channon shared one of his last magnums of Krug 1920 with Averell Harriman, President Roosevelt's "sallow, distinguished" envoy, whom he was getting to know. "Much talk of a possible Japanese invasion of California," Channon wrote. "Averell hopes that the American cities will be blitzed, so as to wake the people up. He attacked the American isolationists bitterly." It was December 9, 1941.

WILLIAM ALLEN WHITE published an editorial in his newspaper, the Emporia *Gazette*. It was about Jeannette Rankin's vote in the House of Representatives.

"The *Gazette* entirely disagrees with the wisdom of her position," White wrote. "But Lord, it was a brave thing!" There were, White said, a hundred congressmen who would have liked to have voted no. "Not one of them had the courage to do it." It was December 10, 1941.

GEORGE GALLUP'S POLLSTERS called people up and asked them a question: "Should the United States air force bomb cities in Japan?" Sixty-seven percent said yes. Some said yes, if Japan bombed the United States first. Some weren't sure. Ten percent—representing twelve million citizens—were wholly opposed.

Twelve million people still held to Franklin Roosevelt's basic principle of civilization: that no man should be punished for the deed of another. Franklin D. Roosevelt was not one of them. It was December 10, 1941.

JOSEPH GOEBBELS remembered the great German boxer Max Schmeling. Schmeling had beaten Joe Louis in one fight, but then, in a later fight, he made the mistake of saving his strength and so was knocked out in the first round. "Maybe the Japanese, too, have the opportunity to hit the Americans so lethally in their first strikes that the USA will be significantly weakened in their naval capacity and will no longer be able to launch successful counter-strikes," Goebbels wrote. Perhaps, also, he thought, the United States wouldn't give so many planes and weapons to England, because it would need them now for its fight with Japan.

There was a change in Hitler, Goebbels observed. "The Führer once again radiates optimism and confidence in victory. It feels good, after having to digest so much unpleasant news for many days, to come in direct contact with him again." It was December 10, 1941.

LORD HALIFAX wrote a letter to a friend in England. "Isn't this Japanese business astonishing?" he said. "I had been betting against their throwing their hats over the fence just yet." Now that they had, though, the good thing was that America was going to work harder: "The President told me today that they were going to get on to a 7-day week and a 24-hour day, and showed me a graph of what they think this will do to their production."

The Japs might "break a good deal of china" in the near term, Halifax predicted, but in the end they would see that they'd made a big mistake. "The little swine—I hope they will get it thoroughly in the neck."

A RESIDENT OF DETROIT wrote an anonymous letter to Roosevelt's press secretary. "That was a good speech the President made the other night," said the writer, "but I do think he tends to be too idealistic.

> To Hell with ideals, until we have licked these international thugs. Blast Hell out of them, and make them cry 'Uncle'. Then blast em again. The treacherous yellow rats under- stand only one language, FORCE. Lets give them 10 times as much as they gave us. Put them back to where they were when we discovered them.

The same went for Hitler and "Muss," too, the letter writer said. It was December 10, 1941.

JAPANESE DIVE-BOMBERS, flying out of Saigon, sunk the *Prince of Wales,* the ship on which Churchill had sailed to meet Roosevelt and sign the Atlantic Charter. Half the men on it died. It was December 10, 1941.

Harold Nicolson, crossing Oxford Circus, read a poster: PRINCE OF WALES AND REPULSE SUNK. The intersection began revolving in the air. "To the Beefsteak as quick as I can," wrote Nicolson, "where I can have a glass of sherry to revive me." It was December 10, 1941.

LORD PORTAL made a suggestion to Churchill. Air Marshal Richard Peirse, the head of Bomber Command, hadn't achieved satisfactory results. Perhaps Peirse could be transferred to the Far East in a month or so and Arthur Harris promoted to take his place? It was December 1941.

Winston Churchill said yes. Churchill, Portal, and Bomber Harris: the British leaders were in place now for the pan-Germanic firestorms of 1942, 1943, 1944, and 1945.

VICTOR KLEMPERER, in Dresden, was at the grocery store. He heard Hitler's voice on the radio but couldn't understand what he was saying. "Has war been declared on the USA?" Klemperer asked the shopkeeper.

"I don't know, I'm busy here," said the shopkeeper.

Later, Klemperer read Hitler's denunciation of Roosevelt: "It was the Jew in all his Satanic vileness, which gathered around this man, but also to whom this man reached out." The language of the empire "pushed to the point of absurdity," Klemperer thought. It was December 11, 1941.

ANOTHER TRANSPORT OF JEWS—men, women, and children—was sent by train from Krefeld to Düsseldorf, about fifteen miles away. It was December 11, 1941.

In Düsseldorf, Gestapo and SS men marched the Jews through the city to a slaughterhouse. The slaughterhouse was being used as a deportation terminal because it was out of the way and because it had long loading ramps—and perhaps also because it was a slaughterhouse. The Jews left for the ghetto in Riga the next day.

In Riga, an SS officer named Friedrich Jeckeln carried out Himmler's orders: "They were shot," he later told an interrogator, "in a little wood three kilometres outside Riga on the left hand side of the road between the road and the railway line."

PRESIDENT ROOSEVELT read a preliminary copy of "Washington Merry-Go-Round," a widely syndicated newspaper column by Drew Pearson and Robert S. Allen. Pearson and Allen said that Pearl Harbor was the "largest naval defeat in this nation's history." Roosevelt was vexed—he was suppressing all details of the disaster—and he asked J. Edgar Hoover, head of the FBI, to get in touch with the columnists and threaten to take away their press privileges. Hoover met with Pearson and Allen, and they withdrew the column. It was December 12, 1941.

GOEBBELS WAS in the Reich Chancellery listening to Hitler talk to party leaders. He talked about Russia and Pearl Harbor and the war with the United States. And then he talked about the Jews. "With respect to the Jewish Question, the Führer has decided to make a clean sweep," Goebbels wrote afterward in his diary. "The world war is here, and the annihilation of the Jews must be the necessary consequence." It was December 12, 1941.

German soldiers were freezing at the front, and Goebbels threw himself into the Winter Relief campaign. In a speech, he asked the German people to donate:

> Overshoes, if possible lined ones, or fur-lined ones; warm woolen clothing, socks, stockings, heavy underwear, vests, or pullovers; warm, especially woolen, underclothing, undershirts, chest and lung protectors; any kind of headgear protection, ear muffs, wristlets, ear protectors, woolen helmets; furs in all senses of the word, fur jackets and fur waistcoats, fur boots of every kind, and every size; blankets, especially fur covers, thick warm gloves, again especially fur-lined leather ones, or knitted gloves, and wool mittens; altogether everything of wool is needed urgently on the front and will be doubly welcome.

The war, Goebbels said, would decide the "existence, or non-existence, of the German nation."

AT COMMUNITY CHURCH IN NEW YORK, John Haynes Holmes, the pacifist and playwright, preached the first sermon he had written since Pearl Harbor. "More significant than any action of America in defense of her national interests was her instant reaction of retaliation, revenge, punishment and death upon the foe," Holmes said. "From such evil can come no good thing, but only disaster and doom immeasurable." He invoked St. Augustine's description of a Roman victory, wherein the conqueror came to resemble the conquered. "The precious treasure of our civilization," he said, "is about to be swept away." It was December 14, 1941.

MIHAIL SEBASTIAN heard that the *Struma,* the refugee ship, had reached Istanbul. "Those people still have a life," he wrote. It was December 15, 1941.

In fact, though, those people didn't have a life. The British government wouldn't let the boat proceed to Palestine, and the Turkish government wouldn't let the passengers get off the boat. After two months, the Turks towed the boat into the Baltic, where it was sunk by a Russian torpedo. One passenger survived.

HANS FRANK, the governor-general of the General Government in Poland, was talking to some of his subordinates. An important conference about the Jews was going to be taking place in Berlin in January, Frank informed them. "A major migration is about to start": The Jews of Germany would be sent east. But when they were sent east—when they arrived in Hans Frank's territory—what would happen to them?

The Jews were pernicious eaters, Frank said—and there were, if one included the mixed-race Jews, three and a half million of them already living in the General Government. "We cannot shoot or poison those 3,500,000 Jews, but we shall nevertheless be able to take measures, which will lead, somehow, to their annihilation," said Frank. "The General Government must become free of Jews, the same as the Reich." It was December 16, 1941.

EZRA KRAUS, a botanist from the University of Chicago, had an idea for how to win the war with Japan. It was December 18, 1941.

Spraying rice fields with toxic levels of growth hormones, Kraus thought, "would be a feasible and comparatively simple means of destruction of rice crops, the staple food supply of the Japanese."

Kraus's work led him to experiment with two synthetic hormones—2,4-D and 2,4,5-T—components of a defoliant that would later came to be called Agent Orange.

ADOLF HITLER fired General Brauchitsch. It was December 19, 1941. Eight hundred thousand Germans and millions of Russians had killed one another, and yet Moscow had not fallen. "I have, therefore, resolved today, under these circumstances, to take over myself the leading of the army in my capacity as Supreme Commander of the German armed forces," Hitler said.

CLEMENTINE CHURCHILL wrote a letter to her husband. Her Russian fund-raising drive was going well, she said—and everywhere she went in London, the people were good and sweet and asked about him, especially the old people. "Well my beloved Winston," she said, "May God keep you and inspire you to make good plans with the President. It's a horrible world at present, Europe over-run by the Nazi hogs & the Far East by yellow Japanese lice." It was December 19, 1941.

THE *BOMBAY CHRONICLE* asked Mohandas Gandhi what he thought of the fact that the United States was now in the war. It was December 20, 1941.

"I cannot welcome this entry of America," Gandhi said. "By her territorial vastness, amazing energy, unrivalled financial status and owing to the composite character of her people she is the one country which could have saved the world from the unthinkable butchery that is going on." Now, he said, there was no powerful nation left to mediate and bring about the peace that all peoples wanted. "It is a strange phenomenon," he said, "that the human wish is paralysed by the creeping effect of the war fever."

CHURCHILL WROTE a memo to the chiefs of staff on the future conduct of the war. "The burning of Japanese cities by incendiary bombs will bring home in a most effective way to the people of Japan the dangers of the course to which they have committed themselves," he wrote. It was December 20, 1941.

LIFE MAGAZINE published an article on how to tell a Japanese person from a Chinese person. It was December 22, 1941.

Chinese people have finely bridged noses and parchment-yellow skin, and they are relatively tall and slenderly built, the article said. Japanese people, on the other hand, have pug noses and squat builds, betraying their aboriginal ancestry. "The modern Jap is the descendant of Mongoloids who invaded the Japanese archipelago back in the mists of prehistory, and of the native aborigines who possessed the islands before them," *Life* explained. The picture next to the article was of the Japanese premier, Hideki Tojo.

IN THE LODZ GHETTO, trucks began taking the Gypsies away. They went to Chelmno, the new death camp, where they were killed with exhaust gases and buried. It was just before Christmas 1941.

RUSSIAN PLANES dropped Christmas cards onto German troops at the front. It was December 24, 1941.

One card reproduced photographs of families of dead German soldiers. "For this woman there is no happy Christmas," it said. "For this child no father's knee. She is a widow. He is fatherless." Another card showed a winter landscape covered with innumerable wooden crosses, each with a German helmet on top, while carrion birds circled overhead. It said: "Living space in the East."

ADAM CZERNIAKOW was sick, feverish, throwing up. It was December 24, 1941.

Czerniakow had gotten an order. "We must surrender all the furs—both men's and women's. I am to be personally responsible." He had until the twenty-eighth of December.

THE POPE gave a Christmas Day message from Vatican City. "There is no place for open or secret oppression of national minorities," he said. "Let a ray of real wisdom descend on the men who rule the peoples, divided in this moment against each other."

MIRIAM KORBER, living with her deported family near Mogilev, in the Ukraine, wrote in her diary that it was very cold. "Last night the north wind started to blow," she wrote. "A true Ukrainian north wind, the wind of the steppe; it blows into our room." Firewood was very expensive, so they had no fire in the daytime. "Will we be able to survive these times?" she wondered. "Everyone asks himself this question, including me." It was December 26, 1941.

DAVID LILIENTHAL, the director of the Tennessee Valley Authority, listened to Winston Churchill give a speech to a joint session of the U.S. Congress. The speech was a masterpiece, Lilienthal thought, one of the best he'd ever heard, enlivened by alliteration and imagery and, at one point, "a growling sound that sounded like the British lion."

"When he promised Japan that she would be roundly punished," Lilienthal wrote in his journal, "the place broke out in yells—the first sound of blood-lust I have yet heard in this war."

Churchill paced in the White House garden afterward. He'd had some doubts about his speech ahead of time, he told his doctor, Lord Moran, but then he knew it was just right. "I hit the target all the time," he said.

It was December 26, 1941.

FRANCES PARTRIDGE listened to the BBC. She heard about German soldiers freezing and dying, and she heard about Churchill's latest triumph in America. "He is 'doing his stuff,' " she wrote in her diary, "and basking in the applause of American journalists and not feeling a pang (I can't help thinking) over all the mistakes, the death and disaster, he is responsible for, and boasting and threatening, and speaking in rolling phrases of what we are going to do to the enemy in 1942, 1943, 1944 and 1945, God help us all!"

THERE WERE MOUNTAINS of furs in the conference room at the Community Authority in the Warsaw ghetto. "All normal work in the offices has stopped," wrote Czerniakow. "Everybody is busy with fur collection." It was December 28, 1941.

Commissioner Auerswald arrived the next morning, angry that he had not received an itemized report. Czerniakow and staff began making an inventory. They counted 690 men's fur coats, 2,541 ladies' fur coats, 4,441 men's fur linings, 4,020 ladies' fur linings, 222 silver-fox pelts, 258 blue-fox pelts, 872 red-fox pelts, 5,118 fur hand warmers, 39,556 fur collars, 7,205 assorted pelts, and 2,201 sheepskin coats, with more coming in.

Czerniakow also noted 3,438 cases of typhus in October and 2,156 in November. There were ten times the number of funerals in the ghetto as there had been the year before.

DOROTHY DETZER wrote a letter to the members of the Women's International League of Peace and Freedom. Membership in the league had dipped since Pearl Harbor, but Detzer was unswayed. "As pacifists, we can never yield our inalienable right to affirm and declare that war between nations or classes or races cannot permanently settle conflicts or heal the wounds that brought them into being," Detzer said. It was December 28, 1941.

Albert Einstein, on the other hand, was a war supporter now. "We must strike hard," he said, "and leave the breaking to the other sides."

GENERAL MACARTHUR listed the cultural treasures of Manila that had been wrecked by Japanese planes. The actions of Japan's sixty-three bombers "can only be deemed completely violative of all the civilized processes of international law," he said. "The beautiful old church of Santo Domingo, with its priceless art treasures and venerated relics, is now a heap of smoking ruins, before which relays of black-robed priests are continually praying for the people." At the proper time, MacArthur added, there would be "retaliatory measures."

Much of Manila was unscathed, however. Three years later, during its recapture, American bombs and shells would flatten the city.

SENATOR ALBEN BARKLEY, majority leader and longtime interventionist, said that Japan's bombing of Manila was the most stupid thing imaginable. "Think of Tokyo," Senator Barkley said, "with ten times as many inhabitants, when the inevitable day of destruction comes, as our bombers swoop down upon the city." It was December 29, 1941.

Senator Burton Wheeler, former isolationist, was in absolute agreement: "One can come to only one conclusion from the action of the Japanese," he said, "and that is that they are an inhuman and half-civilized race and in the future will be treated as such." The tragedy, Senator Wheeler said, was that we had given so many airplanes away to the English that we couldn't yet bomb Nagasaki, Yokohama, and Tokyo.

Senator George W. Norris, from Nebraska, said that Japanese cities were open to the kind of attack that would "burn them off the face of the earth." He added: "And that is what they are coming to."

CHURCHILL WAS IN OTTAWA giving a speech to the Canadian Parliament. It was December 30, 1941.

The tide had turned against the Hun, Churchill told the Canadians. "They shall themselves be cast into the pit of death and shame," he said, "and only when the earth has been cleansed and purged of their crimes and of their villainies will we turn from the task which they have forced upon us."

The enemy had asked for total war, he said. "Let us make sure they get it."

President Roosevelt listened on the radio—he said the speech was perfectly wonderful.

GANDHI ASKED to be removed from the Working Committee of the Indian National Congress. It was December 30, 1941.

"I must continue the civil disobedience movement for freedom of speech against all wars with such Congressmen whom I select and who believe in non-violence," Gandhi said. "If any country has a message for the world, which is groaning under violence unknown perhaps to history, it is India."

Once Gandhi left the Working Committee, members could support England's war, which some of them wanted to do—hoping, mistakenly, that in return Churchill's government would grant India its independence.

IN WASHINGTON, the British and American chiefs of staff reached an agreement on how they would together win the war. It was December 31, 1941.

The five-page document—TO BE KEPT UNDER LOCK AND KEY—was called "American-British Grand Strategy." It revealed that the Allies would fight Germany first: "Once Germany is defeated, the collapse of Italy and the defeat of Japan must follow." A land attack wasn't possible until 1943, the joint strategists decided. For the time being, the Allies would build weapons day and night and wear down Germany's resistance. Bomb, starve, subvert, and sabotage, so as to "close the ring around Germany"—that was the Allied grand strategy.

SOME SOLDIERS who had been hurt in the Pearl Harbor attack landed in San Francisco. It was New Year's Eve 1941. "First came the walking wounded," said an article in the *Chicago Tribune,* "hobbling on crutches or their arms in slings, in a thin trickle down the gangplanks from the tall gray sides of the ships. Later, orderlies began carrying off the stretcher cases and loading them into ambulances." One burn victim had died en route. A paralyzed sailor, interviewed by *Time* magazine, said, "Before this we didn't want to fight anybody. But now all we want is to get well enough to get our crack at those bastards."

CHRISTOPHER ISHERWOOD spent New Year's Eve in Haverford, Pennsylvania, at a party organized by one of the refugees, Carl Furtmueller, a former Viennese school inspector. "The group was holding together well, now," Isherwood wrote. "This was our best period."

GENERAL HIDEKO TOJO, premier of Japan, had a New Year's Eve message. "The war has only just begun," he said.

Generalissimo Chiang Kai-shek had a New Year's Eve message, too: "I believe that when a certain stage is reached the Allies will be in a position to inflict overwhelming punishment upon the enemy on the sea and in the air as a preliminary to a decisive rout of his forces on land."

And Hitler had a New Year's Eve message. "The first year of the titanic struggle against Judeo-Bolshevism has just ended, and the second year is about to commence," he said. "He who fights for the life of his people, for his daily bread and his future will have victory, but he who is moved by Judaic hate and seeks in this war to annihilate all peoples will be destroyed."

President Roosevelt called for prayer.

A MAN WAS SELLING horns on Clark Street in Chicago on New Year's Eve 1941. People bought them and tooted them until they discovered that the horns said MADE IN JAPAN. "When the public discovered the nature of his wares," said the *Chicago Tribune,* "they crushed them under their heels and forced him to flee."

As the year turned, the blast furnaces and the war factories were "ablaze with light," said the *Tribune* reporter. "At midnight the whistles of the plants blew and the workmen stopped long enough to cheer. Then they went on with their work."

AT MIDNIGHT ON NEW YEAR'S EVE, on the train from Ottawa to Washington, Prime Minister Winston Churchill, dressed in his zippered rompers, called together bathrobed reporters and staff in the dining car and lifted a glass. A photographer, Jackie Martin, looked at him with awe and love. "This is the man whose courage, whose will, whose faith in God and Englishmen has saved the civilized world," she thought. "It's this little guy."

Churchill said:

> Here's to 1942—
> A year of toil,
> A year of struggle,
> A year of peril,
> But a long step forward to victory.

The reporters cheered, and Churchill took a puff of his cigar. Holding crossed hands with Sir Charles Portal, head of the Royal Air Force, he led a singing of "Auld Lang Syne." The reporters sang "For He's a Jolly Good Fellow," and Churchill flashed the V-for-Victory sign, which everyone in the car returned.

"May we all come through in safety and with honour," Churchill said. Then he left the dining car.

No bombs fell on England or Germany on that last night of the year. The British bombed La Pallice, a port in France where U-boats were moored.

Stefan Zweig wrote his friend Victor Wittkowski a New Year's Eve letter. Zweig was now living in Petropolis, Brazil. The extension of the war into the Pacific, he said, was history's greatest catastrophe. "When I read that for us in 1941, victory is promised for 1943 or 1944, the hand that holds the paper trembles with terror," Zweig wrote. He and his wife took poison two months later.

Victor Klemperer celebrated New Year's at the Jews' House in Dresden. There were tea and cakes, then vermouth, then a punch bowl. "I made a serious little speech, so serious that when we toasted one another my hand was trembling," wrote Klemperer. It had been their most dreadful year, he said—most dreadful of all because of what others were suffering. But at the end there was optimism. "My adhortatio was: Head held high for the difficult last five minutes!"

Mihail Sebastian wrote a few lines in his journal to end the year. "I carry inside myself the 364 terrible days of the dreadful year we are closing tonight," he said. "But we are alive. We can still wait for something. There is still time; we still have some time left."

Afterword

This book ends on December 31, 1941. Most of the people who died in the Second World War were at that moment still alive.

Was it a "good war"? Did waging it help anyone who needed help? Those were the basic questions that I hoped to answer when I began writing. I've relied on newspaper articles, diaries, memos, memoirs, and public proclamations, each tied as much as possible to a particular date, because they helped me understand the grain of events better than secondary sources did. But I've used many secondary sources as well. All the texts are published and publicly available, one way or another, and all are in English.

The New York Times is probably the single richest resource for the history and prehistory of the war years—more so than British newspapers, which operated under heavy censorship. Radio speeches, official press statements, the texts of air-dropped leaflets, translated foreign news, and snippets of unedited congressional testimony are all to be found in *The New York Times,* as well as good reporting. The New York *Herald Tribune* is another fount of specificity; indeed, my interest in World War II began when, some years ago, I first opened bound volumes of the *Herald Tribune* and read headlines for the bombing of Berlin and Tokyo and wondered how we got there. Martin Gilbert's many books—especially his fascinating, impeccable *Churchill War Papers*—were also useful in preparing this work.

I'm grateful to the librarians at the University of New Hampshire Library, who retrieved things for me from distant places. My editors—Sarah Hochman, David Rosenthal, and Timothy Mennel—and my agent, Melanie Jackson, all made apt queries and suggestions. My dear wife shaped and edited the book; my dear children and parents offered advice, hope, and helpful improvements.

The title comes from Franz Halder, one of Hitler's restive but compliant generals. General Halder told an interrogator that when he was imprisoned in Auschwitz late in the war he saw flakes of smoke blow into his cell. Human smoke, he called it.

I dedicate this book to the memory of Clarence Pickett and other American and British pacifists. They've never really gotten their due. They tried to save Jewish refugees, feed Europe, reconcile the United States and Japan, and stop the war from happening. They failed, but they were right.

Notes

NYT = *The New York Times.*

1 *"my factories"*: Bertha von Suttner, *The Records of an Eventful Life*, p. 437.

1 *"Everybody yelled"*: Stefan Zweig, *The World of Yesterday*, pp. 210–11.

2 *"The British blockade"*: Winston Churchill, *The World Crisis, 1911–1918*, ed. Martin Gilbert, p. 686.

2 *"One crude stretcher"*: Zweig, *World of Yesterday*, p. 249.

2 *"I had recognized"*: Ibid., p. 252.

3 *"I leaned over the gallery"*: "Suffrage Leaders Pardon Miss Rankin," *NYT*, April 7, 1917.

3 *"I want to stand by," "I felt,"* and *"a dupe of the Kaiser"*: Hannah Josephson, *Jeannette Rankin*, pp. 76, 78, 77.

3 *"War is now dropping"*: Harry Emerson Fosdick, *The Challenge of the Present Crisis*, p. 62.

3 *"Your country needs you"*: Ibid., p. 99.

4 *"In matters of war"*: "President Signs Declaration of War," *NYT*, December 8, 1917.

4 *"I've got to go"*: Joseph P. Lash, *Eleanor and Franklin*, p. 214; Jan Pottker, *Sara and Eleanor*, p. 161.

5 *"The Emperor is surrounded"*: "Says Pessimists Cow the Kaiser," *NYT*, November 4, 1918.

5 *"We are enforcing the blockade"*: Suda Lorena Bane and Ralph Haswell Lutz, eds., *The Blockade of Germany after the Armistice, 1918–1919*, p. 720.

6 *"This movement among the Jews"*: Winston Churchill, "Zionism versus Bolshevism," *Illustrated Sunday Herald*, February 8, 1920, quoted in Gisela C. Lebzelter, *Political Anti-Semitism in England, 1918–1939*, p. 19.

7 *"Jihad was being preached"*: Aylmer L. Haldane, *The Insurrection in Mesopotamia*, p. 214.

7 *"The Cabinet have decided"*: Ibid., p. 215.

7 *"I think you should certainly"*: Martin Gilbert, *Winston S. Churchill*, vol. 4, companion vol. 2, p. 1190.

7 *"lively terror"*: Ibid., companion vol. 1, p. 649.

8 *"gas-filled shells"*: David Omissi, "Baghdad and the British Bombers," *The Guardian*, January 19, 1991.

8 *"It is impossible"*: Haldane, *Insurrection*, p. 331.

8 *"Separate parties"*: Ibid., pp. 341–42.

8 *"During these difficult months"*: Ibid., pp. 229–30.

8 *"The attack with bombs"*: James S. Corum, "The Myth of Air Control."

9 *"It was decided"*: Frank Freidel, *Franklin D. Roosevelt*, p. 296.

9 *"Gandhi is disciplining"*: "Gandhi as World Savior," *NYT*, March 13, 1922.

9 *"I am endeavoring to show"*: Homer A. Jack, ed., *The Gandhi Reader*, p. 205.

10 *"Had the War lasted"*: Winston Churchill, *Winston S. Churchill: His Complete Speeches*, p. 3267.

10 *"Now the real witch's sabbath"*: Zweig, *World of Yesterday*, pp. 311–14.

11 *"The French in a bombing duel"*: Charles Webster and Noble Frankland, *The Strategic Air Offensive Against Germany*, vol. 4, p. 66.

12 *"very secret"*: "Britain Denounces Soviet Propaganda in Note to Moscow," *NYT*, October 25, 1924.

12 *Churchill's close ally*: Gill Bennett, *Churchill's Man of Mystery*, p. 80.

12 *"clumsy forgery"*: "Red Plot Confuses British Government," *NYT*, October 26, 1924.

12 *"crude fabrication"*: "Soviet Repudiates Propaganda Letter," *NYT*, October 27, 1924.

12 *"fake"*: "Red Plot Confuses British Government," *NYT*, October 26, 1924.

12 *"malicious hoax"*: "London Still Mystified," *NYT*, October 27, 1924.

12 *"How did Conservative headquarters"*: "Macdonald Explains Action in Red Plot, Believes It Genuine," *NYT*, October 28, 1924.

13 *"You all know"*: Churchill, *Complete Speeches*, vol. 4, p. 3498.

13 *"of every race under the sun"*: Robert Rhodes James, "The Politician," in A. I. P. Taylor et al., *Churchill Revised*, p. 99.

13 *sewn in a sack*: David Marquand, *Ramsey MacDonald*, p. 387.

14 *"I lie awake"*: Viktor Reiman, *Goebbels*, p. 25.

14 *"Who is this man?"* Anthony Read, *Devil's Disciples*, p. 144.

14 *"He jumps to his feet"*: Joachim Fest, *The Face of the Third Reich*, p. 85.

14 *"Hitler is there"*: Ibid.

14 *"I give it all"*: Reimann, *Goebbels*, p. 56.

14 *"Adolf Hitler—I love you"*: Fest, *Face of the Third Reich*, p. 89.

15 *sermon in Geneva*: Robert Moats Miller, *Harry Emerson Fosdick*, p. 180.

15 *"I hate war"*: Ibid., pp. 497–98.

15 *150 tons:* Peter W. Gray, "The Myths of Air Control and the Realities of Imperial Policing," citing David E. Omissi, *Air Power and Colonial Control,* p. 48.

16 *"I could not help":* Churchill, *Complete Speeches,* vol. 4, pp. 4125–26.

16 *"The 'town' ":* "32 Planes to Circle Britain for 2 Days," *NYT,* June 12, 1927.

16 *"Chick, chick":* "Airplanes Will Dance to Tunes of Radio," *NYT,* June 26, 1927.

17 *"mangled flesh":* "Bombs," *Time,* February 27, 1928.

17 *wounding a pilot:* David Killingray, "A Swift Agent of Government," p. 437.

17 *"Not more than 200 Nuers":* Omissi, *Air Power,* p. 153.

17 *March 1929:* P. W. Wilson, "Mr. Churchill Plays With Fire" (review), *NYT,* March 17, 1929.

17 *"Whole nations":* Churchill, *The Aftermath,* p. 481.

17 *"incredibly malignity":* Ibid., p. 482.

17 *"Death stands":* Ibid., p. 483.

18 *"I like things to happen":* Christopher Hassall, *A Biography of Edward Marsh,* p. 565, quoted in James, "The Politician," in Taylor, *Churchill Revised,* p. 95.

18 *speaker's fee:* Martin Gilbert, *Churchill and America,* p. 120.

18 *"profound sources":* Mary Soames, ed., *Winston and Clementine,* p. 345.

18 *"You are the friends":* "Amity With Britain Urged by Churchill," *NYT,* October 26, 1929.

19 *"I was always told":* Frederick, earl of Birkenhead, *Halifax,* p. 282.

19 *"cleaned up":* "Poetess Set to Lead Indians in Salt Raid," *NYT,* May 15, 1930. See also "Benn Reassures Commons on India," *NYT,* May 13, 1930; "Sholapur Reported in Rioters Hands," *NYT,* May 13, 1930; "Bomb Injures Nine in Clash in India," *NYT,* May 20, 1930.

19 *"Words are beautiful things":* H. James Burgwyn, *Italian Foreign Policy in the Interwar Period, 1918–1940,* p. 59.

20 *"Its continued uncensored":* Kirby Page, *National Defense,* p. 230.

20 *"Chastened by a daily rain of bombs":* "Afridis in Full Flight Before British Planes," *NYT,* August 18, 1930.

20 *in an editorial:* "Afridis Repulsed Again at Peshawar," *NYT,* August 11, 1930.

21 *"There is no reason":* "Fascists Walk Out of Berlin Council," *NYT,* September 19, 1930.

21 *"slicked-over fashion-monkey":* F. T. Birchall, "The Man Who Inflames the Nazi Crowds," *NYT Magazine,* April 22, 1934.

21 *"work of filth":* Reimann, *Goebbels,* p. 127.

22 *"Many a proprietor":* "Fascist Youth Riot As 'All Quiet' Runs," *NYT,* December 9, 1930, p. 17.

22 *"The film of shame":* Reimann, *Goebbels,* p. 127.

22 *"Nobody was older":* Hilton Tims, *Erich Maria Remarque: The Last Romantic,* p. 72.

22 *"The truth is":* Churchill, *Complete Speeches,* vol. 5, p. 4938.

478

22 *"Dear Friend"*: Mohandas Gandhi, *Collected Works of Mahatma Gandhi*, vol. 51, p. 130.

23 *"weak, wrong-headed"*: Churchill, *Complete Speeches*, vol. 5, p. 4985.

23 *"If only 2 percent"*: "Einstein Advocates Resistance to War," *NYT*, December 15, 1930.

24 *"mental turmoil"*: Richard Breiting, *Secret Conversations with Hitler*, p. 17 ff.

26 *Richard Breiting returned*: Ibid., pp. 47 ff.

27 *"The hot air rising"*: Willy Ley, *Bombs and Bombing*, pp. 43–44.

27 *"Down with Judea!"*: "Hitler Bids 'Nazis' Shun Violent Steps," *NYT*, December 3, 1931.

28 *Churchill declined to meet*: Louis Fischer, *The Life of Mahatma Gandhi*, p. 31.

28 *ceremony at the Sports Palace*: Lilian T. Mowrer, *Journalist's Wife*, pp. 260–65.

29 *"At eleven o'clock"*: Hallett Abend, *My Life in China, 1926–1941*, p. 187.

29 *towel factory*: "Japanese Threaten Chinese in Shanghai," *NYT*, January 22, 1932; see also "Japanese Set Fire to Shanghai Mills," *NYT*, January 20, 1932.

29 *drastic measures*: "Japanese Threaten Chinese in Shanghai," *NYT*, January 22, 1932; "Japan Ready to Act at Shanghai Today if the Chinese Balk," *NYT*, January 25, 1932.

30 *two American destroyers*: "Joint Action Considered," *NYT*, January 28, 1932.

30 *Marines had paraded*: "President Reveals All Notes on China," *NYT*, January 28, 1932 (see photograph).

30 *British policemen*: Hallett Abend, "Japanese Checked in Taking Shanghai," *NYT*, January 29, 1932. In *My Life in China*, Abend omits the British policemen (p. 190).

30 *machine gun in tow*: Abend, *My Life in China*, p. 190.

30 *"Lights out, you fools!"*: Ibid.

30 *"The little yellow bastards"*: Ibid., p. 191.

30 *"Airplanes Spread Terror"*: "Foreign Zone is Shelled," *NYT*, January 30, 1932.

30 *"Wounded Children"*: "Thousands Flee Japanese Terror in Chapei; Wounded Children Lie All Night in Streets," *NYT*, January 31, 1932.

31 *"I see your American"*: Abend, *My Life in China*, p. 193.

31 *George Westervelt*: William M. Leary Jr., "Wings for China: The Jouett Mission, 1932–35."

31 *"Such planes could"*: Ibid.

31 *"The presence"*: *Foreign Relations of the United States, 1932*, vol. 3, pp. 582–83. See also Leary, "Wings for China."

32 *"The cardinal wrote"*: Edgar Ansel Mowrer, *Triumph and Turmoil*, p. 209.

32 *Only war brings*: Strang, *On the Fiery March*, p. 122.

32 *eighty-eight Chinese*: William M. Leary, "Wings for China."

33 *"After dinner"*: Mowrer, *Triumph and Turmoil*, p. 213.

33 *Hans or Heinrich Arnhold*: Gerald Feldman, "Two German Businessmen," p. 16.

33 *"Forty copies"*: "Hitler Ridiculed as a Writing Man," *NYT*, February 9, 1933.

33 *"I believe"*: "Terror In Germany Amazes Novelist," *NYT,* March 21, 1933.

34 *"Are you mad?"* Alan Bullock, *Hitler: A Study in Tyranny,* p. 263.

34 *"Goering let loose"*: Zweig, *World of Yesterday,* p. 364.

34 *"pure invention"*: "Jews in Reich Deny Atrocities by Nazis," *NYT,* March 25, 1933.

35 *McDonald told Hanfstaengel:* James G. McDonald, "Hitler Foretold Slaughter" (letter), *NYT,* July 17, 1944.

35 *underarm hair:* Mowrer, *Journalist's Wife,* p. 299.

35 *"Our enemies will be brutally"*: Ibid., p. 285.

36 *"The salesfolk stood around"*: Ibid., p. 289.

36 *"Is he going to keep"*: Edgar B. Nixon, ed., *Franklin D. Roosevelt and Foreign Affairs,* vol. 1, pp. 172–73.

36 *"Regarding the Jews"*: Ibid., pp. 174–76.

37 *"The age of extreme"*: Louis P. Lochner, introduction to Joseph Goebbels, *The Goebbels Diaries, 1942–1943,* p. 18.

37 *Lion Feuchtwanger's books:* "Nazi Book-Burning Fails to Stir Berlin," *NYT,* May 11, 1933; "Nazi Fires to Get 160 Writers Books," May 6, 1933.

38 *"un-German"*: "Nazi Book-Burning," *NYT,* May 11, 1933.

38 *most booing:* Mowrer, *Journalist's Wife,* p. 291.

38 *nailed to a pillory:* Zweig, *World of Yesterday,* p. 366.

38 *"seeping poison"*: "Nazi Book-Burning," *NYT,* May 11, 1933.

38 *"Brightened by these flames"*: Lochner, in *Goebbels Diaries, 1942–1943,* p. 18.

38 *"We acknowledge"*: "1,200 Clergymen Sign Nazi Protest," *NYT,* May 26, 1933.

39 *most of a page:* "List of Christian Churchmen Who Signed Protest on Hitlerism," *NYT,* May 26, 1933.

39 *"Nothing so barbarous"*: "Churchmen Score Reich Hysteria," *NYT,* October 27, 1933.

39 *"We will not have you swindle,"* and *He offered to resign:* Mowrer, *Journalist's Wife,* p. 303.

40 *"Think of their love"*: Ibid., p. 305.

40 *"Nowhere have I had"*: Ibid., p. 309.

40 *"insult to the intelligence"*: "Cruelty of Nazis to Jews Asserted," *NYT,* July 11, 1933.

41 *Hitler made Julius Streicher:* Martin Gilbert, *The Holocaust,* p. 40.

41 *"They were made"*: "Nuremberg Jews Brutally Treated," *NYT,* July 31, 1933.

41 *"set to plucking"*: Gilbert, *Holocaust,* p. 40.

41 *"We sold 24"*: "Greater Shanghai," *Time,* July 24, 1933.

42 *Ernst Udet:* Murray Rubenstein and Richard M. Goldman, *To Join with the Eagles,* pp. 124, 125.

42 *American air shows:* "63 Fliers to Start Coast Derby Today," *NYT,* August 23, 1931.

42 *Udet fancied:* Cajus Bekker, *The Luftwaffe War Diaries,* p. 39; Rubenstein and Goldman, *To Join with the Eagles,* p. 125.

42 *"I have offered":* "Nazis Use Penalty of Medieval Days," *NYT,* August 19, 1933.

42 *pronounced mentally ill:* "Nazi Victim Deranged," *NYT,* September 4, 1933.

42 *field mice:* "Famine in Russia Held Equal of 1921," *NYT,* August 25, 1933.

42 *"We are all dying":* "Visitors Describe Famine in Ukraine," *NYT,* August 29, 1933.

43 *"I know there have been":* "Lloyd George Warns on 'Bullying' Reich," *NYT,* September 23, 1933.

43 *in Buffalo:* Bekker, *Luftwaffe War Diaries,* p. 39.

44 *"It is gas":* Frederick Birchall, "Reich is Thinking of War Despite Its Talk of Peace," *NYT,* October 8, 1933.

45 *air pageant:* "Bomb Feat Thrills Air Show Throng," *NYT,* October 8, 1933.

45 *"Single sentences":* "Reich Bans Book Advocating War," *NYT,* October 21, 1933.

45 *His head fell:* Time, January 22, 1934.

46 *"Any one who thinks":* " 'War Utter Futility,' Says Mrs. Roosevelt," *NYT,* January 18, 1934.

46 *"Proselytizing parlor pinks":* "Peace Efforts Hit by Naval Officer," *NYT,* January 26, 1934.

47 *"Maybe Hitler wasn't":* F. W. Winterbotham, *The Nazi Connection,* pp. 49–50, 53, 54, 57.

48 *"Until you have complied":* Denis Richards, *Portal of Hungerford,* pp. 108–10.

48 *bestseller:* "H. C. Engelbrecht Stricken on Train," *NYT,* October 10, 1939.

48 *"Armament is an industry":* "Peace Hope Voiced Amid War Threats," *NYT,* April 15, 1934.

48 *Schneider:* H. C. Engelbrecht, "The Problem of the Munitions Industry."

49 *Vickers:* Ibid.

49 *"to explore whether":* Clarence E. Pickett, *For More than Bread,* p. 93.

49 *Rabbi Baeck said:* Ibid., pp. 99–100.

50 *position paper:* Francis R. Nicosia, "Zionism in National Socialist Jewish Policy in Germany, 1933–39," *The Journal of Modern History,* December 1978.

50 *"The aim of Jewish policy":* Francis R. Nicosia, "Zionism, Antisemitism, and the Origins of the Final Solution," in Wolfgang Mieder and David Scrase, eds., *Reflections on the Holocaust,* p. 130.

50 *"without a future":* Ibid., p. 129.

50 *long, spidery fingers:* Callum MacDonald, *The Killing of SS Obergruppenführer Reinhard Heydrich,* p. 5.

50 *agricultural-training centers:* Francis R. Nicosia, "Zionism in National Socialist Jewish Policy in Germany, 1933–39."

51 *thirty two warships:* "Navy Has Been Strengthened and Army Has New Tasks," *NYT,* March 4, 1934.

51 *visited Pearl Harbor:* "Roosevelt Tours Hawaii Naval Base," *NYT,* July 28, 1934.

51 *"These forces must ever":* "Mr. Roosevelt's Address," *NYT,* July 29, 1934.

51 *"President Roosevelt has traveled":* "Japanese General Finds Us 'Insolent,' " *NYT,* August 5, 1934.

52 *"It is an axiom":* George Seldes, "The New Propaganda for War," *Harper's Magazine,* October 1934.

52 *"Sound strategy requires":* Tami Davis Biddle, *Rhetoric and Reality in Air Warfare,* p. 195.

52 *"Large urban populations":* Conrad C. Crane, *Bombs, Cities, and Civilians,* p. 21.

52 *"Reservoirs can be gassed":* Biddle, *Rhetoric and Reality,* p. 350.

53 *"might be regarded":* "Reich to be Armed in Air with Mighty Fleet by 1936," *NYT,* May 11, 1934.

53 *patent-sharing agreement* and *crankshafts, cylinder heads:* Thomas Etzold, "The (F)utility Factor."

53 *"The islands are natural":* "Japan is Opposed to Pacific Airline," *NYT,* March 15, 1935; see also "Washington Sticks to Pacific Air Plan," *NYT,* March 16, 1935.

54 *tea in the Oval Office:* Pickett, *For More than Bread,* pp. 392–93; see also "Churches Oppose Open Door Force," *NYT,* March 18, 1935.

54 *"One hundred and sixty":* "160 Ships to Begin War Games Friday," *NYT,* April 28, 1935.

54 *largest war games:* Ibid., caption.

54 *"We desire":* "War Games Scored in Letter to Japan," *NYT,* May 3, 1935; see also *Franklin D. Roosevelt and Foreign Affairs,* vol. 2, pp. 515–16.

55 *"drawing a sword":* "Swanson Retorts to Tokyo on Navy," *NYT,* May 16, 1935.

55 *"That's too damn bad":* "Navy Game Fears Arouse Standley," *NYT,* May 22, 1935.

55 *Someone threw a stone:* "Anti-Nazi Artist is Beaten in Raid," *NYT,* May 17, 1935.

55 *Independents' Show:* "Institute Awards Arts Scholarships," *NYT,* August 18, 1934.

55 *Hitler expelling Einstein:* Ibid.

56 *"No Nation Can Afford":* "10,000 Here Join Anti-War Parade," *NYT,* May 19, 1935.

57 *"Signor Mussolini himself":* "Italy Exhibits Chemical War," *NYT,* May 19, 1935.

57 *"deeply encysted":* Leo Rosten, "Men Like War," *Harper's Magazine,* July 1935.

58 *He based his plot:* "Field Notes for a Play on Peace," *NYT,* September 22, 1935.

58 *"They have managed"*: "Anti-War Drama Seen in Westport," *NYT,* July 30, 1935.

58 *"It has been to me"*: John Haynes Holmes, *I Speak for Myself,* pp. 219–20.

58 *"Every child learns"*: David Bankier, *The Germans and the Final Solution,* p. 96.

59 *"The type of immigration"*: Nixon, ed., *Franklin D. Roosevelt and Foreign Affairs,* vol. 3, pp. 50–51.

59 *"persons in the class described"*: Ibid., pp. 64–66.

60 *China was again:* "China Buys War Goods," *NYT,* March 15, 1936.

60 *"I have no objection"*: David G. Anderson, "British Rearmament and the 'Merchants of Death,' " p. 22.

60 *Imperial Chemical Industries wasn't:* "British Arms Man Admits 'Greasing,' " *NYT,* February 7, 1936.

60 *The company broke ground:* Robert Harris and Jeremy Paxman, *A Higher Form of Killing,* pp. 52–53.

60 *"collective security"*: Aldous Huxley, "Notes on the Way," in *Complete Essays,* vol. 4, pp. 118–21.

61 *"Beginning at 7:30 A.M."*: "Two Kinds of Poison Gas Used by Italy in Air Raid," *NYT,* March 17, 1936.

61 *"From a fine rain"*: "Gas Use is Shown in Photographs," *NYT,* May 10, 1936; Harris and Paxman, *Higher Form of Killing,* p. 51.

62 *"Safety will only come"*: Churchill, "How to Stop War," in *Step by Step,* p. 26.

62 *"Led by a red-faced man"*: "Fascisti in Uproar Shriek at Negus at League Session," *NYT,* July 1, 1936.

62 *"Special sprayers"*: "Summary of the Ethiopian Emperor's Address to the League," *NYT,* July 1, 1936.

63 *Newspapers in Tokyo:* "U.S. Loan to China Reported in Japan," *NYT,* July 21, 1936.

63 *"wreathed in smiles"*: Henry Channon, *Chips,* p. 111.

64 *"If our attacks"*: Webster and Frankland, *Strategic Air Offensive,* vol. 4, pp. 88–89.

65 *German War College:* Albert C. Wedemeyer, *Wedemeyer Reports!,* pp. 49–53.

65 *Rossbach:* Ibid., pp. 53–54.

65 *Ernst Röhm:* See Lothar Machtan, *The Hidden Hitler,* pp. 181–230.

65 *"Heil Roosevelt"*: Wedemeyer, *Wedemeyer Reports!,* p. 37.

66 *"What is the difference"*: H. C. Engelbrecht, *Revolt Against War,* pp. 15–16.

66 *"The Polish government"*: "Poles Renew Call for Exile of Jews," *NYT,* January 14, 1937.

67 *A delegation:* Joseph Marcus, *Social and Political History of the Jews in Poland, 1919–1939.*

67 *"the central plateau"*: "Madagascar Studied as a Home for Jews," *NYT,* January 1, 1938.

67 *"unfit for white"*: Ibid.

67 *"veritable paradise"*: "Huge New Colony for Jews Proposed," *NYT,* January 19, 1937.

67 *Trujillo wanted Jewish immigrants:* Henry L. Feingold, *Bearing Witness,* p. 135. Eric Paul Roorda, *The Dictator Next Door,* p. 127.

68 *"Every German boat"*: "Labor Democracy is Bar To Fascism, Lewis Says Here," *NYT,* March 16, 1937.

68 *"I know some of you"*: Philip Williamson and Edward Baldwin, *Baldwin Papers,* p. 432.

69 *"turned three-fifths"*: "Pictures Women Fighting Next War," *NYT,* April 14, 1937.

69 *"It was a pity"*: John Killen, *A History of the Luftwaffe,* p. 77.

70 *He suspected poison:* Breiting, *Secret Conversations,* p. 15.

70 *August 1937:* Winston Churchill, *Great Contemporaries,* p. x.

70 *"Those who have met"*: Ibid., p. 232.

70 *short piece on Leon Trotsky:* Ibid., pp. 167–74.

71 *The Japanese government announced:* "Japan Disturbed by Report 182 Americans Have Enlisted to Fly Warplanes for China," *NYT,* August 6, 1937.

71 *"The worst part"*: Abend, *My Life in China,* p. 257.

72 *two Chinese corpses:* "Two Times Correspondents Injured in Bombing of Department Store," *NYT,* August 24, 1937.

72 *"I threw the car"*: Abend, *My Life in China,* p. 261.

72 *"Peaceful commerce"*: "Envoy for Parleys," *NYT,* August 29, 1937.

72 *A freighter:* "U.S. Planes Off for China," *NYT,* August 29, 1937.

73 *One crewmember was killed:* "1 Fatality on Ship: Chinese Planes Mistake the President Hoover for Foes' Vessel," *NYT,* August 31, 1937.

73 *A niece:* "Bombing of Liner a Tale of Terror," *NYT,* September 1, 1937.

73 *"I want you"*: Royal Leonard, *I Flew for China,* pp. 130–31.

73 *Julius Barr:* "U.S. Flier 'Detained' by Chang's Troops," *NYT,* December 17, 1936.

73 *"Working day and night"*: Leonard, *I Flew for China,* pp. 147–48, 154; see also "Japan, China Preen Wings," *NYT,* August 8, 1937.

73 *"It would be a dangerous"*: Robert Rhodes James, *Churchill: A Study in Failure,* p. 285.

74 *"I have asked them privately"*: Martin Gilbert, *Winston S. Churchill,* vol. 5, companion vol. 3, p. 791.

74 *"It is vitally necessary"*: "Urges Funds to Help Jews Leave Germany," *NYT,* October 18, 1937.

75 *"The police act"*: Aldous Huxley, *Ends and Means,* p. 113.

75 *"We have all seen"*: Ibid., pp. 141–42.

76 *"The room was crowded"*: Leonard, *I Flew for China,* p. 118.

76 *"Leatherface"*: Ibid., p. 177.

76 *"He thinks the regime"*: Channon, *Chips,* p. 141.

77 *"I remember people"*: Leonard, *I Flew for China,* p. 140.

77 *the room of the models:* Albert Speer, *Inside the Third Reich,* pp. 187–89.

78 *"Shall the United States":* U.S. Department of State, *Peace and War,* pp. 400–401.

78 *"I fully realize":* Ibid., p. 401.

79 *"It is for the world":* "Cuza Insists Jews Must Quit Rumania," *NYT,* January 22, 1938.

79 *"While working":* "Jewish Students Beaten in Rumania," *NYT,* January 30, 1938.

79 *A Jew is riding a streetcar:* Milton Mayer, *They Thought They Were Free,* p. 116.

80 *"violet kimono":* Fest, *Face,* pp. 78–79.

80 *"I want to urge":* Ronald Bayly and Nancy Landgren, *Jeannette Rankin, the Woman Who Voted No* (videotape), 1984 PBS.

80 *"Suddenly it does not":* "216 Pastors Sign New Peace Pledge," *NYT,* March 2, 1938.

81 *"Nine Royal Air Force":* "British Mopping Up in Palestine Area," *NYT,* March 6, 1938.

81 *Der Führer ist hier!:* Authentic History Center *WWII: 1938–Dec. 6, 1941* (CD 0400).

81 *"He was told":* "World Reaction to the Anschluss," Mutual Broadcasting Network, Ibid.

81 *"Torture, starvation":* Muriel Lester, *It So Happened,* p. 4.

82 *"Dear brothers and sisters":* Ibid., p. 6.

82 *"Warships themselves":* "Quakers Attack May Bill on War," *NYT,* April 3, 1938.

82 *"the navy is being run":* "Our 'Sailor-President' Charts a Course," *NYT,* April 3, 1938.

83 *"sovereign control of England":* Feingold, *Bearing Witness,* p. 107.

83 *"Messrs. Baruch and Morgenthau":* Richard Breitman and Alan M. Kraut, *American Refugee Policy and European Jewry,* 1933–1945, p. 272n.

84 *got off the* Queen Mary: "British Air Mission Arrives in Washington," *NYT,* April 26, 1938.

84 *big bomb bay:* Walter J. Boyne, *Beyond the Horizons,* p. 91.

84 *"To my astonishment":* John Terraine, *A Time for Courage,* p. 39.

84 *"the largest foreign order":* "400 Planes Bought by Britain in U.S.," *NYT,* June 10, 1938.

84 *"When they speak":* Gandhi, "Interview to a Professor," *Collected Works,* vol. 73, pp. 156–57.

85 *"We were all trained":* Robin Cross, *The Bombers,* p. 70.

85 *twenty-nine Lockheed Model 14:* "British Try U.S. Planes," *NYT,* May 15, 1938.

85 *"very formidable weapon":* "Big Orders Tax Plants," *NYT,* June 19, 1938.

85 *building them under license:* Boyne, *Beyond the Horizons,* p. 82; "Japan," www.lockheedmartin.com; "British Try U.S. Planes," *NYT,* May 15, 1938.

85 *"Please cooperate"*: "Town to 'Black Out' in 'Air Raid' Tonight," *NYT*, May 16, 1938.

86 *Police told drivers*: Associated Press, "Long Island Town Has 'Blackout' Test," in *Nebraska State Journal*, May 17, 1938, available at www.ancestry.com.

86 *eight hundred-million-candlepower*: Ibid.

86 *hundred parachute flares*: "Night Air 'Raid' Awes Long Island," *NYT*, May 17, 1938.

86 *"Is it realistic"*: Associated Press, "Lights Out Order is Obeyed When Planes Stage Attack," in *Reno Evening Gazette*, May 17, 1938, available at www.ancestry.com.

86 *"These national defense exercises"*: Jeffery S. Underwood, *The Wings of Democracy*, pp. 115–16.

86 *They flew around Nagasaki*: "Japan is 'Raided' by Chinese Planes," *NYT*, May 21, 1938.

87 *"War Means Fascism"*: "Fifth Ave. Scene of Anti-War Walk," *NYT*, May 22, 1938.

87 *"one of the surest"*: Churchill, *Step by Step*, p. 218.

88 *"The aircraft manufacturing industry"*: "Aircraft Plants Lead in Industry," *NYT*, June 5, 1938.

88 *"These foreign orders"*: John Morton Blum, *From the Morgenthau Diaries*, vol. 2, p. 118.

88 *"They bring with"*: Lawrence S. Wittner, *Rebels Against War*, p. 18.

89 *"Old books are perfectly good"*: Pickett, *For More than Bread*, p. 139.

89 *quotas were liberal*: Breitman and Kraut, *American Refugee Policy and European Jewry*, p. 60.

89 *"Powers Slam Doors"*: New York *Herald Tribune*, July 8, 1938.

89 *"Jews for Sale"*: Rita Thalmann and Emmanuel Feinermann, *Crystal Night*, p. 22.

90 *"Maria is a Jewess"*: Wedemeyer, *Wedemeyer Reports!*, pp. 37–38.

90 *"I cannot understand"*: Jasper, *George Bell*, pp. 142–43.

91 *"In a situation"*: "Reich's Jews Unit to Deal with Nazis," *NYT*, July 29, 1938.

91 *Henry Ford's birthday party*: "Henry Ford Getting High Honor from Germany," *NYT*, August 1, 1938.

92 *"Abnormal times require deeds"*: Harold C. Deutsch, *The Conspiracy Against Hitler in the Twilight War*, p. 30.

92 *"Now all depends"*: Ibid., p. 31.

92 *both mentally ill and evil*, *detailed coup plan*, and *An overwrought General Halder*: Joachim Fest, *Plotting Hitler's Death*, pp. 84, 87.

93 *shooting grouse*: "Season for Grouse Opens in Scotland," *NYT*, August 13, 1938.

93 *talking to Winston Churchill*: Margaret L. Coit, *Mr. Baruch*, pp. 466–67.

93 *"Everyone knows"*: "Baruch Is Silent on Defense Post," *NYT*, September 20, 1938.

93 *fifty thousand long-range bombers:* Coit, *Mr. Baruch*, pp. 467–68.

93 *"I believe America":* "Baruch in Warning Asks Defense Step," *NYT,* October 14, 1938.

93 *news conference:* "Roosevelt Moves to Rush Expansion of Army and Navy," *NYT,* October 15, 1938.

93 THE JEW BARUCH: Otto Tolischus, "Reich Impressed by U.S. Arms Plan; Baruch Denounced," *NYT,* October 16, 1938.

94 *"Discovery would have":* Lester, *It So Happened,* p. 42.

94 *"It demonstrated":* Ibid., p. 46.

94 *Small groups of Jews:* "Jews Left to Starve Near Czech Frontier," *NYT,* October 23, 1938.

95 *"The Jews living in Germany":* "Reich Intensifies Pressure on Jews," *NYT,* October 27, 1938. Another translation in Ian Kershaw, *Hitler, 1936–45,* p. 151.

95 *a policeman knocked:* Thalmann and Feinermann, *Crystal Night,* pp. 35–36.

95 *"greatest mass deportation":* "Germany Deports Jews to Poland; Seizes Thousands," *NYT,* October 29, 1938.

96 *impending doom:* Pickett, *For More than Bread,* p. 132.

96 *"We may feel penitent":* Lawrence McK. Miller, *Witness for Humanity,* p. 178.

96 *"by order of der Führer":* Charles A. Lindbergh, *The Wartime Journals of Charles A. Lindbergh,* p. 102.

96 *"well-, though heavily, furnished":* Ibid., p. 111.

96 *The owner was Jewish:* Leonard Mosley, *Lindbergh,* p. 237.

97 *"Mr. Churchill said":* "Hitler Assails War Agitators," *NYT,* November 7, 1938, p. 1.

97 *"I have always said":* "Churchill Answers Hitler," *NYT,* November 7, 1938, p. 14.

97 *He bought a gun:* Gerald Schwab, *The Day the Holocaust Began,* p. 1.

98 *Clarence Pickett had lunch:* Miller, *Witness for Humanity,* pp. 178–79.

98 *"We were sure":* Pickett, *For More than Bread,* pp. 132–33.

98 *"I questioned":* Ibid., p. 133.

98 *"Being a Jew":* Time, November 21, 1938.

99 *"He decides":* Herf, *The Jewish Enemy: Nazi Propaganda During World War II and the Holocaust,* p. 45.

99 *"only if there is no danger":* Roderick Stackelberg and Sally A. Winkle, *The Nazi Germany Sourcebook,* pp. 223–24.

99 *favorite books:* Larry Tye, *The Father of Spin,* p. 111.

100 *"In one of the Jewish":* Thalmann and Feinermann, *Crystal Night,* pp. 67–68.

100 *"shocked an almost":* Time, November 21, 1938.

100 *"The population of Cologne":* "Excerpts From the British Government's White Paper on German Concentration Camps," *NYT,* October 31, 1939.

101 *"They have undoubtedly":* Lindbergh, *Wartime Journals,* p. 115.

101 *"I myself could scarcely":* Franklin D. Roosevelt, *The Public Papers and Addresses of Franklin D. Roosevelt,* vol. 7, pp. 597–98.

102 *"begging for visas"*: Martin Gilbert, *Kristallnacht,* p. 152, citing "Throwing Responsibilities on Other Countries," *Manchester Guardian,* November 16, 1938.

102 *"Cables from Germany indicate"*: Miller, *Witness for Humanity,* pp. 180–81.

103 *"On Tuesday, Mr. President"*: Roosevelt, *Public Papers,* vol. 7, p. 602.

104 *"We are a thickly populated"*: "Excerpts from Commons Debate on Refugees," *NYT,* November 22, 1938.

104 *"Tanganyika offers"*: "Tanganyika," *NYT,* November 24, 1938.

105 *"a striking indication"*: "After Munich," *Time,* November 28, 1938.

105 *Tanganyika was too hot:* "Tanganyika Opposed as Haven for Exiles," *NYT,* November 27, 1938.

105 *"I would rather"*: Feingold, *Bearing Witness,* p. 139.

105 *"My sympathies are all"*: Jack, ed., *Gandhi Reader,* pp. 324–26.

106 *One hundred and ninety-six:* "Refugee Children Reach England," *NYT,* December 3, 1938.

107 *went to Germany:* Elizabeth Gray Vining, *Friend of Life,* pp. 281–93; Hans A. Schmitt, *Quakers and Nazis,* pp. 107–11; David Hinshaw, *Rufus Jones, Master Quaker,* pp. 272–82.

107 *"We need the note," "intervene personally" and "they are to investigate"*: Vining, *Friend of Life,* pp. 283, 286, 301.

108 *Cora Berliner:* Schmitt, *Quakers and Nazis,* p. 107.

109 *"We noted a softening"*: Hinshaw, *Rufus Jones,* p. 281.

109 *transient camps:* Vining, *Friend of Life,* p. 291; "Germany Permits Relief by Quakers," *NYT,* January 3, 1939.

109 *"I shall telegraph tonight"*: Hinshaw, *Rufus Jones,* p. 281.

109 *"It is the settled purpose"*: Miller, *Witness for Humanity,* p. 186.

109 *"Don't put food"*: "Germany Permits Relief by Quakers," *NYT,* January 3, 1939.

109 *"This short reprieve"*: Pickett, *For More than Bread,* p. 137.

110 *target shooting:* Lindbergh, *Wartime Journals,* pp. 128–29.

110 *"I suppose this means that Himmler"*: Ibid., p. 129.

110 *"I did not talk"*: Ibid., p. 131.

111 *"I therefore offered"*: Pickett, *For More than Bread,* pp. 140–41.

111 *"It was an extremely unpleasant"*: Miller, *Witness for Humanity,* p. 187.

111 *"I did not pass"*: Gilbert, *Kristallnacht,* p. 181.

111 *"Because of the cold wave"*: "Nazi Camps Release 7,000 Jews," *NYT,* December 24, 1938.

112 *"Herr Hitler is"*: Dennis Dalton, *Mahatma Gandhi: Nonviolent Power in Action,* p. 135.

112 *"Lindbergh Reported Providing"*: Lindbergh, *Wartime Journals,* p. 135.

112 *"If we must arm"*: Ibid., p. 136.

113 *"European refugees are stealing"*: "Anti-Refugee Riots by British Fascists," *NYT,* January 15, 1939.

113 *Reich Bureau for Jewish Emigration:* Arno Mayer, *Why Did the Heavens Not Darken?*, p. 290.

113 *"If the United States could":* "German Proposal on Refugees Near," *NYT,* January 28, 1939.

113 *"Their transit visa having":* Zweig, *World of Yesterday,* pp. 425–26.

114 *Hitler shook his finger:* "Hitler Speaks Before the Reichstag," United States Holocaust Memorial Museum, www.ushmm.org/musuem/exhibit/online/szyk/action/93852.htm.

114 *"one of the most sensational":* "Reactions to Hitler," *Time,* February 13, 1939.

114 *secret meeting:* "Stunning Secrets on Foreign Policy Hinted by Senator," *NYT,* March 2, 1939.

115 *"What can we do":* David Reynolds, *From World War to Cold War,* p. 169.

115 *"Thousands of American families":* *Congressional Record,* February 9, 1939, p. 1279.

116 *"the humanitarian thing to do":* David S. Wyman, *Paper Walls,* p. 97.

116 *"It is all right":* Ibid.

116 *"both for the portion":* "The Child Refugees," New York *Herald Tribune,* February 11, 1939, quoted in U.S. Senate and House of Representatives, *Admission of German Refugee Children,* p. 11.

116 *"If we had a barbed-wire":* "Children in the Dark," *NYT,* February 18, 1939.

116 *"The call":* "Mercy for Refugee Children," Newport News *Times Herald,* February 15, 1939, quoted in U.S. Senate and House, *Admission of German Refugee Children,* p. 27.

116 *visa applications:* "130,000 Ask for U.S. Visas," *NYT,* March 4, 1939.

117 *March 8, 1939:* Edward S. Miller, *War Plan Orange: The U.S. Strategy to Defeat Japan, 1897–1945,* p. 463.

117 *"War with ORANGE"* and *National Mission:* Richardson, *On the Treadmill to Pearl Harbor,* pp. 270–71.

117 *"When you accept":* "Pacifists Denounce War Policy," *NYT,* March 12, 1939.

117 *"handed down to us":* "Hull Statement on Referendum," *NYT,* March 12, 1939.

118 *"I am convinced":* "22,000 in Army Fete Parade in 5th Ave.," *NYT,* April 9, 1939.

118 *"Mass Murder":* "52 Pacifists March in Army Day Protest," *NYT,* April 9, 1939.

118 *near peaceable people:* Jonathan Fryer, *Isherwood,* p. 188.

118 *He planned a trip:* Christopher Isherwood, *Diaries,* p. 14.

118 *"Our way of passive resistance":* Ibid., p. 16.

119 *"I come here with":* "Urge Bill to Admit Refugee Children," *NYT,* April 21, 1939.

119 *"A Jewish child":* U.S. Senate and House, *Admission of German Refugee Children,* pp. 56–57.

119 *"My father's name":* Ibid., p. 85.

119 *"corroding and fearful":* "Declare Germans Abhor Nazi Terror," *NYT,* April 22, 1939.

120 *"No harm," "That issue is whether,"* and *"boring from within":* "Hoover Backs Bill to Waive Quota Act for Reich Children," *NYT,* April 23, 1939.

120 *Boy Scouts:* "Louis Taber Dies," *NYT,* October 17, 1960.

120 *"many distorted minds":* Schmitt, *Quakers and Nazis,* pp. 110, 245.

121 *"Bare, arid spaces":* Lester, *It So Happened,* p. 90.

121 *"This sort of war":* Ibid., pp. 96–97.

121 *"Your dislike of British":* Ibid., p. 98.

122 *"After the period":* Yale Law School, *The Avalon Project,* "British White Paper of 1939," www.yale.edu/lawweb/avalon/mideast/brwh1939.htm.

122 *"Any one aware":* "Britain is Warned by Zionist Leader," *NYT,* May 14, 1939.

122 *"That will not disprove":* Dalton, *Mahatma Gandhi,* p. 136.

123 *very quietly:* "Chamberlain Bares Pledge," *NYT,* April 1, 1939.

123 *His Majesty's government was:* "Chamberlain's Statement," *NYT,* April 1, 1939.

123 *"Mr. Chamberlain's pledge":* "Chamberlain Bares Pledge," *NYT,* April 1, 1939.

123 *soon reciprocated:* Ian Colvin, *The Chamberlain Cabinet,* p. 197.

123 *Secrecy was the precondition:* Stackelberg and Winkle, *Nazi Germany Sourcebook,* pp. 231–35.

124 *Lockheed employees remained:* "Air Experts in Japan Only Fill Contracts," *NYT,* May 27, 1939.

124 *"Never before in history":* "Exiles' Woes Move Writers' Congress," *NYT,* June 5, 1939.

125 *bought a Lockheed 14:* Winterbotham, *Nazi Connection,* pp. 188–98.

125 *"File No action FDR":* Wyman, *Paper Walls,* p. 97.

125 *"The facts and the logic":* Pickett, *For More than Bread,* p. 152.

126 *Registration forms went out:* Henry Friedlander, *The Origins of Nazi Genocide,* p. 45; J. Noakes and G. Pridham, eds., *Nazism, 1919–1945,* vol. 3, pp. 1006–7.

126 *confiscated:* Götz Aly et al., *Cleansing the Fatherland,* p. 40.

126 *One hundred British bombers:* "Britain Posts Warnings For the Nazis to Read," *NYT,* July 16, 1939.

126 *Marseille:* "British Bombers Fly to Marseille," *NYT,* July 20, 1939.

126 *240 planes:* "240 British Planes Soar Over France," *NYT,* July 26, 1939.

127 *"shuttle bombing":* "Shuttle Bombing Raids Face Reich," *NYT,* August 23, 1939.

127 *"within easy striking":* Ibid.

127 *The newspapers said:* "Britain to Assure Status of Danzig in Specific Pledge," *NYT,* July 6, 1939; Gilbert, *Churchill,* vol. 5, pp. 1090–92.

127 *"secret council of war":* "British Army Chief Arrives in Poland," *NYT,* July 18, 1939.

127 *"He is a pacifist at heart":* Gilbert, *Churchill,* vol. 5, p. 1093.

128 *"No doubt Jews":* Gilbert, *Holocaust,* p. 81.

128 *"Huge United States Bomber":* " 'Flying Fortress' Here With Record," *NYT,* August 2, 1939.

128 *noontime signal:* "Army Corps Sends 1,500 Planes in Air," *NYT,* August 3, 1939.

129 *short pants:* Donald Cameron Watt, *How War Came,* p. 444.

129 *"I have called you together":* Stackelberg and Winkle, *Nazi Germany Sourcebook,* pp. 242–46.

129 *"Here a man spoke":* Kershaw, *Hitler,* p. 209.

130 *some sort of mental breakdown:* Watt, *How War Came,* p. 500.

130 *"pacific means of settlement":* Stackelberg and Winkle, *Nazi Germany Sourcebook,* p. 249.

130 *Electrolux's British subsidiary:* Scott Newton, *Profits of Peace,* p. 123.

130 *"abnormal":* Kershaw, *Hitler,* p. 216.

130 *"I will build U-boats":* Watt, *How War Came,* p. 505.

130 *"pledged to defend":* Ibid.

130 *"a wasp at a picnic":* Alexander Cadogan, *The Diaries of Sir Alexander Cadogan,* p. 220.

130 *"unimaginably nervy":* Watt, *How War Came,* p. 511.

131 *"These last few days":* Victor Klemperer, *I Will Bear Witness,* vol. 1, p. 305.

131 *"For almost two hours":* "Hitler Reported Locking Self In To Make Fateful Decision Alone," New York *Herald Tribune,* September 1, 1939.

132 *"So far as I'm concerned":* Ulrich Von Hassell, *The Von Hassell Diaries,* p. 69.

132 *"The sky":* Count Galeazzo Ciano, *The Ciano Diaries, 1939–1943,* p. 134.

132 *"Everybody against":* William L. Shirer, *Berlin Diary,* p. 191.

133 *"To put an end":* New York *Herald Tribune,* September 1, 1939.

133 *"The German Air Force":* Asher Lee, *Goering: Air Leader,* p. 69.

133 *"I had* in fact": Franklin D. Roosevelt, *F.D.R.: His Personal Letters,* vol. 2, p. 915.

133 *"The Germans have invaded":* Zweig, *World of Yesterday,* p. 433.

135 *"Pack up your troubles":* New York *Herald Tribune,* September 1, 1939.

135 *"utterly intolerable":* Stackelberg and Winkle, *Nazi Germany Sourcebook,* pp. 254–56.

136 *weak speech:* Von Hassell, *Diaries,* p. 72.

136 *"amazingly small":* New York *Herald Tribune,* September 2, 1939.

136 *Hitler's breath:* Kershaw, *Hitler,* p. 222.

136 *"At twilight":* New York *Herald Tribune,* September 2, 1939.

136 *The planes would come:* Shirer, *Berlin Diary,* pp. 198–99.

136 *"It was as though":* Isherwood, *Diaries,* p. 46.

137 *"conduct hostilities":* J. R. M. Butler, *Grand Strategy,* p. 568; see also separate statements of France and England, in New York *Herald Tribune,* September 2, 1939.

137 *"I agree to your proposal":* Hans Rumpf, *The Bombing of Germany,* p. 20.

137 Tiger Hill: Bernard Wasserstein, *Britain and the Jews of Europe, 1939–1945,* p. 40.

138 *"The glory of Old England":* Winston Churchill, *The Gathering Storm,* p. 409.

138 *"There was not a murmur"*: Shirer, *Berlin Diary*, p. 200.

138 *"Second Armageddon"*: *Life*, September 11, 1939.

138 *"You would have saved"*: Martin Gilbert, *The Churchill War Papers*, vol. 1, p. 12.

138 *wooden map case:* Churchill, *Gathering Storm*, p. 410; Gilbert, *Churchill War Papers*, vol. 1, p. 8.

138 WINSTON IS BACK: Gilbert, *Churchill War Papers*, vol. 1, p. 6.

139 *Olinda* and *grain and canned meat:* "German Ship Sunk by British Cruiser," *NYT*, September 5, 1939.

139 *"Do not wait"*: Max Caulfield, *Tomorrow Never Came*, p. 13.

140 *"With cold deliberation"*: "Text of British Leaflet," *NYT*, September 5, 1939.

140 *Some planes missed Germany:* Cadogan, *Diaries*, p. 213.

140 *"We are not allowed"*: Harold Nicolson, *The War Years, 1939–1945*, p. 32.

140 *the British sent twenty-nine airplanes:* Anthony Verrier, *The Bomber Offensive*, p. 110.

140 *"Our airmen* say *they bombed"*: Cadogan, *Diaries*, p. 213.

140 *Esbjerg:* "Bombs Drop on Neutral Denmark but 'Raid' is Held Unintentional," *NYT*, September 5, 1939; "First Picture of Bomb Damage in Neutral Danish City," *NYT*, September 15, 1939.

141 *three million more pieces:* "Britain Continues Leaflet 'Bombing,' " *NYT*, September 6, 1939.

141 *"Don't forget that England"*: "Sylt, German Isle, Reported Bombed," *NYT*, September 9, 1939; New York *Herald Tribune*, September 9, 1939.

141 *free toilet paper:* Robin Neillands, *The Bomber War*, p. 39.

141 *The Danish were considering:* "Sylt, German Isle, Reported Bombed," *NYT*, September 9, 1939.

141 *"Germans may not leave"*: "French Interne Germans," *NYT*, September 7, 1939.

141 *fifteen thousand Germans:* "French Speed Aid for Enemy Aliens," *NYT*, December 17, 1939; "France Interns 15,000 Germans," *NYT*, September 19, 1939.

142 *"crushing Poland"*: Otto D. Tolischus, *They Wanted War*, p. 289; "Poles Unprepared for Blow So Hard," *NYT*, September 12, 1939.

142 *keep their swords:* Tolischus, *They Wanted War*, p. 300.

142 *Streets were an inch deep:* "Fires in Warsaw," *NYT*, September 5, 1939.

142 *"I lost my wife"*: New York *Herald Tribune*, September 3, 1939.

142 *"The great roof"*: "Italian Reports Warsaw Bombing," *NYT*, September 9, 1939.

142 *"Destroy and exterminate"*: Christopher Browning, *The Origins of the Final Solution*, p. 17.

143 *"You declared war"*: "Further Excerpts from Speech," *NYT*, September 10, 1939.

143 *"Our love and veneration"*: Ibid.

143 *"laughable flyleaves":* "Summary of Marshal Goering's Speech to the Reich Munitions Workers," *NYT,* September 10, 1939.

143 *"It is his job":* Edward R. Murrow, *This Is London,* pp. 22–23.

143 *"Blockade was enforced":* Churchill, *Gathering Storm,* p. 425.

144 *"The public at":* Mollie Panter-Downes, "London War Notes," *The New Yorker,* September 10, 1939.

144 *"Loraine does not seem":* Colvin, *Chamberlain Cabinet,* p. 255.

144 FOR THE SAKE: Peace Pledge Union, "PPU's Women's Peace Campaign," www .ppu.org.uk; Pat Starkey, *I Will Not Fight,* p. 7.

145 *"peace offensive":* "Allies Prepared to Reject 'Peace,' " *NYT,* September 19, 1939.

145 *no peace was possible:* "Britain Bars Peace Until Hitler Goes," *NYT,* September 12, 1939.

145 *He'd planned to give:* Shirer, *Berlin Diary,* p. 216.

145 *"I have neither":* Otto Tolischus, "Fuehrer at Danzig," *NYT,* September 20, 1939.

145 *"like a pack":* Shirer, *Berlin Diary,* p. 217.

145 *"Some of it rhetorically"* and *"One of two things":* Klemperer, *Witness,* p. 312–13.

146 *"frankly terrified":* Nicolson, *War Years,* pp. 35–36.

146 *"All parts of the Reich":* "Offers Lasting Peace," *NYT,* September 20, 1939.

146 *"The peace that Hitler":* William Shirer, "A Peace of Sorts," track 5 of CD accompanying Mark Bernstein and Alex Lubertozzi, *World War II on the Air.*

146 *"There can be no peace":* "London Shuns Bait," *NYT,* September 30, 1939, citing *The Times* (London), September 30, 1939.

146 *"The People Want Peace":* William L. Shirer, *"This Is Berlin,"* p. 101.

147 *"One looks ahead":* Isherwood, *Diaries,* p. 46.

147 *"The Paris sky":* Ibid.

147 *"He says that Hitler":* Nicolson, *War Years,* p. 39.

148 *A church had been hit:* "Poles Fighting On," *NYT,* September 25, 1939.

148 *"Gentlemen, you have seen":* Jon E. Lewis, ed., *The Mammoth Book of Eyewitness World War II,* p. 40.

148 *detecting blind spots:* Gilbert, *Holocaust,* p. 99.

148 *"It is quite clear":* "Clash in Commons," *NYT,* October 4, 1939.

149 *"I want repeatedly":* Vera Brittain, *Testament of a Peace Lover,* p. 2.

149 *"solution and settlement":* Adolf Hitler, *My New Order,* p. 751, quoted in Louis C. Kilzer, *Churchill's Deception,* p. 169.

149 *"Rather surprisingly":* John Colville, *The Fringes of Power,* p. 32.

149 *"What in the devil's name":* George Bernard Shaw, "Uncommon Sense About the War," in Edward Hyams, ed., *New Statesmanship,* pp. 167–71.

150 *"I make my decision":* Milton S. Mayer, "I Think I'll Sit This One Out," *The Saturday Evening Post,* October 7, 1939.

151 *"The Führer still":* Joseph Goebbels, *The Goebbels Diaries, 1939–1941,* p. 17.

151 *"laughs until the tears":* Ibid., p. 18.

151 *standing stiffly:* "Prime Minister Says Bar to Peace is the Present German Government," *NYT,* October 13, 1939.

151 *"It would be impossible":* Christopher Hill, *Cabinet Decisions on Foreign Policy,* p. 253.

151 *just as horrified:* "Prime Minister Says Bar to Peace is the Present German Government," *NYT,* October 13, 1939.

151 *three hours:* "Blood Bath," *Time,* October 23, 1939.

152 *"In the fishmongers' ":* Klemperer, *Witness,* pp. 315–16.

152 *"The Government's own":* Vera Brittain, "Letters to a Peace Lover," Peace Pledge Union, www.ppu.org.uk.

153 *Owinska Mental Home:* Browning, *Origins,* p. 188; Charles Sydnor, *Soldiers of Destruction,* p. 42; "Owinska Mental Home and Poznan Fort VII," www.deathcamps.org; "Koscian and the Euthanasia in Poland," www.deathcamps.org.

153 *"The little people":* Browning, *Origins,* p. 17.

153 *"Among well-informed people":* Von Hassell, *Diaries,* pp. 78–79.

154 *"Yes, of course":* Cyril Joad, *Journey Through the War Mind,* p. 99.

154 *"Suppose you are right":* Ibid., p. 118.

155 *"perverted morons":* Ibid., p. 89.

155 *"Quite frankly":* Ibid., p. 93.

156 *"reservation":* "2,000 Jews Sent from Vienna," *NYT,* October 22, 1939.

156 *"Jew free":* Associated Press, "Jews Off to Reservation," in *Nebraska State Journal,* November 1, 1939, available at www.ancestry.com.

156 *"our arch-enemies in the Eastern sphere":* Noakes and Pridham, *Nazism,* p. 939.

156 *flogging:* Raul Hilberg, *The Destruction of the European Jews,* vol. 1, p. 191.

157 *"with supposed tolerance":* Browning, *Origins,* pp. 74–75.

157 *carried it around with him:* Gerald Reitlinger, *The SS: Alibi of a Nation,* pp. 134–35, Omer Bartov, *Hitler's Army,* p. 65.

157 *rabid Nazi:* Von Hassell, *Diaries,* p. 67; also, Browning, *Origins,* p. 75.

157 *"Every soldier feels":* Gilbert, *Second World War,* p. 43.

157 *"spread like an epidemic":* Bartov, *Hitler's Army,* p. 66.

157 *"Surprisingly quickly":* Browning, *Origins,* p. 78.

157 *"only the brutal":* Bartov, *Hitler's Army,* p. 66.

158 *"He must either die":* Scott Newton, *Profits of Peace,* p. 145.

158 *A man named Elser:* Kershaw, *Hitler,* pp. 271–73.

159 *"Warships are important":* Tolischus, *They Wanted War,* pp. 324–25.

159 *"Of the many":* Brittain, *Testament of a Peace Lover,* pp. 7–8.

159 *"The ever increasing food":* Klemperer, *Witness,* p. 320.

160 *"All that is needed":* "Goering Threatens Terror for British," *NYT,* December 31, 1939.

161 *Half the money:* New York *Herald Tribune,* January 2, 1940.

161 *"I did a magician's trick"*: Thomas M. Coffey, *Hap,* p. 205.

161 *"How all these people"*: Isherwood, *Diaries,* p. 81.

162 *Hitler was not:* John Gunther, *Inside Europe,* p. 4.

162 *"Nor, as is so widely believed"*: Ibid., p. 8.

163 *"The Group agrees"*: Nicolson, *War Years,* p. 58.

163 *"Am I afraid"*: Isherwood, *Diaries,* pp. 83–84.

164 *"If the war in Europe"*: "Fears for Polish Jews," *NYT,* January 22, 1940.

164 *"Is it that they"*: Churchill, *Complete Speeches,* vol. 6, pp. 6187–88.

165 *more people:* Verrier, *Bomber Offensive,* p. 91.

166 *"A new restlessness"*: Robert MacKay, *Half the Battle,* p. 56.

166 *"The Jewish cemetery"*: Mary Berg, *Warsaw Ghetto,* p. 26.

167 *"Was that deliberate?"*: J. M. Spaight, *Bombing Vindicated,* p. 69.

167 *"I do beg your Lordships"*: H. W. Koch, "The Strategic Air Offensive Against Germany," p. 125.

167 *German island of Sylt:* "Nazis Give British Third Air Warning," *NYT,* April 26, 1940.

167 *Some airplanes overshot:* "British Planes in All-Night Raid Bomb Great Nazi Air Base at Sylt," *NYT,* March 20, 1940.

167 *Peace Hope Dies:* "British Planes in All-Night Raid," *NYT,* March 20, 1940.

167 *War Seen Entering:* Augur, "War Seen Entering New Phase of Violence," *NYT,* March 22, 1940.

167 *"One of the main ideas"*: "Raid on Sylt Acts as Tonic to British," *NYT,* March 21, 1940.

168 *cripple the enemy's:* B. H. Liddell Hart, *History of the Second World War,* p. 57.

168 *"succeed in provoking"*: Gilbert, *Churchill War Papers,* vol. 1, p. 780.

168 *Hints of Churchill's plan:* "Nazi Ship is Sunk; Allies Open Drive to Cut Ore Route," *NYT,* March 25, 1940.

168 *as good as lost:* J. R. M. Butler, *Grand Strategy,* p. 104.

168 *"This will create"*: Nicolson, *War Years,* p. 67.

168 *"Says we have done the silliest"*: Cadogan, *Diaries,* p. 268.

169 *"The Norwegian Government protests"*: "Allied Mines Bring a Protest by Oslo," *NYT,* April 9, 1940.

169 *"Germans seem to have got in"*: Cadogan, *Diaries,* p. 268.

169 *One group commandeered:* "More Allied Norway Units Return," *NYT,* May 9, 1940.

169 *A squadron of RAF planes:* Killen, *History of the Luftwaffe,* p. 111.

169 *delayed-action bombs:* Richards, *Portal of Hungerford,* p. 144.

169 *"The first of our glorious evacuations"*: "H. G. Wells Insists on British Shake-Up," *NYT,* September 8, 1940.

169 *"Norway was Winston's adventure"*: Channon, *Chips,* pp. 251–52.

170 *"The hawk poises herself"*: Richards, *Portal of Hungerford,* pp. 24–25.

171 *"that vast row"*: Clare Boothe, *Europe in the Spring,* p. 156.

171 *"should the Germans"*: Ibid., pp. 158–59.

172 *"thousands and more thousands":* Browning, *Origins,* pp. 131–32.

172 *Germany issued a warning:* "Nazis Warn British of Major Air Raids," *NYT,* April 13, 1940; see also "Berlin Renews Threat to Britain," *NYT,* April 15, 1940.

172 *Heiligenhafen station* and *The British Air Ministry denied:* "Nazis Give British Third Air Warning," *NYT,* April 26, 1940.

172 *British bombed occupied Oslo:* "Allies Warn Oslo of Approaching Air-Raid," *NYT,* April 24, 1940.

172 *third, "final," warning:* "Nazis Give British Third Air Warning," *NYT,* April 26, 1940.

173 *"Here it is":* Gilbert, *Churchill War Papers,* vol. 1, p. 1153.

173 *"He wanted to divert troops":* Edmund Ironside, *Time Unguarded,* p. 278.

173 *"No attack was made":* "Nazis Give British Third Air Warning," *NYT,* April 26, 1940.

173 *dead reckoning:* Hastings, *Bomber Command,* p. 111.

173 *peering down:* Webster and Frankland, *Strategic Air Offensive,* vol. 1, pp. 204–5.

173 *"Normally it was not difficult":* Neillands, *Bomber War,* p. 38.

174 *A photographer began taking:* Friedlander, *Origins of Nazi Genocide,* p. 237.

174 *"Hitler felt that":* Viktor Brack, "Affidavit Concerning the Nazi Administrative System, the Euthanasia Program, and the Sterilization Experiments," p. 5.

174 *The assembly-line killings:* Friedlander, *Origins,* pp. 109–10.

174 *"Reports abounded":* Ibid., p. 237.

174 *bonus checks:* Norman J. W. Goda, "Black Marks: Hitler's Bribery of His Senior Officers."

174 *"closed envelopes":* Kurt von Schuschnigg, *Austrian Requiem,* p. 280.

175 *"The Germans are coming":* Boothe, *Europe in the Spring,* pp. 223–24.

175 *"Germans have relieved us":* Cadogan, *Diaries,* p. 280.

175 *discussed bombing Germany:* Ibid., p. 281; Gilbert, *War Papers,* vol. 1, pp. 1273–75, 1279.

175 *"I sought an audience":* "British Prime Minister Neville Chamberlain Resigns," WWII: 1938–Dec 6, 1941, Authentic History Center, www.authentichistory .com.

176 *"All the hatred":* Nicolson, *War Years,* p. 84.

176 *"a monstrous tyranny":* Churchill, *Their Finest Hour,* p. 25.

176 *"That got the sods":* James, "The Politician," in Taylor, *Churchill Revised,* p. 122n.

176 *dummy paratroopers:* Liddell Hart, *History of the Second World War,* p. 73.

176 *The Luftwaffe targeted:* "French Towns Hit by First Bombings," *NYT,* May 11, 1940.

177 *"I have seldom met":* Birkenhead, *Halifax,* p. 456.

177 *"The mere thought of Churchill":* John Colville, in Sir John Wheeler-Bennett, *Action This Day: Working with Churchill,* p. 48.

177 *"very respectable civil servants":* Ibid., p. 50.

178 *Whitley bombers:* Spaight, *Bombing Vindicated,* p. 69, quoting Arthur Harris.

178 *an Englishwoman:* Rumpf, *Bombing of Germany,* p. 25.

178 *The Germans shot down:* A. C. Grayling, *Among the Dead Cities,* p. 32.

178 *"A German radio broadcast":* "British Airmen Hit Nazi Columns," *NYT,* May 12, 1940.

178 *"Essen was not among":* "Cry for Reprisals Grows in France," *NYT,* May 13, 1940.

179 *Telegrams went out:* Fred Kaufman, *Searching for Justice,* pp. 33–34.

179 *most of them Jewish refugees:* Wasserstein, *Britain and the Jews of Europe,* p. 92; François Lafitte, *The Internment of Aliens,* pp. 76–77.

179 *fixed bayonets:* See, e.g., *The Illustrated London News,* May 25, 1940, p. 706.

179 *"I feel that any move":* George Morgenstern, *Pearl Harbor,* pp. 54–55.

180 *"complete destruction":* Butler, *Grand Strategy,* pp. 569–70.

180 *Oil from a margarine factory:* Killen, *History of the Luftwaffe,* p. 115.

180 *"carried out on open cities":* Koch, "Strategic Air Offensive," p. 127.

181 *"Do you think":* Etty Hillesum, *An Interrupted Life,* March 25, 1941, p. 19.

181 *"very large round-up"* and *was it time:* Gilbert, *Churchill War Papers,* vol. 2, pp. 40–43.

182 *"Cabinet this morning decided":* Cadogan, *Diaries,* p. 283.

183 *"I am looking to you":* Warren F. Kimball, ed., *Churchill and Roosevelt,* pp. 37–38.

183 *Aachen, Düsseldorf, Cologne:* Koch, "Strategic Air Offensive," p. 130.

183 *bombing at random:* "Charge Bombing at Random," *NYT,* May 19, 1940.

183 *air-dropping Colorado beetles* and *bovine plague:* Simon M. Whitby, *Biological Warfare Against Crops,* pp. 78–81.

184 *Colorado-beetle bombings:* Biddle, *Rhetoric and Reality,* p. 40.

184 *"well worth considering":* Ibid., p. 316.

184 *"I strongly emphasized":* Yale Law School, *The Avalon Project,* Nuremberg Trial Proceedings, vol. 9, www.yale.edu/lawweb/avalon/imt/proc/03-15-46.htm.

184 *"Rather unpleasant day":* Hart, *History of the Second World War,* p. 86.

185 *"square search":* Edward B. Westermann, *Flak,* p. 90.

185 *"found difficulty":* Ibid.

185 *"authorised to attack":* H. R. Trevor-Roper, ed., *Hitler's War Directives,* p. 29.

186 *"I should like this nation":* Coffey, *Hap,* p. 211.

186 *"Have greatest possible admiration"* and *"It was painful thus":* Churchill, *Their Finest Hour,* pp. 79, 82.

187 *"It is easy":* William Shirer, *Collapse of the Third Republic,* p. 732.

187 *"prevent a useless massacre":* John Costello, *Ten Days to Destiny,* p. 219.

187 *Goering promised:* John Toland, *Adolf Hitler,* vol. 2, p. 703.

187 *"It is perhaps fortunate":* Nicolson, *War Years,* p. 91.

188 *"in a certain eventuality"* and *"Life will be sustained"*: Butler, *Grand Strategy,* pp. 209, 212–15.

189 *"A few, mainly those"*: "Alien Arrests Net Women in Britain," *NYT,* May 28, 1940.

189 *"To have been arrested"*: Max Perutz, *I Wish I'd Made You Angry Earlier,* p. 75.

189 *"Let the* Mooragh Times*"*: Argus, "Friendly Enemy Aliens"; see also Onlooker, "The Tragedy of the Refugees."

189 *suppressed:* Jennifer Taylor, " 'Something to Make People Laugh'? Political Content in Isle of Man Internment Camp Journals, July–October 1940," in Richard Dove, ed., *"Totally Un-English"?* p. 143.

190 *"Let us therefore avoid"*: Gilbert, *Churchill War Papers,* vol. 2, p. 168.

190 *"I thought Winston talked"*: Birkenhead, *Halifax,* p. 458.

191 *"However cruel and tragic"*: Browning, *Origins,* pp. 69–70.

191 *It must now be abandoned:* Churchill, *Their Finest Hour,* pp. 110–12.

192 *antiwar meeting:* "War Trend is Hit at Peace Session," *NYT,* June 8, 1940.

193 *"I do not know him sufficiently"*: Margaret Gowing, *Britain and Atomic Energy, 1939–1945,* p. 47.

193 *on an aircraft carrier:* Lewis, *Mammoth Book of Eyewitness World War II,* pp. 112–16.

194 *All enemy aliens:* "Britain Interns Elder Aliens," *NYT,* June 11, 1940.

194 *"I am very sorry"*: Wasserstein, *Britain and the Jews of Europe,* p. 96.

194 *At six o'clock, Mussolini:* "Duce Gives Signal," *NYT,* June 11, 1940.

194 *"The news of the war"*: Ciano, *Diaries,* p. 264.

195 *the manager of the Picadilly hotel:* A. W. Brian Simpson, *In the Highest Degree Odious,* p. 194.

195 *"Collar the lot"*: Wasserstein, *Britain and the Jews of Europe,* p. 90.

195 *"extensive Italianization"*: Eric Koch, *Deemed Suspect: A Wartime Blunder,* p. 15.

195 *Canadian mounted police arrested:* "Hundreds of Italians Arrested in Canada," *NYT,* June 12, 1940.

195 *fruit shops:* "Disorders in Toronto," *NYT,* June 13, 1940.

195 *"It's the Jews' fault!"*: Klemperer, *Witness,* p. 343.

196 *"What makes me gnash"*: Nicolson, *War Years,* p. 95.

196 *"A woman in a wheelchair"*: "Swiss Blame British for Killing 4" *NYT,* June 13, 1940.

196 *The British government offered:* "Bombs Fall on Swiss Soil," *NYT,* July 1, 1940.

196 *"pernicious propaganda"*: Peace Pledge Union, "PPU History in Context."

196 *He was shot:* Peace Pledge Union, "1940–1949: Candles in the Dark."

197 *"We have bound ourselves"*: Harris and Paxman, *Higher Form of Killing,* p. 112.

197 *"Let me have"*: Ibid., p. 113.

197 *"Strange how lukewarm"*: Marie Vassiltchikov, *Berlin Diaries,* p. 18.

197 *"life-and-death struggle"* and *"I felt a glow"*: Churchill, *Their Finest Hour*, pp. 194–96, 198.

198 *"It is the most extraordinary brain"*: Birkenhead, *Halifax*, p. 459.

198 *"Nothing will stir them"*: David Reynolds, "Churchill and the British 'Decision' to Fight on in 1940," in Richard Langhorne, ed., *Diplomacy and Intelligence During the Second World War*, p. 162.

199 *returned to drop, machine-gunning fire brigades*, and *"Strong hatred"*: Koch, "Strategic Air Offensive," pp. 121, 131–32.

199 *Franklin Roosevelt fired*: Roosevelt, *F.D.R.: His Personal Letters*, pp. 1041–44.

200 *"We sat downstairs"*: Vassiltchikov, *Berlin Diaries*, p. 20.

201 *"They caused the death"*: "Reporters Find No Raid Havoc in Italian Plants," New York *Herald Tribune*, June 22, 1940.

201 *The Chinese were pleased*: "Senate Hearings Ordered On Stimson's Nomination," *NYT*, June 22, 1940.

201 *"Mr. Stimson is disliked"*: "Nazis See Knox and Stimson as 'Warmongers,' " New York *Herald Tribune*, June 22, 1940.

202 *"One of the men"*: Soames, *Winston and Clementine*, p. 454.

202 *Paris Opera House*: Speer, *Inside the Third Reich*, pp. 235–36.

203 *"It was a great relief"*: Adolf Hitler, *Hitler's Table Talk*, pp. 98–99.

203 *"The press and broadcast"*: Churchill, *Their Finest Hour*, p. 170.

203 *"borne a heavy share"*: "Our Plane Sales to Allies Detailed," *NYT*, June 28, 1940.

204 *"They do it well"*: Raymond E. Lee, *The London Journal of General Raymond E. Lee*, p. 8.

204 *"In this way the Zionist"*: Adam Czerniakow, *The Warsaw Diary of Adam Czerniakow*, p. 169.

204 *Work promptly stopped*: Browning, *Origins*, p. 84.

204 *"superghetto"*: Ibid., p. 85.

204 *One hundred and twenty boats*: Richard Breitman, *The Architect of Genocide*, p. 130; see also Browning, *Origins*, pp. 86–87.

205 *Ciano asked Phillips*: Ciano, *Diaries*, p. 272.

205 *"We reckoned that Somerville"*: Max Arthur, ed., *Forgotten Voices of World War II*, pp. 98–99.

205 *under Churchill's orders*: John Lukacs, *The Duel*, p. 163.

205 *"When he finished"*: Lee, *London Journal*, p. 12.

206 *"Your soldiers are doing"*: Gandhi, "To Every Briton," *Collected Works*, vol. 78, p. 387.

206 *"a general rage"*: Koch, "Strategic Air Offensive," p. 133.

207 *"violent explosion which lit"*: "Violent Explosion at Hamburg," *Times* (London), July 6, 1940.

207 *"Day after day"* and *"Now they'll make peace"*: Klemperer, *Witness*, p. 346–47.

208 *"The blockade is broken"*: Churchill, *Their Finest Hour*, p. 643.

208 *"The essential idea"*: "Educators Assail Peacetime Draft," *NYT*, July 9, 1940.

209   *"If you let the Nazis"*: Isherwood, *Diaries,* pp. 99–100.

209   *"Our action against"*: Nicolson, *War Years,* p. 100.

210   *"firmly resolved"*: "Gandhi's Non-Violence Toward Reich Rejected," *NYT,* July 14, 1940.

210   *"I was grateful to H.E."*: Gandhi, "To Every Briton," *Collected Works,* vol. 79, p. 9.

210   *"The country is gravely," "If you want to fight," "Military conscription is not freedom,"* and *"I would just like to enumerate"*: U.S. Senate Committee on Military Affairs, *Compulsary Military Training and Service,* pp. 21, 25, 148, 255.

211   *"no analogy"*: "Training Bill Wins Senators' Support," *NYT,* July 11, 1940.

212   *"We await undismayed"*: Gilbert, *Churchill War Papers,* vol. 2, p. 518.

212   *"Since England"*: Trevor-Roper, *Hitler's War Directives,* p. 34.

212   *"On its edge"*: Lee, *London Journal,* p. 17.

213   *His voice was under*: Shirer, *Berlin Diary,* p. 454.

213   *"Mr. Churchill has just declared"*: Stackelberg and Winkle, *Nazi Germany Sourcebook,* pp. 264–66.

213   *"unusually humane tone"*: Ciano, *Diaries,* p. 277.

213   *splendid new jacket*: Killen, *History of the Luftwaffe,* pp. 124–25.

213   *"His boyish pride"*: Shirer, *Berlin Diary,* p. 456.

214   *"Let me tell you"*: Sefton Delmer, *Black Boomerang.*

214   *"Late in the evening"*: Ciano, *Diaries,* p. 277.

214   *"I do not propose"*: Gilbert, *Churchill War Papers,* vol. 2, p. 568.

214   *"The reaction to Hitler's"*: Nicolson, *War Years,* p. 103.

214   *"The Prime Minister asked"*: Richards, *Portal of Hungerford,* p. 161.

215   *"But it's too tantalising"*: Frances Partridge, *A Pacifist's War,* p. 51.

215   *Quaker intermediary*: Costello, *Ten Days to Destiny,* p. 347.

215   *"We ought to find out"*: Ibid.

215   *"Philip Lothian telephones"*: Nicolson, *War Years,* p. 104.

216   *"Halifax Adamant"*: *NYT,* July 23, 1940.

216   *"Various sentences"*: "Text of Speech Changed," *NYT,* July 23, 1940.

216   *"iron curtain"*: "Nazis Hint Attack on Britain is Near," Ibid.

216   *"Magnetic attraction"*: "British See Blow Within 2 Weeks," *NYT,* August 6, 1940.

217   *"I recently came"*: Jeanne Guillemin, *Biological Weapons,* p. 49.

217   *"The truth is"*: Isherwood, *Diaries,* p. 115.

218   *"Britain Loses Her Honor"*: Spaight, *Bombing Vindicated,* p. 72.

218   *delayed action bombs*: Koch, "Strategic Air Offensive," p. 135.

218   *"I had expected"*: Shirer, *Berlin Diary,* p. 464.

218   *mad british lies:* "Nazis Call Hamburg 'Pulverization' False," *NYT,* August 4, 1940.

218   *"No man can be turned"*: Gandhi, *Collected Works,* vol. 79, pp. 92–93.

219   *"The whole time"*: Gilbert, *Churchill War Papers,* vol. 2, p. 651.

219   *"A sort of nausea"*: Lester, *It So Happened,* p. 123.

220 *"The obvious truth"*: "Hoover Maps Plan to Feed Europeans," *NYT,* August 12, 1940.

220 *"He was a militarist"* and *"When Churchill succeeded"*: Herbert Hoover, *An American Epic,* vol. 4, pp. 8, 17.

220 *"Speed the Food Ships"*: Lester, *It So Happened,* pp. 233–35.

221 *"I received a warning"*: Ibid., p. 125.

221 *"So they won't come!"*: Charles De Gaulle, *Complete War Memoirs,* p. 104.

222 *"From what I saw"*: Murrow, *This Is London,* pp. 143–44.

222 *"Now the British bombers"*: "Italian Cities Hit," *NYT,* August 20, 1940.

222 *"Combat service will fall"*: "Peace Bloc Assail Conscription Bill," *NYT,* August 20, 1940.

223 *"founded on the highest motives"*: Gilbert, *Churchill War Papers,* vol. 2, pp. 689–90.

223 *"The notion"*: Hoover, *American Epic,* pp. 20–21.

223 *"disgraceful and deplorable"*: "Britain Eases Lot of Interned Aliens," *NYT,* August 23, 1940.

224 *The doorman banged:* Vassiltchikov, *Berlin Diaries,* p. 27.

224 *blew the leg off, "good strafing,"* and *timed-release bombs:* Shirer, *Berlin Diary,* pp. 490, 492–93.

224 *"Small children lie"*: Vassiltchikov, *Berlin Diaries,* p. 28.

224 *"Heanley revealed"*: Cecil King, *With Malice Toward None,* pp. 69–70.

224 *"I am very glad"*: Gilbert, *Churchill War Papers,* vol. 2, p. 747.

225 *They'd tried it before:* Richards, *Portal of Hungerford,* p. 155.

225 *"calling cards"* and *playing card:* Ley, *Bombs and Bombing,* p. 38–39.

225 *Hitler had storehouses:* Kershaw, *Hitler,* p. 300.

225 *"Woods Are Bombed"*: "Woods Are Bombed," *NYT,* September 5, 1940.

226 *"The English come"*: "Talks of Invasion," *NYT,* September 5, 1940.

227 *"Tiny little boys"*: Nicolson, *War Years,* p. 111.

227 *"The planes were so high"*: "Churchill Proud of British Morale," *NYT,* September 10, 1940.

227 *"Several military targets"*: "Capital is Shaken," *NYT,* September 8, 1940.

227 *"After all"* and *"There was a heavy"*: "London Total War Arouses Cold Anger," *NYT,* September 8, 1940.

228 *"Skirting these blank spots"*: "Bases for Invasion Battered by R.A.F.," *NYT,* September 9, 1940.

228 *"we had a very wet August"*: Shirer, *Berlin Diary,* p. 502.

228 *"A large bomb"* and *"It sounded rather like"*: King, *With Malice Toward None,* pp. 74, 76.

229 *A British pilot saw the moon:* "Navy Helps R.A.F.," *NYT,* September 12, 1940.

229 *"Typical of present"*: "The Texts of the Day's War Communiques," September 12, 1940.

229 *What was damaged:* "Raid Nazi Capital," *NYT,* September 11, 1940.

229 *A bomb splinter:* Shirer, *Berlin Diary,* p. 504.

229 *burned in the garden:* Shirer, *This Is Berlin,* p. 403.

229 *Five civilians:* "The Texts of the Day's War Communiques," *NYT,* September 12, 1940.

229 *"Reichstag Bombarded!":* "Berlin Threatens New Fury in Raids," *NYT,* September 12, 1940.

229 *"Now that our Reichstag":* Ibid.

230 *"This wicked man":* "Text of Premier Churchill's Speech," *NYT,* September 12, 1940.

230 *"I am so far," "grotesque," "the situation with socks,"* and *"The Jews' House continually":* Klemperer, *Witness,* pp. 349, 355.

230 *Colorado potato bugs:* "Germans Accuse British of Spreading Potato Bugs," *NYT,* September 15, 1940.

231 *"Planes crashing":* "Canadian Says Germans Man Planes With Boys," New York *Herald Tribune,* September 13, 1940.

231 *"Our Wandsworth family":* Partridge, *Pacifist's War,* p. 60.

231 *"The thought of St. Paul's":* Gandhi, *Collected Works,* vol. 79, p. 217.

232 *played golf:* Richardson, *On the Treadmill,* p. 378.

232 *"Present policy":* Ibid., p. 380.

232 *"I told him":* Ibid., pp. 381–82.

232 *Clarence Pickett asked:* J. Garry Clifford and Samuel R. Spencer Jr., *The First Peacetime Draft,* p. 223.

232 *"We cannot remain indifferent":* Roosevelt, *Public Papers and Addresses,* vol. 9, p. 430.

233 *"knowingly counsels":* "Text of the Selective Service Measure as it Was Finally Passed by Congress Yesterday," *NYT,* September 15, 1940.

233 *"Everybody is worried"* and *In the bomb shelters:* Nicolson, *War Years,* pp. 114–16.

233 *Madagascar Plan:* Christopher Browning, *The Path to Genocide,* pp. 18–19.

234 *"I've seen enough":* Murrow, *This Is London,* pp. 186–87.

234 *"Attacks by the Royal Air Force":* Ciano, *Diaries,* p. 295.

234 *"Every night the citizens":* Ibid., p. 296.

235 *Kinderlandverschickung:* Jost Hermand, *A Hitler Youth in Poland,* p. 6.

235 *Baldur von Schirach:* Ibid., p. xiv.

235 *one of the old comrades:* William L. Shirer, *The Rise and Fall of the Third Reich,* p. 253; Machtan, *Hidden Hitler,* p. 82.

235 *he'd discovered anti-Semitism:* Shirer, *Rise and Fall,* p. 149.

235 *nationalist indoctrination:* Hermand, *Hitler Youth,* p. xiv.

235 *run by the Hitler Youth:* Fest, *Face of the Third Reich,* p. 227.

235 *"The possibility of our having":* Gilbert, *Churchill War Papers,* vol. 2, p. 880.

235 *"A few nights ago":* Vassiltchikov, *Berlin Diaries,* p. 31.

236 *"Hoses are old":* Armstrong, *Preemptive Strike,* pp. 61–62. Smith-Hutton is

identified as the naval attaché in Thomas G. Mahnken, *Uncovering Ways of War,* pp. 22, 47.

236 *"We are confronted":* Alexander S. Lipsett, "Mass Starvation Feared," *NYT,* October 2, 1940.

237 *The British Press Service organized:* Nicholas John Cull, *Selling War,* pp. 120–21.

237 *wheat, rice, and fleas:* Ed Regis, *The Biology of Doom,* p. 17; Peter Williams and David Wallace, *Unit 731: Japan's Secret Biological Warfare in World War II,* pp. 101–2.

237 *Chuhsien:* Now spelled Zhoushan.

238 *released a list:* "200 Points Listed by R.A.F. as Bombed," *NYT,* October 8, 1940.

238 *"Death and sorrow":* Gilbert, *Churchill War Papers,* vol. 2, p. 922.

238 *"The Luftwaffe has changed":* Michael Patterson, *Battle for the Skies,* pp. 59–60.

239 *confrontation* and *"restraining influence":* Richardson, *On the Treadmill,* pp. 425, 434.

239 *"He replied":* Ibid., p. 427; Morgenstern, *Pearl Harbor,* p. 58.

239 *Cecil King's newspapers:* King, *With Malice Toward None,* pp. 80–84.

240 *"Don't panic!":* Jean R. Freedman, *Whistling in the Dark: Memory and Culture in Wartime London,* pp. 106–7.

241 *"Calmly, without fear":* "President Speaks," *NYT,* October 17, 1940.

241 *"You must not hate":* "First Draft Objectors Are Called to Federal Inquiry Here Today," *NYT,* October 17, 1940.

241 *Four members of the Fellowship:* Ibid.; "Subpoenaed for Refusing to Register for Conscription," *NYT,* October 17, 1940; "10 Draft Objectors Are Indicted Here," *NYT,* October 22, 1940.

241 *"You and others":* Nicolson, *War Years,* pp. 121–22.

242 *"blitzkrieg of verbal":* Franklin D. Roosevelt, "Campaign Address at Philadelphia, Pennsylvania," October 23, 1940, in Wooley and Peters, *American Presidency Project.*

242 *In Dresden, air-raid sirens:* Klemperer, *Witness,* p. 360.

243 *new Nazi decree:* Eric A. Johnson, *Nazi Terror,* pp. 386–87.

243 *"directly or indirectly foment":* "India Bans Anti-War Talk," *NYT,* October 27, 1940.

243 *Nehru was arrested:* "Nehru Seized in India for Pacifist Speech," *NYT,* November 1, 1940.

243 *"I fear so much":* Nicolson, *War Years,* pp. 123–24.

243 *One of Halifax's stipulations:* Newton, *Profits of Peace,* p. 150.

244 *"Yesterday news came":* Women's International League for Peace and Freedom, "From a Letter from Camp de Gurs, South France," available at www.wilpf .int.ch/history/1941.doc.

244 *"Much perturbed":* Klemperer, *Witness,* p. 361.

244 *"in age from six months":* "Reich Jews Sent to South France," *NYT,* November 9, 1940.

245 *"Since there is a shortage"*: Noakes and Pridham, *Nazism,* p. 1080.

245 *"Relief work"*: "Reich Jews Sent to South France," *NYT,* November 9, 1940.

245 *blindfold:* Clifford and Spencer, *First Peacetime Draft,* p. 2.

246 *The Red Cross cut:* "Red Cross to Cut Staff in France," *NYT,* November 9, 1940.

246 *"Something deeply damaging"*: Lester, *It So Happened,* p. 126.

246 *"One of the reasons"*: "Hoover Food Plan Defended by Holmes," *NYT,* November 18, 1940.

246 *"If famine and plague"*: *Commonweal,* November 22, 1940.

246 *grand Lowenbrau beerhall:* "R.A.F. Fired Cellar After Hitler Left," *NYT,* November 10, 1940.

246 *"one of the hardest"*: "Hitler Forswears Any Compromise," *NYT,* November 9, 1940; "Adolf Tells the World He's One Tough Fellow," *NYT,* November 10, 1940.

247 *"Then it suddenly occurred"*: Toni Winkelnkemper, "The Attack on Cologne," trans. Randall Bytwerk, *German Propaganda Archive,* www.calvin.edu/academic/cas/gpa/cologne.htm.

247 *"No need to search"*: Isherwood, *Diaries,* p. 124.

248 *"By betraying every rule"*: "Italians Charge Cowardice," *NYT,* November 10, 1940.

248 *"It is so spread out"*: "Bomb-Proof City Shown as Model," *NYT,* November 11, 1940.

248 *"The bombing is not"*: Robert C. Twombly, *Frank Lloyd Wright,* pp. 296–97.

249 *farewell luncheon:* Lee, *London Journal,* pp. 129–30.

249 *Neville Chamberlain's funeral:* Cadogan, *Diaries,* p. 336.

249 *"In view of the indiscriminate"*: "British Still Split on Bombing Nazis," *NYT,* November 15, 1940; Hadley Cantril, ed., *Public Opinion,* p. 1067.

250 *"He believes that riots," "very considerable dimensions,"* and *"It is probably"*: F. H. Hinsley, *British Intelligence in the Second World War,* vol. 1, pp. 539–41.

251 *"War consists of mass murder"*: Staughton Lynd, ed., *Nonviolence in America,* pp. 296–99.

251 *"This is a national emergency"*: "8 Draft Objectors Get Prison Terms," *NYT,* November 15, 1940.

251 *"By three o'clock"*: Aileen Clayton, *The Enemy Is Listening,* p. 71.

252 *"Only to be opened"*: Gilbert, *Churchill War Papers,* vol. 2, p. 880.

252 *"False start"*: Ibid., p. 1095.

252 *Nobody called up Coventry:* Norman Longmate, *Air Raid,* pp. 263–64.

252 *"Major raid expected"*: Ibid., p. 74.

253 *They dropped ten thousand:* Allan W. Kurki, *Operation Moonlight Sonata,* p. 17.

253 *Whitley bomber:* King, *With Malice Toward None,* p. 85.

253 *"All the shops"*: Harry Oakley, "The Worst Night of Our Lives."

253 *"It looked as if"*: "Coventry Plants Razed, Nazis Say," *NYT,* November 16, 1940.

253 *"Coventry as a production center"*: King, *With Malice Toward None*, p. 86.

253 *"In revenge for the attack"*: Carl Henze, "Bombs on Coventry."

254 *"There was a little procession"*: Arthur, *Forgotten Voices of World War II*, p. 107.

254 *"I think they liked"*: Longmate, *Air Raid*, p. 206.

254 *heavy publicity*: Cull, *Selling War*, pp. 103–4.

254 *"just long enough"*: "Hamburg Pounded in Reply by R.A.F.," *NYT*, November 17, 1940.

255 *"Sometimes small explosions"*: "Time Bombs Rock Coventry Anew; Many Dead Are Found in Shelters," *NYT*, November 18, 1940.

255 *"Women were seen to cry"*: Angus Calder, *The People's War*, p. 204.

255 *IT IS GREATLY*: Longmate, *Air Raid*, p. 223.

255 *172 bodies*: "Coventrizing," *Time*, December 2, 1940.

255 *burned beyond recognition*: Cull, *Selling War*, photo and caption f.p. 134.

256 *"a long, narrow, deep gash"*: "Coventry Dead Laid in One Grave; Air Raid Siren is their Requiem," *NYT*, November 21, 1940.

256 *being photographed*: Colville, *Fringes of Power*, p. 298.

256 *"A very pretty young girl"*: Churchill, *Their Finest Hour*, p. 377.

257 *armbands*: "All Antwerp Citiizens Defy Nazis by Donning Armbands," *NYT*, November 23, 1940.

257 *"In Germany we can get"*: Von Hassell, *Diaries*, p. 159.

257 *With Churchill's approval* and *British prison*: Wasserstein, *Britain and the Jews of Europe*, p. 66–68.

257 *"The problem of supplying"*: U.S. Department of State, *Foreign Relaitons of the United States*, 1940, vol. 2, pp. 243–44.

258 *sat on the letter*: "Hull Tells Basis of Refugee Curb," *NYT*, January 10, 1941.

258 *"There are few"*: "Nomura Holds U.S., Japan Need Peace," *NYT*, November 27, 1940.

258 *"There are 136 airfields"*: Alan Armstrong, *Preemptive Strike*, pp. 38–39.

259 *"with the understanding"*: Blum, *From the Morgenthau Diaries*, vol. 2, p. 365.

259 *"The invasion of Norway"*: Milo Perkins, "Exports and Appeasement," *Harper's Magazine*, December 1940.

260 *"You instructed me"*: Gilbert, *Churchill War Papers*, vol. 2, p. 1186.

260 *"With object causing widespread"*: Ibid., vol. 3, p. 353n.

260 *"The moral scruples"*: Colville, *The Fringes of Power*, p. 311.

261 *Morgenthau swore Soong*: Michael Schaller, *The U.S. Crusade in China, 1938–1945*, p. 72.

261 *"To say he was enthusiastic"*: Blum, *From the Morgenthau Diaries*, vol. 2, p. 366.

261 *Could Soong furnish* and *"In connection with"*: Armstrong, *Preemptive Strike*, pp. 36, 39–40.

262 *"The security of the State"*: "Liberty for Mosley Debated in Commons," *NYT*, December 11, 1940; "500 Mosley Aides Ordered Held," *NYT*, July 26, 1940.

262 *"At the moment"*: "Friends to Ignore British Blockade," *NYT*, December 12, 1940.

262 *"We can't build a workable":* "Quakers Planning to Free Draft Foes," *NYT,* December 1, 1940.

263 *"concentrate the maximum amount":* Webster and Frankland, *Strategic Air Offensive,* vol. 1, pp. 225–26.

263 *"like a golden fountain":* "Mannheim District is Bombed 7 Hours," *NYT,* December 18, 1940.

263 *a castle and a hospital:* Ibid.

263 *"We have struck":* "Prime Minister Churchill's Speech in the House of Commons," *NYT,* December 20, 1940.

263 *"I count on the great majority":* Webster and Frankland, *Strategic Air Offensive,* vol. 1, p. 226.

264 *He had a bit of a tan:* Frank L. Kluckhohn, "Aid Plan Outlined," *NYT,* December 18, 1940.

264 *four women:* "Swiss Have Alarms Again," *NYT,* December 24, 1940.

264 *The town asked for permission:* "Swiss Charge British with Bombing Basle," *NYT,* December 18, 1940.

265 *"On other nights also":* "Mannheim Blasted Steadily by R.A.F.," *NYT,* December 24, 1940.

265 *"Is he still willing":* Armstrong, *Preemptive Strike,* p. 51, citing Morgenthau Diary 342-A, China: Bombers, December 3–22, 1940.

265 *The Chinese government charged:* "Plague Declared Sprayed," *NYT,* December 20, 1940.

266 *"They are all fascists":* Nicolson, *War Years,* p. 131.

266 *Henry Morgenthau's dining room:* Armstrong, *Preemptive Strike,* p. 59; Robert Smith Thompson, *A Time for War,* pp. 288–89.

267 *"inasmuch as the Japanese cities":* Schaller, *The U.S. Crusade in China,* p. 75.

267 *"The laws of the United States":* Foreign Relations of the United States, 1940, vol. 2, pp. 245–46.

268 *"Were we to yield":* Ibid.

269 *"Colin thinks":* Partridge, *Pacifist's War,* p. 70.

269 *"Naturally I feel distressed":* Gilbert, *Churchill War Papers,* vol. 2, pp. 1276–77.

270 *"Low-flying planes pumped":* "Berlin Assaulted in Heavy R.A.F. Raid," *NYT,* December 22, 1940.

270 *"The attack on the largest church":* "Berlin Paper Talks of Reprisals," *NYT,* December 23, 1940.

270 *"We have no doubt":* Gandhi, "Letter to Adolf Hitler," *Collected Works,* vol. 79, pp. 452–56.

271 *guildhall was destroyed:* "Guildhall Housed Many Treasures," *NYT,* December 31, 1940.

271 *"They are sowing the wind":* Henry Probert, *Bomber Harris,* p. 110.

271 *"Decided to advertise attack":* Cadogan, *Diaries,* p. 344.

272 *Censorship was suddenly lifted:* "Havoc in 'the City,' " *NYT,* December 31, 1940.

272 *"Buildings have been destroyed":* Ibid.

272 *"quite at liberty":* Webster and Frankland, *Strategic Air Offensive,* vol. 1, p. 221.

272 *"a large shop-building":* Louis MacNeice, *Selected Prose of Louis MacNeice,* p. 103.

272 *"Defense of the people's":* "Briton Hits Parley Supported by Reds," *NYT,* December 18, 1940.

273 *"I firmly believe":* "Text of Senator Wheeler's Speech," *NYT,* December 31, 1940.

273 *cable about milk:* Kimball, *Churchill and Roosevelt,* pp. 11–18.

273 *"If it did not sail":* Pickett, *For More than Bread,* pp. 177–78.

274 KINDNESS BUILDS REAL PEACE: "Peace Trek Ends in a Parade Here," *NYT,* January 2, 1941.

275 *"All along there were":* Nicolson, *War Years,* p. 136.

275 *"I feel sure":* Kimball, *Churchill and Roosevelt,* pp. 125–26.

276 *More than fifty thousand:* René Kraus, *The Men Around Churchill,* p. 165; see also "Many Interned in Britain Freed," *NYT,* January 4, 1941.

276 *"I am very much in favor":* Wasserstein, *Britain and the Jews of Europe,* p. 107; Gilbert, *Churchill War Papers,* vol. 3, p. 18.

276 *"ships, planes, tanks, guns":* "Annual Message to Congress," Roosevelt Library, www.fdrlibrary.marist.edu/4free.html.

277 *"In registering I":* " 'God's Will' Argued by Draft Objector," *NYT,* January 7, 1941.

277 *"Who?," "The politicians and the upper crust," "It has been emphasized," "He looks forward,"* and *"He expressed the hope":* Robert E. Sherwood, *Roosevelt and Hopkins,* pp. 239, 243, 259–60.

278 *"The British People Speak Up!":* *NYT,* January 13, 1941, p. 11.

279 *two thousand delegates met:* "British Leftists Demand Control," *NYT,* January 13, 1941.

279 *threatened to ban:* "Britain May Forbid Anti-War Meeting," *NYT,* December 20, 1940.

279 *The flyer oughtn't:* Gilbert, *Churchill War Papers,* vol. 3, pp. 71–72.

280 *"totalitarian doctrines":* "Blockade Helps Britain's Foes French Assert," *Chicago Tribune,* January 14, 1941.

280 *Catholic priests gathered:* "List Bombed Churches," *NYT,* January 14, 1941.

280 *"Huge overseas naval":* "Hawaiian Position Assailed," *NYT,* January 17, 1941.

280 *It was canceled:* National Committee on the Cause and Cure of War Records, www.swarthmore.edu/library/peace/CDGA.M-R/ncccw.html.

281 *"While fun is fun":* "Britain Prepared to Repress Reds," *NYT,* January 19, 1941.

281 *police from Scotland Yard:* "Daily Worker Office Raided by Scotland Yard Men," *NYT,* January 22, 1941.

281 *"weaken the will"*: "Morrison Defends Curb on Red Paper," *NYT,* January 23, 1941.

281 *"It is not in the interest"*: King, *With Malice Toward None,* pp. 93–94.

282 *"Then study and write"*: Klemperer, *Witness,* p. 370.

282 *with the immigration quota:* Ibid., p. 363.

282 *His English wasn't good:* Ibid., p. 370.

282 *Who would have him?* Ibid., p. 363.

282 *"There is a lot"*: Joseph C. Grew, *Ten Years in Japan,* p. 568.

282 *"Do get some sleep"*: Sherwood, *Roosevelt and Hopkins,* p. 253; Roosevelt, *F.D.R.: His Personal Letters,* p. 1114.

283 *"blue wonders"*: A Reply to Roosevelt, *NYT,* January 31, 1941.

283 *January 31, 1941:* "Japanese Ambassador Given Navy Escort," *Oakland Tribune,* January 30, 1941, available at www.ancestry.com.

283 *"I speak for the officers"*: Richardson, *On the Treadmill,* pp. 409–10.

284 *3:00 A.M. flight to Padua:* "R.A.F. Planes Gun Nazis in Trenches," *NYT,* January 14, 1941.

284 *"lake of fire"*: "Lake of Fire Seen At Wilhelmshaven," *NYT,* January 17, 1941.

284 *"and as many extra fifty caliber"* and *"The maximum number of B-17"*: Sherwood, *Roosevelt and Hopkins,* p. 258.

285 *"The giant bomber"*: "Bomber for Britain Flies Here Non-Stop," *NYT,* February 17, 1941.

285 *18,482:* Allan G. Blue, *The B-24 Liberator,* p. 192.

286 *"to consider the possibility"*: Leo P. Brophy and George J. B. Fisher, *The Chemical Warfare Service: Organizing for War,* pp. 132–33.

286 *manufacturing lewisite:* "James B. Conant is Dead at 84," *NYT,* February 12, 1978.

286 *bombs, fuels, gases:* Brophy and Fisher, *Chemical Warfare Service,* p. 38.

286 *"We must bravely"*: "Conant Backs Aid to Defeat Hitler," *NYT,* February 12, 1941.

287 *two Polish prisoners:* Debórah Dwork and Robert Jan van Pelt, *Auschwitz: 1270 to the Present,* p. 203.

287 *pea-size:* Breitman, *Architect of Genocide,* p. 203.

287 *"I do not have any right"*: "Draft Evaders Get 2 Years in Prison," *NYT,* February 12, 1941.

287 *international bankers:* Edward S. Shapiro, "World War II and American Jewish Identity," *Modern Judaism,* February 1990.

287 *"deplorable note of bigotry"*: "Battle Accuses Wheeler," *NYT,* March 8, 1941.

288 *party leader Baldur:* Kershaw, *Hitler,* p. 351.

288 *"Most of them"*: "Nazi Deportation of Jews Resumed," *NYT,* February 20, 1941.

288 *"His face is devoid"*: Reimann, *Goebbels,* p. 246.

288 *"the freshest and best"*: Robert Menzies, *Dark and Hurrying Days,* pp. 63–64.

289 *"The Jew's car"* and *"We arrived at"*: Klemperer, *Witness,* pp. 376–77.

289 *"Many of our students"*: Berg, *Warsaw Ghetto,* p. 53.

290 *"If we should decide"*: Gilbert, *Churchill War Papers,* vol. 3, p. 289.

290 *"Apart from the dreadful"*: Menzies, *Dark and Hurrying Days,* pp. 70–71.

291 *"Salient points"* and *"a view"*: Von Hassell, *Diaries,* pp. 171–72.

291 *"It is a bedlamite world"*: Menzies, *Dark and Hurrying Days,* p. 82.

292 *"We talked about"*: Gilbert, *Churchill War Papers,* vol. 3, pp. 320–24.

293 *"Chemical Board Crop Subcommittee"*: Biddle, *Rhetoric and Reality,* pp. 178, 355.

293 *Runcol-brand:* Tim Jones, *The X Site,* p. 8.

293 *"aerial distribution over Germany"*: Harris and Paxman, *Higher Form of Killing,* p. 100.

293 *"whole-hogger"*: Menzies, *Dark and Hurrying Days,* p. 84.

294 *"Gentle, magnetic Snakehips"*: Laurel Holliday, *Children in the Holocaust and World War II,* p. 306.

294 *looters moved:* Maev Kennedy, "Sex, Fear, and Looting," *Guardian Unlimited,* October 5, 2006, www.guardian.co.uk; Gavin Mortimer, *The Longest Night,* p. 44.

294 *"That, in the dark"*: John Howells, interviewed in Greg Wilkinson, *Talking about Psychiatry,* p. 212.

294 *"The bombs this spring"*: Murrow, *This Is London,* p. 235.

295 *"Mr. Churchill came"*: Charles De Gaulle, *Complete War Memoirs,* p. 165.

295 *Hitler said he wished:* Shlomo Aronson, *Hitler, the Allies, and the Jews,* p. 28.

295 *"Now we shall let rip"*: Goebbels, *Goebbels Diaries, 1939–1941,* p. 240.

295 *"Reprisals on Jews Hinted"*: "Nazis Deny Alarm Over New U.S. Aid," *NYT,* March 13, 1941.

295 *"I hope we knock"*: Max Hastings, *Bomber Command,* pp. 112–13.

296 *"Everything is going"*: Gilbert, *Churchill War Papers,* vol. 3, p. 353.

296 *"It is the problem"*: Hillesum, *Diaries,* p. 8.

296 *"An indescribable hatred"*: Von Hassell, *Diaries,* pp. 172–73.

297 *"Vienna will soon"* and *Speer's assistant agreed:* Browning, *Origins,* pp. 104–5.

297 *essential work:* Ibid., p. 105; Martin Broszat, "The Genesis of the 'Final Solution,' " in H. W. Koch, ed., *Aspects of the Third Reich,* p. 404.

297 *"Read GERMANY MUST PERISH!"*: "A Modest Proposal," *Time,* March 24, 1941.

298 *"Had he written"*: Randall L. Bytwerk, "The Argument for Genocide in Nazi Propaganda."

298 *"Have you heard"*: Thomas Mann, *Listen, Germany!,* p. 23.

298 *"Street after street"*: Menzies, *Dark and Hurrying Days,* pp. 93–94.

299 *A blending of the western:* Browning, *Origins,* p. 106.

299 *"One practical way"*: Viktor Brack, "Report on Experiments Concerning X-ray Castration," March 28, 1941, HLS (Harvard Law School) item no. 114, nuremberg.law.harvard.edu.

299 *"He has read the report":* Tiefenbacher, "Letter to Viktor Brack Concerning the X-ray Sterilization Experiments," May 12, 1941, HLS (Harvard Law School) item no. 115, nuremberg.law.harvard.edu.

300 *encouraged and funded:* David Stafford, *Britain and European Resistance, 1940–1945,* p. 53; David Stafford, "SOE and British Involvement in the Belgrade Coup d'Etat of March 1941."

300 *took over the radio station:* Liddell Hart, *History of the Second World War,* p. 159.

300 *"Few revolutions":* Winston Churchill, *The Grand Alliance,* p. 162.

300 *"Early this morning":* Ibid., p. 168.

300 *"boa constrictor":* Churchill, "The War Situation" (speech to the House of Commons), in *Unrelenting Struggle,* p. 81.

300 *"unmerciful harshness":* Churchill, *Grand Alliance,* p. 163.

301 *"All that puffy effect":* Nicolson, *War Years,* p. 155.

301 *"Some grim things":* Lyle Wilson, "Greater Air Attacks Due Nazis Know," (Valparaiso, Ind.) *Vidette Messenger,* April 2, 1941, available at www.ancestry .com.

301 *new punitive rule:* "Nazis Put New Curbs on Jewish Workers," *NYT,* April 3, 1941.

301 *six thousand apprentice engineers:* "British Arrest Strikers," *NYT,* April 5, 1941.

302 *Operation Strafgericht:* Gerhard Schreiber et al., *Germany and the Second World War,* vol. 3, p. 497.

302 *Romanian airfields:* Killen, *History of the Luftwaffe,* p. 165.

302 *"Stupefied inhabitants":* "Dead in Belgrade 3,000, U.S. Aide Says," *NYT,* April 14, 1941.

302 *"A stricken stork":* Churchill, *Grand Alliance,* pp. 174–75.

303 *"You cannot have war":* "Anti-War Speakers Ask Public Protests," *NYT,* April 7, 1941.

303 *"All the refugees":* "Havens of Refuge," *Time,* April 7, 1941.

304 *roofless ruin:* Read, *Devil's Disciples,* p. 682.

304 *He spent two weeks:* Kershaw, *Hitler,* pp. 365–66.

304 *"The sorties which":* Churchill, *Unrelenting Struggle,* p. 83.

304 *"We must lament":* "Text of Pope Pius XII's Easter Sunday Broadcast," *NYT,* April 14, 1941.

304 *"I dread the thought":* Klemperer, *Witness,* p. 381.

305 *forty-ninth bombing of Lorient:* "R.A.F. Fires Bases of Nazis' Sea War," *NYT,* April 14, 1941.

305 *"It is impossible":* "Vichy Aide Assails R.A.F.," *NYT,* April 27, 1941.

306 *"I remain far from satisfied":* Gilbert, *Churchill War Papers,* vol. 3, pp. 498–99.

306 *"any excuse":* "Guns Are Removed From 2 Food Ships," *NYT,* April 17, 1941.

306 *in a letter:* "Hoover Food Plea is Made to London," *NYT,* April 17, 1941; *The Times* (London), April 16, 1941.

307 *"The people strike me"*: Lee, *London Journal*, p. 243.

307 *"exposed to the actual"* and *"Explodes above ground"*: Henry H. Arnold, *American Airpower Comes of Age*, vol. 1, pp. 134, 145.

308 *"Clean up the city"* and *"Portal is a brilliant man"*: Ibid., pp. 149, 152.

309 *"If Europe is civilized"*: Jasper, *George Bell*, p. 262; *The Times* (London), April 17, 1941; see also Andrew Chandler, "The Church of England and the Obliteration Bombing of Germany in the Second World War," and Grayling, *Among the Dead Cities*, p. 180.

309 *"In the future"*: "Nazis Explain Raid as One of Revenge," *NYT*, April 18, 1941.

309 *sixty-one million dollars' worth:* "American Machine Guns on the Factory Line," *NYT*, April 18, 1941.

310 *"we should begin"*: Gilbert, *Churchill War Papers*, vol. 3, p. 511.

310 *"It is, therefore, necessary"*: "Rome to be Raided if Cairo or Athens is Hit, British Warn, But Promise to Spare Vatican," *NYT*, April 19, 1941.

310 *"gone west"*: Lee, *London Journal*, p. 250.

311 *Fight for Freedom:* "New A.E.F. Urged to Defeat Hitler," *NYT*, April 22, 1941.

311 *an advertising executive:* "Advertising News and Notes," *NYT*, January 15, 1941.

311 *The group received funding:* Cull, *Selling War*, p. 133.

311 *"whether declared or undeclared"*: "U.S. is Now at War, New Group Holds," *NYT*, April 20, 1941.

311 *"The war is going badly"* and *"Churchill is running the war"*: Stephen Roskill, *Hankey: Man of Secrets*, vol. 3, pp. 496–97.

312 *Howard Schoenfeld, in prison:* Howard Schoenfeld, "The Danbury Story," in Holley Cantine and Dachine Rainer, eds., *Prison Etiquette*, pp. 12ff.

313 *new, more pragmatic paper:* Webster and Frankland, *Strategic Air Offensive*, vol. 1, p. 244 and n.

313 *"congested industrial towns"*: Ibid., vol. 4, pp. 137–41.

313 *"Here I am stumping"*: Lindbergh, *Wartime Journals*, p. 478.

314 *looting:* Murrow, *This Is London*, p. 213; "Looting Epidemic Stirs London to Action; Press Suggests Hanging," *NYT*, November 4, 1940; "Crime Boom," *Time*, November 11, 1940; MacKay, *Half the Battle*, p. 84.

314 *rat population:* "Rat Plague Begun in Britain by Raids," *NYT*, January 24, 1941.

314 *"blasted into rubble-heaps"*: Churchill, "Westward, Look, the Land is Bright," in *Unrelenting Struggle*, p. 81.

315 *"It may be taken"*: Gilbert, *Churchill War Papers*, vol. 3, p. 556.

316 *"I consider the prolongation," "You do not need,"* and *"defend Habbaniya to the last"*: Churchill, *Grand Alliance*, pp. 257, 259, 261.

316 *almost two hundred flights:* Kelly Bell, "World War II: Air War Over Iraq."

316 *Iraqi airplanes:* San Diego Aerospace Museum, "History Makers," *Flight Lines*, fall 2005, www.aerospacemuseum.org.

317 *"Iraq situation pretty bad"*: Cadogan, *Diaries*, pp. 375–76.

317 *"When war broke"*: "Textual Excerpts from Reichsfuehrer Hitler's Address," *NYT,* May 5, 1941.

317 *"I like the oratory"*: Ciano, *Diaries,* p. 347.

318 *Henry Ford was breaking ground:* "Ford Asks to Make Complete Bomber," *NYT,* February 5, 1941; "Ford Will Turn Out 205 Bombers a Month," *NYT,* June 26, 1941.

318 *German economic miracle:* Charles Higham, *Trading with the Enemy,* p. 163.

318 *"Let's get going"*: "Roosevelt Urgent," *NYT,* May 6, 1941.

318 *"A reinforcing column"*: Churchill, *Grand Alliance,* p. 259.

319 *Curtiss Tomahawk fighters:* "British in U.S. Planes Driving Iraqis Back," *NYT,* May 26, 1941.

319 *flown out, sedated:* Bell, "Air War Over Iraq."

319 *"It was a mass catharsis"*: Schoenfeld, "Danbury Story," p. 26.

320 *A rumor:* Newton, *Profits of Peace,* p. 188.

320 *"eminently credible"*: "The World and Hess," *Time,* May 26, 1941.

320 *double coup:* Newton, *Profits of Peace,* pp. 179–89.

320 *now being bombed:* "German Aircraft Attacking Crete Fought by British Planes and Guns," *NYT,* May 6, 1941.

320 *"I am the one whose head"*: Gilbert, *Churchill War Papers,* vol. 3, p. 623.

320 *Three MPs voted no:* D. N. Pritt, socialist lawyer; Alfred Salter, doctor; William Gallacher, communist. "Churchill Upheld," *NYT,* May 8, 1941.

321 *An armada of three hundred:* "300 Planes Smash at German Ports," *NYT,* May 10, 1941; "American-Built Planes Used," *NYT,* May 10, 1941.

321 *"big show"*: "Biggest R.A.F. Raid," *NYT,* May 10, 1941.

321 *"fires were seen raging"*: "The Texts of Day's Communiques on Fighting in Europe and the Middle East," *NYT,* May 10, 1941.

321 *basement of the Anatomical Institute:* Aly et al., *Cleansing the Fatherland,* pp. 125–27.

321 *a stick of explosives:* "Biggest R.A.F. Raid," *NYT,* May 10, 1941.

321 *sixty-eighth time:* "American-Built Planes Used," *NYT,* May 10, 1941.

321 *Ninety-four people:* "Casualties in Hamburg," *NYT,* May 11, 1941.

322 *"We are staging"* and *diamonds glittering on velvet:* Richard Collier, *The City that Would Not Die,* pp. 66–67.

322 *Coins and Medals Room* and *Queen's Hall:* Mortimer, *The Longest Night,* pp. 280–81.

322 *More Christopher Wren churches:* Collier, *City That Would Not Die,* p. 238.

322 *Streetlamps drooped:* Mortimer, *Longest Night,* p. 213.

322 *stood crying:* Ibid., pp. 186–87.

323 *"Our eyes were blinded"*: "100,000 Fire Bombs Dropped," *NYT,* May 12, 1941.

323 *"All that day"*: Mortimer, *Longest Night,* p. 282.

323 *"I hate Germans"*: Ibid.

323 *"I have no bombs"*: "Fugitive Nazi Tells Guards How He Bailed Out When Unable to Land," *NYT,* May 14, 1941.

323 *"puckered with incredulous"*: Collier, *City That Would Not Die,* p. 107.

323 *"No, he'll be put"*: Ibid., p. 108.

324 *"Oh, my God"*: John Toland, *Adolf Hitler,* vol. 2, p. 760.

324 *"R. is a little jealous"*: Menzies, *Dark and Hurrying Days,* pp. 126–29.

324 *"a Gorki in literature"*: Kenneth Saunders, "Toyohiko Kagawa, the St Francis of Japan," pp. 308–17.

325 *"very pale"*: Isherwood, *Diaries,* p. 160.

325 *The purpose of their trip:* "Japan's Christians Discount U.S. War," *NYT,* May 15, 1941; "Peace Talk with Japan," *Time,* April 21, 1941.

325 *several thousand Jews:* "Internees Routed from Beds," *NYT,* May 16, 1941; "5,000 Paris Jews off to Labor Camps," *NYT,* May 16, 1941; Browning, *Origins,* p. 201.

325 *locked trains:* "New Vichy Moves Strike Alien Jews," *NYT,* May 17, 1941.

325 *again bombed Lorient:* "Nazi Raid Strikes West Midlands," *NYT,* May 17, 1941.

325 *Mr. and Mrs. Otto Suesser:* "Berlin Exiles Here After Many Voyages," *NYT,* May 18, 1941.

327 *"History has proved"*: Webster and Frankland, *Strategic Air Offensive,* vol. 4, pp. 194–97.

327 *concurred:* Ibid., p. 200.

328 *"This struggle requires"*: Noakes and Pridham, *Nazism,* p. 1090.

328 *"I explained"*: Czerniakow, *Warsaw Diary,* pp. 237–83.

328 *"The situation in the Jewish quarter"*: Browning, *Origins,* p. 158.

328 *"He pointed out"* and *Auerswald said he wanted:* Czerniakow, *Warsaw Diary,* pp. 237–40.

329 *rejected Sorensen's suggestion:* "Ban on Night Bombings is Rejected by Britain," *NYT,* May 22, 1941; "Night Bombing," *The Times* (London), May 22, 1941.

329 *"The news about the destruction"*: Gandhi, *Collected Works,* vol. 80, p. 273.

329 *about fourteen thousand:* Judith M. Brown, *Gandhi,* p. 331.

330 *"As soon as he learns"*: Delmer, *Black Boomerang.*

330 *"In view of the anti-Jewish"*: "Cancels Anti-War Talk," *NYT,* May 24, 1941.

331 *"When I receive my ration"*: Dawid Sierakowiak, *The Diary of Dawid Sierakowiak,* p. 94.

331 *"Chinese aviators have been"*: "Chinese Air Force to Take Offensive," *NYT,* May 24, 1941.

332 *"Every day that I stayed"*: "Japanese Believed Still Against War," *NYT,* May 26, 1941.

332 *The bishop began summarizing:* Jasper, *George Bell,* pp. 262–63; Chandler, "The Church of England and the Obliteration Bombing of Germany."

332 *"I do not think you can complain"*: Jasper, *George Bell,* p. 263.

333 *"Listening to this disgusting blabber"*: Sierakowiak, *Diary of Dawid Sierakowiak,* p. 96.

333 *The potato crop:* "Bread Ration Cut Restored by Vichy," *NYT,* May 29, 1941.

333 *"A total economic boycott"*: "Avoidance of War Urged as U.S. Aim," *NYT,* June 1, 1941.

334 *"Cheese!"*: "First U.S. Food Under Aid Law Reaches Britain," New York *Herald Tribune,* June 1, 1941.

334 *Wisconsin cheddar:* "Our 1st Food Ship Unloads in Britain," *NYT,* June 1, 1941.

334 *Nearly twice:* "Civilian Deaths Twice British Military Losses," New York *Herald Tribune,* June 1, 1941.

334 *"Reports from within"*: "British Photos Show Havoc of Hamburg Raids," New York *Herald Tribune,* June 2, 1941.

334 *Rhys Davies:* "British Laborites Back War Policy," *NYT,* June 4, 1941.

335 *"Hitler started out"*: New York *Herald Tribune,* June 5, 1951.

335 *Eleven thousand workers:* "Huge Plane Plant Halted by Strike," *NYT,* June 6, 1941.

335 *two hundred million dollars:* "Coast U.A.W. Votes on Aircraft Strike," *NYT,* May 24, 1941.

335 *"Our sole desire"*: "He Sets a Deadline," *NYT,* June 8, 1941.

336 *"the next logical field"*: "Hitler Ridicules U.S. Fears, Holds Nazi Attack Wild Idea," *NYT,* June 6, 1941.

337 *"It is a distinct disadvantage"*: "Quakers Issue Bid to 'Dynamic Peace,' " *NYT,* June 8, 1941.

337 *"Is there no one"*: "Quakers Offer Roosevelt Plan to End the War," New York *Herald Tribune,* June 8, 1941.

337 *Jones sent copies:* "Quakers Issue Bid to 'Dynamic Peace,' " *NYT,* June 8, 1941.

338 *Dashiell Hammett:* "Hammett Elected by Writers League," *NYT,* June 9, 1941.

338 *Richard Wright's* Native Son: "Native Son Wins Award for Novel," *NYT,* June 8, 1941.

338 *Theodore Dreiser:* "Theodore Dreiser Gets Peace Award," *NYT,* June 7, 1941.

338 *"Today, we must ask"*: "Leftist Writers Denounce War as 'Imperialist,' " New York *Herald Tribune,* June 7, 1941.

338 *"Our country is in danger"*: "Roosevelt Explains Seizure," *NYT,* June 10, 1941.

338 *"Here comes the army"*: "Troops' Arrival Brings Quick Shift," *NYT,* June 10, 1941.

339 *"has had a profound"*: Nelson Lichtenstein, *Labor's War at Home,* p. 63, quoted in Lawrence W. Levine and Cornelia R. Levine, *The People and the President,* p. 477.

339 *"I always grieve"*: "Roosevelt Explains Seizure," *NYT,* June 10, 1941.

339 *"On the floor"*: Berg, *Warsaw Ghetto,* p. 69.

340 *"Germany is busy"*: Gabriel Gorodetsky, *Grand Delusion: Stalin and the German Invasion of Russia,* p. 279.

340 *"This oven was built"*: Aly et al., *Cleansing the Fatherland,* p. 130.

341 WHAT ARE WE WAITING FOR: Fight for Freedom advertisement, *NYT,* June 15, 1941, p. 29.

341 *"If everybody did"*: "Draft Evader Jailed," *NYT*, June 17, 1941.

342 *"If Hitler realizes"*: Mihail Sebastian, *Journal, 1935–1944*, pp. 366–67.

342 *"far reaching effects"*: "U.S. Bars Refugees with Kin in Reich," *NYT*, June 18, 1941.

342 *"Is our government so destitute"*: Justus D. Doenecke, "Non-Interventionism of the Left," p. 299.

343 *"Our people are being turned"*: Jervis Anderson, *A. Philip Randolph*, pp. 256–59.

344 H. G. Wells *wrote a letter*: Churchill Archive, www.chu.cam.ac.uk, catalog entry CHAR 20/30/59–62.

344 *"taken care of things"*: Adam Grolsch, interview in Eric A. Johnson and Karl-Heinz Reuband, *What We Knew*, p. 237.

345 *"Tell the BBC"*: Churchill, *The Grand Alliance*, p. 331.

345 *"So now this bloodthirsty"*: Churchill, *Unrelenting Struggle*, p. 171.

346 *"We buried 48 people"*: Jan Cherniak et al., *Pobediteli: Soldiers of the Great War*.

346 *"This unheard of attack"*: "Text of Molotoff Address," *NYT*, June 23, 1941.

346 *"Well, you sounded"*: Edvard Radzinsky, *Stalin*, pp. 462–63.

347 NOW IS THE TIME!: Fight for Freedom advertisement, *NYT*, June 23, 1941, p. 10.

347 *"What is the position"*: Gilbert, *Churchill War Papers*, vol. 3, p. 842 and n.

348 *"If we see that Germany"*: "Our Policy Stated," *NYT*, June 24, 1941.

348 *"military defeat of the fascist"*: "Reds Here Shift in Stand on War," *NYT*, July 27, 1941.

349 There were no air-raid shelters: Cherniak et al., *Pobediteli*.

349 a Jew loomed: Sebastian, *Journal*, p. 370.

349 *"Every German woman and child"*: Partridge, *Pacifist's War*, p. 99.

349 sealed trains: International Commission on the Holocaust in Romania, *Final Report*, chap. 5, pp. 24–26.

350 *"The city is like an oven"* and *"The food supply situation"*: Goebbels, *Goebbels Diaries, 1939–1941*, pp. 433–34.

350 *"Everyone in uniform"*: Gilbert, *Churchill War Papers*, vol. 3, p. 871.

350 stocks of poison gas: Ibid., p. 927.

351 small Trotskyist group: "29 Reds Indicted in Overthrow Plot," *NYT*, July 16, 1941.

351 *"What did these people do?"*: I. F. Stone, *The War Years*, pp. 72–74.

352 oyster method: Ley, *Bombs and Bombing*, p. 37.

353 *"The Greek people face"*: "Famine Spread Menaces Greece," *NYT*, July 2, 1941.

353 *"Special care must be taken"*: Noakes and Pridham, *Nazism*, vol. 3, p. 1092.

354 *"Heavy English air raids"*: Goebbels, *Goebbels Diaries, 1939–1941*, p. 445.

354 bombenfrischler: Ibid., p. 444.

354 Baltimore Fried Chicken: "All Britain Honors Independence Day," *NYT*, July 5, 1941.

355 *"To read the papers"*: Sebastian, *Journal*, p. 375.

355 *"three-star blasting"*: David Anderson, "Britain is Prepared to Press Her Air Offensive," *NYT*, September 7, 1941; "RAF Blasts Reich Cities in Vast 24-Hour Offensive," *NYT*, July 9, 1941.

355 *"You will direct"*: Denis Richards, *The Royal Air Force*, chap. 13.

355 *"One of our great aims"*: Gilbert, *Churchill War Papers*, vol. 3, pp. 908–9.

356 *Nissen huts:* James A. Donovan, *Outpost in the North Atlantic*.

356 *"running after the war"*: "Nazis Assail U.S. on Step in Iceland," *NYT*, July 10, 1941.

356 *Surely, thought Victor Klemperer:* Klemperer, *Witness*, p. 417.

356 *"Although the procedure"* and *"Thus I became"*: Wedemeyer, *Wedemeyer Reports!*, pp. 14–17.

357 *"I saw Warsaw drowning"* and *"For that reason"*: Berg, *Warsaw Ghetto*, pp. 80–81.

357 *"Hitler is now"*: "Hitler is Plotting Peace Drive Here with Pacifist Help, Mayor Warns," *NYT*, July 15, 1941.

357 *seconded LaGuardia's warning:* "Supports Warning of Mayor on Peace," *NYT*, July 16, 1941.

358 *Reviewed six thousand:* "Defense Workers' Day," *NYT*, July 15, 1941.

358 *"All these people"*: "Text of Churchill's Address to Londoners," *NYT*, July 15, 1941.

359 *"About 7 we got Japanese intercepts"*: Cadogan, *Diaries*, p. 392.

359 *"This is no sadistic"*: "Civilian Morale," *NYT*, July 15, 1941.

360 *"splinters find very few"*: Gilbert, *Churchill War Papers*, vol. 3, pp. 948–49.

360 *"I am pleased to note"*: Ibid., p. 990.

361 *Charles Darwin, "We should like to emphasize,"* and *"Are our own Prime Minister"*: Gowing, *Britain and Atomic Energy*, pp. 94, 86, 394–98.

362 *"There is an imminent danger"*: Lucy S. Dawidowicz, *The War Against the Jews*, p. 162.

362 *"a source of bacilli"*: Broszat, "Genesis of the 'Final Solution,'" p. 400.

362 *This thousandth airplane:* "Halifax Praises American Planes," *NYT*, July 18, 1941.

363 *"Duesseldorf is little more"*: "German Cities Reported Hard Hit," *NYT*, July 18, 1941.

364 *"He may then start"*: Nicolson, *War Years*, p. 178.

364 *"I think on the widest"*: Gilbert, *Churchill War Papers*, vol. 3, p. 968.

365 *thirty thousand feet:* Alexander P. De Seversky, *Victory Through Air Power*, p. 246.

365 *Their guns froze:* Wesley Frank Craven and James Lea Cate, *The Army Air Forces in World War II*, vol. 1, p. 601.

365 *no success:* Terraine, *Time for Courage*, pp. 279–80.

365 *Flying Targets:* Geoffrey Perret, *Winged Victory*, p. 98.

365 *Flying Coffins:* Craven and Cate, *Army Air Forces in World War II,* vol. 1, p. 601.

365 *"incendiary bombing of Japan":* Schaller, *The U.S. Crusade in China,* p. 79.

365 *okayed it:* Armstrong, *Preemptive Strike,* pp. 103, 118.

365 *"I am very happy to be able":* Armstrong, "Secret Documents," www.preemp tivestrikethebook.com; Armstrong, *Preemptive Strike,* p. 138; Duane Schultz, *The Maverick War,* p. 14.

365 *relayed detailed reports:* Armstrong, *Preemptive Strike,* pp. 124–26, 133–35.

366 *"There are a lot of things":* "U.S. Policy Stated," *NYT,* July 25, 1941; "President on Defense and Far East," *NYT,* July 25, 1941.

366 *"Big four-motored":* "Boeings Strike from Great Height," *NYT,* July 25, 1941.

366 *"The raids were built":* "Bombing from 40,000 Feet Up," *NYT,* July 26, 1941.

367 *"From altitudes of seven miles":* Martin Caidin, *Flying Forts,* p. 116.

367 *reported for active duty:* "Professor at Columbia is Called by the Army," *NYT,* July 8, 1941; "Col. Zanetti Goes on Army Duty," *NYT,* July 25, 1941.

367 *fire warfare:* "Professor at Columbia is Called by the Army," *NYT,* July 8, 1941.

367 *partly burned Italian firebomb:* Leo P. Brophy, Wyndham D. Miles, and Rex-mond C. Cochrane, *The Chemical Warfare Service: From Laboratory to Field,* p. 168.

367 *"Gas dissipates while fire propagates":* Brooks E. Kleber and Dale Birdsell, *The Chemical Warfare Service: Chemicals in Combat,* p. 616.

367 *Slums were particularly vulnerable:* " 'Ineptitude' Is Seen in Fire Bomb At-tacks," *NYT,* February 3, 1941.

367 *Zanetti was put in charge:* Brophy, Miles, and Cochrane, *From Laboratory to Field,* p. 342.

367 *brought back blueprints:* Kleber and Birdsell, *Chemicals in Combat,* p. 617.

367 *magnesium-thermate bomb:* Brophy, Miles, and Cochrane, *From Laboratory to Field,* pp. 172–73.

367 *roof-piercing properties:* Kleber and Birdsell, *Chemicals in Combat,* p. 622.

368 *"In view of the unlimited":* "Freezing Statement's Text," *NYT,* July 26, 1941.

368 *"must always deal":* Walter Laqueur, *The Terrible Secret,* p. 91.

368 *"This spell of dry weather":* Gilbert, *Churchill War Papers,* vol. 3, p. 982.

369 *"The war with the Russians":* Sebastian, *Journal,* p. 385.

369 *American journalist:* "Quentin Reynolds Is Dead at 62," *NYT,* March 18, 1965.

369 *"I did not come":* Sherwood, *Roosevelt and Hopkins,* p. 320.

369 *"A little while ago":* Gilbert, *Churchill War Papers,* vol. 3, p. 991.

370 *"During the last two":* Lord Alanbrooke, *War Diaries,* p. 174.

370 *"Japan Smolders over Oil Threat":* *NYT,* July 30, 1941.

370 *"I would like to see":* Harold L. Ickes, *The Secret Diary of Harold L. Ickes,* vol. 3, p. 593.

370 *"How many children":* Vera Brittain, *Testament of a Peace Lover,* p. 86.

371 *"Complementing the task"* and *"The Final Solution"*: Breitman, *Architect of Genocide*, pp. 192–94.

372 *Ninety Jewish children:* Raul Hilberg, *Perpetrators, Victims, Bystanders*, pp. 58–60.

372 *"heaved like a volcano"*: "Nazi Capital Bombed Hard," *NYT*, August 4, 1941.

372 *"The vast British air"*: "Biggest Air Attack Staged by R.A.F.," *NYT*, August 13, 1941.

372 *"R.A.F.'s latest pride"*: "Nazi Capital Bombed Hard," *NYT*, August 4, 1941.

373 *"For some months"*: Clemens von Galen, sermon, in Noakes and Pridham, *Nazism*, pp. 1036–38.

373 *"Children call each other names"*: Stackelberg and Winkle, *Nazi Germany Sourcebook*, pp. 332–33.

373 *moved east to Lublin:* Brack, "Affidavit," p. 6.

373 *Alexander Cadogan was on the train:* Cadogan, *Diaries*, p. 395.

374 *"When I went out"* and *"Whenever I see a Jew"*: Sebastian, *Journal*, pp. 389–91.

374 *"The way to lick Hitler"*: Crane, *Bombs, Cities, and Civilians*, p. 32.

375 *"First there was the creation"*: "Japanese Insist U.S. and Britain Err on Thailand," *NYT*, August 8, 1941.

375 *knew nothing about encirclement:* "Hull Declares Japan Encircles Herself by Acts," *NYT*, August 9, 1941.

375 *"Food is a weapon"*: "President Urges More Food Crops," *NYT*, August 13, 1941.

376 *"vastly entertaining"*: Churchill, *Grand Alliance*, p. 429.

376 *deeply moving:* Gilbert, *Churchill War Papers*, vol. 3, p. 1043.

376 *each box:* Walter Henry Thompson, *Assignment: Churchill*, p. 233.

376 *plan to grow Christmas trees:* Cadogan, *Diaries*, p. 398.

376 *trading compliments:* Thompson, *Assignment: Churchill*, pp. 238–39.

377 *hard language:* Churchill, *Grand Alliance*, p. 446.

377 *parallel British and American declaration:* Maurice Matloff and Edwin M. Snell, *Strategic Planning for Coalition Warfare, 1941–1942*, pp. 68–69.

377 *Max Beaverbrook:* "London Expects More from Talks," *NYT*, August 15, 1941.

377 *"British want 6,000"*: Arnold, *American Airpower*, p. 224.

377 *"They are sending us"*: Churchill, *Grand Alliance*, pp. 446–47.

377 *"There could be little"*: Sherwood, *Roosevelt and Hopkins*, p. 362.

378 *two lightning bolts:* "Big Fires are Seen in Berlin as R.A.F. Pilots Hover Over City for Two Hours," *NYT*, August 14, 1941.

378 *"The first wave"*: "300 Big Bombers Raid Nazi Cities," *NYT*, August 16, 1941.

378 *A tanker filled:* "U.S. Tanker Sails With Soviet Fuel," *NYT*, August 15, 1941.

379 *biggest propaganda campaign:* "Our Role in Pacific," *NYT*, August 16, 1941.

379 *Himmler noticed:* Breitman, *Architect of Genocide*, p. 195.

379 *"Himmler had never seen"*: Gilbert, *Holocaust*, p. 191.

379 *"Look at the eyes"*: Browning, *Origins*, p. 353.

380 *"Seldom has history"*: "Nazis See Bluff in Bid to Stalin," *NYT,* August 17, 1941.

380 *"THE B & B COCKTAIL"*: *NYT,* August 17, 1941.

380 *Churchill drank a Benedictine:* Cadogan, *Diaries,* p. 402.

381 *"The President had said"*: "War-Entry Plans Laid to Roosevelt," *NYT,* January 2, 1972.

381 *Lord Cherwell's personal secretary:* Maurice W. Kirby, *Operational Research in War and Peace: The British Experience from the 1930s to 1970,* p. 135.

382 *"We have 1,000"*: "Prisons Roll Out Defense Products," *NYT,* August 19, 1941.

382 *"I am afraid"*: Lester, *It So Happened,* p. 163; "Trinidad Holds Muriel Lester," *NYT,* August 29, 1941.

382 *Lester's passport:* Lester, *It So Happened,* p. 211.

383 *"Immediately after the conclusion"*: Broszat, "Genesis of the 'Final Solution,'" p. 401.

383 *The victims fell:* Paul Ginsburg, "Engelbert Kreuzer: Butcher of Sudilkov," Max Grossman, "The Holocaust," www.grossmanproject.net/the_holocaust.htm.

383 *"In case of a new"*: "Nazis Will Hold French Hostages; Officer is Slain," *NYT,* August 23, 1941.

384 *"We earnestly hope"*: "Text of Prime Minister Churchill's Address," *NYT,* August 25, 1941.

384 *"What Churchill said"*: "Accusation of Falsehood," *NYT,* August 26, 1941.

384 *"I find that it takes"*: Lee, *London Journal,* p. 377.

385 *It was supposed:* Brophy and Fisher, *From Laboratory to Field,* p. 342.

385 *magnesium plant:* Ibid., p. 173; "Company to Build Magnesium Plants," *NYT,* August 14, 1941; "The Nation: Critical Material," *NYT,* April 12, 1942.

385 *Half of Great Britain's:* Thompson, *Generalissimo Churchill,* p. 76.

385 *"Mr. Churchill was"*: John Noble Kennedy, *The Business of War,* p. 96.

385 *"Although personally"*: Churchill, *Grand Alliance,* p. 814.

386 *small-town program:* Webster and Frankland, *Strategic Air Offensive,* vol. 4, pp. 140–41.

386 *"level" German cities:* "See British Gain in Control of Air," *NYT,* August 31, 1941.

386 *"There wasn't any fire"*: "All Day Attacks Staged by R.A.F.," *NYT,* September 1, 1941.

386 *heavy reprisal:* "Nazis Bomb English Port Hard," *NYT,* September 1, 1941.

387 *"The Germans cannot take it"*: "Morale Among Germans Held to be Weakening," *NYT,* September 7, 1941.

387 *"flaunting this oil"*: "Tokyo Press Scores U.S.," *NYT,* August 23, 1941.

387 *"slow death"*: "Tokyo Army Aide Bids Japan Fight If Parleys Fail," *NYT,* September 2, 1941.

388 *"Führer of Immediate Measures"*: Robert Gellately, *Backing Hitler,* p. 211.

388 *"For bombing to be effective"* and *"We need two or three thousand"*: David Garnett, *War in the Air,* pp. 225–26, 269.

389 *"A pacifist between wars"*: Miller, *Fosdick,* p. 491.

389 *An American boat:* "Press Ignores Tanker Arrival," *NYT,* September 6, 1941.

389 *Hans Hirschfeld and Inge Korach:* Alison Owings, *Frauen,* p. xxi.

390 *"Crestfallen people"*: Sebastian, *Journal,* p. 405.

390 *"The star consists"*: "Nazis Order Jews Over Six Labeled," *NYT,* September 7, 1941.

390 *"People looked pained"*: Owings, *Frauen,* pp. 457–58.

391 *"Today's was the first"*: "100 Leading Jews Seized in Paris," *NYT,* September 9, 1941.

391 *"of all ages and both sexes"*: Associated Press, "Jews of Hanover ordered to Evacuate Homes in 24 Hours," in the Lethbridge *Herald,* September 8, 1941; "Jews of Hanover Forced from Homes," *NYT,* September 9, 1941.

391 *"The enemy air force"*: New York *Herald Tribune,* September 9, 1941.

391 *"The bombing offensive"*: Aronson, *Hitler, the Allies, and the Jews,* p. 297; see also pp. 40, 291.

392 *"Berliners crept out"*: New York *Herald Tribune,* September 9, 1941.

392 *"In the list of criminal attacks"*: "Berlin Accounts Rail at British," *NYT,* September 9, 1941.

392 *"I saw it"*: Sebastian, *Journal,* pp. 407–8.

393 *"I panicked"*: Owings, *Frauen,* p. 458.

393 *"To overcome the enemy"*: "Nazis May Use Gas, Gen. Porter Warns," *NYT,* September 11, 1941.

394 *Roosevelt drove around Hyde Park:* "President Shuts Self from World," *NYT,* September 9, 1941.

394 *The U-boat fired torpedoes:* Kimball, *Churchill and Roosevelt,* p. 236.

394 *"Roosevelt," said a German communiqué:* "Accuse President," *NYT,* September 7, 1941.

395 *"They planned"*: "Lindbergh Sees a Plot for War," *NYT,* September 12, 1941.

396 *"You have seen"*: "Assail Lindbergh for Iowa Speech," *NYT,* September 13, 1941.

396 *"Each one of us"*: "Two Jewish Groups Reply to Lindbergh," *NYT,* September 20, 1941.

396 *"Many groups and elements"*: "Thomas Assails Speech," *NYT,* September 13, 1941.

397 *"A large proportion"*: "Death Rate Soars in Polish Ghettos," *NYT,* September 14, 1941.

397 *"It is clear"*: "Britain's 'Silent War' Tightening Pinch," *NYT,* September 21, 1941.

398 *Alfred Rosenberg thought:* Browning, *Origins,* p. 324.

398 *"nest of poison"*: Peter Witte, "Two Decisions," *Holocaust and Genocide Studies,* vol. 9 (1995).

398 *"The Führer is considering"*: Peter Witte, "Two Decisions"; Christopher Browning, *Nazi Policy, Jewish Workers, German Killers*, p. 38; Roseman, *Wannsee Conference and the Final Solution*, p. 60.

399 *"Nebe and I came to the conclusion"*: Eugen Kogon et al., *Nazi Mass Murder: A Documentary History of the Use of Poison Gas*, p. 53.

399 *Zyklon B pesticide:* Browning, *Origins*, pp. 357, 526–27.

399 *"When the gas was thrown"*: Noakes and Pridham, *Nazism*, p. 1178.

399 *"I must even admit"*: Yitzhak Arad, *Belzec, Sobibor, Treblinka*, p. 10.

400 *"The Problem of Defeating Japan"*: Thompson, *Time for War*, pp. 365–66; Armstrong, *Preemptive Strike*, pp. 153–55.

400 *"Stupid, pretentious"*: Sebastian, *Journal*, p. 414.

401 *"The Whitley bomber factory"*: Colville, *Fringes of Power*, p. 441.

401 *"I didn't wait"*: Ilya Ehrenburg and Vasily Grossman, *The Complete Black Book of Russian Jewry*, p. 9.

402 *"The four-engine heavy bomber"*: "A Tool for Mr. Churchill," *Fortune*, October 1941.

403 *Fifteen German policemen:* Breitman, *Architect of Genocide*, pp. 200–201.

403 *"a little unfair"*: "Text of Prime Minister Churchill's Review of War in House of Commons," *NYT*, October 1, 1941.

404 *"Because of the dangers"*: Williams and Wallace, *Unit 731*, p. 93.

404 *Edwin B. Fred:* Regis, *Biology of Doom*, p. 20; Guillemin, *Biological Weapons*, p. 59.

404 *"cases of unsuitable compassion"*: Bankier, *Germans and the Final Solution*, p. 128.

405 *"It's Fun to Be Free"*: "Freedom Rally Thrills 17,000," *NYT*, October 6, 1941.

405 *talked over the uranium bomb:* John C. Culver and John Hyde, *American Dreamer: The Life and Times of Henry A. Wallace*, p. 167.

405 *"It appears desirable"*: Kimball, *Churchill and Roosevelt*, p. 249.

406 *"shot securely"*: Browning, *Origins*, p. 298.

406 *Eighty-two Wellington bombers:* Grayling, *Among the Dead Cities*, p. 296.

406 *ended up over Stuttgart:* "Campaign Diary 1941," *Bomber Command*, www.raf.mod.uk/bombercommand/diary1941_3.html.

407 *British Bombers Sear: NYT*, October 14, 1941.

407 *"A barbaric war"*: Gandhi, *Collected Works*, vol. 81, p. 192.

407 *"guarantees of human liberties"*: "Gandhi for a Peace Without a Defeat," *NYT*, October 13, 1941.

408 *"stand a better chance"*: United States Congress, *Arming American Merchant Vessels*, p. 64; see also "Foes of Ship Arming Demand President Make Peace Move," *NYT*, October 15, 1941.

408 *"in munitions factories"*: "Rules Against Jews Multiply in Berlin," *NYT*, October 16, 1941.

409 *arrived at the train station, "an aristocratic Jewish Dante,"* and *"Caroline, is thee"*: Isherwood, *Diaries*, pp. 182, 185, 186.

409 *"To get on there"*: Sebastian, *Journal*, p. 427.

409 *"Jews were being evicted"*: "Berlin Evicts Jews to Get Apartments," *NYT*, October 18, 1941.

410 *"Keep the Germans"*: "R.A.F. Units Strike in Industrial Ruhr," *NYT*, October 18, 1941.

410 *"Tanks in what are described"*: "Defense Heads Draft Plan for 100 Billions for Arms," *NYT*, October 18, 1941.

410 *"By its emphasis"*: Wedemeyer, *Wedemeyer Reports!*, pp. 28–29.

410 *twenty-one people were injured*: Jones, *X Site*, pp. 16–17.

411 *All Jewish emigration*: Browning, *Origins*, p. 197.

411 *"Their pleas for food"*: "Feed Starving War Children, Hoover Pleads," *Chicago Tribune*, October 20, 1941.

411 *Two men rushed up*: "Nazi Commander Slain at Nantes," *NYT*, October 21, 1941.

412 *"55,000 of an estimated"*: "55,000 of Berlin's Jews Reported to Face Exile," *NYT*, October 21, 1941.

412 *"When the eviction started"*: "Anti-Jewish Drive Renewed in Reich," *NYT*, October 22, 1941.

412 *"Ever more shocking"*: Klemperer, *Witness*, p. 440.

412 *"Their energies"*: "Berlin Calls Action on Jews Military," *NYT*, October 24, 1941.

412 *"catastrophe apartment"*: "Nazis Seek to Rid Europe of All Jews," *NYT*, October 28, 1941.

412 *"According to a Speer directive"*: Joachim Fest, *Speer*, p. 118.

413 *"Since Saturday"*: Helmuth James von Moltke, *Letters to Freya*, p. 175.

413 *"The German Jews keep"*: Sierakowiak, *Diary*, pp. 142–43.

413 *a German officer was walking*: "Frenchmen Slay a German Major," *NYT*, October 23, 1941.

413 *A commander* and *the Romanian army shot*: Gilbert, *Holocaust*, pp. 217–18.

414 *"terrible scenes"*: Von Hassell, *Diaries*, p. 222.

414 *"Every Jew"*: "Anti-Jewish Drive Renewed in Reich," *NYT*, October 22, 1941.

414 *"It has repeatedly"*: Noakes and Pridham, *Nazism*, vol. 3, p. 1111.

415 *practice air-raid blackout*: "Tokyo Blackout Stresses Crisis," *NYT*, October 23, 1941.

415 *"You will pass"* and *"The Japs will take Manila"*: Mowrer, *Triumph and Turmoil*, pp. 323, 325.

416 *prayers for the Jews*: "Berlin Dean Held; Prayed for Jews," *NYT*, November 9, 1941; Yad Vashem, "Lichtenberg, Bernhard."

416 *Lichtenberg had also been praying*: Pope Paul II, "Address During a Meeting with the Central Council of the Jews in Germany."

416 *His interrogators threatened*: von Moltke, *Letters to Freya*, p. 185.

417 *"the only thing I heard"*: "Excerpts from the Press Conference," in Wooley and Peters, *American Presidency Project*.

417 *"Civilized peoples long ago"*: "President Flays Hostage Killings," *NYT,* October 26, 1941.

417 *"Retribution for these crimes"*: "Churchill to Avenge Crimes," *NYT,* October 26, 1941.

418 *"fanatic, gloomy Japanese"*: "Tokyo, Capital of Shadows," *NYT,* October 26, 1941.

418 *"They all took"*: Ciano, *Diaries,* p. 398.

418 *"Look what luck"* and *"Isn't this shoot"*: Felix Kersten, *The Kersten Memoirs, 1940–1945,* pp. 112–13.

419 *"I told him of the fears"*: Alanbrooke, *War Diaries,* p. 194.

420 *torpedo hit its boiler room*: Robert Sinclair Parkin, *Blood on the Sea,* p. 3.

420 *Mayflower Hotel*: "Answer to Enemy," *NYT,* October 28, 1941.

420 *"workshops of Jewish forgers"* and ROOSEVELT, THE VICEROY: "Nazis Excoriate Navy Day Speech," *NYT,* October 29, 1941.

421 *"scream"*: "Nazi Ire Over 'Secret Map' Is a 'Scream' to Roosevelt," *NYT,* October 29, 1941.

421 *some basket on his desk*: Ibid.

421 *routes in South America*: Joseph E. Persico, *Roosevelt's Secret War,* pp. 127–28.

421 *British forgery*: Cull, *Selling War,* pp. 170–73.

421 *"We urge the President"*: "Nazi Ire Over 'Secret Map' Is a 'Scream' to Roosevelt," *NYT,* October 29, 1941.

422 *"Let's try not"*: Sebastian, *Journal,* p. 435.

422 *"The entire block"*: Lindbergh, *Wartime Journals,* p. 551.

422 *rang cowbells*: "Lindbergh Sees Trickery on War," *NYT,* October 31, 1941.

422 *"The war we are asked"*: "Text of Lindbergh's Address at America First Rally," *NYT,* October 31, 1941.

422 *"The thing that I think"*: Lindbergh, *Wartime Journals,* p. 552.

423 *"Eleven Poles"*: Aly et al., *Cleansing the Fatherland,* p. 137.

423 *map of the Far East*: United States News, October 31, 1941, reproduced in Thompson, *Time for War,* f.p. 210.

423 *"That hit me hard"* and *"We heard from several"*: Klemperer, *Witness,* pp. 442–43.

424 *"The doors were very"*: Yitzhak Arad, " 'Operation Reinhard': Extermination Camps of Belzec, Sobibor and Treblinka," pp. 4–5.

424 *"During the period"*: Fest, *Speer,* p. 118.

425 HALIFAX IS A WAR MONGER: "Women Hurl Eggs and Tomatoes at Lord Halifax on Detroit Tour," *NYT,* November 5, 1941; "War of Workshops Depicted by Halifax," *NYT,* November 4, 1941; "Realtors Discuss Impact of Defense," *NYT,* November 5, 1941.

425 *"This is a war of the workshops"*: Earl of Halifax, *The American Speeches of the Earl of Halifax,* pp. 94–101.

425 *"national hara-kiri"* and *"If war should occur"*: Grew, *Ten Years in Japan,* pp. 468, 470.

426 *Air-raid sirens:* Regis, *Biology of Doom,* pp. 18–19; Williams and Wallace, *Unit 731,* pp. 95–96.

426 *"My only feeling":* "Halifax Envies Wasters of Eggs," *NYT,* November 6, 1941; see also Cull, *Selling War,* p. 167.

426 *"He is, after all":* von Moltke, *Letters to Freya,* p. 177.

427 *new mesh of barbed wire* and *"The overwhelming majority":* Lucjan Dobroszycki, ed., *The Chronicle of the Lodz Ghetto, 1941–1944,* pp. 82, 86.

427 *"Accidents were frequent":* J. D. V. Ludlow, *Bridgend Royal Ordnance Factory,* p. 116.

428 *"During the first night":* Miriam Korber, "Transnistria," in Alexandra Zapruder, ed., *Salvaged Pages,* pp. 250–51.

428 *"In a healthy society":* von Moltke, *Letters to Freya,* pp. 179–80.

429 *"Bunny frankly":* Partridge, *Pacifist's War,* p. 111.

429 *"peace offensive"* and *"We must regard them":* Churchill, "A Warning to Japan," in *Unrelenting Struggle,* pp. 295, 298–99.

430 *"After much pressure":* Kersten, *Kersten Memoirs,* pp. 119–20; see also Noakes and Pridham, *Nazism,* p. 1121.

430 *"Since I labour":* Kersten, *Kersten Memoirs,* p. 121.

430 *Thirty-seven bombers* and *"Our catastrophic losses":* Cadogan, *Diaries,* pp. 411–12.

431 *"Every House in Berlin":* Stewart Halsey Ross, *Strategic Bombing by the United States in World War II,* p. 138.

431 *"Undoubtedly a release":* Gilbert, *Churchill War Papers,* vol. 3, pp. 1446–47.

431 *"We are preparing an offensive":* Michael S. Sherry, *The Rise of American Air Power,* p. 109; Thompson, *Time for War,* p. 375.

431 *"blanket the whole":* Thompson ibid., p. 376.

432 *red bathrobe:* Killen, *History of the Luftwaffe,* pp. 184–85.

432 *"Your allies aren't helping you":* "U.S. Plane Downs Nazi at Moscow," *NYT,* November 24, 1941.

432 *The Gestapo in Bremen:* Bankier, *Germans and the Final Solution,* p. 134.

432 *The transport left Bremen:* Christopher Browning, *Ordinary Men,* p. 42.

433 *"November 9 was a day":* Benno Müller-Hill, *Murderous Science,* pp. 47–48.

433 *"The question was how":* Richard N. Current, "How Stimson Meant to 'Maneuver' the Japanese," p. 67.

434 *Two students sat:* "2 Quaker Objectors Sent to Prison Farm," *NYT,* November 27, 1941.

434 *"For a man eager"* and *"I cannot understand":* Parents of Arnold Satterthwait and Frederick Richards, *Federal Convicts Numbers 1128 and 1129, College to Prison.*

434 *"The morale of the British people":* Lee, *London Journal,* p. 468.

435 *slave laborers:* Gellately, *Backing Hitler,* p. 213.

435 *"a comprehensive solution":* Roseman, *Wannsee Conference,* p. 81.

435 *"There are no problems":* "U.S. Ultimatum is Seen by Japan," *NYT,* November 29, 1941.

435 *"May they be conscious"*: "Peace with Japan is Asked in Prayer," *NYT,* November 30, 1941.

436 *"Chennault and I had"*: Leonard, *I Flew for China,* pp. 186–87.

436 *"Everywhere you go"*: Berg, *Warsaw Ghetto,* p. 117.

436 *praying continuously:* "Prayers for Peace Revealed in Tokyo," *NYT,* April 22, 1942.

437 *"Jews will fight"*: "Jewish Army Urged to Win Just Peace," *NYT,* December 5, 1941.

437 *"The only meaning"*: "India Frees 500 Including Nehru," *NYT,* December 5, 1941.

438 *late edition*: Wedemeyer, *Wedemeyer Reports!,* f.p. 178.

438 *"Popular support of the war"*: *Congressional Record,* vol. 87, 77-1, 1941–42, A5450.

438 *"strategic methods"*: "A.E.F. Plan Laid to Army and Navy," *NYT,* December 5, 1941.

439 *"I don't think"*: Betty Houchin Winfield, *FDR and the News Media,* p. 200.

439 *Senator Burton Wheeler, "I have no hard evidence,"* and SECRET UNITED STATES PLANS: Thomas Fleming, *The New Dealers' War,* pp. 12, 27, 29.

439 *"Current opinion is that"*: *Congressional Record,* vol. 87, p. A5446, December 4, 1941.

440 *"You know the unspeakable crimes"*: Mann, *Listen, Germany!,* pp. 61–62; another translation is in "Mann Bids Reich Break Nazi Yoke," *NYT,* December 7, 1941.

440 *"The only method technically"*: Harris and Paxman, *Higher Form of Killing,* pp. 88–90.

441 *nose drops:* Persico, *Roosevelt's Secret War,* p. xxii.

441 *"I got him there"*: David E. Lilienthal, *The Journals of David E. Lilienthal,* vol. 1, p. 506.

441 *"I address myself to Your Majesty"*: Yale Law School, *The Avalon Project,* "Message from the President to the Emperor of Japan," www.yale.edu/lawweb/avalon/wwii/p2.htm.

441 *"That will be fine"*: Lilienthal, *Journals,* p. 506.

441 *stamp collection:* Persico, *Roosevelt's Secret War,* p. xxiii.

442 *"You damned!"* "Leaflets Carried by Raiders," *NYT,* December 25, 1941. Image at Naval Historical Center, photo no. 80-G-413507, available at www.history.navy.mil.

442 *Dozens of Honolulu civilians:* Jack G. Henkels, "Civilians Died on Dec. 7, Too," *Honolulu Star Bulletin,* December 7, 1996, available at www.starbulletin.com.

442 *"recovering from his lethargy"*: W. Averell Harriman and Elie Abel, *Special Envoy to Churchill and Stalin, 1941–1946,* pp. 111–12.

442 *"Mr. President, what's this"*: Churchill, *The Grand Alliance,* p. 605.

443 *"Winant's dominant reaction"*: Martin Gilbert, *In Search of Churchill,* p. 184.

443 *"with admirable fortitude"*: Churchill, *The Grand Alliance,* p. 605.

443 *"He had out"*: *Newsweek,* December 12, 1966, p. 42, partially quoted in Mark Emerson Willey, *Pearl Harbor,* p. 108.

444 *sitting in his study:* Harry Emerson Fosdick, *The Living of These Days,* p. 295.

444 *"This radio audience"*: Authentic History Center, *WWII: December 7–8, 1941* (CD0410), www.authentichistory.com.

445 *"Knox feels something terrible"*: Blum, *From the Morgenthau Diaries,* vol. 3, p. 1.

445 *The man in the bar:* Mowrer, *Triumph and Turmoil,* p. 327.

446 *"Finally, the blow"*: Eleanor Roosevelt, "Pearl Harbor," in *My Day,* p. 60.

446 *one exported pearls:* "F.B.I. Rounding Up Germans in Nation," *NYT,* December 9, 1941.

446 *"This is an unfortunate situation"*: "Entire City Put on War Footing," *NYT,* December 8, 1941.

446 *Fort Missoula held a thousand:* "Japanese Arrests in Country at 345," *NYT,* December 9, 1941.

446 *"A great man hunt"*: Peter H. Irons, *Justice at War,* p. 19.

447 *"Russia saved the government"*: Channon, *Diaries,* pp. 313–14.

447 *"Being saturated and satiated"*: Gilbert, *Churchill War Papers,* vol. 3, p. 1580.

448 *wearing a cape:* Robert Smith Thompson, *Empires on the Pacific,* p. xi.

448 *black armband:* Jan Pottker, *Sara and Eleanor,* p. ix.

448 *army soldiers and marines:* James Reston, "Capital Swings Into War Stride," *NYT,* December 9, 1941.

448 *smiled and waved:* Ibid.

448 *"The Japanese, like murderous"* and *"Yes, perish"*: *Congressional Record,* vol. 87, pp. 9529, 9536.

448 *"Mr. Speaker, I would like"*: Josephson, *Jeannette Rankin,* p. 161.

448 *Later, she told a colleague:* Bayly and Landgren, *Jeannette Rankin.*

449 *Chelmno:* Breitman, *Architect of Genocide,* p. 202; "Chelmno," in *Aktion Reinhard Camps,* www.deathcamps.org; "Chelmno," United States Holocaust Memorial Museum, www.ushmm.org.

449 *gray van* and *"After a few minutes"*: Noakes and Pridham, *Nazism,* p. 1138–40.

449 *"The fruits of appeasement have burst"*: Freda Kirchwey, "Fruits of Appeasement," *The Nation,* December 13, 1941.

449 *"The war is spreading"*: Sebastian, *Journal,* p. 450.

450 *"continue to support"*: "Pacifist Group Shifts to Negotiated Peace," *NYT,* December 9, 1941.

450 *Reinhard Heydrich hastily:* Roseman, *Wannsee Conference,* p. 86.

450 *"Swiftly and quietly"*: "Schools Emptied Quickly in 'Raid,' " *NYT,* December 10, 1941.

451 *"Most people believe"*: Berg, *Warsaw Ghetto,* p. 117.

451 *"sallow, distinguished"*: Channon, *Chips,* p. 314.

451 *"The* Gazette *entirely disagrees"*: Josephson, *Jeannette Rankin,* p. 162.

452 *Sixty-seven percent:* Cantril, *Public Opinion,* p. 1067, cited in Crane, *Bombs, Cities, and Civilians,* p. 29.

452 *"Maybe the Japanese, too"* and *"The Führer once again"*: Stackelberg and Winkle, *Nazi Germany Sourcebook*, pp. 291–92.

453 *"Isn't this Japanese business"*: Birkenhead, *Halifax*, p. 532.

453 *"That was a good speech"*: Lawrence W. Levine and Cornelia R. Levine, *The People and the President*, p. 405.

454 *"To the Beefsteak"*: Nicolson, *War Years*, p. 155.

454 *made a suggestion*: Probert, *Bomber Harris*, p. 122.

454 *"Has war been declared"* and *"It was the Jew"*: Klemperer, *Witness*, pp. 449–50.

455 *Another transport*: Johnson, *Nazi Terror*, p. 402.

455 *"They were shot"*: Noakes and Pridham, *Nazism*, p. 1121.

455 *"largest naval defeat"*: Patrick S. Washburn, *A Question of Sedition*, p. 47.

456 *He talked about Russia*: Kershaw, *Hitler*, p. 490.

456 *"With respect to the Jewish Question"*: Stackelberg and Winkle, *Nazi Germany Sourcebook*, p. 292.

456 *"Overshoes, if possible"*: "Text of Goebbels Plea for Clothing for the German Troops," *NYT*, December 21, 1941.

457 *"More significant than any"*: Holmes, *I Speak for Myself*, pp. 205–8; "Holmes as Pacifist Offers to Resign," *NYT*, December 15, 1941.

457 *"Those people still have"*: Sebastian, *Journal*, p. 452.

458 *pernicious eaters*: Frank's phrase is *"aussergewöhnlich schädliche Fresser"*; Hilbert, *Destruction of the European Jews*, vol. 2, p. 483, renders this as "very parasitical eaters."

458 *"would be a feasible"*: Nicolas Rasmussen, "Plant Hormones in War and Peace," p. 302.

459 *"I have, therefore, resolved"*: "Reich Statement and Hitler's Appeal," *NYT*, December 22, 1941.

459 *"Well my beloved Winston"*: Mary Soames, *Clementine Churchill*, pp. 410–11.

459 *"I cannot welcome"*: Gandhi, *Collected Works*, vol. 81, p. 387.

460 *"The burning of Japanese cities"*: Gilbert, *Churchill War Papers*, vol. 3, p. 1652.

460 *"The modern Jap"*: "How to Tell Japs from the Chinese," *Life*, December 22, 1941, p. 81.

460 *They went to Chelmno*: Dobroszycki, ed., *Chronicle*, p. 108n.

461 *Russian planes dropped*: "Red Yule Cards for Foe," *NYT*, December 25, 1941.

461 *"For this woman"*: "Russians Bombard Nazis with Taunts," *NYT*, December 26, 1941.

461 *"We must surrender"*: Czerniakow, *Warsaw Diary*, p. 309.

461 *"There is no place"*: Sister Margherita Marchione, *Pope Pius XII: Architect for Peace*, p. 109.

461 *"Let a ray"*: "Pope Broadcasts Five Peace Points," *NYT*, December 25, 1941.

462 *"Last night the north wind"*: Korber, "Transnistria," in Zapruder, ed., *Salvaged Pages*, pp. 254–55.

462 *"growling sound"*: Lilienthal, *Journals*, p. 419.

462 *Churchill paced* and *"I hit the target"*: Moran, *Churchill*, pp. 16–17.

463 *"He is 'doing' "*: Partridge, *Pacifist's War*, p. 118.

463 *"All normal work"* and *They counted*: Czerniakow, *Warsaw Diary*, p. 310.

464 *"As pacifists"*: Wittner, *Rebels Against War*, p. 52.

464 *"We must strike"*: "Must Strike Hard, Dr. Einstein Asserts," *NYT*, December 30, 1941.

464 *"can only be deemed"*: "MacArthur Bids U.S. Take Raid Revenge," *NYT*, December 31, 1941.

465 *"Think of Tokyo"*: New York *Herald Tribune*, December 30, 1941.

465 *"One can come to only"*: "Washington Asks Revenge Bombings," *NYT*, December 28, 1941.

465 *"burn them off the face of the earth"*: "Hot Talk," *Time*, January 5, 1942.

465 *"They shall themselves"*: Gilbert, *Churchill War Papers*, vol. 3, p. 1711.

465 *perfectly wonderful*: "Roosevelt Awaiting Return of Churchill," *NYT*, December 31, 1941.

466 *"I must continue"*: "Gandhi Steps Down in War Policy Rift," *NYT*, December 31, 1941; Gandhi, *Collected Works*, vol. 81, pp. 397–98.

466 *"If any country has"*: Gandhi, *Collected Works*, vol. 81, p. 399.

466 *"American-British Grand Strategy"*: Franklin D. Roosevelt Presidential Library and Museum, Safe Files, Box 1, www.fdrlibrary.marist.edu/psf/box1/a05s19 .html.

467 *"First came the walking wounded"*: "Wounded Pour Into Frisco From Bombed Hawaii," *Chicago Tribune*, January 1, 1942.

467 *"Before this we didn't"*: "The Wounded Return," *Time*, January 5, 1942.

467 *"The group was holding"*: Isherwood, *Diaries*, p. 201.

468 *"The war has only"*: "Tojo Tells Japan War Will Be Long," *NYT*, January 1, 1942.

468 *"I believe that when"*: Chiang Kai-shek, *All We Are and All We Have*, p. 4.

468 *"The first year"*: "Hitler Says Reich Will Break Russia," *NYT*, January 1, 1942.

468 *"When the public"*: "War Factories Roar New Note in Din of 1942," *Chicago Tribune*, January 1, 1942.

469 *At midnight*: Jackie Martin, "A Night to Remember: New Year's Eve with Winston Churchill," pp. 155–60.

469 *"Here's to 1942"*: "Churchill Toasts New Year on Train," *NYT*, January 2, 1942. Other versions are in Winston Churchill, *The End of the Beginning*, p. 3, and Martin, "Night to Remember."

469 *Holding crossed hands*: Thompson, *Assignment: Churchill*, p. 257.

470 *"No bombs fell"*: "No Bombs Disturb English New Year," *NYT*, January 1, 1942.

470 *history's greatest catastrophe*: D. A. Prater, *European of Yesterday*, p. 322.

471 *"I made a serious"*: Klemperer, *Witness*, p. 456.

471 *"I carry inside myself"*: Sebastian, *Journal*, p. 458.

474 *Human smoke*: Leon Goldensohn, *The Nuremberg Interviews*, p. 288.

References

Abend, Hallett. *My Life in China, 1926–1941*. New York: Harcourt, Brace, 1943.

Alanbrooke, Lord. *War Diaries*. Berkeley: University of California Press, 2001.

Aly, Götz. *"Final Solution": Nazi Population Policy and the Murder of the European Jews*. London: Arnold, 1999.

Aly, Götz, Peter Chroust, and Christian Pross. *Cleansing the Fatherland: Nazi Medicine and Racial Hygiene*. Baltimore: Johns Hopkins University Press, 1994.

American-Israeli Cooperative Enterprise. *Jewish Virtual Library*. www.jewishvirtual library.org

Anderson, David G. "British Rearmament and the 'Merchants of Death,' " *Journal of Contemporary History*, January 1994.

Anderson, Jervis. *A. Philip Randolph: A Biographical Portrait*. New York: Harcourt, 1973.

Arad, Gulie Ne'eman. *America, Its Jews, and the Rise of Nazism*. Bloomington: Indiana University Press, 2000.

Arad, Yitzhak. *Belzec, Sobibor, Treblinka: The Operation Reinhard Death Camps*. Bloomington: Indiana University Press, 1987.

———. " 'Operation Reinhard': Extermination Camps of Belzec, Sobibor and Treblinka." Shoah Resource Center. www.yadvashem.org.

Argus. "Friendly Enemy Aliens." *The Contemporary Review*, January 1941.

Armitage, John. "The Internment of Aliens" (book review). *The Fortnightly*, December 1940.

Armstrong, Alan. *Preemptive Strike: The Secret Plan That Would Have Prevented the Attack on Pearl Harbor*. Guilford, Conn.: Lyons Press, 2006.

Arnold, Henry H. *American Airpower Comes of Age: General Henry H. "Hap" Arnold's World War II Diaries*. Ed. John W. Huston. 2 vols. Maxwell Air Force Base, Ala.: Air University Press, 2002.

Aronson, Shlomo. *Hitler, the Allies, and the Jews.* New York: Cambridge University Press, 2004.

Arthur, Max, ed. *Forgotten Voices of World War II.* Guilford, Conn.: Lyons Press, 2004.

Authentic History Center. *WWII: 1938–Dec. 6 1941* (CD0400). Audio CD.

———. *WWII: December 7–8 1941.* Audio CD. Available at www.authentic history.com.

Bane, Suda Lorena, and Ralph Haswell Lutz, eds. *The Blockade of Germany after the Armistice, 1918–1919.* Stanford, Calif.: Stanford University Press, 1942.

Bankier, David. *The Germans and the Final Solution.* Oxford: Blackwell, 1992.

Bartov, Omer. *Hitler's Army: Soldiers, Nazis, and War in the Third Reich.* New York: Oxford University Press, 1991.

Bayly, Ronald and Nancy Landgren. *Jeannette Rankin, the Woman Who Voted No* (videotape). Alexandria, Va.: PBS Video, 1984.

Bekker, Cajus. *The Luftwaffe War Diaries.* New York: Da Capo, 1994.

Bell, Kelly. "World War II: Air War Over Iraq." *Aviation History,* May 2004. Available at www.historynet.com.

Bennett, Gill. *Churchill's Man of Mystery.* London: Routledge, 2007.

Berg, Mary. *Warsaw Ghetto: A Diary.* Ed. S. L. Shneiderman. New York: L. B. Fischer, 1945.

Biddle, Tami Davis. *Rhetoric and Reality in Air Warfare.* Princeton, N.J.: Princeton University Press, 2002.

Birkenhead, Frederick, earl of. *Halifax: The Life of Lord Halifax.* London: Hamish Hamilton, 1965.

Blue, Allan G. *The B-24 Liberator: A Pictorial History.* New York: Scribner's, 1975.

Blum, John Morton. *From the Morgenthau Diaries,* vol. 2, *Years of Urgency, 1938–1941.* Boston: Houghton Mifflin, 1959.

———. *From the Morgenthau Diaries,* vol. 3, *Years of War, 1941–1945.* Boston: Houghton Mifflin, 1967.

Boothe, Clare. *Europe in the Spring.* New York: Knopf, 1941.

Borg, Dorothy. *The United States and the Far Eastern Crisis of 1933–1938.* Cambridge, Mass.: Harvard University Press, 1964.

Boyne, Walter J. *Beyond the Horizons: The Lockheed Story.* New York: St. Martin's, 1998.

Brack, Viktor. "Affidavit Concerning the Nazi Administrative System, the Euthanasia Program, and the Sterilization Experiments." Harvard Law School Library, Nuremberg Trials Projects, nuremberg.law.harvard.edu.

Breiting, Richard. *Secret Conversations with Hitler: The Two Newly-Discovered 1931 Interviews.* Ed. Édouard Calic. Trans. Richard Barry. New York: John Day, 1971.

Breitman, Richard. *The Architect of Genocide: Himmler and the Final Solution.* New York: Knopf, 1991.

Breitman, Richard, and Alan M. Kraut. *American Refugee Policy and European Jewry, 1933–1945.* Bloomington, Ind.: Indiana University Press, 1987.

Brittain, Vera. *Testament of a Peace Lover.* Ed. Winifred and Alan Eden-Green. London: Virago, 1988.

Brooks, Collin. *Fleet Street, Press Barons and Politics: The Journals of Collin Brooks, 1932–1940.* Ed. N. J. Crowson. London: Royal Historical Society, 1998.

Brophy, Leo P., and George J. B. Fisher. *The Chemical Warfare Service: Organizing for War.* Washington, D.C.: Department of the Army, 1959.

Brophy, Leo P., Wyndham D. Miles, and Rexmond C. Cochrane. *The Chemical Warfare Service: From Laboratory to Field.* Washington, D.C.: Department of the Army, 1959.

Broszat, Martin. "The Genesis of the 'Final Solution.' " In H. W. Koch, ed., *Aspects of the Third Reich.* New York: St. Martin's, 1985.

Brown, Judith M. *Gandhi: Prisoner of Hope.* New Haven, Conn.: Yale University Press, 1989.

Browning, Christopher. *Ordinary Men: Reserve Police Battalion 101 and the Final Solution in Poland.* New York: HarperCollins, 1992.

———. *Nazi Policy, Jewish Workers, German Killers.* New York: Cambridge University Press, 2000.

———. *The Origins of the Final Solution: Evolution of Nazi Jewish Policy, September 1939–March 1942.* London: Heinemann, 2004.

———. *The Path to Genocide.* New York: Cambridge University Press, 1992.

Bullock, Alan. *Hitler: A Study in Tyranny.* New York: Harper, 1962.

Burgwyn, H. James. *Italian Foreign Policy in the Interwar Period, 1918–1940.* Westport, Conn.: Praeger, 1997.

Butler, J. R. M. *Grand Strategy,* vol. 2, *September 1939–June 1941.* London: Her Majesty's Stationery Office, 1957.

Bytwerk, Randall L. "The Argument for Genocide in Nazi Propaganda." *Quarterly Journal of Speech* vol. 91, no. 1 (February 2005).

Cadogan, Alexander. *The Diaries of Sir Alexander Cadogan.* Ed. David Dilks. New York: Putnam, 1972.

Caidin, Martin. *Flying Forts: The B-17 in World War II.* New York: Bantam, 1990.

Calder, Angus. *The People's War: Britain—1939–1945.* New York: Pantheon, 1969.

Cantril, Hadley, ed. *Public Opinion.* Princeton, N.J.: Princeton University Press, 1951.

Caulfield, Max. *Tomorrow Never Came: The Sinking of the SS. Athenia.* New York: Norton, 1959.

Chamberlain, Neville. "British Prime Minister Neville Chamberlain Resigns" (audio file). *Authentic History.* www.authentichistory.com.

Chandler, Andrew. "The Church of England and the Obliteration Bombing of Germany in the Second World War." *English Historical Review* 108, no. 429 (October 1993).

Channon, Henry. *Chips: The Diaries of Sir Henry Channon.* London: Weidenfeld and Nicolson, 1967.

Cherniak, Jan, et al. *Pobediteli: Soldiers of the Great War.* English.pobediteli.ru.

Churchill, Winston. *The End of the Beginning: War Speeches by the Right Hon. Winston S. Churchill C.H., M.P.* Ed. Charles Eade. Boston: Little, Brown, 1943.

———. *Great Contemporaries.* Freeport, N.Y.: Books for Libraries, 1971 [1937].

———. *Winston S. Churchill: His Complete Speeches.* Ed. Robert Rhodes James. London: Chelsea House, 1974.

———. *The Aftermath.* New York: Scribner's, 1929.

———. *The Second World War,* vol. 1, *The Gathering Storm.* Boston: Houghton Mifflin, 1948.

———. *The Second World War,* vol. 2, *Their Finest Hour.* Boston: Houghton Mifflin, 1949.

———. *The Second World War,* vol. 3, *The Grand Alliance.* Boston: Houghton Mifflin, 1950.

———. *Step by Step, 1936–1939.* Freeport, N.Y.: Books for Libraries, 1971 [1939].

———. *The Unrelenting Struggle: War Speeches by the Right Hon. Winston S. Churchill.* Freeport, N.Y.: Books for Libraries, 1971.

Ciano, Galeazzo, Count. *The Ciano Diaries, 1939–1943.* Ed. Hugh Gibson. New York: Doubleday, 1946.

Clayton, Aileen. *The Enemy Is Listening.* New York: Ballantine, 1982.

Clifford, J. Garry, and Samuel R. Spencer Jr. *The First Peacetime Draft.* Lawrence, Kan.: University Press of Kansas, 1986.

Coffey, Thomas M. *Hap: The Story of the U.S. Air Force and the Man Who Built It, General Henry H. "Hap" Arnold.* New York: Viking, 1982.

———. *Iron Eagle: The Turbulent Life of General Curtis LeMay.* New York: Avon, 1988.

Coit, Margaret L. *Mr. Baruch.* Boston: Houghton Mifflin, 1957.

Collier, Richard. *The City That Would Not Die.* New York: Dutton, 1960.

Colville, John. *The Fringes of Power: Downing Street Diaries, 1939–1955.* New York: Norton, 1985.

Colvin, Ian. *The Chamberlain Cabinet.* New York: Taplinger, 1971.

Corum, James S. "The Myth of Air Control." *Aerospace Power Journal* (winter 2000), www.airpower.maxwell.af.mil/airchronicles/apj/apj00/win00/corum.htm.

Costello, John. *Ten Days to Destiny.* New York: Morrow, 1991.

Crane, Conrad C. *Bombs, Cities, and Civilians: American Airpower Strategy in World War II.* Lawrence, Kan.: University Press of Kansas, 1993.

Craven, Wesley Frank, and James Lea Cate. *The Army Air Forces in World War II,* vol. 1. Chicago: University of Chicago Press, 1948.

Cross, Robin. *The Bombers: The Illustrated Story of Offensive Strategy and Tactics in the Twentieth Century.* New York: Macmillan, 1987.

Cull, Nicholas John. *Selling War: The British Propaganda Campaign Against American "Neutrality" in World War II.* New York: Oxford, 1995.

Culver, John C, and John Hyde. *American Dreamer: The Life and Times of Henry A. Wallace.* New York: Norton, 2000.

Current, Richard N. "How Stimson Meant to 'Maneuver' the Japanese." *The Mississippi Valley Historical Review* 40, no. 1 (June 1953).

Czerniakow, Adam. *The Warsaw Diary of Adam Czerniakow.* Ed. Raul Hilberg, Stanislaw Staron, and Josef Kermisz. New York: Stein and Day, 1979.

Dalton, Dennis. *Mahatma Gandhi: Nonviolent Power in Action.* New York: Columbia University Press, 1993.

Davis, Mike. *Dead Cities.* New York: New Press, 2002.

Dawidowicz, Lucy S. *The War Against the Jews, 1933–1945.* New York: Holt, Rinehart, and Winston, 1975.

De Gaulle, Charles. *The Complete War Memoirs.* New York: Simon and Schuster, 1964.

Delmer, Sefton. *Black Boomerang.* www.seftondelmer.co.uk.

De Seversky, Alexander P. *Victory Through Air Power.* Garden City, N.Y.: Garden City, 1943.

Deutsch, Harold C. *The Conspiracy Against Hitler in the Twilight War.* Minneapolis: University of Minnesota Press, 1968.

Dobroszycki, Lucjan, ed. *The Chronicle of the Lodz Ghetto, 1941–1944.* New Haven, Conn.: Yale University Press, 1984.

Doenecke, Justus D. "Non-Interventionism of the Left: The Keep America Out of War Congress, 1938–41." *Journal of Contemporary History* 12, no. 2 (April 1977).

Donovan, James A. *Outpost in the North Atlantic: Marines in Defense of Iceland* (Washington, D.C.: Marine Corps Historical Center, 1991). HyperWar Foundation, www.ibiblio.org/hyperwar/USMC/USMC-C-Iceland.html.

Dwork, Debórah, and Robert Jan van Pelt. *Auschwitz: 1270 to the Present.* New York: Norton, 1996.

Ehrenburg, Ilya, and Vasily Grossman. *The Complete Black Book of Russian Jewry.* Trans. David Patterson. New Brunswick, N.J.: Transaction, 2003.

Engelbrecht, H. C. *Revolt Against War.* New York: Dodd, Mead, 1937.

———. "The Problem of the Munitions Industry." *Annals of the American Academy of Political and Social Science* 174 (July 1934).

———. "The International Armament Industry," *Annals of the American Academy of Political and Social Science* (September 1934).

Etzold, Thomas "The (F)utility Factor: German Information Gathering in the United States." *Military Affairs* 39, no. 2 (April 1975).

"Evolution of the Hudson Bomber." www.hudsonbomber.com.

Feingold, Henry L. *Bearing Witness: How America and Its Jews Responded to the Holocaust.* Syracuse: Syracuse University Press, 1995.

Feldman, Gerald. "Two German Businessmen." *Berlin Journal: Newsletter of the American Academy in Berlin,* no. 2 (summer 2001), www.americanacademy.de/fileadmin/berlinjournal/BJ21.pdf.

Fest, Joachim. *The Face of the Third Reich.* London: Weidenfeld and Nicolson, 1970.

———. *Plotting Hitler's Death: The Story of the German Resistance.* New York: Metropolitan, 1996.

———. *Speer: The Final Verdict.* New York: Harcourt, 2001.

Fischer, Louis. *The Life of Mahatma Gandhi.* New York: Harper, 1950.

Fleming, Thomas. *The New Dealers' War: Franklin D. Roosevelt and the War Within World War II.* New York: Basic Books, 2001.

Fosdick, Harry Emerson. *The Challenge of the Present Crisis.* New York: Association Press, 1918.

———. *The Living of These Days: The Autobiography of Harry Emerson Fosdick.* New York: Harper, 1956.

Freedman, Jean R. *Whistling in the Dark: Memory and Culture in Wartime London.* Lexington: Kentucky University Press, 1999.

Freidel, Frank. *Franklin D. Roosevelt: A Rendezvous with Destiny.* Boston: Little, Brown, 1990.

Friedlander, Henry. *The Origins of Nazi Genocide.* Chapel Hill: University of North Carolina Press, 1995.

Friedrich, Jörg. *The Fire: The Bombing of Germany, 1940–1945.* New York: Columbia University Press, 2006.

Fryer, Jonathan. *Isherwood.* New York: Doubleday, 1978.

Gandhi, Mohandas. *The Collected Works of Mahatma Gandhi.* www.gandhiserve.org/cwmg/cwmg.html.

Garnett, David. *War in the Air: September 1939–May 1941.* New York: Doubleday, Doran, 1941.

Gellately, Robert. *Backing Hitler.* London: Oxford, 2001.

Gilbert, Martin. *Churchill and America.* New York: Free Press, 2005.

———. *The Churchill War Papers,* vols. 1–3. London: Heinemann, 1993–2000.

———. *The Holocaust.* New York: Holt, 1985.

———. *In Search of Churchill: A Historian's Journey.* New York: John Wiley, 1994.

———. *Kristallnacht: Prelude to Destruction.* New York: HarperCollins, 2006.

———. *Winston S. Churchill,* vols. 4–7. London: Heinemann, 1975–1986.

Ginsburg, Paul. "Engelbert Kreuzer: Butcher of Sudilkov." Internet Archive, web.archive.org/web/*/http://www.sudilkov.com.

Goda, Norman J. W. "Black Marks: Hitler's Bribery of His Senior Officers during World War II." *The Journal of Modern History* 72, no. 2 (June 2000).

Goebbels, Joseph. *The Goebbels Diaries, 1939–1941.* Ed. Fred Taylor. New York: Putnam, 1983.

———. *The Goebbels Diaries, 1942–1943.* Ed. Louis P. Lochner. New York: Doubleday, 1948.

Goldensohn, Leon. *The Nuremberg Interviews.* New York: Knopf, 2004.

Gorodetsky, Gabriel. *Grand Delusion: Stalin and the German Invasion of Russia.* New Haven, Conn.: Yale University Press, 1999.

Gowing, Margaret. *Britain and Atomic Energy, 1939–1945.* London: Macmillan, 1964.

Gray, Peter W. "The Myths of Air Control and the Realities of Imperial Policing." *Aerospace Power Journal* (fall 2001), www.airpower.maxwell.af.mil/airchronicles/apj/apj01/fal101/gray.html.

Grayling, A. C. *Among the Dead Cities.* New York: Walker, 2006.

Grew, Joseph C. *Ten Years in Japan.* New York: Simon and Schuster, 1944.

Guillemin, Jean. *Biological Weapons: From the Invention of State-Sponsored Programs to Contemporary Bioterrorism.* New York: Columbia University Press, 2005.

Haffner, Sebastian. *The Meaning of Hitler.* Cambridge, Mass.: Harvard University Press, 1983.

Haldane, Aylmer L. *The Insurrection in Mesopotamia, 1920.* Edinburgh: Blackwood, 1922.

Halifax, earl of. *The American Speeches of the Earl of Halifax.* Freeport, N.Y.: Books for Libraries, 1970.

Harris, Robert, and Jeremy Paxman. *A Higher Form of Killing: The Secret History of Chemical and Biological Warfare.* New York: Random House, 2002.

Harvard Law School Library. *Nuremberg Trials Project.* www.nuremberg.law.harvard.edu.

Harvey, Oliver. *The Diplomatic Diaries of Oliver Harvey.* New York: St. Martin's, 1970.

Hastings, Max. *Bomber Command.* New York: Dial Press, 1979.

"The Heavy Bomber." *Fortune,* October 1941.

Henze, Carl G. B. "Bombs on Coventry: Experiences of a Ju 88 in Action Against England." Trans. Randall L. Bytwerk. German Propaganda Archive, www.calvin.edu/academic/cas/gpa/index.htm.

Hermand, Jost. *A Hitler Youth in Poland: The Nazis' Program for Evacuating Children During World War II.* Evanston, Ill.: Northwestern University Press, 1997.

Higham, Charles. *Trading with the Enemy: The Nazi-American Money Plot, 1933–1949.* New York: Barnes and Noble, 1995.

Hilberg, Raul. *The Destruction of the European Jews.* Rev. ed. 3 vols. New York: Holmes and Meier, 1985.

———. *Perpetrators, Victims, Bystanders: The Jewish Catastrophe, 1933–1945.* New York: HarperPerennial, 1993.

Hill, Christopher. *Cabinet Decisions on Foreign Policy: The British Experience, October 1938–June 1941.* Cambridge: Cambridge University Press, 1991.

Hillesum, Etty. *An Interrupted Life: The Diaries of Etty Hillesum, 1941–1943.* New York: Pantheon, 1983.

Hinshaw, David. *Rufus Jones, Master Quaker.* New York: Putnam, 1951.

Hinsley, F. H. *British Intelligence in the Second World War: Its Influence on Strategy and Operations.* 5 vols. New York: Cambridge University Press, 1979.

Hitler, Adolf. *My New Order.* Ed. Raoul de Roussy de Sales. New York: Reynal and Hitchcock, 1941.

———. *Hitler's Table Talk: His Private Conversations.* New York: Enigma, 2000.

Holliday, Laurel. *Children in the Holocaust and World War II: Their Secret Diaries.* New York: Washington Square Press, 1996.

Holmes, John Haynes. *I Speak for Myself.* New York: Harper and Brothers, 1959.

Hoover, Herbert. *An American Epic,* vol. 4. Chicago: Regnery, 1964.

Höss, Rudolph. *Death Dealer: The Memoirs of the SS Kommandant at Auschwitz.* Ed. Steven Paskuly. New York: Da Capo, 1996.

"How to Tell Japs from the Chinese." *Life,* December 22, 1941.

Huxley, Aldous. *Complete Essays,* vol. 4, *1936–1938.* Ed. Robert S. Baker and James Sexton. Chicago: Ivan R. Dee, 2001.

———. *Ends and Means.* London: Chatto and Windus, 1965.

Ickes, Harold. *The Secret Diary of Harold L. Ickes.* New York: Simon and Schuster, 1954.

International Commission on the Holocaust in Romania. *Final Report.* United States Holocaust Memorial Museum, www.ushmm.org.

Irons, Peter H. *Justice at War.* Oxford: Oxford University Press, 1983.

Ironside, Edmund. *Time Unguarded: The Ironside Diaries.* New York: D. McKay, 1962.

Isherwood, Christopher. *Diaries,* vol. 1. Ed. Katherine Bucknell. New York: HarperCollins, 1996.

Jack, Homer A., ed. *The Gandhi Reader: A Sourcebook of His Life and Writings.* Unabridged ed. New York: Grove Weidenfeld, 1989.

James, Robert Rhodes. *Churchill: A Study in Failure, 1900–1939.* New York: World, 1970.

James, Ronald Michael, and John Bevis Reid, eds. *Uncovering Nevada's Past.* Reno: University of Nevada Press, 2004.

Jasper, Ronald C. D. *George Bell: Bishop of Chichester.* London: Oxford University Press, 1967.

Joad, Cyril. *Journey Through the War Mind.* London: Faber, 1940.

John Paul II, Pope. "Address During a Meeting with the Central Council of the Jews in Germany." June 23, 1996. Service International de Documentation Judéo-Chrétienne (SIDIC), www.sidic.org.

Johnson, Eric A. *Nazi Terror: The Gestapo, Jews, and Ordinary Germans.* New York: Basic Books, 1999.

Johnson, Eric A., and Karl-Heinz Reuband. *What We Knew: Terror, Mass Murder, and Everyday Life in Nazi Germany.* New York: Basic Books, 2005.

Jones, Simon. *World War I Gas Warfare Tactics and Equipment.* New York: Osprey, 2007.

Jones, Tim. *The X Site: Britain's Most Mysterious Government Facility.* Rhyl, Wales: Gwasg Helygain, 2000.

Josephson, Hannah. *Jeannette Rankin: First Lady in Congress.* New York: Bobbs-Merrill, 1974.

Kai-shek, Chiang. *All We Are and All We Have: Speeches and Messages Since Pearl Harbor.* New York: John Day, 1943.

Kaufman, Fred. *Searching for Justice: An Autobiography.* Toronto: University of Toronto Press, 2005.

Kershaw, Ian. *Hitler, 1936–45: Nemesis.* New York: Norton, 2000.

Kersten, Felix. *The Kersten Memoirs, 1940–1945.* New York: Macmillan, 1957.

Killen, John. *A History of the Luftwaffe.* New York: Doubleday, 1968.

Killingray, David. "A Swift Agent of Government: Air Power in British Colonial Africa." *The Journal of African History* 25, no. 4 (1984).

Kilzer, Louis C. *Churchill's Deception.* New York: Simon and Schuster, 1994.

Kimball, Warren F., ed. *Churchill and Roosevelt: The Complete Correspondence,* vol. 1. Princeton, N.J.: Princeton University Press, 1984.

King, Cecil. *With Malice Toward None: A War Diary.* London: Sidgwick and Jackson, 1970.

Kirchwey, Freda. "Fruits of Appeasement." *The Nation,* December 13, 1941.

Kleber, Brooks E., and Dale Birdsell. *The Chemical Warfare Service: Chemicals in Combat.* Washington, D.C.: U.S. Army, 1966.

Klemperer, Victor. *I Will Bear Witness: A Diary of the Nazi Years,* vol. 1, *1933–1941.* Trans. Martin Chalmers. New York: Random House, 1998.

Koch, Eric. *Deemed Suspect: A Wartime Blunder.* Toronto: Methuen, 1980.

Koch, H. W. "The Strategic Air Offensive Against Germany: The Early Phase, May–September 1940." *The Historical Journal* 34, no. 1 (March 1991).

Kogon, Eugen, et al. *Nazi Mass Murder: A Documentary History of the Use of Poison Gas.* New Haven, Conn.: Yale University Press, 1993.

Korber, Miriam. "Transnistria." In Alexandra Zapruder, ed., *Salvaged Pages: Young Writers' Diaries of the Holocaust.* New Haven, Conn.: Yale University Press, 2002.

"Koscian and the Euthanasia in Poland." Aktion Reinhard Camps. www.death camps.org.

Kraus, René. *The Men Around Churchill.* Freeport, N.Y.: Books for Libraries, 1971 [1941].

Kurki, Allan W. *Operation Moonlight Sonata: The German Raid on Coventry.* Westport, Conn.: Praeger, 1995.

Lafitte, François. *The Internment of Aliens.* London: Libris, 1988 [1940].

Laqueur, Walter. *The Terrible Secret: Suppression of the Truth about Hitler's "Final Solution."* Boston: Little, Brown, 1980.

Lash, Joseph P. *Eleanor and Franklin.* New York: Norton, 1971.

Leary, William M. "Wings for China: The Jouett Mission, 1932–35." *The Pacific Historical Review* 38, no. 4 (November 1969).

Lebzelter, Gisela C. *Political Anti-Semitism in England, 1918–1939.* New York: Holmes and Meier, 1978.

Lee, Asher. *Goering: Air Leader.* New York: Hippocrene, 1972.

Lee, Raymond E. *The London Journal of General Raymond E. Lee.* Boston: Little, Brown, 1971.

Leonard, Royal. *I Flew for China.* New York: Doubleday, Doran, 1942.

Lester, Muriel. *It So Happened.* New York: Harper and Brothers, 1947.

Levine, Lawrence W. and Cornelia R. Levine. *The People and the President*, Boston: Beacon, 2002.

Lewis, Jon E., ed. *The Mammoth Book of Eyewitness World War II*. New York: Carroll and Graf, 2002.

Ley, Willy. *Bombs and Bombing*. New York: Modern Age, 1941.

Lichtenstein, Nelson. *Labor's War at Home: The CIO in World War II*. New York: Cambridge University Press, 1982.

Liddell Hart, B. H. *History of the Second World War*. London: Pan, 1973.

Lilienthal, David E. *The Journals of David E. Lilienthal,* vol. 1, *The TVA Years, 1939–1945*. New York: Harper and Row, 1964.

Lindbergh, Charles A. *The Wartime Journals of Charles A. Lindbergh*. New York: Harcourt Brace Jovanovich, 1970.

Lindqvist, Sven. *A History of Bombing*. New York: New Press, 2001.

Lipsett, Alexander S. *Famine Stalks Europe*. New York: Craft Union Publishers, 1941.

Longmate, Norman. *Air Raid: The Bombing of Coventry, 1940*. New York: McKay, 1976.

Ludlow, J. D. V. *Bridgend Royal Ordnance Factory: A Brief History, 1936–1946*. www.bridgend.co.uk, 2003.

Lukacs, John. *The Duel: 10 May–31 July 1940*. New Haven, Conn.: Yale University Press, 2001.

Lynd, Staughton, ed. *Nonviolence in America: A Documentary History*. New York: Bobbs-Merrill, 1966.

MacDonald, Callum. *The Killing of SS Obergruppenführer Reinhard Heydrich*. New York: Free Press, 1989.

MacKay, Robert. *Half the Battle: Civilian Morale in Britain During the Second World War*. Manchester, Eng.: Manchester University Press, 2002.

Machtan, Lothar. *The Hidden Hitler*. Trans. John Brownjohn. New York: Basic Books, 2001.

MacNeice, Louis. *Selected Prose of Louis MacNeice*. Ed. Alan Heuser. Oxford: Clarendon Press, 1990.

Mahnken, Thomas G. *Uncovering Ways of War: U.S. Intelligence and Foreign Military Innovation*. Ithaca, N.Y.: Cornell University Press, 2002.

Mann, Thomas. *Listen, Germany! Twenty-Five Radio Messages to the German People over BBC*. New York: Knopf, 1943.

Mansfield, Harold. *Vision: A Saga of the Sky*. New York: Duell, Sloan, and Pearce, 1956.

Marcus, Joseph. *Social and Political History of the Jews in Poland, 1919–1939*. Berlin: Mouton, 1983.

Martin, Jackie. "A Night to Remember: New Year's Eve with Winston Churchill." In *Memorial Addresses in the Congress of the United States and Tributes in Eulogy of Sir Winston Churchill*. Washington, D.C.: Government Printing Office, 1965.

Matloff, Maurice, and Edwin M. Snell. *Strategic Planning for Coalition Warfare, 1941–1942.* Washington, D.C.: Department of the Army, 1953.

Mayer, Arno. *Why Did the Heavens Not Darken? The Final Solution in History.* New York: Pantheon, 1988.

Mayer, Milton. "I Think I'll Sit This One Out," *Saturday Evening Post,* October 7, 1939.

———. *They Thought They Were Free: The Germans, 1933–1945.* Chicago: University of Chicago Press, 1955.

Menzies, Robert. *Dark and Hurrying Days: Menzies' 1941 Diary.* National Library of Australia, 1993.

Miller, Edward S. *War Plan Orange: The U.S. Strategy to Defeat Japan, 1897–1945.* Annapolis: Naval Institute Press, 1991.

Miller, Lawrence Mek, *Witness for Humanity: A Biography of Clarence E. Pickett.* Wallingford, Penn.: Pendle Hill, 1999.

Miller Robert Moats. *Harry Emerson Fosdick: Preacher, Pastor, Prophet.* New York: Oxford, 1985.

[Ministry of Information?]. *The Air Offensive Against Germany.* 1941.

Moltke, Helmuth James von. *Letters to Freya, 1939–1945.* New York: Knopf, 1990.

Moran, Lord. *Churchill: Taken from the Diaries of Lord Moran.* Boston: Houghton Mifflin, 1966.

Morgenstern, George. *Pearl Harbor: The Story of the Secret War.* New York: Devin-Adair, 1947.

Mortimer, Gavin. *The Longest Night: The Bombing of London on May 10, 1941.* New York: Berkley, 2005.

Mosley, Leonard. *Lindbergh: A Biography.* New York: Doubleday, 1976.

Mowrer, Edgar Ansel. *Triumph and Turmoil: A Personal History of Our Time.* New York: Weybright and Talley, 1968.

Mowrer, Lilian T. *Journalist's Wife.* New York: Morrow, 1937.

Müller-Hill, Benno. *Murderous Science: Elimination by Scientific Selection of Jews, Gypsies, and Others, Germany 1933–1945.* Trans. George Fraser. New York: Oxford University Press, 1988.

Murrow, Edward R. *This Is London.* New York: Simon and Schuster, 1941.

National Committee on the Cause and Cure of War Records. Swarthmore College Peace Collection. www.swarthmore.edu/library/peace/CDGA.M-R/ncccw.html.

Neillands, Robin. *The Bomber War: The Allied Air Offensive Against Nazi Germany.* New York: Barnes and Noble, 2005.

Newton, Scott. *Profits of Peace: The Political Economy of Anglo-German Appeasement.* Oxford: Clarendon, 1996.

Nicolson, Harold. *The War Years, 1939–1945: Diaries and Letters,* vol. 2. Ed. Nigel Nicolson. New York: Athenaeum, 1967.

Nicosia, Francis R. "Zionism, Antisemitism, and the Origins of the Final Solution." In Wolfgang Mieder and David Scrase, eds., *Reflections on the Holocaust: Fest-*

schrift for Raul Hilberg on His Seventy-Fifth Birthday. Burlington, Vt.: Center for Holocaust Studies, 2001.

———. "Zionism in National Socialist Jewish Policy in Germany, 1933–39." *The Journal of Modern History* 50, no. 4, on-demand supplement (December 1978).

Nixon, Edgar B., ed. *Franklin D. Roosevelt and Foreign Affairs,* vols. 1–3. Cambridge, Mass.: Harvard University Press, 1969.

Noakes, J., and G. Pridham, eds. *Nazism 1919–1945.* Exeter: University of Exeter, 1988.

Oakley, Harry. "The Worst Night of Our Lives." *WW2 People's War: An Archive of World War Two Memories.* BBC, www.bbc.co.uk.

Omissi, David E. *Air Power and Colonial Control: The Royal Air Force 1919–1939.* Manchester: Manchester University Press, 1990.

———. "Baghdad and The British Bombers." *The Guardian,* January 19, 1991. Available at www.globalpolicy.org.

Onlooker. "The Tragedy of the Refugees." *The Contemporary Review,* August 1940.

Owings, Alison. *Frauen: German Women Recall the Third Reich.* New Brunswick, N.J.: Rutgers University Press, 1993.

"Owinska Mental Home and Poznan Fort VII." *Aktion Reinhard Camps,* www.deathcamps.org.

Page, Kirby. *National Defense: A Study of the Origins, Results, and Prevention of War.* New York: Farrar and Rinehart, 1931.

Parents of Arnold Satterthwait and Frederick Richards. *Federal Convicts Numbers 1128 and 1129, College As Prison.* Pamphlet [1942]. Swarthmore College Peace Collection.

Parkin, Robert Sinclair. *Blood on the Sea: American Destroyers Lost in World War II.* Cambridge, Mass.: Da Capo, 2001.

Partridge, Frances. *A Pacifist's War.* London: Phoenix, 1978.

Paterson, Michael. *Battle for the Skies.* Newton Abbot, Eng.: David and Charles, 2004.

Peace Pledge Union. "1940–1949: Candles in the Dark." www.ppu.org.uk/century/century5.html.

———. "PPU History in Context." www.ppu.org.uk/ppu/history1.html.

Perkins, Milo. "Exports and Appeasement." *Harper's Magazine,* December 1940.

Perret, Geoffrey. *Winged Victory: The Army Air Forces in World War II.* New York: Random House, 1993.

Persico, Joseph E. *Roosevelt's Secret War: FDR and World War II Espionage.* New York: Random House, 2001.

Perutz, Max. *I Wish I'd Made You Angry Earlier: Essays on Science, Scientists, and Humanity.* Plainview, N.Y.: Cold Spring Harbor Laboratory Press, 1998.

Pickett, Clarence E. *For More than Bread: An Autobiographical Account of Twenty-Two Years' Work with the American Friends Service Committee.* Boston: Little, Brown, 1953.

Ponting, Clive. *1940: Myth and Reality.* Chicago: Ivan R. Dee, 1991.

Pottker, Jan. *Sara and Eleanor: The Story of Sara Delano Roosevelt and Her Daughter-in-Law, Eleanor Roosevelt.* New York: St. Martin's, 2004.

Prater, D. A. *European of Yesterday: A Biography of Stefan Zweig.* Oxford: Oxford University Press, 1972.

Probert, Henry. *Bomber Harris: His Life and Times.* London: Greenhill, 2003.

Radzinsky, Edvard. *Stalin.* Trans. H. T. Willetts. New York: Doubleday, 1996.

Rasmussen, Nicolas. "Plant Hormones in War and Peace: Science, Industry, and Government in the Development of Herbicides in 1940s America." *Isis* 92, no. 2 (June 2001).

Read, Anthony. *The Devil's Disciples.* New York: Norton, 2004.

Regis, Ed. *The Biology of Doom.* New York: Holt, 1999.

Reimann, Viktor. *Goebbels.* New York: Doubleday, 1976.

Reitlinger, Gerald. *The SS: Alibi of a Nation.* New York: Viking, 1968.

Reynolds, David. "Churchill and the British 'Decision' to Fight on in 1940." In Richard Langhorne, ed., *Diplomacy and Intelligence During the Second World War: Essays in Honour of F. H. Hinsley.* Cambridge: Cambridge University Press, 1985.

———. *From World War to Cold War: Churchill, Roosevelt, and the International History of the 1940s.* Oxford: Oxford University Press, 2006.

Richards, Denis. *Portal of Hungerford.* New York: Holmes and Meier, 1977.

———. *The Royal Air Force,* vol. 1, *The Fight at Odds.* London: Her Majesty's Stationery Office, 1953. Available at HyperWar Foundation, www.ibiblio.org/hyperwar/UN/UK/UK-RAF-I/UK-RAF-I-13.html.

Richardson, James O. *On the Treadmill to Pearl Harbor.* Washington, D.C.: Department of the Navy, 1973.

Roosevelt, Eleanor. *My Day: The Best of Eleanor Roosevelt's Acclaimed Newspaper Columns, 1936–1962.* Ed. David Emblidge. Cambridge, Mass.: Da Capo, 2001.

Roosevelt, Franklin D. *The Public Papers and Addresses of Franklin D. Roosevelt.* New York: Russell & Russell, 1938–1950.

———. *F.D.R.: His Personal Letters,* vol. 2, *1928–1945.* New York: Duell, Sloan, and Pearce, 1950.

Rose, Norman. *Churchill: The Unruly Giant.* New York: Free Press, 1995.

Roseman, Mark. *The Wannsee Conference and the Final Solution: A Reconsideration.* New York: Picador, 2002.

Roskill, Stephen. *Hankey: Man of Secrets.* New York: St. Martin's, 1972.

Ross, Stewart Halsey. *Strategic Bombing by the United States in World War II.* Jefferson, N.C.: McFarland, 2003.

Rosten, Leo. "Men Like War." *Harper's Magazine,* July 1935.

Rubenstein, Murray, and Richard M. Goldman. *To Join with the Eagles: Curtiss Aircraft, 1903–1965.* New York: Doubleday, 1974.

Rumpf, Hans. *The Bombing of Germany.* New York: Holt, 1962.

Saunders, Kenneth. "Toyohiko Kagawa, the St Francis of Japan." *Pacific Affairs* 4, no. 4 (April 1931).

Schaller, Michael. *The U.S. Crusade in China, 1938–1945.* New York: Columbia University Press, 1979.

Schmitt, Hans A. *Quakers and Nazis: Inner Light in Outer Darkness.* Columbia, Mo.: University of Missouri Press, 1997.

Schoenfeld, Howard. "The Danbury Story." In Holley Cantine and Dachine Rainer, eds., *Prison Etiquette.* Bearsville, N.Y.: Retort Press, 1950.

Schreiber, Gerhard, et al. *Germany and the Second World War,* vol. 3. New York: Oxford University Press, 1995.

Schultz, Duane. *The Maverick War: Chennault and the Flying Tigers.* New York: St. Martin's, 1987.

Schuschnigg, Kurt von. *Austrian Requiem.* New York: Putnam, 1946.

Schwab, Gerald. *The Day the Holocaust Began: The Odyssey of Herschel Grynszpan.* New York: Praeger, 1990.

Scott, Robert Lee. *Flying Tiger: Chennault of China.* Westport, Conn.: Greenwood, 1973.

Sebald, W. G. *On the Natural History of Destruction.* New York: Modern Library, 2004.

Sebastian, Mihail. *Journal, 1935–1944.* Chicago: Ivan R. Dee, 2000.

Seldes, George. "The New Propaganda for War." *Harper's,* October 1934.

Shapiro, Edward S. "World War II and American Jewish Identity." *Modern Judaism* 10, no. 1 (February 1990).

Shaw, George Bernard. "Uncommon Sense About the War." In Edward Hyams, ed., *New Statesmanship: An Anthology.* London: Longmans, 1963.

Sherry, Michael S. *The Rise of American Air Power.* New Haven, Conn.: Yale University Press, 1987.

Sherwood, Robert E. *Roosevelt and Hopkins: An Intimate History.* New York: Harper and Brothers, 1948.

Shirer, William L. *Berlin Diary: The Journal of a Foreign Correspondent, 1934–1941.* New York: Penguin, 1979.

———. *Collapse of the Third Republic.* New York: Simon and Schuster, 1969.

———. "A Peace of Sorts." In audio CD accompanying Mark Bernstein and Alex Lubertozzi, *World War II on the Air.* Naperville, Ill.: Sourcebooks Media-Fusion, 2003.

———. *The Rise and Fall of the Third Reich.* New York: Simon and Schuster, 1960.

———. *"This Is Berlin": Radio Broadcasts from Nazi Germany.* Woodstock, N.Y.: Overlook, 1999.

Sierakowiak, Dawid. *The Diary of Dawid Sierakowiak.* New York: Oxford University Press, 1996.

Simpson, A. W. Brian. *In the Highest Degree Odious: Detention Without Trial in Wartime Britain.* Oxford: Clarendon, 1992.

Soames, Mary. *Clementine Churchill: The Biography of a Marriage.* Boston: Houghton Mifflin, 1979.

Soames, Mary, ed. *Winston and Clementine: The Personal Letters of the Churchills.* Boston: Houghton Mifflin, 1998.

Spaight, J. M. *Bombing Vindicated.* London: Bles, 1944.

Speer, Albert. *Inside the Third Reich.* New York: Avon, 1970.

Stackelberg, Roderick, and Sally A. Winkle. *The Nazi Germany Sourcebook: An Anthology of Texts.* London: Routledge, 2002.

Stafford, David. *Britain and European Resistance, 1940–1945: A Survey of the Special Operations Executive, with Documents.* Toronto: University of Toronto Press, 1980.

———. "SOE and British Involvement in the Belgrade Coup d'Etat of March 1941." *Slavic Review* 36, no. 3 (September 1977).

Starkey, Pat. *I Will Not Fight: Conscientious Objectors and Pacifists in the North West During the Second World War.* Liverpool: Liverpool University Press, 1992.

Stone, Dan. *Responses to Nazism in Britain, 1933–1939.* London: Palgrave MacMillan, 2003.

Stone, I. F. *The War Years, 1939–1945: A Nonconformist History of Our Times.* Boston: Little, Brown, 1988.

Sydnor, Charles. *Soldiers of Destruction: The SS Death's Head Division, 1933–1945.* Princeton, N.J.: Princeton University Press, 1977.

Taylor, A. J. P., et al. *Churchill Revised: A Critical Assessment.* New York: Dial, 1969.

Taylor, Jennifer. " 'Something to Make People Laugh'? Political Content in Isle of Man Internment Camp Journals, July–October 1940." In Richard Dove, ed., *"Totally Un-English"?: Britain's Internment of "Enemy Aliens" in Two World Wars.* Amsterdam: Rodopi, 2005.

Terraine, John. *A Time for Courage: The Royal Air Force in the European War, 1939–1945.* New York: Macmillan, 1985.

Thalmann, Rita, and Emmanuel Feinermann. *Crystal Night: 9–10 November 1938.* New York: Holocaust Library, 1980.

Thompson, Robert Smith. *Empires on the Pacific: World War II and the Struggle for the Mastery of Asia.* New York: Basic Books, 2001.

———. *A Time for War: Franklin Delano Roosevelt and the Path to Pearl Harbor.* New York: Prentice Hall, 1991.

Thompson, R. W. *Generalissimo Churchill.* New York: Scribner's, 1973.

Thompson, Walter Henry. *Assignment: Churchill.* New York: Farrar, Straus, and Young, 1955.

Tims, Hilton. *Erich Maria Remarque: The Last Romantic.* New York: Carroll and Graf, 2003.

Toland, John. *Adolf Hitler,* vol. 2. New York: Doubleday, 1976.

Tolischus, Otto D. *They Wanted War.* New York: Reynal and Hitchcock, 1940.

Trevor-Roper, H. R., ed. *Hitler's War Directives, 1939–1945.* London: Sidgwick and Jackson, 1964.

Twombly, Robert C. *Frank Lloyd Wright: His Life and Architecture.* New York: Wiley, 1979.

Tye, Larry. *The Father of Spin: Edward L. Bernays and the Birth of Public Relations.* New York: Crown, 1998.

Underwood, Jeffery S. *The Wings of Democracy: The Influence of Air Power on the Roosevelt Administration, 1933–1941.* College Station: Texas A&M University Press, 1991.

United States Congress, House of Representatives, Committee on Foreign Affairs. *Arming of American Merchant Vessels Hearings.* Washington, D.C.: Government Printing Office, 1941.

U.S. Department of State. *Foreign Relations of the United States.* Washington, D.C.: Government Printing Office.

———. *Peace and War: United States Foreign Policy, 1931–1941.* Washington, D.C.: Government Printing Office, 1943.

U.S. Senate Committee on Military Affairs. *Compulsory Military Training and Service Hearings.* Washington, D.C.: Government Printing Office, 1940.

U.S. Senate and House of Representatives. *Admission of German Refugee Children.* Washington, D.C.: Government Printing Office, 1939.

Vassiltchikov, Marie. *Berlin Diaries, 1940–1945.* New York: Knopf, 1987.

Verrier, Anthony. *The Bomber Offensive.* London: Batsford, 1968.

Vining, Elizabeth Gray. *Friend of Life: The Biography of Rufus M. Jones.* Philadelphia: Lippincott, 1958.

von Hassell, Ulrich. *The Von Hassell Diaries, 1938–1944.* Westport, Conn.: Greenwood, 1971.

von Suttner, Bertha. *The Records of an Eventful Life,* vol. 1. Boston: Ginn, 1910.

Washburn, Patrick S. *A Question of Sedition: The Federal Government's Investigation of the Black Press During World War II.* New York: Oxford University Press, 1986.

Wasserstein, Bernard. *Britain and the Jews of Europe, 1939–1945.* Oxford: Clarendon, 1979.

Watt, Donald Cameron. *How War Came: The Immediate Origins of the Second World War.* New York: Pantheon, 1989.

Webster, Charles, and Noble Frankland. *The Strategic Air Offensive Against Germany,* vols. 1, 4. London: Her Majesty's Stationery Office, 1961.

Wedemeyer, Albert C. *Wedemeyer Reports!* New York: Holt, 1958.

Westermann, Edward B. *Flak: German Anti-aircraft Defenses, 1914–1945.* Lawrence, Kan.: University Press of Kansas, 2001.

Wheeler-Bennett, John, ed. *Action This Day: Working With Churchill.* New York: St. Martin's, 1969.

Whitby, Simon M. *Biological Warfare Against Crops.* New York: Palgrave, 2002.

Wilkinson, Greg. *Talking about Psychiatry.* London: RCPsych, 1993.

Willey, Mark Emerson. *Pearl Harbor: Mother of All Conspiracies.* Philadelphia, Penn.: Xlibris, 2000.

Williams, Peter, and David Wallace. *Unit 731: Japan's Secret Biological Warfare in World War II.* New York: Free Press, 1989.

Williamson, Philip, and Edward Baldwin. *Baldwin Papers.* Cambridge: Cambridge University Press, 2004.

Winfield, Betty Houchin. *FDR and the News Media.* Urbana, Ill.: University of Illinois Press, 1990.

Winkelnkemper, Toni. "The Attack on Cologne." Randall Bytwerk, trans. *German Propaganda Archive,* www.calvin.edu/academic/cas/gpa/cologne.htm.

Winterbotham, F. W. *The Nazi Connection.* New York: Harper, 1978.

———. *The Ultra Secret.* New York: Harper, 1974.

Witte, Peter. "Two Decisions Concerning the 'Final Solution to the Jewish Question.' " *Holocaust and Genocide Studies* 9, 1995.

Wittner, Lawrence S. *Rebels Against War: The American Peace Movement, 1941–1960.* New York: Columbia University Press, 1969.

Women's International League for Peace and Freedom. "From a Letter from Camp de Gurs, South France." www.wilpf.int.ch/history/1941.doc.

Wooley, John T., and Gerhard Peters. *The American Presidency Project.* University of California, Santa Barbara, www.presidency.ucsb.edu.

Wyman, David S. *Paper Walls: America and the Refugee Crisis, 1938–1941.* Amherst: University of Massachusetts Press, 1968.

Yad Vashem. "Lichtenberg, Bernhard." In *The Righteous Among Nations,* www.yadvashem.org.

Yale Law School. *The Avalon Project.* www.yale.edu/lawweb/avalon/avalon.htm.

Zinn, Howard. *Passionate Declarations.* New York: Perennial, 2003.

Zweig, Stefan. *The World of Yesterday.* Lincoln: University of Nebraska Press, 1964.

Index

About the Author

Nicholson Baker was born in 1957 and attended the Eastman School of Music and Haverford College. He is the author of seven novels and three previous works of nonfiction, including *Double Fold,* which won a National Book Critics Circle Award in 2001. He lives in Maine with his family.